Theory and Practice of Corporate Governance

Theory and Practice of Corporate Governance explains how the real world of corporate governance works. It offers new definitions of governance and new conceptual models for investigating governance and corporate behaviour, based on both practical experience and academic investigation. In examining the historical development of corporate governance, it integrates issues of company law, regulatory practice and company administration with contemporary corporate governance policies and structures. An extensive range of international examples, both recent and historical, is used to compare theoretical explanations of governance behaviour with practical outcomes. The book will be particularly suitable for students taking an ICSA-accredited course – giving a necessary critical view on governance, law and regulation – and through utilising new conceptual models, it will stimulate debate among both theorists and practitioners.

STEPHEN BLOOMFIELD leads the Corporate Governance Unit at Anglia Ruskin University. He was a visiting fellow in Corporate Governance at Kingston University and London South Bank University and, prior to his academic career, he was a stockbroking analyst and then a director of a major venture capital fund. He has been a director of numerous venture capital funded companies and is a fellow of the Institute of Chartered Secretaries and Administrators.

Theory and Practice of Corporate Governance

An Integrated Approach

STEPHEN BLOOMFIELD

CAMBRIDGE
UNIVERSITY PRESS

CAMBRIDGE UNIVERSITY PRESS
Cambridge, New York, Melbourne, Madrid, Cape Town,
Singapore, São Paulo, Delhi, Mexico City

Cambridge University Press
The Edinburgh Building, Cambridge CB2 8RU, UK

Published in the United States of America by Cambridge University Press, New York
www.cambridge.org

Information on this title: www.cambridge.org/9781107612242

First published 2013

Printed and bound in the United Kingdom by the MPG Books Group

A catalogue record for this publication is available from the British Library

Library of Congress Cataloguing in Publication data

Bloomfield, Stephen.
  Theory and practice of corporate governance : an integrated approach / Stephen Bloomfield.
    p.   cm.
  ISBN 978-1-107-01224-0 – ISBN 978-1-107-61224-2 (Paperback)
1. Corporate governance.   I. Title.
  HD2741.B575 2013
  658.4′2–dc23   2012029372

ISBN 978-1-107-01224-0 Hardback
ISBN 978-1-107-61224-2 Paperback

Contents

List of Figures and Tables

Introduction

It is the central contention of this book that much of what currently passes for the theory of corporate governance and which forms the foundation of regulatory policy is based on a description of forces, relationships and actors that holds very little similarity to the way that the real world operates. Sometimes, the suggestions of the theory will turn out to be supported by the reality of practice; at other times the two will be in disagreement. But because the current explanations of corporate governance used by policy-makers do not correctly explain the real world, much of the practical superstructure of governance is directed towards the wrong purpose or works only partially. There are examples throughout the text of good (and bad) governance practice to support this view.

The traditional/conventional view

In discussing the existing dominant descriptions of the way that corporate governance is supposed to work, the terms traditionalist or conventional approaches to (or sometimes theories of) governance will be used.

The conventional view typically emphasises the primacy of the shareholder; concentrates on the ownership rights of shareholders; and dwells on the consequences of the relationship between shareholders and managers through the legal and economic prism of the principal-and-agent relationship. Occasionally the traditionalist view may admit additional players (stakeholders) to the governance game but usually only grudgingly or by allocating walk-on parts.

This view is also based largely on the economic characteristics of the period which, in British history, starts with the Victorian era and ends about a century and a half later, towards the end of the twentieth century. That was a very different world from that which now exists; what held true then may not hold true now in terms of the relative significance of the components that go to make up the commercial world.

One of the arguments that will be developed in this book is that, ironically, just as the paradigm of governance for this period was being articulated by the report of the Cadbury Committee of 1992, so the characteristics of the commercial world were changing radically. The resulting changes were beyond the scope of description that the Cadbury Committee arrived at. The shape of the economy to which the Cadbury definition would have applied (at least in Britain) was receding into the distance of history: the Cadbury Committee's world view was focused on an economy which was on the cusp of changing into something that the Committee had not recognised.

Reviewing the existing accepted and conventional definitions and formulations of corporate governance to see if they do reflect reality helps to explain one of the puzzles of the impact of governance, which is why – if all this activity in developing policies, proposals and principles has taken place in the past twenty years – governance lapses seems to have become more frequent and their consequences more damaging. In the argument advanced in this book Cadbury's definitions and prescriptions become a bit like the Anglo-Saxon legend of King Canute in reverse – with the King not commanding the waves to stop but with them leaving him watching the tides race away, while he gesticulates futilely from what was once the shoreline, admonishing them to come back to what he understood.

The investigation in the book of what corporate governance is – and by implication what constitutes good corporate governance – extends, then, beyond the repetition of the paradigms of the Cadbury model, to highlight the disparities between the theory and the way that governance operates (or not) in practice.

The gap between theory and practice

The disparity between theory and practice is particularly striking when comparisons are made between the mechanisms and effects of corporate governance in listed public limited companies and unlisted private companies. The unlisted companies – especially smaller ones – appear to follow the broad projections of the conventional definitions (although this has now been changed slightly by the effects of the Companies Act 2006). But in large companies it is very difficult to see how corporate governance conforms to the conventional descriptions: the existence of shareholder primacy can be questioned on a number of fronts; the characteristics of shareholder ownership are not met in practice; stakeholders occupy a much more significant role than the traditionalist view accords them.

In practice, the effective regulation of large companies is hamstrung by regulators, stakeholders and shareholders pulling on policy levers, which the theory holds should work but where, in fact, no linkage exists to real world environments or the behaviour of those involved in managing those organisations, either practically or legally. This then means that if changes in governance practice are sought they do not work in the way intended or perhaps not at all. The impact and significance of Einstein's dictum – 'In theory practice and theory are the same; in practice they are not' – is sorely neglected in developing and improving corporate governance structures.

In considering what constitutes good corporate governance the main focus in this book is therefore on large companies – usually, but not exclusively, those with some form of stock market listing or those with large numbers of shareholders who are distant from day-to-day contact with the company but where there may not be a public market in the shares.

These two sets of companies are where ownership and control are starkly contrasted. Concentration on them effectively excludes the vast majority of small limited liability businesses – which while numerically superior, tend to be less significant economically because of being small in turnover and capitalisation and often with very few shareholders. But if bigger companies are run properly on the vaunted characteristic of principle-based governance that 'a rising tide lifts all boats', the rising tide effect will presumably eventually improve standards in all, by example and gradual cultural change.

Failures of governance in large stock market-listed companies have far greater and more widespread economic impact than those of a plethora of small ones. The failure of a Barings, a Parmalat or even a Farepak is of far greater economic consequence than that of several modestly-capitalised local engineering companies or building firms, however important they may be locally to stakeholders.

The necessity of context

One strand of the argument throughout this book is that to effectively understand the processes of corporate governance it cannot be removed from the contextual issues that have shaped it.

So a significant part of this book is devoted to analysis of the underlying factors concerned with corporate governance as it now stands. These are the factors that have brought about the current processes of governance of the major commercial organisations and public bodies so important to our collective economic well-being.

The global financial crisis that erupted in 2008 brought the issues of corporate governance into sharp relief. But much of the substantial body of commentary that the crisis generated is still little more than description of events and so lacks any prescriptive value. This is largely because the basic terms on which debate about governance rests are poorly formulated; the contributing factors which bring about effective corporate governance are poorly described. Debate often lacks any appreciation of context so progress in corporate governance flounders because the origins of the issues are inadequately understood and there is little common ground from which to develop proposals for change.

To take an example from geography: a simple description of the landscape – rolling hills, sharp valleys, flat plains – does not really help to understand its development. For that an understanding of geology is needed – an account of how the effect of glaciers, the winds and the rivers interacted to produce the shape of the landscape. To relate this analogy to corporate governance, most existing accounts and theories are mere description of the governance landscape when what is really needed is an attempt at a better understanding of the geological processes – the linkages between procedure, behaviour and systems – which produced it. Throughout the book attempts will be made to consider why corporate governance structures are the way they are or why they do not appear to work, rather than just describing how they appear to be.

Appropriate historical examples which illustrate why procedures, behaviour and systems were changed are the most useful tools for illuminating change. So this book – and the accompanying website – contains many examples of governance failures (and some examples of good governance) to assist an understanding of context. Given the propensity of organisational managers to flout the rules of governance, there is no lack of examples.

An effort has been made to extend the range of examples used in the book beyond the normal Anglo-American boundary found in the majority of textbooks on corporate governance. The Anglo-Americans have no exclusivity on good governance and little cause for congratulation on the sturdiness of their governance structures (despite official pronouncements and political complacency) but they are not alone in recording examples of poor governance. In fact the examples that are reported nearly every week in the financial press which, during the course of writing this book, included (in no particular order) the Southern Cross Scandal; the HSBC pay regime and chairmanship controversy; the Galleon Fund insider dealing trial; the ENRC directorships; failures of ethics and good governance at News International; remuneration arguments at Thomas Cook, William Morrisons, Tesco and William Hill indicate that poor governance is alive and flourishing. A companion website to this book – www.stephenbloomfield.co.uk – gives details of many instances of governance breakdown (both contemporary and historical) and is constantly updated with new examples.

One of the weaknesses of much of the teaching of corporate governance is that it usually considers each discipline separately – administration and secretaryship; law; and accounting. But in governance terms they are different lenses through which the same subject is viewed. It is impossible when discussing corporate governance effectively to separate the individual components of the practical operation and hold them sterile and apart. To do so is like describing a fruit cake only in terms of its ingredients: technically accurate but it does not convey the texture or flavour of the finished article.

This does give rise to some boundary problems however. The strength of the 'single ingredient' approach is that it allows a clear distinction between all the sub-disciplines which facilitates description of each area without elaborate cross-referencing. But its weakness is that it does not convey the complex inter-related nature of the subject matter of governance – a complicated blend of law, finance, administrative practice and ethics. By avoiding the monocular approach in favour of trying to identify the way that governance works in the real world, this book will sometimes touch on subjects more than once in different places, occasionally a partial but relevant explanation of an event may be provided initially which is then elaborated more fully elsewhere.

Consideration of how the conventional description of governance might be improved uses a classification of dimensions of governance – described more fully in the first chapter – which breaks the blunt instrument approach of the conventional description into a more subtle set of distinctions.

The book is laid out in a series of sections. The first section, Chapters 1, 2 and 3, deals with the governance landscape (rather than the geology). Here governance is divided into two specific types, which are considered separately: the inward-facing aspect of governance – that which concerns principally shareholder relationship – and the outward aspect – the relationship of the company with its stakeholders. This first part establishes the broad boundaries of the subject area and the bones of the argument that the traditionalist/legalist theories of governance which form the basis for the regulatory structures of governance are inadequate to describe what really happens. The concepts of 'procedural', 'behavioural', 'structural' and 'systemic' governance are also introduced: these operate at different levels within companies and throughout the economy to reinforce individual governance practices and activities.

The second part (Chapters 4 and 5) then looks at the legal framework within which companies operate – paying particular attention to developments from the 1970s and 1980s to the passage of the latest Companies Act in 2006. The chapters examine the relationship between law and governance both at the theoretical level and again how things work out in practice – in particular taking into account the rule of unintended consequences and extending the argument about existing descriptions not working well and developing the 'geological' approach.

The third part (Chapters 6, 7 and 8) looks at the overlap between law, regulation and governance; and contends that the abiding characteristic of regulatory activity – in particular that of auditing activity – is that it fails. The basis for this claim is that even with the thicket of regulation that surrounds financial activity, governance failures are very prevalent. Regulators and legislators have been facing a losing battle that has accelerated over the past thirty years, as they seek perpetually to catch up with a market place where 'innovation' has often been allowed to dominate at the expense of suitability for purpose, and the interests of a small minority have been allowed to outweigh the well-being of the many. The situation has been made worse since this innovation was subject only to the lightest of regulatory touches in the first decade of the new millenium, and regulation that was implemented appears to have been unable to check in a timely way activity that has proved subsequently to be inimical to the interests of stakeholders in general. A good and effective corporate governance system would surely act as a prophylactic, not a sticking plaster.

Chapters 9, 10 and 11 (Part 4) look at what might be called the secretarial or administrative aspects of governance, including a more detailed revisiting of the prickly issue of remuneration that was briefly introduced in Part 1. Again, the traditionalist/legalist theories are drawn upon to explain the operation of governance where unintended consequences are once more apparent in regulatory practices based on these precepts.

Part 4 also looks, in Chapters 12, 13 and 14, at the environment in which the listed company operates and reviews in particular the development of the separate reports and recommendations that constitute the UK Corporate Governance Code. The UK reports are found mostly to lack impact, because their underlying assumptions about the operation of governance arrangements are faulty. If anything this tendency seems to have accelerated as the reports have been produced – with the notable exception of the 1999 Turnbull Report. It also describes the anticipated framework of the regulatory environment following the forthcoming break-up of the Financial Services Authority (FSA) into the Prudential Regulation Authority and the Financial Conduct Authority, and the regulatory implications of new and fragmented markets for shares and financial instruments.

Part 5 of the book draws together the aspects of failure of governance in its various components of procedural, behavioural and systemic dimensions. Taken together these may be considered to be *counter-governance* when they are pursued as matters of policy or *contra-governance* when policies are occasionally instituted which are intended to by-pass laws or regulations through criminality, recklessness and market abuse. Needless to say there are subjects and instances which re-appear here having made their first appearance in other chapters, but this section is intended to deal with the issues in a coherent way, placing them against the background of the extended definitions of governance developed earlier in the book.

The final chapter makes some observations about the development of governance policies and in particular the fashionable – but no less valuable for that – concept of stewardship and its relationship to the areas covered in the argument.

Stephen Bloomfield

PART 1

THE DISCIPLINE OF GOVERNANCE

CHAPTER 1

The landscape and definitions of governance: the major actors

This chapter:

- establishes the area for review;
- examines existing theories of governance and indicates where and how they do not describe the real world accurately;
- introduces the concepts of procedural, behavioural, structural and systemic governance;
- suggests alternative definitions for governance.

Introduction

Corporate governance has been the single most significant issue on the business agenda nationally, internationally and globally for the past thirty or more years. Although it may not have always appeared under the same title, its successes – and more particularly its failings – will have affected every working individual in every economy across the world during that time. Most importantly, the financial cost of recent failures of corporate governance (since the turn of this century) and the worldwide governmental response to them, will affect at least two generations of workers yet to enter the workforce worldwide, with incalculable political and social consequences.

Given this level of importance and impact, it seems important that we get the study of corporate governance issues right. This might reasonably be expected to include not simply a tour of what exists now but also an examination of how we got here – since to mix up a couple of aphorisms, those who do not understand the lessons of history are condemned to repeat them: the first time as tragedy, the second time as farce.

Not everyone is convinced of the need to undertake this examination. In 2002, ten years after the publication of the Cadbury Report – which in definitional terms, provided the benchmark for most future examinations of the subject, the Economist Intelligence Unit (EIU) produced a survey entitled 'Corporate Governance – the New Strategic Imperative'.[1] In the terms of the argument of the introduction it

---

[1] EIU/KPMG, *Corporate Governance: The New Strategic Imperative* (London: EIU/KPMG, 2002).

reviewed the landscape of corporate governance and decided to stick with the basic Cadbury definition as being the platform from which to consider the issue of how businesses are run and for whom. The use of the Cadbury Report's conclusions was grudging: the EIU suggested at one point in the review that the pendulum may have swung too far and that business was being actively inhibited by regulation. Seeing no reason to recommend change it only nodded towards a further (evolutionary) definition prepared by the Organisation for Economic Co-operation and Development (OECD) three years earlier.

Five years after the EIU's report came the events of 2007–8 and the financial paralysis which followed – these events can quite correctly be ascribed to failures of governance. Ten years on from the EIU's report, and twenty years after its initial publication, the definition used in the Cadbury Report is still the standard starting point for most examinations of corporate governance. The longevity of the definition and the endorsement of it as recently as 2009 in the UK's Walker Review,[2] might suggest that the problems of corporate governance had been cracked. Yet, since 1992, the private sector has suffered the collapse of Barings Bank (1995); the extinction of GEC plc through governance failures (1996); the double-dip collapse of Railtrack (1997 and 1999); the dot.com bust of 2000–01; the Equitable Life Scandal (2000); the scandal over the false oilfield reserves claimed by Royal Dutch Shell (2004); the blast at BP's Texas City Oil refinery which cost the lives of 15 workers and injured 170 others (2005) and resulted in record fines on the company; the purchase of Amro Bank by RBS (2007) which is widely attributed as the factor that toppled the bank into public ownership eighteen months later; the BAE Al-Yamani scandal (2008) which again resulted in record fines; political scandal and legislative changes; the 'Phoenix 4' affair at British Leyland (more political noise); the Sirbir, Keydata and Farepak scandals, together with directorial misbehaviour at JJB and Carphone Warehouse – all in 2009; and the loss of at least £250 million of shareholder value at Mitchells and Butlers because of poor governance. Obviously there was something in the water in 2009, since it was such a bad year for ethical behaviour.

The behaviour of companies overseas was no better in the same period: among the more notable instances are the collapse of HIH Insurance in Australia; the carbon trading scandals of 2009/10, again in Australia; corruption problems at Siemens which led to record fines for that company in 2006 and appear to have arisen again in 2011; the Satyam affair in India, uncovered in 2009 but running for at least six years previously; governance problems at Societe Generale in 2009/10; the overambitious expansion and then collapse of the Icelandic banks; and, repeating the mistakes of five

---

[2] Sir D. Walker, *A Review of Corporate Governance in UK Banks and Other Financial Industry Entities: Final Recommendations* (London: HM Treasury, 2009).

years earlier, the governance failures at BP which brought about the Mexican Gulf disaster in 2010, costing yet more lives as well as stupendous amounts of treasure; and continuing corporate scandals in the telecoms and extractive industries in India. During this time Goldman Sachs was also doing 'God's Work' on the sovereign debt burdens of Greece, Portugal and municipal bonds in Germany, while losing $1.3 billion of Libya's investment fund. And of course the collapse of the Western financial sector in September 2008 – the biggest failure of corporate governance ever – the cost of which is mind-bendingly high.

It doesn't seem as though the problem has been cracked since, from the time of the publication of the Cadbury Report's definition, trillions of pounds have been wiped off the value of businesses worldwide; thousands of jobs lost; personal savings and pensions have been reduced or eliminated; economic prospects have been retarded and governments have been tainted by their contact with bribery, incompetence, peculation and fraud – all through failures of governance of one sort or another. And, if this were not enough, the number and value of private sector scandals (this recital takes no account of public sector problems) has accelerated since the 1990s in comparison with previous decades as the list below shows:

The 1960s

Rolls Razor (1964)

Emil Savundra and Fire Auto and Marine (1966)

The 1970s

Secondary Banks Crisis (1973–75)

Lloyd's: the Sasse syndicate collapse (1974)

The 1980s

de Lorean (1982)

Lloyd's: Christopher Moran (1982)

The Guinness Affair: Ernest Saunders and Gerald Ronson (1986)

Blue Arrow 1/Manpower (1987)

The Herald of Free Enterprise (1987)

The Kings Cross fire (1987)

The Barlow Clowes affair (1980–)

The Piper Alpha disaster (1988)

Lloyd's Insurance collapse (1988)

The Marchioness disaster (1989)

The 1990s

BCCI (1990)

Polly Peck (1991)

Maxwell and Mirror Group Pensions (1991)

British Gas and the 'fat cats' row (1994)

Barings Bank – Nick Leeson (1995)

The GEC collapse (1996)

Railtrack (1997 and 1999)

The 2000s

Equitable Life (2000)

Administration of Turner and Newall (2001)

Collapse of HIH Insurance (2001)

RDS reserves restatement (2004)

Langbar International (2005)

BP Texas City blast (2005)

BAE ethics report (Woolf Report – 2008)

RBS/ABN Amro (2007)

Northern Rock failure (2008)

Sirbir (2009)

Carphone Warehouse (2009)

JJB Loans scandal (2009)

Keydata (2009)

Farepak (2009)

The Phoenix 4 – Leyland (2009)

Arch Cru failure (2009)

Qinetiq privatisation (2002)

CDC and Aventis (2004)

The Australian carbon trading scandals (2009/10)

Satyam (2009)

Mitchells and Butler (2009–)

The 2010s

BP/Florida Gulf (2010)

The Cadbury takeover (2010)

Marks and Spencer's succession problems (2009–10)

Southern Cross Scandal (2011)

ENRC (2011)

William Hill pay controversy (2011)

Thomas Cook pay controversy (2011)

William Morrison pay controversy (2011)

Prudential Chairmanship controversy (2011)

The increase in the number of scandals and uncovering of misbehaviour could be due simply to increased public awareness of the incompetence or greed of some directors of public companies, more eagerly investigated by a Press alerted to the prevalence of corporate scandal. But with a record as extensive as this, it is appropriate to ask if there is something more significantly wrong: are the measures by which we gauge corporate good behaviour and the standards to which we hold company managers insufficiently rigorous?

Some experts tend to favour a positive attitude towards the evidence. The most recent examination of the structures of UK governance – the Review prepared by Sir David Walker in 2009 into the UK's Banks and other Financial Institutions (BoFIs) concluded that, as far as the banks were concerned, the existing corporate governance code needed only minor tweaking. In sum, the review concluded, corporate governance in the financial sector was working pretty much as it should. Others might say that such a conclusion is absurd after the record of the last three decades and that we really should look again at the definitions of corporate governance that we work with to see if they are still fit for the uses to which we put them.

The Cadbury Committee definition and others

The Cadbury Committee was set up jointly by the City of London and the accounting profession in the summer of 1991[3] to look at what actions might be taken to soothe public disquiet about how major companies were being run, especially in light of the BCCI and Maxwell/Mirror Group scandals of the immediately preceding years.

The Committee's purpose was to review those aspects of corporate governance that related to financial reporting and accountability. The formal set of instructions (included as Appendix 1 to the Report) was as follows:

> To consider the following issues in relation to financial reporting and accountability and to make recommendations on good practice:
> a) the responsibilities of executive and non-executive directors for reviewing and reporting on performance to shareholders and other financially interested parties;
> b) and the frequency, clarity and form in which information should be provided;
> c) the case for audit committees of the board, including their composition and role;
> d) the principal responsibilities of auditors and the extent and value of the audit;
> e) the links between shareholders, boards, and auditors;
> f) any other relevant matters.

Despite the final clause of the remit, the Committee was not expected (either implicitly or explicitly) to undertake a root-and-branch review of what was happening in the City; nor to concern itself with the specific details of individual cases; not even to look outside the City or to speculate or recommend on anything beyond what the current

---

[3] Sir A. Cadbury, *Report of the Committee on the Financial Aspects of Corporate Governance* (London: Gee, 1992).

best practice was. Since the definition was supposed to act as the benchmark for examination of the processes by which commercial organisations were run and managed, this was equivalent to freezing the current set of practices. The remit pretty much established the conclusions.

Following on from its deliberations, which lasted a little over eighteen months and involved taking over 200 pieces of individual evidence, it produced a report which contained the following definition:

> Corporate governance is the system by which business corporations are directed and controlled. Boards of directors are responsible for the governance of their companies. The shareholders' role in governance is to appoint the directors and the auditors and to satisfy themselves that an appropriate governance structure is in place. The responsibilities of the board include setting the company's strategic aims, providing the leadership to put them into effect, supervising the management of the business and reporting to shareholders on their stewardship. The board's actions are subject to laws, regulations and the shareholders in general meeting.[4]

It is this definition which forms the starting point for most other reviews of governance – despite its obvious shortcomings over the passage of time. There are four obvious limitations of the Cadbury definition – first, that the definition of corporate governance is highly limited in identifying the actors who are involved in the determination of policy. Only three groups of individuals are identified in the Cadbury definition – directors, shareholders and auditors. Governance, in the Committee's view, is limited to the interplay between these parties. One of those parties (the shareholder) is almost immediately out of the action as soon as the company has been established, receiving only backward-looking information and only able to intervene on retrospective intelligence – which is all the company is legally obliged to reveal. The definition almost appears to suggest that the shareholders' job is done when the structures have been set up: there is no reference to continuing oversight.

Second, the formulation lacks any dynamic aspect in that the definition can be interpreted to suggest that structures of governance appear to need setting once and then be left alone ('The shareholders' role in governance is to appoint the directors and the auditors and to satisfy themselves that an appropriate governance structure is in place').

Third, it is a 'blunt instrument' offering only the barest of elaborations about the context or form of governance, with no attempt to go beyond a shallow description. While this is probably a deliberate choice, it renders the description unfit for any form

---

[4] Cadbury, *Report of the Committee on the Financial Aspects of Corporate Governance*, para. 2.5

of prescription about how governance should be developed: some members of the committee were unconvinced from the outset that anything needed to be done.[5]

Finally, the definition appears to apply only to business corporations acting for profit.

In short, the definition begs further questions:

- Against what ethical framework or context does the control and direction of businesses take place?
- How do the shareholders exercise a continuing oversight to ensure that the appropriate governance structures are maintained in place? (Assuming of course that they were able to do so in the first place.)
- Are the only constraints on manager/directors the law, informal rules and initial shareholder involvement possibly with a highly ritualised subsequent involvement?
- What mechanisms exist to develop the organisation in line with the changing dynamics of the business world, to protect good governance?
- Do similar strictures apply only to commercial organisations or more widely to, for instance, public sector organisations?

If the public sector collectively stated that the principles of good corporate governance did not apply to the management of public resources, there would be a justifiable outcry. A definition of the proper governance of corporate bodies in the public sector is required, not least given the political trend to attempt to re-balance economies worldwide by encouraging public sector service providers to both include and ape the techniques and practices of the commercial sector.

Recognition that Cadbury left some areas unresolved came in the form of reports by subsequently-convened committees – the Greenbury,[6] Hampel,[7] Higgs,[8] Myners,[9] and Smith[10] Reports. Some issues still remain unresolved, as will be shown in Chapter 6.

The most glaring omission from the Cadbury Report, the refusal to include any participants other than shareholders, directors and auditors, was partially rectified by the next report from a committee of experts tasked with reviewing the issue. The OECD produced an 'official' definition, which arrived seven years later in 1999.[11] By that time most of the developed economies had begun to review the problem, anyway,

---

[5] Correspondence with Mike Sandland in CAD-0121, Cadbury Archives, Judge Business School, University of Cambridge.

[6] R. Greenbury, *Directors' Remuneration: Report of a Study Group Chaired by Sir Richard Greenbury* (London: CBI, 1995).

[7] R. Hampel, *Report of The Committee on Corporate Governance* (London: Gee, 1998).

[8] D. Higgs, *Review of the Role and Effectiveness of Non-Executive Directors* (London: DTI, 2003).

[9] P. Myners, *Institutional Investment in the UK: A Review* (London: HM Treasury, 2001).

[10] FRC, *Audit Committees Combined Code Guidance* (London: FRC, 2003).

[11] OECD, *Principles of Corporate Governance* (Paris: OECD, 1999).

from their own perspectives but still mostly working on the basis of the Cadbury Committee's definition. As a consequence, the OECD's formulation was unlikely to depart far from what had become received wisdom. The definition from the OECD 'Ad Hoc Task Force on Corporate Governance' is as follows:

> Corporate governance is the system by which business corporations are directed and controlled. The corporate governance structure specifies the distribution of rights and responsibilities among different participants in the corporation, such as, the board, managers, shareholders and other stakeholders, and spells out the rules and procedures for making decisions on corporate affairs. By doing this, it also provides the structure through which the company objectives are set, and the means of attaining those objectives and monitoring performance.

This definition suffers from the same problems as the Cadbury definition – hardly surprising given its obvious parentage.

Other definitions

In the years that followed, economists and auditors also had a stab at defining governance, with even greater brevity than Cadbury:

> Corporate governance deals with the ways in which suppliers of finance to corporations assure themselves of getting a return on their investment.[12]

> Governance is the combination of processes and structures implemented by the board in order to inform, direct, manage and monitor the activities of the organisation toward the achievement of its objectives.[13]

These definitions extend the scope of the description very little: in the seven years that elapsed after the initial publication by Cadbury – and all that had transpired in that time – all that the OECD managed to develop out of the Cadbury definition was a nod to the inclusion of stakeholder involvement and a wink to subsequent monitoring by shareholders.

Yet, in the UK alone, there had been further developments which had impacted on the basic Cadbury definition. The Nolan Committee[14] had reported on ethical standards in public life in 1995, setting out the qualities required of those involved in public

---

[12] A. Shleifer and R. W. Vishny, *A Survey of Corporate Governance*, NBER Working Paper 5554 (Cambridge, MA: NBER, 1996).

[13] Chartered Institute of Internal Auditors (UK), www.iia.org.uk/en/Knowledge_Centre/Resource_Library/corporate-governance.cfm.

[14] Lord R. Nolan, *First Report of The Committee on Standards in Public Life* (London: Committee on Standards in Public Life, 1995).

sector governance. The report had been prompted by more public disquiet, this time about the behaviour of those placed in charge of public resources. Committees had also been convened to review issues of managerial remuneration because of public anger about: 'fat cats'; the implications of the Barings Bank collapse of 1995, brought about supposedly by a rogue trader but actually by poor managerial controls and even poorer auditing practices; the extent of the role and influence of non-executive directors; and reviews of the role of committee structures and the control of issues of risk to companies.

Overseas, even more had been done. The most far-sighted report of all came from South Africa – until recently a pariah state, on the fringes of world trade and, it might be assumed, consequently one of the less likely candidates to produce an enlightened response to corporate governance issues.

However, partly because of the context of the political changes that had occurred in South Africa after the collapse of apartheid, the King Committee[15] took a different attitude from that of Cadbury. To quote from the second report, particularly:

> Unlike its counterparts in other countries at the time, the King Report 1994 went beyond the financial and regulatory aspects of corporate governance in advocating an integrated approach to good governance in the interests of a wide range of stakeholders, having regard to the fundamental principles of good financial, social, ethical and environmental practice. In adopting a participative corporate governance system of enterprise with integrity, the King Committee in 1994 successfully formalised the need for companies to recognise that they no longer act independently from the societies and the environment in which they operate.

This report began to bring in wider concepts than the limited ones used by both the OECD task force and the Cadbury Committee's report on which it was based. It is hardly surprising that, for a brief while at least, given the far-sightedness of the definition, South African companies were also among the leaders worldwide in experimenting with different methods of presenting their financial information to stakeholders.

In 2002 the second King Report[16] back-tracked slightly from the view it had expressed previously about integrating a wide range of stakeholders:

> The stakeholder concept of being accountable to all legitimate stakeholders must be rejected for the simple reason that to ask boards to be accountable to everyone would result in their being accountable to no one.

In following years, other definitions arose. This was partly through a need to be seen to be doing something (since no country was immune from corporate scandal) and partly

---

[15] M. King, *The King Report on Corporate Governance I* (South Africa: IoD, 1994).
[16] M. King, *The King Report on Corporate Governance II* (South Africa: IoD, 2002).

as a means to reassure international investors. The Australians, who had significant corporate governance problems after the boom years at the turn of the twentieth century, produced a definition of their own which elaborated on the common statements found in most of the reports:

> Corporate governance is the framework of rules, relationships, systems and processes within and by which authority is exercised and controlled in corporations. It encompasses the mechanisms by which companies ands those in control are held to account. Corporate governance influences how the objectives of the company are set and achieved; how risk is monitored and assessed and how performance is optimized. Effective corporate governance structures encourage companies to create value through entrepreneurialism, innovation, development and exploration and provide accountability and control systems commensurate with the risk involved.[17]

This definition includes elements complementary to the South African definition: risk; the implication that there are various measures and levels of governance; and a suggestion that there are rules, relationships and perhaps even an ethical framework.

But by the time the Australian formulation was written there had been nearly thirty major failures of corporate governance since the publication of the original Cadbury Report. Given this poor record, it seems likely that the effort expended on corporate governance reform has not achieved much. Shareholder-rule proponents will have been disappointed by the extent of the failures that have occurred and the economic damage done; proponents of stakeholder rule will have found their suspicions about the inadequacy of the in-place regime vindicated, while seeing no indication of development of a more wide-ranging structure of governance that will satisfy their concerns.

The weakness of principle-based structures

Both principle-based (essentially voluntary) and rule-based (legalistic) systems have suffered examples of very significant failure. The corporate governance regime employed in the UK – with which this book is mostly concerned – is that of a principle-based structure which relies on three major factors:

- the goodwill of the participants to adhere to the principles because they are seen to be 'the right thing to do' and because the case for doing so is intrinsically persuasive;
- the pressure on companies from investors to implement corporate governance structures that comply with best practice because such companies will find it easier

---

[17] Australian Stock Exchange, *Principles of Good Corporate Governance and Best Practice Recommendations* (Sydney: Australian Stock Exchange, 2007).

to raise funding in the marketplace[18] and those that do not will find that the cost of capital increases to offset the increased risk perceived by investors of putting their money is less well-run businesses;

- peer pressure – the argument that 'a rising tide lifts all boats'[19] and improved standards of behaviour of corporate leaders will gradually improve the behaviour of all companies.

But in order to work properly, principles-based regimes have to define their terms correctly and it could be, therefore, that the failure to define terms – as suggested above – is one of the factors that has led to the continuing prevalence of corporate governance failure. As a leader column in the *Financial Times* noted in June 2011:[20]

> Britain's vaunted governance code can only work in controlled companies if the majority shareholders are inclined to follow its spirit. Otherwise, the requirement to comply or explain has no force.

The definition is only part of the problem, however. The definition can be internally consistent and 'correct' but if it applies to a putative system where the descriptions of who is involved and how they are involved are wrong, then its effectiveness will be minimised; the levers being pulled to control the system will not connect to the points of pressure in the system.

Crisis highlights need to step up governance

Discussing corporate governance just days before Invensys abruptly parted company with its chief executive, Sir Nigel Rudd, who chairs the FTSE 100 company, put it like this: 'The thing about boards is that you only know how good they are in a crisis. Otherwise, it's a case of "Everything's all right while it's going all right". It's when there's a BP situation or a scandal that you find out when a board works or not.'

While not a crisis, the boardroom move is still sufficiently out of the normal run of corporate life to be a test. So Sir Nigel may well feel pleased that the news did not leak and the company was able to announce the new chief executive at the same time as Ulf Henriksson's swift exit.

Sir Nigel's comments also neatly sum up what has driven corporate governance reform over the past 20 years or so. As successive reports revealed flaws in how

---

[18] See the special issue of *Journal of Financial Economics*: A. Shleifer et al., 'Investor protection and corporate governance', *Journal of Financial Economics*, 58(1–2) (2000), 3–27.

[19] Attributed to J. F. Kennedy: remarks in Heber Springs, Arkansas at the dedication of Greers Ferry Dam, 3 October 1963.

[20] Leader Column, *Financial Times*, 12 June 2011.

Britain's boardrooms operated, codes of conduct developed to embed best practice without leaving reforms to the inflexibility of legislation.

The results have changed corporate behaviours – in areas such as deciding executive pay and improving relationships with shareholders – based on a regime requiring companies either to abide by the code or explain publicly why not.

They have also created something of a governance industry, with the attendant risk that it is seen as a specialist subject rather than a mainstream concern.

Baroness Hogg, chairman of the Financial Reporting Council which looks after the corporate code and last year's newly-minted stewardship code setting out investors' duties, believes people sometimes get hung up on the language. 'If you put it in terms of "Do you care how the company is run?" you can have a very interesting conversation with a fund manager. Every fund manager understands that's important, unless they're short-term traders.'

After years in which the spotlight of reform shone mainly on companies, the focus has now turned to the other side of the coin – the shareholders. Like so many other participants, they are widely perceived to have been asleep at the wheel during the financial crisis.

The stewardship code sets out seven principles intended to encourage better scrutiny of companies by the investors who own them. More than 140 fund managers, asset owners and advisory firms have signed up. The question now is what difference it can make.

It faces some scepticism. Sir Richard Lapthorne, chairman of Cable & Wireless Communications, takes issue with the idea of shareholder stewardship. 'The stewards of a company are the board, not the shareholders, because they don't have the necessary information, knowledge and access,' he says. 'Their job is to choose the people to whom they delegate and then make sure we report back to them in an honest manner.'

Among those who favour shareholders being more active on governance issues, there is a worry that pressure to sign up may encourage participation that is no more than lip service.

'If you force people who are not concerned about things like independence to vote [in general meetings], you often get votes automatically in favour of management, meaning concerned investors' votes are diluted,' says Georgina Marshall, regional head of corporate governance at Aviva Investors. 'We would rather that those who are not really interested stay off the playing field.'

Lady Hogg believes the key to making the code effective is convincing shareholders and companies that active involvement on both sides is valuable.

'It is intrinsic in the equity shareholding model that boards carry responsibility for looking after shareholder interests. If shareholders don't engage with boards then a bit of the system is not operating as it should.'

Jennifer Walmsley, a director of Hermes Equity Ownership Services, agrees. 'We're not doing engagement to make the world a better place but because we believe it enhances value. The corporate governance code relies on "comply or explain", and it is perfectly justified for companies to explain departures from the code. But if those explanations are to have any meaning, there need to be shareholders on the other side of the table to listen.'

The stewardship code is still bedding down, but there are already suggestions that further regulation is needed.

Andrew Tyrie, chairman of the cross-party Treasury committee of MPs, raises the question of extra obligations for investors in financial institutions.

'Shareholder activism has to play a part in addressing moral hazard in banking,' he says. 'Shareholders are beneficiaries of the implicit subsidy to banking – and arguably with those benefits should come some duties.'

There is also the prospect of legislation from the European Commission, with a green paper on corporate governance expected in April.

'It's important that the stewardship code works because it has been made clear by the UK government and the EU that the next step would be legislation,' says Ms Walmsley. 'Given we have the "comply or explain" regime for companies, it would be incongruous to legislate investor behaviour.'

Even so, unless the code can swiftly be shown to have improved shareholder behaviour, incongruity alone may not be enough to stop the Brussels initiative.

Source: A. Smith, *Financial Times*, 27 March 2011

Two years after the OECD report, Sir Adrian Cadbury had revised his own views:

> Corporate governance is concerned with holding the balance between economic and social goals and between individual and communal goals ... the aim is to align as nearly as possible the interests of individuals, corporations and society.[21]

Very obviously this description does not negate the more formal wording of the Committee's Report. But it does recognise that the limited scope of the original definition needs to be widened to encompass a bigger horizon (to be fair, by the time

---

[21] Sir A. Cadbury, *Corporate Governance Overview*, World Bank Report (Washington DC: World Bank, 1999).

of the UK's Hampel Report in 1998 the significance of stakeholders had been recognised: the report stated that 'the directors as a board are responsible for relations with stakeholders but they are accountable to the shareholders').[22]

Additional considerations

In keeping with these propositions – first, that the definitions on which the current debate is founded do not go far enough in describing what corporate governance is and, second, that there are better definitions available and that the practice of corporate governance would be better if the definitions were better adjusted to what is being monitored – two alternative definitions of corporate governance will be advanced and used throughout this book. One definition is for general use and one is slightly more specific to cover activities in the public and non-profit sectors. However, care has to be exercised when talking about governance in the public sector, since there is an absence of the primary mechanism used in the private sector – the price mechanism – by which resources are allocated to different purposes. This, coupled with the elective nature of much public sector oversight, results in the primary mechanism of governance being political – not necessarily subject to the constraints of commercial governance.

The private commercial sector is able to allocate resources by determining whether or not the use of those resources makes a profit and then comparing that profit against alternative uses to choose the most efficient (in terms of profit generation). The public sector has no such yardstick. It can employ resources in different uses but it cannot conclusively say whether those resources are being used effectively or not in comparison with other alternative uses. It has no 'rational economic calculator' to help it decide where to place resources for maximum benefit across different purposes (although much ingenuity and effort has been spent on trying to derive and apply proxy measures for profit – but not always to beneficial effect). The lack of a 'rational economic calculator' – a profit and loss account – makes the business of good governance in the public sector even more difficult.

Governance as risk management

The formulation that profit is the reward for risk is a basic one in economic theory: labour receives wages; capital receives rent; the entrepreneur receives profit for accepting risk. Risk is universal: regardless of whether they are operating with the intention of making a profit or not, all organisations have to contend with uncertainty – effectively,

[22] Hampel, *Report of The Committee on Corporate Governance*.

a synonym for risk. They have to put assets and resources at risk without the knowledge that their ambitions will be realised. In return for this acceptance of risk, in the case of private commercial organisations, a reward in the form of profit is usually expected. (In the case of public sector organisations they have only the option to impose controls to try to mitigate risk, hence the inclusion of that phrase in the formulation of the terms in the separate definition of governance for the public sector.)

The shareholder is of course equally well aware of risk from his or her standpoint. There is substantial academic evidence which suggests that firms which can evidence good corporate governance procedures and records are more highly regarded by capital markets and therefore able to raise funds at lower rates than those businesses in which investors may consider their money to be at greater risk of loss by negligent managers.[23] Their cost of capital is lower, simply because the perceived risks to investors of speculating in the shares of the company are lower. Fundamental to this concept of risk reduction is the concept of the development of appropriate procedures which protect the base capital of the company. This protection is concerned both with operational routines that are effective, and the issue of ownership and distibution of the rewards from trading. This basic level of governance is the *procedural* dimension of governance.

Good corporate governance therefore can be said to be provably connected with the reduction of risk, through effective routines which safeguard the company. By extension, if risk is reduced then, all other things being equal, the potential for securing profit is greater.

Governance and management: the dimensions of governance

At a slightly deeper level of analysis, appropriate supervision is required to oversee the processes by which limited resources are efficiently directed to competing purposes for the use of the organisation and its stakeholders. This is a *behavioural* issue, which will include ensuring the maintenance of the organisation and its long-term sustainability. It is this reliance on the behaviour of the managers of the business which provides confidence in the operational basis on which the investor's inward-looking perception of good governance is based. In terms of the internal operation of a business, greater profit is likely to result from more efficient organisation of the means of production. The existence of good *behavioural corporate governance*, combined with procedural integrity, therefore becomes the catalyst of a virtuous cycle of stewardship.

The maintenance of good governance is then an essential part of managerial activity – not simply an optional extra which shareholders may choose to include in setting up a

---

[23] Shleifer et al., 'Investor protection and corporate governance'.

business (or managers may choose to flout in running one). To be effective, good governance must exist at all levels and is therefore not simply the province of the board – as in the Cadbury definition – but stretches all the way through the organisation. The recognition of this gives the further key to appreciating the essential character of outward-facing governance as being absolutely nothing to do with charitable giving or corporate philanthropy (which is an oxymoron, as we shall see in Chapter 3), but rather a central factor in the efficient operation of any form of organisation.

This means that the definitions expressed above can be used not only for the inward facing aspect of corporate governance – the triangular relationships between the company as a legal entity, shareholders and directors – but are also central to an appreciation of the risks confronting an organisation in the outward-facing aspects of governance too – the relationships between the company and stakeholders in the business like employees; pensioners; customers; suppliers; financiers; the State and so on.

The UK Bribery Act 2010 requires that companies establish an anti-corruption regime of 'appropriate procedures' that indicates the commitment of the company as a whole to a repudiation of corruption, from the very top level down. It implies that there must be a cultural dimension to the repudiation of bribery as a means of doing business. The intention is to inculcate a culture in business which regards correct ethical behaviour as the norm. Good corporate governance will be like this, in that it will be a cultural characteristic of the company that pervades the entirety of its activities. In fact, the procedural requirements of the Bribery Act 2010 might well be taken as a template for effective corporate governance procedures. This type of governance is identified in this book as *structural governance*: it is the cultural glue which holds the business together; the framework of ethics referred to in the definition developed below, as a consequence of these components.

However, there is a distinction which needs to be made about the responsibility for corporate governance policies. The distinction is one that mirrors the distinction between the executive functions of management conducted through 'line' and 'hierarchy' and the strategic activities of boards conducted through 'staff' functions. Since the central function of good governance is the effective management of corporate risk, it is an activity which is carried on day-to-day within the company. But the methods and policies by which risk is controlled, or the organisation adjusts for risk, are the province of the board to determine and establish and for management then to follow.

This description of governance is not contentious. It is recognised as a pervasive operational characteristic of companies by the Cadbury Committee definition and all subsequent generally-accepted definitions, including the King Report's definition and the ones advanced in this book. There is an implicit acceptance that good governance is not a 'tick-box activity' but one which has to become a cultural component of companies if they are to work well for the benefit of all parties. It is a vital component in terms of defining the shape of the company – as necessary as a skeleton is to defining the shape of a human body.

Overarching all of this is the framework of laws and regulations imposed externally (some formally by the State as stakeholder; some informally by other stakeholders such as customers; suppliers; financiers; employees) which the company has to work within. These form the umbrella of 'systemic governance'.

Two suggested definitions: private sector and public sector

Whatever the exact form of the definition used, it seems that to be properly descriptive it should contain some specific reference to a number of important groups involved in determining the way that companies behave and to the four forms of governance identified above.

The first definition of corporate governance applies to the private or commercial sector, and is as follows:

> Corporate governance is the governing structure and processes [procedural governance] in an organisation that exist to oversee the means by which limited resources are efficiently directed to competing purposes for the use of the organisation and its stakeholders; including the maintenance of the organisation and its long-run sustainability [behavioural governance], set and measured against a framework of ethics [structural governance] and backed by regulation and laws [systemic governance].

The second definition applies to governance issues in the public sector and is necessarily slightly more elaborate because of the significant difference alluded to above between the materials and context of governance in the private sector and the public sector:

> A series of principles, which are usually embodied in formal controls, in agencies which seek to redress market imperfections by acting for, on behalf of and with the express approval of the State, through all or some of the activities of policy-making, management, and regulation; mostly using resources without the intention of generating a profit and providing more or less appropriately-transparent information about the means of arriving at the allocation of resources in the absence of a set of rational economic methods of achieving those ends.

Having indicated that there are differences between the activity of governance in the private sector and in the public sector, this book will confine itself to further examination of only the private sector.

Both the alternative definitions of governance have at their heart the concept of risk (and reward where appropriate) as being the determinant of how organisations should be managed. The implicit function of management then is to preserve the long-term basis on which wealth is created and distributed, and to treat each group of stakeholders appropriately. This then dovetails with the issue of treating governance as the management of risk, which itself unites the distinctions of inward- and outward-facing corporate governance into one concept. There are other dimensions – the *longitudinal* and the *operational* – which will be covered in subsequent chapters.

The main actors in governance: shareholders and stakeholders

Almost everyone who comes into some form of commercial contact with a company becomes a stakeholder (even if only on the basis of a temporary relationship) and so using this term covers all the individual actors who might become involved. However, in current conventional usage there is a marked distinction between shareholders and stakeholders – although the one is really only a subset of the other (shareholders are part of the wider collection of stakeholders). Shareholders' interests are generally elevated above those of stakeholders, probably because the simple activity of definition renders the group more distinct, more identifiable in terms of supposedly common interests and therefore more easily dealt with and more significant to commercial managers. It also accords better of course with the traditionalist view of the supremacy of the shareholder in the priority order of those who receive benefits from the company.

Stakeholders' interests, by contrast, are manifold, probably competing and possibly, collectively, conflicting. Appeals to shareholders' interests are usually given consistency and simplicity (even though a description of their interests on this basis is itself usually simplistic and unrealistic; shareholders will have many different interests with respect to the company). But there can be few compelling and consistent appeals to the interests of disparate stakeholders since they are unlikely to hold a completely unifying and common interest other than to see the continued existence of the company (although this issue of sustainability is ultimately of the greatest importance). The point made by the King II Report quoted earlier is relevant here – working for stakeholder interests may mean effectively working for no-one.

The effect of this somewhat artificial distinction serves to cloud the important issues of corporate governance in many respects, rather than to illuminate them. There are obviously certain circumstances where the use of the term shareholder in preference to stakeholder is both inevitable and accurate (and consequently desirable). But this is not always the case. As Chapter 3 suggests there are very compelling reasons for using the term 'stakeholder' in preference to 'shareholder' for describing the status of those who own the rights to participate in dividend payments in listed companies, if the real basis of corporate governance in listed companies is considered.

Subsequent minimal reworkings of the basic definition have not taken into acount changes in the dynamics of governance since the early 1990s because they have, for the most part, sought to squeeze in an additional term without any consideration of whether the basic structure requires an overhaul.

Beyond that precautionary signal about a subject which recurs later, the specific groups that fall into the category of 'major actors' and which will be considered in the rest of this book include the following:

- the company (as a separate legal entity);
- shareholders, including the subset of shareholders known as 'institutional investors';
- directors; both executive and non-executive;
- the company secretary;
- employees, past and present;
- auditors, as a separate component in the governance process;
- 'reputational intermediaries' – auditors, again, but in a different capacity; stockbrokers; the Press;
- regulators;
- customers;
- the State, as the promulgator of law and regulation.

Of these parties, the most significant are usually taken to be the company, shareholders and directors. The dichotomy between the inward aspect of corporate governance and the outward aspect makes dealing with the relationships between these parties easier – if slightly artificial – since, as we have seen, corporate governance should be regarded as an essential component of organisational activity rooted in the basic structures of operation, rather than an optional later addition to the structure.

Examining the specific relationship between shareholders and directors in isolation can also produce illuminating insights into the relationships that should exist between the company, the directors and managers of the company, and other parties to the stakeholder group.

The actors and ownership and control: distinguishing theories

There are four main theories which describe the governance interaction. These are:

- agency theory;
- transaction cost theory;
- stewardship theory; and
- 'the nexus of contracts' theory.

Each gives particular insight into the operation of the company and the context within which the processes of governance are determined. None describes the real world completely since they are all subject to greater or lesser degrees of abstraction. The most useful description of the real world is probably one that incorporates elements of all of them.

Agency theory is a concept largely borrowed from company law. It describes the relationship between the shareholders and the managers that they choose to appoint to run their business for them in legalistic terms, using a contractual relationship as the foundation of the governance process. The impact of some of the concepts of contract law for the processes of governance will be considered in detail in Chapters 4 and 5 but the idea is based on the presumption that after a certain (indeterminate) size it becomes more efficient for shareholders (principals) to delegate the operation of their company to appointees (agents) rather than to attempt to run it themselves. The nub of this idea has a very long provenance[24] and goes back as far as the concept of the company as an economic unit, certainly to Phoenician times, when bands of merchants collaborated, in what we might now call venture capital operations, to trade with other countries, appointing ships' captains and managers to act for them.[25]

The significant factor arising from this – and one which has been identified and examined at length by researchers – is that the ownership of the business and the control of the business are separated and that different individuals are involved in each function.[26]

The agent, the operational controller, is bound by the relationship to do certain things for the principal, the owner, who also has reciprocal obligations to the agent. The relationship between the two is based on the principle of a fiduciary duty and '*uberimae fides*' or utmost good faith. The agent may do nothing which harms the interests of the principal and is required to put the principal's interest above his own in the execution of tasks relating to the contractual relationship. However, human nature being what it is, the owner has to take steps through regulation and law to enforce the moral and ethical basis on which the contract is founded.

Proponents of the principle-based system of governance used in the UK tend to favour the agency model since they contend that the contractual nature of the relationship makes the relative positions of director/agent and shareholder/principal clear and it also has the beneficial effect of aligning the interests of the two parties if the proper arrangements are put in place.[27] However, it has a number of flaws when applied to modern corporate structures and its overuse as a foundation of current

---

[24] J. Mickelthwait and A. Wooldridge, *The Company: A Short History of a Revolutionary Idea* (London: Wiedenfield and Nicholson, 2003).

[25] S. Moscati, *The World of the Phoenicians* (New York, NY: Praeger, 1965).

[26] For a legalistic definition see S. Judge, *Business Law*, 4th edn (Hampshire: Palgrave Macmillan, 2011).

[27] O. Williamson, *The Mechanisms of Governance* (Oxford University Press, 1996).

governance structures leads to a number of problems – especially when remuneration is concerned. The flaws include the question of who the agent is working for; the problem of multiple obligations; and the operational basis of the arrangement between the agent and the principal (whoever that may be). These issues will be examined in more detail in Chapter 3.

Transaction cost theory goes on from the basis established in the agency arrangement to suggest that the owner will put in place safeguards in respect of the delegation of managerial duties to the point where their cost is equal to the benefit returned by putting them in. Transaction cost theory is based on economic explanations of behaviour, rather than legal ones, and suggests that all the players in the arrangement are primarily motivated by rational intentions and seek to maximise their own economic advantage, usually by minimising the costs of transactions.[28] The theory is most appropriate to large companies where the internal allocation of resources effectively provides market-like conditions inside the business, so that the organisation of the business supposedly then determines allocative efficiency. The description of the internal relationships in transaction theory substitutes economic terms for legal ones, so that while the principal and agent arrangement describes the potential of the agent to work for himself rather than for his principal as 'moral hazard', transaction theory describes it as 'opportunism'. The theory offers potentially useful insights into describing managerial behaviour in respect of trading-off personal gain against the interest of shareholders – usually short-term advantage against long-term benefits – but its practical application tends to act as a reinforcement to, rather than a substitute for, agency arrangements.

Stewardship theory[29] – sometimes known as stakeholder theory – is less formalised than either the legalistic or the economic alternatives, drawing on economics, ethical philosophy and sociology for many of its insights. It proposes that individuals have more than simply economic aims and values that are brought into play in their interactions with companies. In contrast to the individualistic motives ascribed to agency theory, stewardship theory suggests that human behaviour is composed of a much larger range of motives – among them achievement, responsibility and recognition (all of which can be regarded as being interchangeable with money, of course) together with ethical principles that are not readily or automatically subordinated to economic rationalism.

Stakeholder theory also often goes under the name of 'corporate social responsibility' (CSR). CSR is a much-abused concept which labours under many misapprehensions, most often that of 'good corporate citizenship' – which will be

---

[28] Williamson, *Mechanisms*.
[29] J. Freeman et al., *Stakeholder Theory* (Cambridge University Press, 2010).

discussed in Chapter 3. Utilisation of the concepts in the alternative definitions above – encompassing aspects of economic competition, ethical behaviour, sustainability and inter-stakeholder relationships – retrieve it from the ditches of so-called corporate philanthropy and charitable giving into which negligent drivers have propelled it.

In contrast to agency theory, stewardship theory sees no real conflict between managers and owners and would take a relaxed view of the needs identified in agency theory to check activities or separate roles between the two. Its focus is very much to the fore in ethical considerations of so-called 'good corporate citizenship'.

The company as an actor

When it is considered further, as will be seen in Chapter 2, the company is an individual legal entity which has a number of capabilities, rights and powers. In this respect, for the purpose of the law, it resembles a person: it can sue and be sued; it can enter into contracts; it can dispose of economic goods. However, in some respects there are good grounds for suggesting that this view of the company as a person gives rise to unnecessary complications in describing relationships between the company and other parties to the governance process – particularly in considering the company's interaction with stakeholders and the relationships between shareholders. The Canadian legal academic Professor Joel Bakan[30] has suggested that if the company is to be considered a legal person then it must be considered a psychopath. In matters of damage done to others for instance, how can the company as a legal entity be punished? Less vividly, but equally prickly, one of the areas where the traditionalist view of the relationship between shareholders and managers is least persuasive is because the company is interposed between the two, so the normal relationship of the principal and agent cannot apply.

The last theory of the four takes this set of problems into account and offers a rather more limited view of the effective status of the company – as opposed to its legal status as defined in the traditionalist view. It recognises the essential contribution of the principal-agent arrangement in identifying the separation between ownership and control of the company but goes on to regard the firm as a junction of all the activities it undertakes with the co-ordination of traffic through this junction undertaken by managers. The company becomes a 'nexus of contracts'[31] – a series of relationships often backed by legal agreements, which are constantly fluid, occupy ever-changing priorities and compete for resources: company-customers; company-suppliers;

---

[30] J. Bakan, *The Corporation: The Pathological Pursuit of Profit and Power* (London: Constable and Robinson, 2005).
[31] R. H. Coase, 'The Nature of the Firm', *Economica*, 4(16) (1937), 386–405.

company-employees; company-state; company-competitors even. In this respect the nexus theory draws on a body of social and political theory from the social contractualists like Hobbes, Locke and Rousseau, as well as the anti-contractualists like Marx and modernists like Rawls and Nozick. However, in common with transaction theory, the nexus of contracts suggest that the driving force behind all this constant change is the economic concept of self-maximising the utility of all the parties and, not least, of the managers.

A review of the formulation of the alternatives offered above to the Cadbury definitions and the brief explanations of alternatives to traditional theory should indicate that they deliberately contain elements of agency theory, transaction cost theory, stewardship theory and the nexus of contracts principle. To revisit the main definition and make this plain:

> The governing structure and processes in an organisation [*nexus of contracts*] that exist to oversee the means by which limited resources are efficiently directed to competing purposes [*transaction cost theory*] for the use of the organisation and its stakeholders, including the maintenance of the organisation and its long-run sustainability [*stewardship theory*], set against a background of managerial and shareholder behaviour implicitly measured against a framework of ethics and backed by regulation and laws [*agency theory*].

CHAPTER 2

Inward-facing governance

This chapter:

- looks at and describes the governance relationships between shareholders, directors and companies;
- reviews the roles of the major actors in the governance relationships;
- discusses limited liability;
- looks at the 'shareholders contract' – the articles of association;
- tests the role of the actors against existing theory.

The first chapter looked at the broad landscape of governance and surveyed the theoretical background; it offered new definitions of corporate governance that seek to overcome the shortcomings of established definitions and, in particular, included notions that go beyond the limited concept of shareholder primacy. It mentioned the chief component of corporate governance – the company – only in passing.

This chapter will deal with some of the formal characteristics of the company and other actors in the governance process. It will conclude by developing an argument that a more realistic description of what a shareholder is in these companies is not the owner of the company at all but the possessor of a different piece of property – the share itself. The argument for this requires an examination of the positions of the other parties who are involved in the company.

The company

The primary effect of setting up a company is to create a new legal person. Since the company can enter into contracts, sue and be sued and dispose of economic property, it has a separate life from its shareholders. But for all these things to happen, because the company has no mind or its own, someone has to control it. This then produces tension about who the beneficiaries of the company's activities are; how they should be rewarded; how the company is controlled to bring that about; and what powers each of these parties has in respect of the others – in short, the discipline of corporate governance. The act of creation of the company is the event that brings about consequential governance issues.

Once established – incorporated – the company becomes separated from its shareholders by what is called 'the veil of incorporation'.[1] A legal distinction descends between the shareholders – as individuals and as a group – and the business that they have created. Money that they have put into the company in subscribing for shares is now no longer theirs but belongs to the company; the assets it buys with those subscribed funds belong to it and not to individual shareholders; the company is the entity which contracts with external agents, not they. And from this arises the creation of a contract between the parties – company, directors and shareholders – about how the company will behave. This contract is the Articles of Association and its impact will be considered in more detail below.

Common structural factors of companies

In conventional descriptions of corporate governance companies are created by shareholders, who therefore own the company and go on to appoint directors to run the company on their behalf. Sometimes of course, particularly in smaller companies, the owning shareholders are also the directors. Conventional interpretations of corporate governance usually emphasise the legalistic elements of the relationships between the company, its shareholders and the directors, particularly that of the ownership of the company by the shareholders. For small companies these descriptions work well. They begin to break down as shareholder numbers get larger and the 'control-distance' between individual shareholders and directors increases.

In the UK, for most practical purposes, there are two types of commercial company – the private limited company and the public limited company. The minimum legal, technical characteristics of these companies are shown below.

Private limited companies must:
- have at least two shares;
- have at least one director who is a natural person;
- not offer shares to the public;
- designate themselves *Ltd* or *ltd.*

Public limited companies must:
- have a minimum of £50,000 of share capital;
- have at least two shareholders;
- have at least two directors;
- be designated *plc* or *PLC* or *public limited company;*

---

[1] See S. Judge, *Business Law*, 4th edn (Hampshire: Palgrave Macmillan, 2011).

- not take advantage of any relaxation of the accounts regulations which may apply to Small and Medium-sized Enterprises (SMEs) even though they may otherwise qualify for such exemptions in certain respects;
- elect directors separately and not *en bloc*;
- observe regulations regarding the purchase of their own shares;
- not issue shares to the public except by means of a prospectus (which is subject to regulatory restriction).

There is no threshold which must be crossed in respect of status: private limited companies do not have to become PLCs on achieving a certain size; they can remain private if they wish.

Other incorporated possibilities

It is technically still possible to come across *unlimited* companies (but there is little purpose for them, other than for very specific tax reasons). Corporations sole which have only one shareholder (and are usually connected with some form of statutory or clerical office) also exist; and companies limited by guarantee (where shareholders agree to stump up some further sum on the dissolution of the company) are prevalent in the charity sector. All these forms of organisation take advantage of the longevity of the corporate structure – it exists with a life of its own that may exceed that of its shareholders.

The company has a number of characteristics – some of which depend upon whether it is a private limited company or a public limited company. Apart from the already-mentioned feature that the company is an independent legal entity with legal consequences, the common structural characteristics between the two types are:

- both have shareholders, who possess limited liability for the debts of the company;
- both must have directors to act as 'the controlling mind' of the company;
- both have a document called the Articles of Association which governs the relationships between the parties.

The description of the essentials of governance in this chapter will concentrate on these four elements: shareholders; limited liability; directors; and the articles. For all types of company, all the other actors in governance – auditors; financiers; stakeholders of whatever description – fit somewhere into this structure like pieces of a jigsaw puzzle and will be considered in subsequent chapters. But, since they are essential to the creation of a company, the foremost among the actors are the shareholders.

Shareholders

There can be no company without shareholders. The conventional (legal) view is that having established the company by subscribing for shares, the shareholders then go on to own the company.[2] For as long as an individual holds a share in a company he remains a shareholder and member of the company and, by extension, an owner of the company.

Shareholders have certain legal rights, regardless of whether the company is a private company or a public one – these are:

- the right to convene general meetings (provided enough fellow-shareholders agree);
- the approval of accounts prepared by the directors;
- the election/approval of directors;
- the right to call for the dismissal of directors (subject to certain rules again);
- approval (or reduction) of dividend – but not an increase in the amount – proposed by the directors;
- the approval of auditors;
- the right to vote at General Meetings on proposals put to the meeting by the directors (or fellow shareholders, always providing sufficient have agreed to the proposals being placed before the meeting);
- the right to require provision of certain documents pertaining to ownership of shares;
- the right to scrutinise certain documents relating to contracts with directors at specific times;
- the right to trade shares (subject to some very modest constraints in public companies but often subject to more serious ones in private limited companies).[3]

All of these rights are essentially backward-looking. In both types of company, public limited and private limited, shareholders are not entitled to see any of the detailed minutes of board meetings; they are not entitled to be given details of future trading, except in a formalised fashion; they may not challenge the right of directors (other than in very exceptional circumstances) to refuse to make a dividend payment; they cannot increase the dividend; they have only limited rights to investigate the accounts prepared by the directors and approved by the auditors who nominally work on the shareholders' behalf.[4] They have traded these privileges in order to be protected from the attentions of the company's creditors.

---

[2] *Ibid.*   [3] *Ibid.*, p. 219.
[4] PriceWaterhouseCoopers, *A Practical Guide to the Companies Act 2006*, 2nd edn (Kingston upon Thames: CCH, 2010).

The shareholders' advantage: limited liability

The most significant thing that happens when a company is formed is that a new legal entity enters the world. The existence of a company is indissolubly linked with the actions of its founding shareholders: there can be no companies without shareholders.

For the shareholders one of the purposes of creating the separate legal entity is that the company can enter into contracts by itself for the supply of goods and services without having to get all the shareholders to agree all the time on every issue. This is one of the most significant ways in which the incorporated entity differs from a partnership. For individual shareholders the major consequence of this separate personality is that, when things go wrong commercially, the liability of the shareholder to stand behind the company's uncovered obligations is limited to the money originally subscribed (or, technically, to any outstanding commitment that they might have to subscribe).[5] This is precisely because the company's commercial behaviour is that of an individual legal entity; as a result the shareholders are not responsible for its debts.

The directors have taken over control of the company (at least in large companies with many shares issued to lots of shareholders) and become responsible to the shareholders – the traditionalist view holds that they have the position of *agents* of the shareholders[6] – in controlling and directing the activities of the company. The obligations that the company enters into as a result of the 'controlling minds' of the directors steering its actions, place a barrier between the company's creditors and the shareholders.

This concept of limited liability, which places a cap on what any individual can be called upon to contribute financially to a business venture in the event of its failure, has been the great engine of economic development since the middle of the Victorian era.[7] It stands in marked contrast to the liabilities of partners to contribute to the debts of the partnership (even if debts are incurred by other members of the partnership, individual partners are still liable under 'joint and several' liability); and to the position of sole traders, who bear all the debts of their trading themselves. It was an innovation in itself which took the form of a political battle – rather than simply an economic one – and in the UK was undertaken, at least in part, under the pressure of the popularity of incorporating in France or the USA where limited liability was available earlier.

---

[5] PriceWaterhouseCoopers, *A Practical Guide*, para. 8.1.3.
[6] Williamson, *Mechanisms*.   [7] Mickelthwait and Wooldridge, *The Company*.

The development of limited liability

Limited liability as a concept dates from the time of the chartered trading companies, which undertook adventures of exploration that might be regarded as equivalent in risk and cost to the exploration of space.

The stupendous costs and risks could only be borne if members of the company were granted some form of barrier to their liabilities. Although the performance of these companies was patchy in profit terms, they were a convenient way of harnessing private activity to State ambitions (they have ghostly echoes to the Private Finance Initiatives of the late twentieth century). However, they sometimes went spectacularly wrong – one such failure being the South Sea Company. The company assumed government borrowings (£10 million in the value of the currency of the time) in return for a monopoly on trade with South America and then took on more government debt while extravagant rumours of its trading prospects circulated.[8]

Following the resulting scandal of the South Sea Bubble, the British Government enacted legislation in 1720 which prohibited the creation of joint stock companies without specific Parliamentary approval, granted through the award of a charter. This was difficult to obtain and the process was designed to limit the possibility of a recurrence of the unbridled speculation which had surrounded the South Sea Company's shares (partly because of the steadying effects of the Act, the company survived, was restructured and continued trading for more than a century).

The restrictive effects of the Bubble Act were not greatly resented by the early industrialists, who often preferred the closeness of partnerships built on family or friendship ties.

However, the need for development capital in the United States, inter-state competition and change in the common law (the *Dartmouth College* case[9]), which gave clarity to the rights of legal corporate entities, prompted a loosening of the same strictures that existed in the UK. Similar trends occurred in France, where sleeping partners were given limited liability in 1807.

In 1825 the Joint Stock Companies Act repealed some of the provisions of the Bubble Act and enabled companies to be set up, but still at considerable cost.

A series of insurance and railway company frauds retarded further progress in the 1840s (the growth of the railways exerted a heavy pressure for liberalisation

---

[8] For the history of the South Sea Bubble see M. Balen, *A Very English Deceit* (London: Fourth Estate, 2002).

[9] *Trustees of Dartmouth College* v. *Woodward*, 17 U.S. (4 Wheat.) 518 (1819).

and reform of company law) but liberal political reformers like John Stuart Mill, Richard Cobden and Robert Lowe all argued for the law to be altered on the grounds that it would allow the poor to participate in wealth creation. According to Walter Bagehot,[10] editor of the Economist newspaper, the rich were against the idea for the same reason.

In 1844, with the passage of the Joint Stock Companies Act, Parliamentary approval was dispensed with. By 1855 the Vice-President of the Board of Trade, Edward Pleydell-Bouverie was complaining that companies were being established in France and America that would otherwise have been set up in Britain[11] to satisfy the demand for capital projects, mostly railways. In that year the Limited Liability Act provided the privilege of limited liability to incorporated companies, but retained capital requirements to restrict expansion.

A year later, in 1856, in the midst of the Crimean War, these restrictions were lifted and a company could be established by registering an office and using the abbreviation 'ltd', provided seven shareholders signed a memorandum of association (a document which lasted for 150 years until it was largely dispensed with by the Companies Act 2006). In 1862 a consolidating act was passed and the grandfather of the dynasty of the Companies Acts was established.

The existence of limited liability enabled entrepreneurs to mobilise the modest individual savings of the many; it provided a route for the innovative and the energetic who were not the beneficiaries of inherited wealth to create industrial businesses. But limited liability, being intimately connected with the independence of the legal entity, is also at the root of the problem of defining how, and for whom, corporate governance works.

The potential pitfalls resulting from limited liability are not lost on critics of incorporation (nor on fraudsters), who contend that by releasing promoters and owners of companies from their obligations to act prudently in trading and borrowing, the company carries within itself the seeds of its downfall. Adam Smith identified the problem in *The Wealth of Nations*, first published in 1776.

> The directors of such companies, however, being the managers rather of other people's money than of their own, it cannot well be expected that they should watch over it with the same anxious vigilance with which the partners in a private copartnery frequently watch over their own. Like the stewards of a rich man,

---

[10] W. Bagehot, *Lombard Street: A description of the Money Market* (New Jersey: Wiley, 1999).
[11] Parl. Deb. vol. 138, ser. 3, cols 293–4 10 May 1855.

they are apt to consider attention to small matters as not for their master's honour, and very easily give themselves a dispensation from having it. Negligence and profusion, therefore, must always prevail, more or less, in the management of the affairs of such a company.[12]

Although as a consequence of its economic potential, the incorporated business is now the dominant form of business organisation world-wide, Smith's words still resonate: the processes of corporate governance are principally directed towards ensuring that the effects of the shortcomings which he identified are kept to a minimum – the shareholders try to exercise residual control over the company even though they have appointed directors to run it for them.

Directors

The law does not define the term 'director' in any great detail.[13] The usual operational and legal definitions are that a director is 'a person who manages the company's business', and this may be supplemented with the attribute that he or she 'is accustomed to exercising the powers of the company for any purpose connected with managing the company's business'. The 2006 Act also recognises *de facto* directors – any person occupying the position of director by whatever name called (s. 250).

Strictly speaking, a director is a person who is registered as such on the company's documents at Companies House. However, it is quite common for the title to be bestowed for some operational purpose – 'director of south west region' or 'director of communications' – which does not mean that the holder of the post is a registered director of the company. Case law would probably extend that definition to include something to the effect of 'any person holding themselves out as a director with ostensible authority to do so'.[14]

Directors are (nominally) appointed by shareholders at general meetings but this disguises much of the reality of the situation. The situation in large companies is usually very different from that in small companies where directors may very well be elected from among the ranks of the shareholders. In fact, in many small companies some form of shareholding is a necessary qualification for directorship (particularly in companies funded by venture capital).

In most cases in larger companies, with shares listed on a Stock Exchange, shareholders will be presented with a number of candidates whose appointments they are usually asked to confirm, since the appointment has already been made – subject to scrutiny by the nominations committee if everything is working as it

---

[12] A. Smith, *The Wealth of Nations, Books IV-V* (London: Penguin, 1995).
[13] PriceWaterhouseCoopers, *A Practical Guide*, s. 1.   [14] *Ibid.*

should. Listed company shareholders are effectively expected to support the individuals nominated by the board and approved by the nominations committee.[15] Competition for places on the board by proposals from shareholders for alternative candidates is usually heavily discouraged by incumbent directors – and probably by other shareholders too.

The detail of the different types of director – executive, non-executive, alternate and shadow – and the significance of each type for the detail of governance are dealt with below. All that needs to be recognised is that all properly-appointed directors are equal in the eyes of the law and they all owe a fiduciary duty to the company – and to no-one else – while acting as directors.

Directors

Confusion sometimes arises over the different terminology employed to identify directors.

A *director* of a company is a person who has been identified as such on the company's statutory registers at Companies House. A director may be a real person or a legal person (a company).

An *alternate director* is someone nominated by the registered director to act as proxy for him or her – or for a company acting as director – when the registered director is unable to perform his or her (or its) duties on a temporary basis. This may be through illness, holiday or unavoidable absence, for instance. The alternate acts as a representative unless specifically mandated and accepts the liabilities of the post as well as the privileges of the position.

A *shadow director* is not a director at all – but is someone in accordance with whose instructions registered directors are accustomed to act. Since this is a position, effectively, of illegality – since directors owe their allegiance, loyalty and fiduciary duty to the company and no other – descriptions of shadow directors owing the same obligations to the company as other directors are perverse.

An executive director is usually the recipient of a contract of employment and is paid a salary.

A non-executive director is usually paid by way of fees and has letters of engagement.

---

[15] See *ibid.* in respect of the powers of nominations committees. Recent activity by the FSA goes even further and requires that the FSA scrutinise the candidates to board positions in companies in the finance sector.

They are not delegates of shareholders, nor are they representatives, and may not be mandated by shareholders, while acting as directors, except in very specific circumstances. Their fiduciary duty is owed to the company – although the Companies Act 1985 was the first to require directors to consider the impact on employees of their actions[16] and this has been further elaborated by the 2006 Companies Act.

However, if shareholders resolve a course of action in a general meeting then directors are expected to adhere to the instructions given by the shareholders. This is a consequence of the impact of the articles of association, discussed below, and the effect of the agency relationship which, despite its inappropriateness, appears to be embedded in the concept of the articles, as interpreted under the traditionalist view of governance.

Considerable discretion is thus allowed to directors to proceed along paths that they consider to be in the best interests of the company. In practice it would be difficult to organise the affairs of a large company any other way: having appointed others to undertake the work of direction and management, it would be absurd for individual shareholders to try to involve themselves in the detail of decisions.

However, while this nice, clear-cut distinction may be plain in simple matters and where men of goodwill are in place, it becomes murkier where issues become multi-faceted (as they do in the real world). Nowhere does this happen more blatantly than where the issue of directorial remuneration is concerned – the issue of how much directors take out of the business in relation to what shareholders are to receive. Much of the recent discussion about corporate governance revolves around this single issue and its ramifications, although as a problem it has existed since the first principal engaged the first agent. The text box about Lord and Lady Docker – two colourful figures from the austerity Britain of the 1950s – shows that the problems we complain of now have been around for some time.

Sir Bernard and Lady Docker – the shareholders' revenge

Sir Bernard Docker was a flamboyant industrialist who, together with his wife, Norah, appeared regularly in the society pages of British newspapers after the Second World War. Pictures of Lady Docker frequently appeared: playing marbles with factory workers, at parties given by London criminals; and dancing the hornpipe for an audience of sheepish miners aboard the Dockers' 878-ton yacht Shemara. The Dockers made generous use of the expense account and position of Sir Bernard, who had been chairman of the Birmingham Small Arms Co (a company his father had founded) since 1938. The company produced

---

[16] Companies Act 2006, s. 172.

everything from air rifles to luxury Daimler limousines. The Dockers used two gold-plated Daimlers – one of them upholstered in six zebra skins – which, although owned by Daimler, were built to Lady Docker's specifications. Lady Docker justified this by saying that: 'We bring glamour and happiness into drab lives. The working class loves everything I do.'

In conditions of post-war austerity, B.S.A.'s business began falling off: the other B.S.A. directors and the insurance companies that held blocks of B.S.A. shares began to become disillusioned with the antics of Lord and Lady Docker.

The final straw was one of Lady Docker's dazzling schemes. She had wanted to open a Gold Showroom in Paris featuring one of the gold-plated Daimlers, wearing a gold lame dress that would have cost over £5,000 (or roughly £100,000 in 2010 prices). She decided to charge it against tax and when the Inland Revenue objected, Sir Bernard tried to bill B.S.A. The board of B.S.A. also objected and finally Sir Bernard paid.

This led to other issues being raised by the directors and after a heated three hour meeting early in June 1956 they turfed Sir Bernard out – not only as chairman and managing director, but even as a director.

The contract between the parties: the Articles of Association

One of the methods that shareholders use to assert their interest in the company is the documentary description of the rights and duties of all the parties to the governance of the company. This document is the Articles of Association.

Aside from issues of separate legal personality and consequential limited liability, the Articles represent the second common characteristic of all incorporated businesses. The Articles of Association are effectively a governance contract between the parties engaged in the company – determining their respective rights and duties.

The Articles explain how the company is structured by describing the type ('classes') of shares and the rights attaching to them; they elaborate the rights of shareholders; they set out the procedures for the appointment and removal of directors and they also detail the powers of directors (although these are also subject to the provisions of the Companies Act 2006 in the UK). The Articles will also give details of the conduct of board and general meetings – although, again, the Companies Act 2006 contains certain provisions which also provide for these issues.[17]

---

[17] For instance, Companies Act 2006, s. 248(2) concerning the retention of board minutes.

The articles complement the statutory obligations laid out in the Companies Act by indicating some of the detail of the mechanism by which companies are administered and governance is conducted. Most companies use the standard sets of Articles published in the Companies Act 2006 (these used to be called Table A, Table C and Table F but these titles have been replaced by the simpler title of 'Model Articles'). Public limited companies are obliged to use a different set of articles from private limited companies.

The model sets are effectively pitched at the lowest common denominator rather than the highest common standard and so for small companies they will contain very little material on detailed mechanisms of corporate governance. Larger public companies – or small private companies backed by outside financiers – may well have their own sets to cater for specific circumstances which therefore contain more elaborate details.

Since the UK operates under a principle-based governance regime for listed companies (and there is none for private companies), most of the recommended procedures for effecting good corporate governance are contained not in company documents but in the UK Corporate Governance Code. Listed companies have to enter into a separate arrangement with the Stock Exchange – the Admission Rules – to ensure that they abide by this Code. This arrangement therefore takes the form of another contract between the company and another stakeholder – the Stock Exchange.

In the previous chapter an alternative description of the company was offered: that it derives its operational powers and income generative ability from its position as a holder of individual contracts which have to be synthesised and co-ordinated (the nexus of contracts theory). The pinnacle of this arrangement is the 'Super Contract' of the Articles, since this regulates the standing of the various parties of the shareholder group with each other in a four-way relationship – between shareholder and shareholder; between shareholder and company; between the directors and the shareholders; and between the directors and the company.

Challenges to the traditionalist interpretation

The structure and terms of the Articles can also be used in the traditionalist/legalist view, in conjunction with the historical development of the company, to offer support for the interpretation of the relationship between directors and shareholders as being one of principal and agent.

While the relationship between directors and shareholders might be interpreted this way in a very small company (or at least could have been so until the passage of the 2006 Companies Act, as will be discussed in Chapter 5) it does not describe the situation at all well for a company with listed shares. There the principal-agent relationship – if it exists at all because of the complications of deciding to whom it applies – could better be interpreted as being between the company and the directors, since the contractual relationship exists between those two and not in any way with the shareholders, who have no direct contract with the directors: the company is not the agent of the shareholders and the directors *cannot* be the agent of the shareholders since they are contracted to the company. The fiduciary duty is owed very plainly by the directors to the company. The impossibility of having more than one fiduciary duty at any one time to multiple 'clients' renders impossible any further claims on the directors.

This reinforces very strongly the idea that the shareholders are 'residual claimants' – as described by the nexus theory – and that their ownership is of something other than the company.

By purchasing shares in the company, either as founding shareholders or subsequently, members of the company agree to abide by the terms of the articles – to be bound by the contract, *without negotiation as to its terms*. This is although the articles are deficient in one particular aspect which is regarded as normally central to legal contracts in general.

Contract and uncertainty

Freedom of contract – the ability to make your own mistakes as you see fit – is a fundamental principle of English contract law. But the courts are unsympathetic to sorting out the problems of litigants who have entered into contracts which are uncertain in their impact or imprecise in their terms. From the parties' standpoint however, precision can often be at odds with the commercial reality of the principles of a deal, since in order to allow for the natural vagaries of commercial life, some flexibility has to be left in the arrangements between the parties. However, in legal terms, flexibility shades at its limits into uncertainty. Uncertainty can then become a major obstacle to enforceability.

Shareholder ownership

The problem is that while all these relationships are governed by individual contracts (supplier contracts; employment contracts and so on) which have specific terms and anticipated conclusions (the terms of the supply of goods; the rate for the supply of labour; the cost of bank loans), the fundamental one – between company and shareholders – has no certainty in terms of outcome. While the imputation of this statement may be stretching to the limit a lawyer's definition of certainty, it is certainly impossible to predict the outcome of the shareholder arrangement in financial terms.

The shareholders have no control over the outcome: they cannot be guaranteed a capital return in terms of growth in share price (that will be partly dependent on the way the managers run the business); they cannot be guaranteed a dividend – if they are they become something other than shareholders; they cede the right to determine the dividend policy to the directors; and they may not see the records of directors' meetings to enable them to take a more informed stance on company strategy.

But there has to be some 'finalising power' in respect of all the contracts that arrive at the nexus of contracts. So, under the arrangement where the managers receive delegated powers to run the business on behalf of the shareholders (in the view of the traditionalist/legalist argument), the delegated control rights (the rights to make decisions on issues not foreseen in the contract) have to be allocated to the managers, and tempered by their fiduciary duty (which has already been shown to be owed to the company and not to the shareholders). The problem for the shareholders then becomes one of trying to constrain the managers' intentions to maximise their own utility (the transaction cost argument) out of this arrangement at the expense of the shareholders. This finalising power is represented by the Articles of Association.

Since every right has to have a countervailing obligation (or there is no contract, since there is no promise and no consideration) the shareholders achieve this aim by assuming a residual financial claim on the company's resources to match the residual operational control exercised by the managers, using the powers contained in the Articles as their lever.

In the traditional/legal view shareholders make use of the rights offered by the Articles by using the powers of the marketplace to bring about control. There are markets for efficient corporate control (takeovers), for managerial labour (engaging and sacking) and for corporate information (auditing). Shareholders can sell their businesses (or their stakes in the business) if they want to change control; they can, theoretically, dispose of managers by not re-electing them; and they can ask other competent parties to review the information provided by managers.

By utilising these markets, the traditional/legal view suggests that shareholders who believe that there is opportunity for mischief of some sort do have some effective levers to make management bear the cost of its own misconduct. The supposition is that management will be encouraged to limit its own utility maximisation (a behaviour called 'bounded rationality'[18]) in the face of shareholders potentially utilising market power to displace them or make them uncomfortable. Thus, corporate governance can be viewed in one light as being concerned with the constraints managers place on themselves or have placed upon them by other parties to the nexus, in order to restrain

---

[18] H. Simon, 'A behavioral model of rational choice' in H. Simon, *Models of Man* (New York, NY: Wiley, 1957).

individual attempts to maximise utility to the disadvantage of shareholders. This has significant implications for the use of information which is disclosed to shareholders; for the relationships between shareholders and managers; and between managers in one company and other managers in other companies.

The additions to the traditionalist/legalist view to make it work in an environment where a company's shares are listed, begin to make the principle of shareholder primacy and shareholder ownership look a bit less than watertight. But it is still a more realistic interpretation of the relationship between shareholders and managers in the modern world than the old flat shareholder-ownership/primacy model, which was developed at the turn of the twentieth century (which is when the legal cases which defined shareholder primacy arose).

When modern service businesses are considered as the archetype rather than the industrial companies of the late nineteenth and early twentieth centuries it becomes even easier to see how shareholders of listed companies are not the owners of companies at all, in the way that the legalistic interpretations of ownership propose. They are owners, agreed, but of something very different from the interpretation offered by the traditionalist/legalistic view.

As economies evolve, the preponderance of primary industries – extractive and exploitative – gives way to secondary activities – manufacturing industry – and then, in the most developed economies, to tertiary activity – service-based and knowledge-based businesses of all types. In terms of economic output and simple numbers, tertiary businesses now largely dominate highly-developed Western economies: typically industrial activity equals about half to two-thirds of the service sector in such economies.[19] Two of the characteristics of such businesses are that first, they employ proportionately little physical capital in relation to their worth, and second, their balance sheets are not really representative of their true value. These have significant implications for shareholders.

In 1999, Bill Gates, the founder and chairman of Microsoft gave an interview[20] in which he said that Microsoft's 'primary assets, which are … (software and) … software-development skills, do not show up on the balance sheet at all'. One of the reasons for the invisibility of these assets, is that one set of them can – and does – walk out of the company's doors every evening (and the other half are subject to the accounting rules concerning intangible assets).

Much of the value of the service-based or knowledge-based business lies in the people it employs. If some cataclysmic event hit Microsoft, wiping it out financially, the shareholders would not gain much residual value out of the soft assets, over which

---

[19] Office of National Statistics: estimates of GDP.
[20] Business Strategy Review, *London Business School Journal*, 10(2) (1999).

they supposedly have a residual claim. They are assets which 'belong' in the business not because they have been bought and can be disposed of (like old-style assets of buildings, plant and machinery) but because they have been the subject of a temporary contract for hire. Once they see no future in staying, they leave. In the past ten to fifteen years there has been a much greater recognition that businesses are collections of people first and foremost: consequently lay-offs and reductions in headcount are recognised as having huge costs in terms of the longevity and culture of businesses affected – and thus of the residual value of the shareholders' interest.[21]

The controllers of the contractual nexus – the directors – are therefore, in practical terms, the dominant party in the governance relationship since they are able to control the future of the company because of the power that they exercise over the terms of this nexus, and because of the asymmetry of the information which they possess in respect to shareholders and others parties to the company's operations in so doing. In the description offered by the nexus theory the shareholders are one of the subordinate parties in the relationship – like all the other contractual parties to the arrangement.

If this description of the world is accepted as being more realistic, then a redefinition of what shareholders own is required. This redefinition has to be not principally in terms of what was identified above, not 'the company', but rather in terms of the attributes of the share itself:

- the right to a small percentage of the company's dividend fund, equal in proportion to the holding of shares;
- the possibility of achieving a capital gain in the value of that right to income;
- the right to trade ownership freely and, as a means of protecting their position, shareholders are entitled to pre-emption rights (considered further in Chapter 4), which protect the other two rights from being arbitrarily affected by managerial action.

This description of the relegation of the shareholder from a position of primacy and ownership, as held by the traditionalist view, accords well with observed behaviour in listed companies and better than the legalist theory, as can be seen by examining the circumstances of ownership and control in both small and listed companies.

Shareholder control of companies

Shareholders are nominally able, in the traditionalist theory of governance, to exercise control over companies by four means: over policy, in the first instance, through picking the right people as directors (election); then getting rid of those that they do

---

[21] S. Moore et al., 'Physical and mental health effects of surviving layoffs: a longitudinal examination', Institute of Behavioral Science Working Paper PEC 2003–0003, University of Colorado.

not want (forcible retirement); then ensuring that the information they receive from directors is properly assembled and accurate; and lastly through some form of prohibiting or enabling resolution to provide them with outcomes they want (although this is, practically, an extremely limited option). After the first of these actions – selection/election – is completed most of these controls are exercised in general meetings – which until the passage of the 2006 Act took place annually for all companies, private and public.

Prior to the passage of the 2006 Act practical activity, at least in private companies, accorded fairly well with the traditionalist theory of governance and provided solid ground for the formulation of the legal view of shareholders as owners. If normal methods of discussion and persuasion failed, the shareholders could take action against the directors by holding them to account through formal questioning at the AGM; by refusing to re-appoint them; and by requiring a new set of auditors to check the books; and by formulating special resolutions to mandate actions. The balance of the principal and agent theory was maintained by the legal structures – largely centred around the general meeting of shareholders of the company for companies of modest size which conducted their activity through shareholder meetings.

Under the provisions of the Companies Act 2006, these powers previously exercisable by shareholders have largely been dispensed with for private companies and the circumstances of large companies render them largely sterile. The long-standing proposition that shareholders control businesses – which could point to law and practice as its foundation – is now rendered largely inaccurate for companies where shareholders and directors are not the same people.

The reason for this radical action was not any corporatist view of company regulation but the far more mundane explanation that the superstructure of administration seemed unnecessary for most small companies. The Company Law Reform Steering Group, whose work provided the platform for the 2006 Act, suggested that the majority of small private companies were actually administered by consensus in an atmosphere of harmony and minimum formality and, by its recommendations, sought to protect this situation.[22]

This is not surprising since the detailed mechanisms of governance had never been intended for the use of very small businesses – perhaps where long-term associates or even family members form the bulk of the shareholders. In family companies, blood is thicker than governance (to use a phrase of Andrew Hill, from the *Financial Times*);[23] in businesses where the shareholders are also working directors then the Company

---

[22] *Company Law Reform Steering Group Report*, June 2001, vol. 1, s. 2.13.
[23] A. Hill, 'All I am saying is give CEOs a chance', *Financial Times*, 23 May 2011.

Law Reform Steering Group's opinion probably does hold good – the companies are run by consensus and mostly in harmony.

But the administrative procedures had grown up for very specific reasons. They had been developed at a time when complete strangers came together to form businesses and required formal protection for their interests from 'almost-strangers' of whom they may have had little or no long-term knowledge but who had asked them for the use of their money. The success of this process in protecting investors who were strangers to each other – by combining good administrative provision with the attractions of limited liability, rather than limiting money-raising to the circle of friends or acquaintances who could rely on personal knowledge and judgement – had commended itself widely. The utility of the process was readily apparent to those engaged in investing who sought not the *economic power of the association* but the *individual protection of limited liability* (and also, as time progressed, the effects of the beneficial tax advantages that had been awarded to companies over the years by politicians seeking to encourage industry and commerce).

In order to understand the general processes and operation of governance in this respect, it is appropriate to consider the private company first and then to move on to the listed company to investigate how recent developments have affected the ideal of shareholder control and shareholder supremacy in each case.

... in smaller companies

The vast majority of newly-incorporated companies are picked 'off the shelf' by those who want a corporate vehicle for the purposes of their business. The first set of founding directors (formation agents) 'resigns' – a pure formality – and the new shareholders usually appoint themselves (or some of their number) as directors in their place. For many small companies this is the only directorial change that ever occurs because, as noted above, the company has been formed principally to act as shield against personal liability and for certain tax advantages. In such cases there is very little need for the mechanisms of administration or governance associated with large shareholder registers and formal meetings.

But for other slightly larger companies – those that have not chosen to be plcs or have not made the necessary administrative changes to their articles – then the position might be more complicated. Here, large numbers of shareholders may be distant from the operation of the business and dependent upon the protection of the law to safeguard the value of their investments – especially as there may be no available market for them to resort to. Harmony, consensus and reason rarely prevail for long in human affairs and it is the purpose of regulatory structures to provide for their possible shortfalls.

For these companies, what the changes have done is to throw the burden of making sure that the shareholders are properly consulted in a frequent manner squarely on the provisions of the Articles of Association. If no provision for such meetings previously existed then the Companies Act 2006 has done away with the possibility of it being made available as of right, while the directors can say with complete accuracy that they are complying with the law. Similarly, for those companies that did not stipulate a fixed period of office for their directors in their Articles, the new Act has effectively given the directors a job from which disgruntled shareholders will only be able to eject them if they can surmount some stiff hurdles. First, they have to organise a special resolution to convene a general meeting and, second, mobilise support by the use of written resolutions for the appointment to be terminated.

They will also find their way strewn with obstacles; the Companies Act 2006 states that:

Shareholders' reserve power
4.   – (1) The shareholders may, by special resolution, direct the directors to take, or refrain from taking, specified action.
   (2) No such special resolution invalidates anything which the directors have done before the passing of the resolution.[24]

The shareholders may well therefore assure themselves of only Pyrrhic victories using this mechanism.

In addition, since the Articles are usually in the form of a take-it-or-leave-it contract where negotiation is both discouraged and unlikely, the removal of the governance safeguards for small companies has the effect of deteriorating the standard of shareholder control. It may, again, not matter very much for the numerical majority of companies – small, tight shareholder groups; modest family businesses (and even for those that are being newly-formed with venture capital backing, for instance where there will be tough provisions to protect the venture capitalists' position) – but the principle has been established by making these changes that shareholder control is something of a distraction and an irritation to management's abilities to get on and *do*.

This is not to say that effective governance has suddenly been dealt a death blow. Rather, what it points to is the gap that is now visible between the reality of company governance and the way that the traditionalist explanation previously held that it should work. For it was among the small companies where direct interaction between shareholders and directors should have produced, according to the traditionalist theory, the sharpest-defined structures of shareholder supremacy and minimal scope for the pernicious effects of the principal and agent theory (even after allowing for the problems of applying the principal-agent relationship).

---

[24] Companies Act 2006, Sched. 1, Model Articles for private companies limited by shares.

The pragmatic position of making the administrative and legal burden fit the requirements of those it was supposed to serve, may be understandable in light of the circumstances of many private companies (that is, the ones run harmoniously, by consensus and with minimal formality). But it does nothing to further habits of good governance generally and chips away further at the accepted definitions and the traditionalist/legalist view points of what governance is; at the supposed supremacy of the shareholder; and at the principle of shareholder ownership.

These habits of good governance are important since they condition the beliefs of those involved in management at progressively more sophisticated levels and those who aspire to become directors of larger companies, having grown their organisations from small beginnings. The changes are wide and significant: they include no automatic mechanisms for shareholder control of directorial appointments; no consistent and regular control of auditors; no regular meetings of shareholders; the possibility of gradual accretion of the numbers of like-minded directors through unapproved appointments; potential for the block-building of share stakes. Looked at in this light, the supposed supremacy of the shareholder in the small company looks a little moth-eaten.

... in larger companies

Paradoxically, governance in larger companies looks slightly stronger at first blush than it does for small companies – once the effects of the 2006 Act are considered.

There is, first, an extensive code of corporate governance – The UK Corporate Governance Code – to which all listed companies are supposed to adhere, by virtue of the bargain that they strike with the Stock Exchange when they accept the Listing Rules.[25] There are, second, numerous rules regarding how directors are to behave in respect of the release of information; the transfer of shares between parties; buying and selling shares in the company. Third, there is the potential for a (relatively) strong financial police force in the Financial Conduct Authority (FCA) (that part of the old FSA that will be concerned with market regulation from 2013 – see Chapter 11) and last, there is a (relatively) strong social culture which respects the rule of law.

In addition, for the first time the 2006 Act placed a definition (of sorts) on what directors are supposed to do (ss. 172–6 of the Act) – a definition which also applies to directors of private companies. And there are pre-emption rights which public companies must observe which prevent shareholders having their stake diluted without their approval.

---

[25] FSA, *The FSA Handbook: Listing Rules*, available at www.fsa.gov.uk/pubs/other/listing_rules.pdf, continually updated.

So, superficially, everything looks as if it conforms to the traditionalist/legalistic ideal of shareholder ownership and the primacy of the shareholder. Unfortunately, superficial appearances and practical reality are different things.

The sheer operational distance between most shareholders and the companies in which they hold shares is the key factor. Shareholdings are atomised in the modern world; many listed companies have hundreds of millions of shares in issue; laws exist in the most developed stock markets to compel those who wish to accumulate large stakes to identify themselves and then bid for the entirety of the company, thereby keeping individual shareholdings proportionately low and minimising the prospects for organised shareholder collaboration. The shareholders are at the *edge* of the nexus – not central to it. Because of this the primacy of the managers is strengthened as Berle and Means[26] and Chandler[27] identified in the 1930s and 1970s respectively. The invisible hand identified by Adam Smith and so beloved by market theorists had by then – in the 1930s and even more evidently by the 1980s – become the visible hand of management.

The second feature is that the majority of shareholders do not wish to exercise any ownership function. They are not long-term holders of shares. Professional shareholders – the large insurance companies and pension funds which dominate the holding, buying and selling of shares – are not primarily interested in exercising a long-term stewardship role and so have no interest in residual rights: in fact they positively want them to belong to someone else. They are totally engaged by the need to maximise the value of their own products and services, towards maximising value for the funds that they operate. Their own economic existence depends critically upon the success of their investment strategies and they would rather have the ability to buy and sell shares to maximise returns for these than be forced into being corporate policemen on the side.[28]

As a consequence of this, too many professional operators in the market for listed shares have a vested interest in a continual turmoil in collective perceptions of the value of individual shares, in order to make money through dealing in them. For shares to be considered in the same way as they were a generation or more ago – as long-term property – they would have to be held long term. The UK stock market has a churn rate of nearly 60 per cent according to research[29] and this has not changed

[26] A. A. Berle and G. C. Means, *The Modern Corporation and Private Property* (New Jersey: Transaction, 1999).

[27] A. Chandler, *The Visible Hand* (Cambridge, MA: Harvard University Press, 1977).

[28] IoD, *Evidence to FRC Consultation*, www.iod.com/MainWebSite/Resources/Document/Takeover_Panel_Review_0710.pdf.

[29] Ø. Bøhren, R. Priestley and B. A. Ødegaard, 'The duration of equity ownership', BI Norwegian School of Management Working Paper 2006, http://finance.bi.no/~bernt/wps/

much since 2003, with the median churn rate varying between 55 per cent and 59 per cent. While this is a crude measure subject to distorting factors, including the effects of the new factor of High Frequency Trading (HFT), its thrust is broadly accurate: most shares in the UK are held for an average of just under two years – hardly an indication of a sustained interest in stewardship on the part of fund managers.

Furthermore, this tendency is accelerating: HFT cannot be described as share owner-ship in the conventional sense since the shares of a company involved in speculation by HFT traders can 'change hands' hundreds of times in the space of seconds. Three separate academic studies from the Universities of Bristol, Cambridge and the London School of Economics[30] have found no link between volatility and HFT – but this is an entirely different matter from ownership. Such activity can confer no entitlement to 'ownership' in any meaningful way and is merely highly-advanced arbitrage activity, equally highly-distanced from the legalist/traditionalist view of ownership. The market is changing dramatically in this way – but the traditionalist/legalistic theory cannot recognise such change.

It is also difficult to think of something which conveys rights to ownership when it is perpetually up for sale. Shares in a listed company are, by their nature, continually available for purchase by others. In addition to the free float of shares that enables markets to be made continually, an adequate price will tempt all current shareholders out of ownership and into a position where they are willing to sell. It is irrational to presume that a share in a company cannot be levered out of the possession of a shareholder if sufficient money is offered – even though individual shareholders may have different prices at which they are willing to sell, of course. The rights of ownership therefore attach themselves to a temporary possession which may, as indicated above, be of a very temporary nature indeed – in fact, with such a short life that none of the attributes of stewardship attach.

Shares are also one of a very few categories of asset which can be compulsorily disgorged. In the event of the purchase of a company by another a rump of sharehold-ers who have not consented to the sale may be compelled to sell their shares under the rules of the Stock Market.[31] The reasons for this are obvious and sensible, but go against the ownership characteristics of most other assets.

If the shareholder supremacy argument were valid then it could presumably dem-onstrate the primacy of shareholders in the outcome of the nub of the principal-agent

---

ownership_duration/durationpaper_dec_2005.pdf; R. Sullivan, 'Brussels drubs managers over short-termism', *Financial Times*, 24 April 2011.

[30] Jean-Pierre Zigrand of the London School of Economics, Dave Cliff of the University of Bristol and Terrence Hendershott at the University of Cambridge reported in J. Grant and P. Stafford, 'Studies say no link between HFT and volatility', *Financial Times*, 8 September 2011.

[31] Companies Act 2006, ss. 974–991.

relationship – how much each side gets out of the bargain. Yet while lip service is paid to the issue of directorial pay being decided by shareholders, the real world apparently operates differently. There is some evidence from the USA (April 2011)[32] that ever-rising levels of executive pay may be affected by the impact of the Dodd-Frank Act's 'say-on-pay' reforms; but in the UK – as the High Pay Commission showed in May 2011[33] – the differential in pay between the managing directors of the largest listed companies and the rest of the population is reaching levels not seen since Victorian times. In April 2010 the then chief of the CBI[34] said that 'if leaders of big companies seem to occupy a different galaxy from the rest of the community they risk being treated as aliens', yet the pay of senior managers marched upward unperturbed – even though share prices overall have fallen relatively over the past eight years.[35]

One of the main reasons why the directorate of listed companies is able to exert such a stranglehold over pay in the UK is the toothlessness of the Remuneration Report which all listed companies must produce in their annual reports and which must be put to a shareholder vote. The problem is that the result of the vote is not binding on management. Consequently they ignore it – or when there is a hoo-ha the chairman of the remuneration committee is wheeled out to explain to shareholders why they are wrong in complaining – as was the case with Thomas Cook in February 2011.

Thomas Cook and the manipulated share option schemes

In February 2011, the Association of British Insurers took the unusual step of issuing a 'red-topped' voting advisory notice about the executive bonus scheme operated by Thomas Cook, the travel firm.

The firm had a long-running bonus scheme, worth about £1m, available to about 100 directors and senior employees which was linked to the share price of the company. Following the effects of the ash cloud from the Iceland volcano, Eyjafjallajokull which erupted in 2010, the company decided to change the terms of the bonus scheme to reflect the 'exceptional nature' of the disruption caused, bringing forward the date of the exercise of the bonus scheme to the day before the

---

[32] E. Crooks and D. McCrum, 'GE changes share option plan for Immelt', *Financial Times*, 20 April 2011.

[33] *Cheques with Balances*, Report of the High Pay Commission available from http://highpaycommission.co.uk/facts-and-figures/final-report-cheques-with-balances-why-tackling-high-pay-is-in-the-national-interest/.

[34] J. Finch, J. Treanor and R. Wachman, 'Critics unite over executive pay to force the "aliens" of business down to earth', *The Guardian*, 31 March 2010.

[35] FT Markets data.

eruption began and airspace was closed across Europe. Other travel firms had not taken such action in reporting their figures or accounting for their bonuses.

The company's shares traded at 335p when the scheme started in 2007 but had fallen to 198p by the time of the 'red-top' issued to coincide with the AGM.

At the AGM 39 per cent of shareholders in the company voted against the remuneration report and a further 7 per cent abstained or failed to vote.

The company issued a statement saying that 'it took the issues raised by shareholders seriously' and offered a meeting with the remuneration committee chairman to explain the company's stance.

The Pru and HSBC – the feeble impact of the shareholder vote

At the Annual General Meeting of the Hong Kong and Shanghai Banking Corporation in May 2011, one-fifth of shareholders failed to back the board's pay policy at what was described by one newspaper (*The Guardian*) as a 'rowdy' meeting. (One in ten investors also failed to back the appointment of the new chairman, Douglas Flint.)

The deal had been constructed internally after the remuneration committee chairman, John Thornton – a former Goldman Sachs banker – 'stood down all the pay consultants' hired by the bank, to use his words. He described the idea as 'the original private partnership where 100% of all net worth is tied up until retirement'. The bank was thus trying to emulate for paid directors and senior employees of the bank the arrangements that exist in private partnerships where partners are unable to 'cash in' the value of their share of the partnership until they leave the partnership but where crucially *all the partners are jointly and severally liable – and there are no external shareholders*. Partnership arrangements are also particularly popular in venture capital funds where there is often a 'carried interest' arrangement to reward senior staff on the basis of an increase in the underlying value of the fund – even though they may not have hazarded their own real wealth by participating in investments.

Thornton appeared to be implying therefore that the directors of the bank and the senior staff involved in the scheme were acting as a partnership unit – and therefore not part of the principal–agent relationship that otherwise governs the traditionalist/legalist view.

One week before, at the Prudential AGM, shareholders had been advised by a firm of corporate governance advisers to vote against the re-election of one of the non-executives, Keki Dediseth, who had failed to attend 75 per cent of board meetings. They described this as a failure to fulfil a fundamental responsibility. One-fifth of the shareholders failed to back the re-election of the chairman, Harvey McGrath, in protest at the disastrously expensive bid made for AIG's assets in the Far East, which had cost shareholders more than £300 million.

The chairmen of both companies shrugged off the contrary votes. Mr Dediseth was re-elected.

One of the alternatives attempted in trying to take the sting out of allegations of excessive directorial remuneration has been to require (as the UK Corporate Governance Code does) that a proportion of senior executives/directors pay be made in the form of share options, exercisable at some point in the future. This will be dealt with in more detail in Chapter 14 but it is enough to say at this point that such exercises are fundamentally misguided in the expectation that they will benefit shareholders. All they do is fundamentally imbalance the principal-agent relationship by replacing the shareholder as the focus of the agent's attention with the exercise of options (see Chapter 14).

Lest anyone still doubt the primacy of directors in the relationship an example can be drawn from the USA. In the 1980s and 1990s it was popular for managers to attempt to prevent the operation of the shareholders' right to sell the company by putting in place 'poison-pill' provisions to prevent takeovers[36] – this involved share-trigger arrangements that forced a potential acquirer to negotiate with the board of the company rather than approach shareholders. While this was nominally to ward off the attentions of so-called 'green-mailers', what it really did was to protect incumbent management whose performance had been less than satisfactory given the assets at their command. Such arrangements are illegal in the UK (and discouraged in Europe) where the Takeover Code requires a board to be consulted by an acquirer before shareholders are approached directly.[37]

On a slightly surreal note, one of the fundamental characteristics of ownership of an asset is the right of the owners to destroy the asset if he or she wishes. It is not possible for the owner of an individual share to destroy the share. Even if the tangible evidence of ownership – the share certificate – is destroyed, the shareholder is still a member of the company. All this stems of course from the fact that company is an independent

[36] R. A. Heron and E. Lie, 'On the use of poison pills and defensive payouts by takeover targets', *Journal of Business*, 79(4) (2008).
[37] UK Takeover Code, Rule No 1.

legal entity with, as far as the law is concerned, a legal life of its own. Admittedly, by acting in concert the shareholders are able to dissolve the company (that is, the arrangements which brought them together) but in practical terms, for a publicly listed company, this is a theoretical power only and one which is beyond the power of any single shareholder to perform.

Lastly, the asymmetrical nature of the amount and quality of information available to directors and to shareholders means that the initiative always lies with the directors as to when they reveal information to shareholders. All the information provided to shareholders is historical, allowing them little chance to make an informed view about prospects for their (listed) companies. By contrast, the directors initiate, control the content and control the release of information to shareholders. There have been numerous scandals about erroneous information passed to shareholders in recent years. Of these, the scandal over reserves at Royal Dutch Shell[38] in 2004 was the most noteworthy since it impacted directly on the share price and consequently on executive bonuses and then resulted in fines for the company and payment of compensation to shareholders; but instances of deliberate falsification of accounting information are reported with alarming frequency in the financial press. And the lesser brothers of falsification – concealment and obfuscation – are probably equally as prevalent. This usually results in false markets being created – a phenomenon which will be reviewed in Chapter 17.

Royal Dutch Shell and the revaluation of reserves

Much of the stock market value of oil companies is linked to the estimates of proven reserves that they can draw on in the future – the Reserve Replacement Ratio (RRR). High RRRs are regarded as healthy and act as a bolster to the share price. However, exploration is a very expensive activity for oil companies – with much expenditure often taking place for no commercial return.

In 2004 the chairman of Royal Dutch Shell, Sir Philip Watts, was deposed from office by the other members of the RDS board in the wake of a scandal concerning the company's reserves of oil, which, it turned out, had been overstated for many years. The precipitating event was an analysis of reserves and the chronology of the sequence of revelations carried out by an American firm of lawyers which was presented to Shell's 'Committee of Managing Directors'.

In the 1980s and 1990s Watts had been responsible for the exploration and planning arms of Shell's business worldwide (as well as its managing director in Nigeria; see Chapter 3). Shell's policy during this time had been to cut back on

---

[38] S. Pfeifer, 'Shell settles last reserves misreporting claim', *Financial Times*, 6 March 2008.

exploration as a heavy cost that could be reduced while oil prices wallowed during a period of international recession. While this move had initially been welcomed by institutional investors, once the amalgamations of other oil companies produced businesses that could better afford the high cost of exploration Shell was seen as having lagged behind.

In 2001 Watts was appointed chairman of the company. Organisationally the position of chairman was very powerful, since the non-executive directors of the group were heavily circumscribed in their effectiveness, and strategic direction was accomplished mostly outside the boards. Shell's structure had complicated corporate decision-making since it was effectively two separate companies joined in an agreed alliance rather than one company with subsidiaries. Meetings of the two holding companies were regarded as principally ritualistic rather than commercially valuable. Watts's appointment was initially welcomed as signalling a new aggressiveness in the company's commercial attitude, but he was later criticised as an abrasive manager and a poor communicator with shareholders and other members of staff. By the time he became chairman he had few friends left in the company because of the behaviour displayed in getting to the top.

In 2004 the company announced that it would be reducing the estimates of proven reserves that it had given to the stock market over many years by roughly 20 per cent – 3.9 billion barrels – reducing the life of reserves from thirteen years to eleven years. The company presented the reduction as a technical reclassification to comply with new US Securities and Exchange Commission regulations but the share price plummeted, wiping $15 billion off Shell's market capitalisation at one point. Watts had not made the announcement himself and did not make himself available to shareholders for some time after. Institutional investors began to call for his resignation, since it was held he must have been complicit in knowledge of the true situation (all the while of course the company's financial statements had been audited and signed off by KPMG: see Chapter 8). It later emerged that he had indeed known about the reserves position for some time, certainly without doing anything about informing the market – as e-mails from senior staff members criticising the company's public stance at the time the problem came to light began to be made public.

Sir Philip Watts was questioned under caution by the FSA after his resignation and he later counter-claimed against them that his rights had been infringed in respect of rebutting their allegations. The company offered compensation to investors without acknowledging wrongdoing (see below).

Summary

The contention of the traditionalist/legalist view that shareholders own companies still works quite well in small private companies with relatively few shareholders. It probably held up quite well for the time when listed companies were industrially-based and had smaller amounts of issued share capital, the ownership of which, although large, was geographically concentrated. The traditionalist view may have been valid in explaining the way that the relationship worked even up to the late 1980s when the nature of passing information about the company out to the market-place was not quite as antiseptically regulated as it now is.

But it does not appear to explain at all well the relationship as it now stands. This is not necessarily surprising: the environment for listed companies has changed out of recognition over the last thirty years and there is no reason why a theory or an explanation should not change as circumstances change. As Keynes is reputed to have said, 'When the facts change I change my mind.'

Listed companies have changed considerably from the time the doctrine of shareholder primacy was formulated by the courts in the late Victorian/early Edwardian age. Even more significantly, the power balance between shareholders and directors has changed – and very markedly – over the past thirty years. In the interests of a supposed equality of treatment between investors, companies are now required to observe very different rules about the release of information to shareholders than they were thirty years ago. In the 1980s stockbroking analysts would routinely meet with companies to discuss in great detail the companies' performance. The function of the finance director at those meetings was often interpreted as being to make sure that there was an 'orderly market' in the company's shares. In order for that to happen, information was then routinely disclosed to analysts for onward transmission to their clients so that the market would not be 'surprised' about results. That information would now render the analysts – and the finance director – guilty of insider trading, without a hope of defence.

It is for these reasons that the traditionalist/legalistic explanations about shareholder primacy in the listed company appear outdated and inadequate, just as the definition of governance produced by the Cadbury Committee does after twenty years. The regulatory environment in which the listed company operates promotes the practical effect of director supremacy and undermines the few remaining shreds of support for the notion of shareholder ownership.

In truth, the purchase of shares in a listed company resembles much more gambling than investing, given the organisational remoteness of the shareholder from the company. The maintenance of a secondary market in shares, which is the larger of the two functions of most Stock Markets, is more akin to going to a racecourse in terms of its purpose and effects than taking ownership of part of a company.

Of course the existence of a primary market – the raising of capital for companies; the release of equity holdings by owners – is predicated on the existence of a strong secondary market. The two have to go together to work efficiently. But that does not mean that incorrect or inaccurate explanations have to persist about how companies are run and for whose benefit.

In many cases, it is the stakeholders who have a longer continuing relationship with a company than the temporary possessors of its shares and it is this class of relationships and the governance issues that surround them that forms the subject of the next chapter.

CHAPTER 3

Outward-facing governance

This chapter will:
- introduce the concepts of operational and longitudinal dimensions of governance;
- describe the concept of stakeholders and their role in governance;
- introduce the concept of the Governance Equation as a means of relating theoretical governance to practice, referring to the operational and longitudinal concepts;
- discuss the idea of corporate social responsibility and civil society.

Traditionalist/legalist theories of governance relegate the significance of stakeholders to a subordinate position. The Cadbury definition did not include them at all; the OECD definition gave them a grudging inclusion as a subordinated element – 'other stakeholders' – to the primacy of the shareholders.

The traditionalist view places the shareholder at the centre of governance – but still as only one of the legs of the triumvirate of shareholder, director and auditor. Yet in practical terms the claims of the stakeholders en masse outweigh the claims of the shareholders as a group. To take only four of the potential herd of stakeholders: without customers there could be no income; without suppliers there would be no raw materials; without workers there would be no production; without the State there would be – at the absolute minimum – no enforceability of contracts. Consideration of these parties' claims to involvement in the governance process again underlines the inaccuracy of regarding the shareholder as the pivotal point of governance, and emphasises the position as the holder of the residual contract. The shareholder is not so much central to governance but might well be regarded as being at either the periphery or at the beginning and the end of the governance process – depending on the world view taken: operational or longitudinal (discussed below).

By downgrading the significance of the shareholder in terms of the operational decisions regarding to what purpose the company is being run, and integrating the stakeholder into the fullness of the picture, it becomes possible to illuminate and define the true purpose of governance in terms of other aspects of activity. This then produces an alternative theory of corporate activity – stakeholder theory, which was touched upon in the previous chapter. At its simplest, this is effectively a body of theory that describes the outward-facing arm of governance – that behaviour which deals with relations that are external to the traditionally-defined triumvirate. At its most complex, it challenges assumptions about the purpose of the company that are central to the current constructs of corporate governance.

By reviewing the phrasing of the suggested new definition of governance made in Chapter 1 it is possible to see how the interests of stakeholders, rather than shareholders, are central to the proper operation of governance. It also becomes apparent how governance is ultimately reducible to a consideration of the management of the risks that the company faces.

The revised definition (Chapter 1) suggested that governance is:

> The governing structure and processes in an organisation [nexus of contracts] that exist to oversee the means by which limited resources are efficiently directed to competing purposes [transaction cost theory] for the use of the organisation and its stakeholders, including the maintenance of the organisation and its long-run sustainability [stewardship theory], set against a background of managerial and shareholder behaviour implicitly measured against a framework of ethics and backed by regulation and laws [agency theory].

In this environment the purpose of the directorate becomes one of balancing all the competing resource claims against each other and against some (un-prescribed) background of ethics, law and regulation (all of which are, of course, linked together into business culture). This is a much more satisfactory way of explaining what directors do than simply indicating a list of unlinked responsibilities (the Cadbury definition) or a minimalist list of outcomes (the OECD definition). Neither of these mainstream definitions produces anything more than a hint of the existence of some form of unelucidated behaviour that simply results in governance, because neither goes any further in trying to explain what governance is, other than indicating – in the analogy of the introduction to this book – the landscape of governance and not the geology of the processes that bring it about.

The concept of governance as sophisticated risk management comes from the consideration of the significance of competing claims for resources for different stakeholders. In order to resolve the competing claims it is necessary for directors of a company to consider some form of prioritisation against which to rank the competing claims. This prioritisation is, effectively, a form of allocation of values of risk to the issues which the directorate have to deal with: for instance, how much resource must go to improving production processes in any given set of market conditions? How much resource should be devoted to developing new customers as against retaining old ones? How can retaining a workforce adequate to the company's needs be achieved? How much resource should be allocated to pursuing new growth opportunities as against cultivating organic development of the company? How much dividend can be prudently paid out? How much pay is needed to get the most appropriately qualified and experienced staff?

Longitudinal and operational dimensions of governance

One of the voids in the study of corporate governance is that we have only clumsy phrases to describe the distinctions between the governance issues that apply mostly to shareholders and those that apply mostly to stakeholders. This book favours the use of the terms 'inward-facing' and 'outward-facing'. But neither of these terms adequately describes the 'geological nature' of governance which was referred to at the outset. The absence of this sense of past and projection is a shortcoming that affects adequate description of the processes, since it does not include an appreciation of the influence of the past and the fact that actions taken now can project into the future.

Some of the questions listed above which face managers refer to the immediate present while some obviously have implications for the future development of an organisation; nearly all will be influenced by past decisions. In this respect those aspects of governance which have immediate impact can be thought of as operationally based, since they mostly affect the short-term. It is likely that they also mostly affect – but not exclusively – the relationships between shareholders, directors and the company.

By contrast those which affect the company into the future are longitudinal in nature since they affect relationships yet to develop. In this respect governance activity in the longitudinal dimension is going to mostly affect the relationships between the company and its stakeholders.

Thought of like this (and bearing in mind the procedural, behaviour and structural dimensions already mentioned) it becomes easier to frame and comprehend the description of the responsibilities of directors as prudent controllers of the company, who balance the underlying requirements of the shareholders to see a return over the long term against other demands on the company's resources from other stakeholders. Operational activity involves the balancing of shareholders' demands; longitudinal activity involves responding to the tensions placed on the organisation by the competing demands of stakeholders. This description then holds good even for encompassing those owners of shares who have no interest in exercising the responsibilities of ownership – or, at best, of only avoiding the exercise of the residual contractual rights of ownership.

It then becomes possible to describe the purpose of governance more exactly, following on from the description of the process of governance stated in Chapter 1. The description integrates the operational and inward-facing aspect of directorial functions – responding to the relationships between the company and directors and shareholders – with the longitudinal and outward-facing aspect of responding to the demands on the combination of the shareholders, the directors and the incorporated entity of the company, from others – the stakeholders – who have some interest in the company's existence.

Good governance then becomes, effectively, the fulcrum in the continual process of balancing resource allocation – which is a proxy for balancing risk against reward for all the parties to the nexus of contracts that forms the company. It is important to recognise that this does not mean to say that the nexus theory or stakeholder theory is supreme and has knocked shareholders out of the picture or eliminated their importance. It does emphasise, though, that good governance is more than merely considering the interests of the shareholder over all others.

In summary terms, using the concept of governance as risk management described earlier, the principle that brings about good governance can be expressed in this way for a profit-seeking enterprise:

- Profit is the reward for risk.
- All companies face continually varying degrees of risk.
- The purpose of management is to choose the 'most appropriate form of action' which mitigates these risks and balances the interests of all stakeholders.
- Choosing 'the most appropriate form of action' is aided by good governance – acts of both operational governance and longitudinal governance.
- Good governance therefore should contribute to the longevity of the company by mitigating risk and maximising the potential for profit.

From the point of view of this proposal, it now becomes easy to see that satisfying the demands of stakeholders – rather than simply shareholders – for an appropriate share of resources is an integral part of the responsibilities of the directorate and not some appendage tacked on as an afterthought.

The inclusion of this additional dimension of time to the relationship produces a longitudinal appreciation of what governance is and its effects rather than the merely horizontal review of the details of the actors involved. By considering this longitudinal view of governance – both who is involved and over what periods of time – the analogy made at the start of this book returns: it is the geology of governance that gives the true platform for its implementation rather than a simple tour of the landscape.

The stakeholders of a business – groups like employees (past and present); suppliers; distributors; customers; non-shareholding financiers; the State; and so on – are often much longer associated with companies in their individual capacities than are shareholders. Their futures and their prosperity are often intimately bound up with the company in a way that the temporary nature of the shareholder in the modern listed company is not. Their interest may persist over several years in comparison with the relatively short-term involvement of the typical shareholder who, research suggests, may have no more than a couple of years association, at most, with any given company.[1]

---

[1] See Sullivan, 'Brussels drubs managers over short-termism'.

Stakeholder theory

The company has not always been seen as the vehicle for delivering returns solely to the shareholder. In the years immediately after the Second World War and until about 1960, 'labour', the 'progress of the company', '[t]he well-being of the customer' and 'the community' were all cited by *The Economist, The Investors Chronicle* and leading academic experts as being the main concern of the commercial enterprise.[2]

The term stakeholder, used in the sense of persons having some interest in the company, first occurred in internal memoranda at the Stanford Research Institute in the early 1960s;[3] the term was then taken to mean 'those groups without whose support the organisation would cease to exist'. Later work was done at the research department of Lockheed and in the 1970s by R. Edward Freeman (now of the University of Virginia) who, in 1984, derived the classic definition of the term as:

> any group or individual who can affect or is affected by the achievement of the organisation's objectives.[4]

The birth of stakeholder theory therefore probably slightly pre-dates the emergence of the term 'corporate governance' which impacted on academic and popular consciousness some years later, having made its first appearance as a book title (in the UK) in 1984[5] – although of course the concepts of corporate governance had been widely practised, examined and discussed (not least by company secretaries) for many years previously.

Like the portmanteau term 'corporate governance' there is no accepted single description of stakeholder theory. Rather than having the characteristics of a theory in the scientific sense, it is more a series of descriptions of the relationships of the company with other parties and how they work together.

However, there are two elaborations (the validity of which are still contested) which extend the basic concept.

The principle of corporate legitimacy

The corporation should be managed for the benefit of its stakeholders: its customers; suppliers; owners; employees; and local communities. The rights of these groups must be ensured and, further, the groups must participate in some sense in decisions that substantially affect their welfare.

---

[2] B. Cheffin, *Corporate Ownership and Control* (Oxford University Press, 2008), p. 341.
[3] See Freeman et al., *Stakeholder Theory.*   [4] *Ibid.*
[5] R. I. Tricker, *Corporate Governance* (London: Gower, 1984).

The stakeholder fiduciary principle

Management bears a fiduciary relationship to stakeholders and to the corporation as an abstract entity. It must act in the interests of the stakeholders as their agent and it must act in the interests of the corporation to ensure the survival of the firm, safeguarding the long-term stakes of each group.[6]

Much work has been done on elaborating these relationships and their consequences: interrogating Google Scholar will indicate something like 400,000 references to the term. But stakeholder theory can never get around a fairly basic problem, which is its Achilles Heel in comparison with the prescriptions of the traditionalist view of shareholder primacy.

The problem is that it becomes impossible to say, unless very contorted arguments are produced, who the company is being run for and why (the King Report alluded to this problem – see Chapter 1). It is logically impossible to have an agent acting in the same field for two or more principals and maintain a fiduciary obligation to both that is consistent – especially when those principals may have competing intentions. Furthermore, it becomes very difficult under the terms of the two Freeman–Evans principles to see how success can be achieved or how it is defined. Would success be mere stasis where all competing claims are effectively balanced (and nothing happens)? Has the company been gifted to managers, effectively, by the founding shareholders once it has been floated on a public market for them to act in the interest of all stakeholders without any form of priority? And if this is the case, then if the shareholders do not own the company, do the stakeholders – or indeed does anyone? And if the function of the managers is to simply balance the competing claims of the myriad stakeholders how are they able to measure their success if they are not producing profits for the benefit of shareholders?

Measurement of performance

The issue of measuring the return to individual classes of stakeholders for whom the company is being run, under the Freeman–Evans principles, is problematic. The presentation of information about a company's performance – the accounting information which directors are legally obliged to prepare – is intended for the use of the shareholders. There are problems in trying to adapt it for stakeholders.

British law does not stipulate how company accounts are to be compiled. The Companies Act 2006 requires directors to keep books of account and leaves it to them how this shall be done.[7] Accounts, however they are kept, have at least five purposes:

---

[6] W. R. Freeman and R. E. Evans, 'Corporate governance: a stakeholder interpretation', *Journal of Behavioural Economics*, 19(4) (1990).
[7] Companies Act 2006, s. 386.

1. for the use of shareholders;
2. for the use of tax authorities;
3. to fulfil the company's obligations to Companies House or to the Stock Exchange – effectively to outsiders who may be interested in the company;
4. for internal management control;
5. to raise additional finance from external sources.

While this list is not exhaustive, nowhere does it include information specifically prepared for the use of stakeholders. The State and outside financiers should be considered as stakeholders, but both these categories have specific financial interests in play which can largely be satisfied by the provision of standard financial information prepared for shareholders. In addition by virtue of their relationships with the company both of these parties may require and obtain additional information, above and beyond that provided to shareholders.

The structure of company accounting is directed towards the needs of shareholders – not surprisingly, since the company is originally set up for the benefit of shareholders. It is they who are the main users of both the type of information prepared and the presentation of that information for their own purposes – and it is them to whom the law pays attention in requiring books of account be kept. But the regulations surrounding the probity of accounts, in terms of the modern understanding of the 'true and fair view', are a comparatively recent development.

The *Royal Mail* case: the 'true and fair' view

The veracity of publicly-available audited accounts is taken for granted. But agreement on the precision of the term 'true and fair' is itself quite recent.

Until the mid-1920s it was common practice for public companies to present their accounts – with the active involvement of their auditors – in such a way that they could be not simply unreliable but occasionally actively misleading. To be fair, such instances were not always active attempts to dissemble: the accounting conventions of the time could be interpreted in a number of ways. But it was only when the manipulations involved the concealment of a serious financial problem that the ambiguity of the accounting conventions came to be discredited. The subterfuges that could be undertaken beneath the surface of apparently accurate audited accounts were revealed in 1931 in the case of *R* v. *Kylsant and Others* [1932] 1 KB 442.

Owen Cosby Phillips had been the chairman of the Royal Mail Steam Packet Company since 1902. He had been a Conservative Member of Parliament, High Sheriff of Pembrokeshire and was created first Baron Kylsant in 1923. The Royal Mail Steam Packet Company became the largest shipping company in the world when it purchased the White Star line (which had owned the

Titanic) for £7 million (about equivalent to £200 million in 2010's purchasing power) in 1927. The purchase of that company had been the culmination of a buying policy that had seen the Pacific Steam Navigation Company, the Union-Pacific Line and Harland and Wolff shipyards all absorbed into 'the Royal Mail'.

During the First World War the company had prospered substantially from government contracts for shipping but with the world-wide economic slump of the 1920s and the need to pay back excess profits from its war-time activities, its profitability – and cash position – declined dramatically.

In 1928 the company issued a prospectus inviting potential investors to buy £2 million of 5 per cent debentures. The prospectus claimed that the company had produced an average yearly profit of £500,000 in the last decade. But only a year later it asked for time to pay back loans owing to the Treasury.

The Government asked a senior member of the accountancy profession, Sir William McLintock, to investigate the company's finances (McLintock was senior partner in the firm that eventually produced the modern pan-national practice KPMG). He reported that far from being profitable, the company had not made a trading profit since 1925, and that over £1.25 million had been drawn from reserves to pad the profit and loss account in the last two years. Over a period of ten years, more than £5 million had been paid out in dividends that had been – effectively – unearned. By 1928 the trading deficit was running at about £300,000 a year and the reserves were exhausted.

As a result of the report, Kylsant and the company's auditor John Moreland were arrested and charged with three counts of false accounting.

Although technically complex, the case against the men appeared to be conclusive, given the financial state of the company and McLintock's report. But Kylsant's lawyers contended that although some of the statements in the prospectus and the accounts may have been misleading, none of them were actually false. They were also supported by other prominent accounting experts whose views differed from McLintock's.

The main support for the use of secret reserve accounting came from Sir William Plender – one of the most respected accountants of the time, who appeared as a witness for the defence. In the witness box he stated that it was routine for firms 'of the very highest repute' to use secret reserves in calculating profit without declaring it.

John Moreland's barrister, Patrick Hastings KC, was then able to say that 'if my client … was guilty of a criminal offence, there is not a single accountant in the City of London or in the world who is not in the same position.'

Possibly swayed by Plender's testimony the jury acquitted both Kylsant and Moreland of falsifying records but Kylsant was found guilty of fraud in respect of the 1928 prospectus and was sentenced to twelve months. The Court of Appeal upheld the verdict, rejecting the contention that there had been concealment but no mis-statement and at sixty-eight Kylsant served a prison term and was stripped of his knighthood.

There was an echo in the arguments of the prosecution and the public's reaction to them, of Adam Smith's dislike of the incorporated business. Smith had believed that the creation of a new legal commercial entity would enable the unscrupulous to escape debts that they had incurred behind the shield of the incorporated business.

It was not until 1947 that the Companies Act of that year made it clear that failing to disclose the use of secret reserve accounting was unacceptable and that its use undermined the value of the statements that otherwise purported to give a true and fair view.[8]

Only with the passage of the 1985 Companies Act, did the law give recognition to the concept of anyone other than shareholders being entitled to benefit from the company's activity. In that piece of legislation, directors were required, for the first time, to contemplate the effects of their policies on employees of the business – although the phrasing, the obligation and the encouragement were all half-hearted. That inclusion started a process which resulted in the inclusion of the statement of directors' responsibilities in the 2006 Companies Act[9] which explicitly requires directors to consider the long-term well being of their companies.

The 1985 Act, passed by a Conservative government – a party traditionally hostile to regulation (but not to ordered markets) and State interference in economic activity – was prompted by the damaging activities of the 'asset-strippers' who had begun to use the powers of the stock markets to break up and re-organise British industry, often to the detriment of employees' immediate interests. Some of the provisions of the Act, in particular the ones relating to the interests of the company's employees were attempts to curtail the excesses of the major players in this area – Jim Slater and Peter Walker; Roland 'Tiny' Rowland; James Goldsmith; James Hanson; and Gordon White.

---

[8] *Bulletin of the Business Historical Society*, 27(1) (March 1953), 1–25 and *The Royal Mail Case; Notable British Trials* (Edinburgh and London: Wm Hodge & Co, 1935).

[9] Companies Act 2006, ss. 171–7.

Other stakeholders' interest in the company

Takeover panel urged to consider M&A pension toll

Representatives of some of the UK's largest corporate pension schemes are pressing the Takeover Panel to ensure that acquiring companies take account of a target company's retirement plan when making a bid.

They want the panel to force bidders to set out in formal documents how an offer will affect a pension scheme and its members.

The move, which could make some takeovers more expensive and derail others, comes as part of one of the biggest shake-ups of UK dealmaking rules in decades. It comes after the outcry over plant closures in the wake of Kraft's successful bid for Cadbury last year.

A panel consultation document aims to spell out how bidders must clarify their intentions towards employees of a target company and offers employees an opportunity to express their views.

If the proposals are put in place, pension scheme representatives believe they could amount to a 'speed bump' in the path of bidders hoping to acquire a target quickly.

'In our view, there is no logical justification for recognising employees as "persons who are affected by takeovers" whilst failing to recognise pension fund members as such,' said David Gee, chairman of ICI Pensions Trustee in a letter to the panel.

ICI Pensions is the trustee for the £7.5bn ($12.4bn) pension scheme of ICI which was bought by Akzo Nobel, the Dutch based coatings company, in 2008.

Law Debenture Trust, an independent trustee company which sits on the boards of more than 200 schemes with more than 1m members and £100bn in assets, is pressing the panel to insist that acquiring or bidding companies make several disclosures.

Among these are a requirement that the bidder must disclose its intentions towards the scheme. The scheme trustee must also be allowed to express an opinion about how the deal is likely to affect members.

One senior adviser explained that this might require the trustee to seek an actuarial valuation of the scheme and publish a report for members.

The panel's consultation on these proposals ended last week. It declined to comment.

Advisers said that the pension scheme requests were not likely to be included in the final document, although they were 'reasonable'. If there is sufficient support, pension disclosure could be included in future drafts, they said.

In recent years, pension schemes have emerged as effective poison pills in hostile transactions because of the scale of their unfunded liabilities.

The pension scheme became a stumbling block during a 2007 hostile bid for Sainsbury's, a deal which led the Takeover Panel to rule that the public statements of scheme trustees are covered by its code.

Trustees say that when a bidder is not hostile, they are often the last to know that the company which sponsors the plan is about to be acquired.

In deals financed by debt, the transaction places another set of senior creditors ahead of the scheme members who are unsecured lenders with little access to assets in the event of insolvency.

Source: N. Cohen, *Financial Times*, 30 May 2011

At the time of the passage of the 1985 Act there was as yet no real debate about the position of stakeholders and the concept of corporate governance was still rudimentary. This first legislative wedge in the door could go no further than require recognition of the effects of corporate policies on stakeholders: its effect was exhortatory. Directors were still bound, in the common perception and that of the law, to work primarily for the benefit of shareholders as the legally-recognised owners of the company. The collection of information about the benefits to other stakeholders of the company's activities was not provided for, although some companies had long provided such information of their own volition.[10] There was not seen to be any great need to consider stakeholders' interests.

In this respect the aggressive takeover specialists had recognised in the 1970s what the traditionalist theory underlying most current corporate governance policies still does not: that the institutional holders of shares do not hold them for any interest in stewarding the businesses. They want to make as great a return out of their holdings as is possible. They do not want to be involved in the management of the businesses they invest in – even at a high level. And nor, most importantly, do the customers of the institutional shareholders want that either. Most shareholders – private or institutional – have no economic interest in acting as benign enlightened owners, working for the interests of all stakeholders by collaborating with managers of these companies, potentially at the expense of their own investment returns. Most listed shares – around 60–70 per cent of holdings in public companies[11] – are held by institutions (domestic and foreign) acting on behalf of pension funds, who act under a legal obligation to maximise the return to their beneficiaries.

---

[10] N. Buhr, 'History of and rationales for sustainability reporting' in J. Unerman et al. (eds), *Sustainability Accounting and Accountability* (Abingdon: Routledge 2007), pp. 57–69.

[11] Office of National Statistics, Table MQ5, available at http://www.ons.gov.uk/ons/rel/fi/mq5–investment-by-insurance-companies–pension-funds-and-trusts/2nd-quarter-2011/stb-mq5-statistical-bulletin.html.

They have little interest in acting as corporate policemen; they are not interested in the benefits accruing from the residual value that the shares possess after all the other stakeholders have received their due. What is most important to them is the continued flow of dividend payments and, associated with that, the prospect of capital growth.

Equally they have little interest in extending the scope of information contained in the standard requirement for accounts to enable other stakeholders to derive any value from them, since this would be burdensome on companies and might reduce profitability, as well as reducing their own grip on the flow of information. They will co-operate with companies through conversations with directors in trying to ensure that companies install and observe effective corporate governance practices – but such activities are intended to preserve the value of their own shareholdings by avoiding problems rather than producing a more enlightened view about the purpose of companies: in terms of for whom they work or by whom they are owned. Institutional funds are not really involved in being stewards at the expense of return. In this respect their interest in the development of stakeholder theory or stakeholder policies is – according to the traditionalist theories – marginal. But if acts of governance are also distinguished as operational and longitudinal then the need to sponsor and cultivate managerial attitudes to stakeholder-responsive policies and benign stewardship becomes self-evidently beneficial for the company and for investors. This is where the issues embedded in the term corporate social responsibility have to be considered since this forms a portmanteau concept for much of what is really company responsiveness to stakeholders.

Stakeholder theory and corporate social responsibility

The term 'corporate social responsibility' is unfortunately often applied as a substitute term for describing the company's response to the legitimate expectations of stakeholders. Used in this way it seems to suggest some greater distinction between the two aspects of governance – inward-facing and outward-facing – than is desirable or necessary.

In recent years, the shortened term 'corporate responsibility' has tended to supplant the older longer phrase. This is a welcome development since it leads thought away from the use of one particularly confused concept – that of 'corporate citizenship'.

Views on what corporate responsibility is range from the practical management of risk outside the immediate confines of the shareholder-company-director tripod – the view favoured here – to the supposed concept of 'being a good citizen'. In this last manifestation, the company is presumably supposed to be capable of some form of altruistic behaviour.

This anthropomorphism has numerous faults: it seems to conflate and confuse a number of issues about who controls the company; it flies in the face of legal theory; it ignores economic argument; and it discards beliefs about the primacy of the shareholder (whether or not that may be right or wrong). In short, it seems to upset just about everyone who does not believe in the case for a company being a citizen. Yet there is no reason or logical basis for this extension of real human characteristics on to the legal entity. By the crucial measures of citizenship companies do not – cannot – qualify to be called such. Quite simply, companies cannot meet any of the tests of citizenship. Companies cannot vote; companies cannot sit in the legislature; companies cannot sit on juries – only (human) citizens can do these things. These objections render the use of the term 'corporate citizen' completely fatuous – one might as well talk of 'corporate goldfish' or 'corporate jelly babies'. Since the company cannot be a citizen the term is therefore a complete distortion of the real issue – that CR is merely a phrase to indicate or describe the state of mind of managers in behaving properly towards stakeholders.

Arguments which suggest a separateness of CR from good governance or 'the business case for CSR' (see the text box below) therefore miss the point: it should be like making the case for breathing to a human being; if you want to survive no other reason is necessary. No case needs to be made at all for CR if the arguments for any form of governance are accepted, since they are one and the same thing; they just point in slightly different directions.

Making the business case: a growing body of evidence

When in 2003, Business in the Community and Arthur D. Little, the consultancy, researched and published a report on the business case for corporate responsibility, they found that while companies believed corporate responsibility delivered financial impact and business opportunity, few could cite hard evidence for this. In the updated report,* whose online version launches today, the results are very different.

'There's much more clarity around business opportunity, competitive advantage and financial impact, certainly, than in 2003,' says Charlotte Turner, BITC research director, 'By the time we got to 2011, there was substantial evidence.'

The report – researched between June and December 2010 by BITC and the Doughty Centre for Corporate Responsibility at Cranfield School of Management – drew on independent research from management consultancies and other work including academic papers, as well as from case studies from business.

'The academic material and what the companies themselves said showed remarkable consistency,' says David Grayson, professor of corporate responsibility and director of the Doughty Centre.

Moreover, the team was helped by a wealth of data and research, material that was not available in such volumes in 2003. 'Not that amount had been written about the business case back then,' says Ms Turner.

The goal of the report was to find evidence of the business benefits to companies that had embraced sustainability strategies and understand how this business case had evolved since 2003, while also predicting how it would be likely to develop over the coming years.

The result of the search was the identification of more than 60 business benefits, which could be grouped into seven key advantages:

- Brand value and reputation
- Employees and future workforce
- Operational effectiveness
- Risk reduction and management
- Direct financial impact
- Organisational growth
- Business opportunity

In addition, the report found two further business benefits – responsible leadership and macro-level sustainable development – that had materialised only more recently for companies whose corporate responsibility strategies were well established.

'We therefore suggest these benefits can be better realised as companies become more sophisticated, in their efforts to be responsible,' write the report's authors.

However, differences between companies emerged from the research, particularly when comparing small and medium-sized businesses (SMEs) with their larger counterparts. While SMEs tended to see benefits in the development of their employees and their potential future workforce, larger companies more often cited 'operational effectiveness'.

Even so, companies of all sizes cite employee engagement as a benefit of corporate responsibility whether at home or overseas. Mid-Counties Co-operative, for example believes that its community funding, company-led volunteering and project work has contributed to a fall in turnover rates at the company.

Meanwhile, Marks and Spencer has worked to improve process efficiency in its Bangladeshi factories as a way of increasing wages and cutting working hours while maintaining product quality. As a result, productivity at the factories increased by 42 per cent, while staff turnover fell from 10 per cent to 2.5 per cent.

'The whole idea of brand value and reputation is also a very strong driver,' says Prof Grayson. 'But also the idea of innovation – and that is likely to become more important with growing resource constraints, which means you need to increase the business while also reducing environmental impact.'

Another business benefit emerging strongly from the report is the operational effectiveness resulting from business responsibility and efficiency improvements gained through responsible sourcing, waste reduction and other practices.

When, for example, Adnams, the brewer, invested in an energy-efficient distribution centre, which uses 58 per cent less gas and 67 per cent less electricity per square metre than the old warehouse, while also taking 3.2 pints of water from the production of each pint of beer (the industry average is 8 pints), the company found it could save £50,000 a year.

And while companies have more recently tended to focus on the opportunities rather than the risk mitigation advantages of managing their operations responsibly, risk management does feature in the report's results.

Company case studies and academic research point to the ability for organisations to identify and reduce exposure to present and future disruptions to their businesses arising from environmental disasters and extreme weather events or social disruptions such as local conflict or community resistance to corporate projects.

Interestingly, however, the report's researchers found this benefit was less frequently cited at the end of the study period than at the beginning. 'We suggest that once processes are in place, this becomes integrated into standard risk protocol,' write the report's authors.

While many debate the ability of a sustainability or corporate responsibly strategy to deliver more than intangible benefits, the BITC-Doughty report found evidence of direct financial benefit to companies, albeit longer-term in nature. This might include better access to capital, lower penalty payments, cost savings, enhanced investors relations and increased shareholder value.

The lesson, suggest the authors of the report, is that 'companies who measure and link actions with results can quantify the impact better, and in turn reinvest in activities with a better understanding of their impact on the business'.

*The Business Case for being a Responsible Business, Business in the Community and the Doughty Centre for Corporate Responsibility at Cranfield School of Management, March 2011.

Source: S. Murray, *Financial Times*, 7 June 2011

However, in order to illuminate further what CR is or is not it is necessary to do the equivalent of investigating the provenance of the term – just as was suggested in the Introduction that geology was the proper comparison for corporate governance and not topology – and not simply concentrate on irregularities of the landscape which do little to aid evaluation or development of the concept.

The acronym CSR could equally stand for 'common sense really' or 'company society relationships' as well as the more common expansion. CR certainly has nothing to do with 'corporate giving' or 'corporate philanthropy'. In September 1970 Milton

Friedman wrote an article for the *New York Times* which was headlined 'The social responsibility of business is to increase its profits'.[12] Friedman said in the body of the article that:

> there is one and only one social responsibility of business – to use its resources and engage in activities designed to increase its profits, so long as it stays within the rules of the game, which is to say, engages in open and free competition without deception or fraud.

If this is accepted as statement of what companies should do then the other definitions of CR fall away as redundant. The principle purpose of CR, as the outward facing aspect of governance, is wholly to do with assessing the risk to the company of not satisfying the legitimate expectations of stakeholders. It is completely distant from any activity involving the provision of gifts to charities favoured by the chief executive, or by the board of directors collectively, unless there is some business purpose in so doing – which is usually unlikely. Bluntly, any description of CR which suggests some form of philanthropy is completely mistaken – almost maliciously so. In most circumstances[13] so-called corporate philanthropy is little more than disguised theft: conversion to the use of others of resources owned by the company or the shareholders without the approval of either.

Similarly, on the other side of the coin, CR is often mistaken by its supposed practitioners as an excuse for the manipulation of 'image', in the worst form of public relations activity. It is possible that sponsorship of a charity might just about be regarded as an example of CR for some companies in very specific circumstances, but it is difficult to see how a monetary gift to an international tiger charity, for instance, can be of benefit to stakeholders of an oil company – unless a very tortuous chain of logic is followed. What is passed off as CR is more often than not manipulative advertising – an attempt to contrive to associate a preferred set of fashionable values with a company for the purpose of concealing other less palatable facts. Such activities are not instances of the execution of corporate social responsibility but merely attempts by companies, which are transgressing on their business obligations to their stakeholders, to assuage public opinion by giving money to alter public perceptions of their behaviour. CR is too often regarded as a means of brushing up a company's image after some actual grievous failure of governance to stakeholders – a sort of corporate apology to the injured that costs no one (except the shareholders) anything of value and is a cosmetic air-brushing of significant managerial failure.

---

[12] M. Friedman, 'The social responsibility of business is to increase its profits', *The New York Times Magazine*, 13 September 1970.

[13] The statement refers to listed companies with very large shareholder bases. What private companies do, where there are fewer shareholders, is a different matter.

BP has been forced to sell off $20 billion of assets to meet obligations to make restitution to those affected by the spill and the loss of life which was promised to the US Government – a forced transfer of one-quarter of its market capitalisation from the shareholders – and twelve months later the company's share price had not recovered half the value it had achieved immediately prior to the explosion and onset of the disaster.[15]

Bhopal and Union Carbide – the extinction of a company through governance failure

During the night of 2–3 December 1984 a pesticide plant exploded in Bhopal, a city of about a million people and the capital of the Indian State of Madhya Pradesh, releasing about thirty-two tons of poisonous gas. The immediate loss of life ran into thousands, caused by asphyxiation and chemical poisoning, and the total loss of life caused by the blast and its after-effects is estimated to have amounted to tens of thousands. Many more casualties since have suffered psychological and neurological disorders; serious skin problems; blindness; or respiratory disorders. There is a much higher than normal incidence of birth defects locally. The incident is believed to be the world's worst industrial disaster in terms of loss of life and subsequent injury.

The plant was a joint venture between Union Carbide and Indian investors (including banks and the Government of the state of Madhya Pradesh). Union Carbide held a 50.1 per cent stake. The plant had been established fifteen years before to produce a pesticide called Sevin, which used highly toxic and very volatile methyl iso-cyanate (MIC) as a feedstock, at a time when the market for chemical pesticides was buoyant. In the intervening years market conditions altered and the production of the pesticide became less profitable.

By 1984, staffing levels at the plant had been reduced; staff training was poor; the plant was in a poor state of repair; pipework was corroded; numerous safety measures were ignored or not working; crucial safety and environmental equipment was out of commission and even when it had worked was of a lower standard than that which was mandatory in Union Carbide's other plants in the United States. The plant still used MIC, although much less hazardous feedstock

---

[15] B. Elder and N. Hume, 'Oil spill continues to put skids under BP's share price', *Financial Times*, 25 May 2010.

was available for the process of pesticide manufacture. Most significantly however, the plant was located adjacent to a densely populated area.

The local authorities had been warned of these failings by local staff but no action had been taken and no contingency plans existed for civil evacuation.

There is no dispute that the trigger for the disaster was introduction of water into a tank containing MIC. This could have been caused by poor maintenance regimes and procedures (work was being done on the plant at the time) but official reports into the incident after the disaster were not released. Union Carbide's own investigations suggested that the plant was sabotaged by a disgruntled worker.

The settlement of the claims made by the State government were consequently disputed – although in 1989, a settlement was reached under which UCC agreed to pay $470 million (the insurance sum, plus interest) in a full and final settlement of its civil and criminal liability. The parent company Union Carbide's reputation internationally became as toxic as the products it manufactured. The Indian Authorities issued an arrest warrant for the chief executive of the company and demanded his extradition – which was refused.[16]

Union Carbide effectively no longer exists as an independent company, having been absorbed by Dow Chemical in 1999.

The Bhopal incident took place, of course, before the world had become hardened by corporate misbehaviour on the grand scale of the 2008 financial collapse, when the extent of the governance lapses were so great as to almost overwhelm the system.

It is almost certainly a general feature of failures of outward-facing governance that, if anything more than trivial, they go on to affect the inward-facing aspect too. Failure to treat stakeholders properly nearly always results in collateral damage to shareholders' interests, usually, in listed companies, in terms of the share price. In this regard, failures of the outward-facing aspect of governance are perhaps more serious. When governance fails in terms of the relationship between shareholders, the company and directors, the damage is usually more localised in its effects. True there may be some reputational damage, which may spill over into some particular stakeholder areas but the effects are largely contained to the parties to the corporate contract (although there is one very significant exception to this – the financial crisis of 2008 – which will be discussed later). In the case of a failure like that of the Deepwater Horizon rig or Bhopal, the knock-on effects to the shareholders are extremely serious (although this should not cloud the fact that the effects to some of the stakeholders were even more so – since fatalities resulted).

[16] 'India PM to ask US to extradite ex-CEO in Bhopal case', *The Economic Times*, 29 June 2010.

Of the stakeholding parties, there are two in particular who are probably more powerful than others because of the influence they can exert on the company. The first of these is the customer, since he or she can, if they wish, usually take their business elsewhere. If a business upsets customers it is almost certain the shareholders will suffer. The second major stakeholder which can damage shareholders' interests is the State. Through levying fines, enacting specific legislation or withholding licences to trade in some specific area, the State can exercise a powerful influence over a company and can – as the example of the mis-selling of payment protection insurance in the UK shows – impose serious costs on companies which find their way back directly to the shareholders.

UK banks and PPI – bad treatment for stakeholders results in multi-billion costs for shareholders

Since 2005 sixteen million payment protection insurance policies have been sold by banks.[17] These policies are supposed to cover the borrower in the event of sickness, unemployment or some other misfortune which results in them being unable to make loan payments. But many of the policies were sold to self-employed people, who would not have been able to claim; some were sold to customers with the implied condition that they were necessary for the loan to be given; others were included in the loan without any form of option.

As a consequence of these obviously improper sales the banks were challenged by the Financial Services Authority. The banks fought the case through the Courts but eventually conceded the issue in May 2011 and agreed to make restitution. Barclays will be paying at least £1 billion; Lloyds TSB provided £3.2 billion; RBS provided at least £1 billion. In addition to these sums for restitution, the banks' operating expenses will also be affected, since staff time will be used to comb through their records to see which of their customers have been badly treated, tying up resources and costs in untangling records. They represent an absolute drain on the amount of money that could go to shareholders in dividends and, through their depressive effect on earnings, they result in a further reduction in the capital value of shareholdings.

CR and civil society

For the concept of corporate responsibility to be effective, certain market conditions are important, which are themselves linked to issues of political and legal structure. In fact, the development of effective corporate responsibility regimes requires many of the same conditions as those required for the existence of free markets:

---

[17] FSA as reported in E. Moore, 'Banks face £3bn bill in PPI Scandal', *Financial Times*, 6 March 2012.

- free association of individuals and multiple routes for them to associate with each other;
- freely available information and access to it;
- minimal controls over access to markets;
- a developed political structure with participants familiar with concepts of justice and regulatory probity.

These are effectively also the basic conditions for development of civil society – the arrangement of society where pressure groups – stakeholders by another name and in a more diffuse form – make their views known and mobilise for action. It is not surprising that consequently the links between the development of active civil society and the growth of effective CR are strong and deep. In societies where there is strong civil society there will be active stakeholders and the pressure on companies from stakeholder groups will be greater.

Summary and conclusion

Over a hundred years elapsed from the time when accepted managerial practice took little real account of the shareholder, to the point where legislation gradually entrenched the distant shareholder's right to information and then to the realisation, incorporated in the statement of directors' obligations in the Companies Act 2006, of the extended nature of the relationships between stakeholders that govern the well-being of companies. As these legal changes occurred, so theoretical development of the concepts of governance took place, with the realisation that the short-term interest of the shareholder alone was not necessarily compatible with ensuring the long-term survival of commercial organisations.

Much of the language of governance theory still takes no account of the distinction between the short- and long-term effects of governance action – and certain concepts (the pernicious misconception of 'corporate citizenship' and the often wilful confusion of corporate responsibility with mere image manipulation) have impeded understanding of what corporate governance really is. Furthermore, the developing realisation of the need for effective stewardship of commercial organisations to ensure their long-term future has been conflated with the supposed proprietorial responsibility stemming from the ownership of shares, pushing on to institutional investors a supposed duty that produces a conflict with their obligations to their customers.

If the premise that companies are perpetually in some form of tension with the competing demands of the market for resources and customers is accepted, then managers resolve these pressures by effective governance, balancing risk and the competing short- and long-term needs of shareholders and other stakeholders. The policies which they employ have both operational and longitudinal consequences – the first being principally concerned with the interests of shareholders and the second with the issues of stewardship that support the long-term well-being of the company through their impact on stakeholders.

If governance is thought of in this way – as an activity of management that has both an operational and a longitudinal component – then the pressures on institutional investors to act also as stewards of the businesses in which they have stakes resolve themselves away, since they are no longer faced with the conflicting position of being asked to involve themselves in the high-level management of a business at the expense of investment return.

However, as too many recent instances in the finance and energy sectors have shown, managers have not yet got to grips with this concept. Managers with an eye only to short-term profit-maximisation will jeopardise the long-term prospects of their companies – perhaps even their long-term existence. Yet it appears that an inability to understand the relationship between operational governance and its longitudinal consequences pervades the boardrooms of even the largest companies, as the BP example, and numerous others, suggest. Since the structures of voluntary governance, even though they may be supported by the moral force of public censure developed through the activities of pressure groups of stakeholders, lack the power to compel certain action in the absence of penalties, the law must step in to support the rights of shareholders and some stakeholders. It is with the issues of legal support for the behavioural and longitudinal dimensions of corporate governance that Chapters 4 and 5 are concerned.

PART 2

THE RELATIONSHIP BETWEEN LAW AND GOVERNANCE

CHAPTER 4

The protection of the laws

This chapter will look at the impact of the law on governance and considers:
- the background to the Companies Act 2006;
- the ways that the law impacts on governance;
  - the concept, functions and purpose of the share;
  - protecting the shareholder individually;
  - protecting capital;
  - protecting shareholders collectively;
  - in meetings;
  - protecting value and power;
- meetings and votes;
- remedies available to shareholders to protect their rights;
- the company.

Introduction

This chapter and the next will look at the legal framework inside which issues of governance mostly rest. The overall framework is considered in this chapter with more details of how law and governance interact in specific examples in Chapter 5.

The chapter also includes a development of the further classification of governance activity into procedural, behavioural and structural types and relates these to issues of law and regulation.

Effective corporate governance is a compound of many things – administration, management, accounting and law all figure in the mixture. Separating them out and studying them individually unfortunately potentially isolates them from the necessary interaction they have with each other. But a familiarity with the mechanics of operational governance – the legal/administrative aspects – is essential in order to comprehend the way that governance actually works as an activity. This chapter concentrates on some of the necessary preliminaries involving how the law impacts on governance which can then be developed into showing how governance works in practice (on the foundation of a legally-prescribed administrative structure) and how it sometimes differs from descriptions based on theory.

Additional dimensions of governance

The concepts of operational and longitudinal governance have already been dealt with in discussing the inward and outward-facing aspects of a company's governance activities. The introduction indicated additional dimensions; these will now be considered in more detail since they have significance to much of the interaction of the company with shareholders and other stakeholders in a legal sense. These dimensions are those parts of governance which might be called purely *procedural* or *administrative* and those parts which might be called *behavioural* (another dimension will be added later – the *structural* dimension). The impact of these dimensions is on both shareholders and stakeholders but with procedural aspects concentrated most on shareholders; behavioural affecting both, but concentrated mostly on shareholders; and structural governance infusing both.

The procedural/administrative aspects are essentially those which have now become so deeply embedded in the common administration of companies that they could not be realistically dispensed with. The essential purpose of the procedural set of governance provisions is to establish basic standards of governance that enable shareholders to have some confidence that money they use to purchase a company's shares will be protected from the ravages of criminal fraudsters and charlatans. This applies particularly, of course, to private companies or companies where there is no liquid market for the shares in the company. They are the foundations upon which the superstructure of the behavioural aspects of governance is erected. Examples of the procedural aspects would be matters relating to the efficient and fair administration of shareholdings; the conduct of meetings of shareholders; maintenance of capital structures and so on – they apply centrally to issues of legal ownership.

A consequent characteristic of procedural governance is that it is often a legal requirement (although some common procedural governance issues may not be specifically mandated by law). Normally, procedural aspects of governance fall within those measures which are required by law in the form of the Companies Act 2006 or associated or subordinate legislation (although the legal obligation to include them in company administration does not preclude more elaborate procedures being employed).

The behavioural aspects of governance then are those activities and features which form that part of the framework of corporate governance which extends beyond the basic legal structure established by law. These involve aspects which are not mentioned in the Companies Act 2006 (and associated legislation) but are often required by some accepted regulatory control or supervision. They revolve principally around the use of appropriate monitoring mechanisms such as board committees and the subjects that they are set up for: nomination of directors; remuneration of directors; audit and oversight; the powers and duties of non-executives; stakeholder involvement; stewardship.

Categorising such aspects as 'procedural' or 'administrative' does not mean that these issues are insignificant: the legal requirement that they have to be in place indicates how important they are judged to be by both legislators and by investors – both existing and potential. Nor does it indicate that they may be regarded as uncontentious: some of the changes made by the Companies Act 2006 to procedural matters of governance are *highly* contentious as well as being highly significant, e.g. the removal of annual general meetings as an obligation on private limited companies is a case in point.

A further significant point about the procedural aspects of governance is that although they are now the minimum standard common to all companies, their collective existence is comparatively recent[1] with some of the most important dating as obligatory only from the middle of the twentieth century (see, for instance, the *Royal Mail* case text box in Chapter 2). This emphasises again how the changing characteristics of shareholdings have not been matched by accompanying theoretical development in concepts of governance. To date the requirements of European law have not had a major direct impact on the procedural aspects of governance since for the most part UK law has enjoyed the position of 'super-equivalence' in such issues;[2] European Union directives have merely served to increase the thicket of law surrounding governance issues rather than to change the effect of regulations.

The Companies Act 2006

The law, through the Companies Act, is therefore mostly concerned with establishing the detail of procedural governance. It does this through strictures on company administration and controlling the detail of the administrative relationship that the company – listed or private – has with its shareholders. The most recent of the Companies Acts – the 2006 Act – was the result of review of the suitability of the then existing legislation against a widespread belief that the law had grown too large and cumbersome.[3] The Company Law Reform Steering Group (CLRSG) noted that the structure had to be gradually added to over 150 years as successive scandals indicated weaknesses in the procedural provisions. The procedural governance provisions provided by successive Companies Acts grew up like a coral reef – a huge structure, gradually added to over many years, providing shelter for many yet still offering plenty of places for the rapacious to hide.

---

[1] Cheffin, *Corporate Ownership*, Chapter 10.
[2] Temporarily allowed under the Markets In Financial Instruments Directive of the EU, Directive 2008/10/EC.
[3] See the *CLRSG Report*.

To quote the Final Report of the CLRSG:

> the approach to reform has been to add detailed provisions to deal with the particular corporate scandal of the times ... The result is that companies labour under unnecessary costs and burdens. Those seeking to streamline their administration and increase efficiency have to pick their way through the obstacles to be found in the [existing] Companies Act.[4]

The CLRSG went on to say that among the anomalies were that small and medium sized companies operated under regulations designed for listed companies; that directors who wanted to act honestly and in good faith were given no guidance (by existing legislation) and that the dishonest minority could find refuge in the gaps and obscurity of the law. 'And those who make up the wide range of interests to whom any company is accountable are not receiving the information necessary to assess the nature of the company and its business.'[5]

In attempting to cover all the changes in approach (if not all the detailed proposals) recommended by the CLRSG, the Companies Act 2006 became the largest single piece of legislation to be enacted by Parliament, at the time of its passing. Its stated purpose, as expressed in the CLRSG Report, was to clean up, consolidate and overhaul the principles by which companies are legally administered in respect of specific administrative obligations to shareholders and, innovatively, to certain stakeholders. (It is perhaps not surprising that in consequence it took over four years to fully engage – with the final provisions only becoming operative in 2010 – or that it produced confusion in certain aspects of its proposed reforms and appeared to back-track on the significance of good governance across the entirety of the corporate spectrum, as has already been noted in respect of small company governance.)

In pursuit of remedying this situation, what the CLRSG did *not* recommend (and what the eventual law did not do) was to impose any form of overall *behavioural* corporate governance structure on companies, since to have done this would have offended its desire to simplify and make appropriate to purpose the framework of company law. In the UK much of the impact of the law on corporate governance behaviour is, therefore, mostly indirect in its impact, since it establishes the procedural platform and leaves the development of behavioural governance to other parties. The law, in the shape of the Companies Act, does not concern itself with behavioural governance issues. This is left to others to do – principally in the case of listed companies through the listing obligations.

For listed companies the supervision of the behavioural dimension of governance (as opposed to the mechanisms of administrative governance) rests with a contractual

---

[4] *Ibid.*, para. 4.   [5] *Ibid.*, para. 5.

obligation which they enter into with the Stock Exchange – the Listing Rules and its continuing obligations. This contract, although carrying the force of law as subordinate legislation (because of the statutory powers of the Listing Authority) is largely dependent for its effect upon the 'intentions to adhere' of the companies who are supposedly bound by it. This is because the system of corporate governance for listed companies in the UK is one of principle, not of legal rule, and companies – if they do not wish to follow the recommendations of the UK Corporate Governance Code, which is at the heart of the Listing Rules – may *explain* their way out of compliance, *without formal sanction or penalty.*

In summary the situation is that all companies – private limited; public limited; or public limited and listed – must follow the procedural provisions of the Companies Act (unless they are expressly exempted from so doing by the Act itself); but only listed companies are required to observe the behavioural aspects of governance set out by the UK Corporate Governance code (the corporate governance of listed companies is dealt with in detail in Chapter 9).

The way that the law – the Companies Act and other legislation – affects companies is therefore very specific in that it has a number of distinct characteristics:

- it provides a procedural framework inside which the larger mechanism of governance fits;
- it does not prescribe governance behaviour;
- it concerns itself mostly with the basic rights protecting a certain type of property (the share);
- it protects the right to trade those shares; and
- it protects the right to be informed of issues that might affect perceptions of value in shares.

The ways that the law impacts on governance

The law sets the framework for procedural governance which provides a springboard for the development of efficient and effective behavioural governance beyond the basic level. The impact of the law is focused on certain areas: in this respect the provisions of the law in both procedural *and* behavioural terms (in the UK at least) generally interact with matters of corporate governance in six main ways:

1. on the shareholder as an individual;
2. on the shareholders collectively;
3. on the company – as a separate legal entity;
4. on the directors of the company and their obligations to the company as 'controlling minds';
5. on the company in the market place – principally in two forms: in terms of the contract that the company enters into with the listing authority if it is a quoted

company; and under general legislation regarding commercial trading (which it is beyond the scope of this book to cover);

6. on other stakeholders of the company – principally when they are in the form of creditors: suppliers; financiers; employees and pensioners; and, of course, the State.

Each of these areas will be reviewed further to describe how the basic governance platforms are established and then how they may or may not accord with the theoretical constructs which are supposed to describe governance.

The descriptions and elaborations are not intended to be authoritative guides to the law or its application but are illustrations of how the law supports (or occasionally hinders) the application of corporate governance. Readers wishing to pursue the detail of legislation or case law further are advised to consult one of the many excellent textbooks available.

The shareholder individually: protecting capital subscribed

Liability

The capital of a company is the amount which shareholders subscribe to establish and sustain the company, in return for which they receive a limitation on their liability for its debts. The amount of liability is limited to the amount agreed to be paid for the shares on their issue by the company. Accordingly, once shares are fully paid, members have no further liability. (This applies both to private limited companies and to public limited companies.) The majority of shares are issued 'fully paid' and accordingly there is no further liability on the part of the owners for any trading or other debt of the company.

Capital

The share capital of a company is usually referred to variously as authorised share capital, nominal share capital, issued share capital or paid-up share capital. Each refers to a different aspect of the overall share structure.

Authorised capital

The authorised share capital refers to the maximum number of shares available for issue at the nominal value of each share.

Issued capital

Issued share capital is that part of the company's total authorised or nominal capital which has been issued and taken up by the members of the company, after it has been issued for cash or for a consideration other than cash. It is expressed by reference to the aggregate nominal value of the shares issued. For example, a company may have an issued share capital of £250 divided into 250 shares of £1 each; or the same sum of issued capital composed of 2,500 shares of 10p or 25,000 1p shares.

Paid-up capital

If a company has an issued share capital of £250 comprising 250 shares of £1 each and the shares are fully-paid, the paid-up share capital will be £250. However, if the shares are issued only partly paid, for example 50p paid up on each share, with the balance due at some point in the future, the paid up capital will be £125. In the event of a winding-up the holders of partly paid shares are obliged to pay the balance of the share subscription outstanding. A 'call' for the balance may in addition be made at any time and failure to honour the call may result in the shares being forfeited by the putative holder.

Share premium

A share premium is the difference between the issue price of a share and its nominal value. For example, if the nominal value of a share is £1 and it is issued for £1.50, the premium is 50p. When a company states its share capital, only the nominal amount of the shares is included. The amount of any share premium is credited to a share premium account. The use of a share premium account is restricted as set out in CA 2006, s. 610 – initial costs may be set off against share premium; the premium may be capitalised to give bonus or scrip shares and certain other charges may also be set off. No dividend may be paid out of share premium, since this would be a reduction in capital.

Shares as evidence of ownership

It is commonly stated in law that shareholders own the company in which they have shares. The legal position is that:

> The share is the interest of the shareholder in the company measured by a sum of money, for the purpose of the liability in the first place and of interest in the second, but also consisting of a set of covenants entered into by all the shareholders *inter se* in accordance with [CA 2006, s. 33].[6]

[6] Farwell, J in *Borland's Trustee* v. *Steel Brothers & Co Ltd* [1901] 1 Ch 279.

So the money paid for shares can be construed as 'the price of the promise' – the consideration for the contract enabling the shareholder to engage in the affairs of the company and participating in its value; or, to put it another way, the consideration paid for the residual rights.

While this certainly holds good for private companies (as has been discussed), in companies where the shares are listed, the conventional theories of corporate governance begin to break down – issues such as the sheer number of shares in listed companies (the 'atomisation' of individual holdings); the 'control distance' between the individual shareholder and the director; and the significance of some procedural mechanisms all begin to play a part (and will be considered in due course). What can be said, regardless of which doctrine is being advanced, is the following:

- Shareholders own shares which are a fraction of the total capital of a company; therefore a share denotes a financial stake in a business.
- The share denotes a right to vote and assume the other rights and duties of membership of an association.
- The share is type of property *in itself*.

Consequent upon these initial characteristics, the main features of ordinary shares are as follows:[7]

- They have a right to participate in dividend payments (unless the articles or class rights say otherwise).
- They have a right to vote at general meetings.
- They have a right to receive whatever distribution is made to the holder of similar shares on a winding up.
- They are under an obligation to pay capital of a given amount (the subscription).
- They have whatever rights of membership are attached to the shares by virtue of the articles.
- The possessor of the share has the right to transfer shares freely in accordance with the terms of the articles of association.

The law is then concerned to protect these aspects of the contract between company and shareholder through establishing procedural requirements which companies must observe. These include provisions that share transfers must be registered before they can become valid (CA 2006, ss. 770–78), which obviously requires a register of shareholders (CA 2006, s. 113) to be kept. If a person's name is not on the register then he or she is not a member and so is not entitled to attend meetings, vote or receive dividends. Furthermore, since the share transfer certificate has to have the approval of the selling shareholder, no-one can be relieved of their shares without their consent

---

[7] This applies to listed companies. Private companies may have restrictions on some of these issues in their Articles, e.g. the contract between shareholders.

(at least, not easily).[8] Transfers supposedly accomplished without a valid transfer form being completed and presented to the company are, consequently, unlawful.[9]

However, again as a protection against fraud on the (anonymous) mass of their fellows, shareholders acting either individually or collectively have no right to compel the payment of dividends (CA 2006, Pt 23, ss. 829–53 and the Model Articles), unless recommended by the board and may not adjust the dividend above the recommendation of the board (although there are certain overseas cases which have been decided in favour of shareholders when dividends were wilfully withheld). Dividends may only be paid of course out of distributable profits anyway (CA 2006, s. 831). So a crooked promoter could not grab all of the cash out of a company by paying a spurious dividend to himself and leaving shareholders high and dry in much the same way as if there had been a reduction of capital. This is a comparatively modern innovation: until the 1950s in Britain it was still quite common to find shares being issued without voting rights,[10] which enabled blocks of shares to be held by owners who then controlled distribution policy.

Shareholders collectively (1)

Collectively, the primary protection which the law offers all shareholders is embodied in the Articles of Association.

This contract between all the parties to the company identifies the relationship of all parties to each other and gives details of their rights and powers. Its significance is such that it cannot be changed except by special resolution of the shareholders and requires a majority of 75 per cent of the shareholders to agree before changes can be made. The Articles are of sufficient significance that the law recognises they can override statute in some cases, as will be seen below in respect of pre-emption (subject always of course to the provision that nothing can be enshrined in the articles which is itself unlawful).

The individual subscriptions for shares of individual shareholders collectively form the capital of the company. This is what gives the company its individual legal identity. Capital serves four major purposes in a business:

1. its primary purpose is in creating the business legally;
2. it indicates proportions of ownership (these first two collectively forming evidence of the contract between shareholder and company);
3. it provides initial working capital;
4. it acts as a protection for creditors (up to a point).

---

[8] Companies Act 2006, s. 770(1).   [9] Companies Act 2006, s. 776(3).
[10] Cheffin, *Corporate Ownership*, p. 31.

In addition there are three subordinate purposes:
1. enabling growth, through the acquisition of real – or possibly intangible – assets;
2. providing a method of enabling shareholders to participate in the company's profitability through distributions;
3. acting as a measure of the company's ability to trade – through measures of its ability to meet its debts.

Of both these sets of functions, the last of each set is the most legally important. Because of this, capital cannot normally be returned – in the Companies Act 2006 the relevant section governing this is s. 658 – but this is only the most recent embodiment of a chain of provisions in the Companies Acts over time. It was recognised very early on[11] in providing the legislative support to limited liability companies that to allow unfettered return of capital would obviously be a fraud on the shareholders – and possibly the equivalent of murder of an independent legal entity – since otherwise unscrupulous promoters could raise money for the company and then withdraw it piecemeal leaving holders of share certificates with nothing more than the pieces of paper that signified membership of the company which would have degenerated into a cashless shell.

In exceptional circumstances, however, it is possible to return capital but only through a very specific set of statutory procedures which involves Court-authorised reduction of capital (CA 2006, ss. 641 *et seq*) or the repurchase of shares and their subsequent cancellation (CA 2006, ss. 684 *et seq*). It is possible, too, to alter the structure of a company's capital by redemption of shares designated initially as redeemable, through the proceeds of another issue. This amounts to the effective replacement of one subscription of capital with another; since the sum raised to redeem the original capital must be at least as large as that which is redeemed and may be greater than the original sum.

The CLRSG complained in its Report that much of the structure of company law had been determined by the effects of adjustments being made to statute brought on by the effects of financial scandals and misdeeds. The rightness – or wrongness – of actions was often tested in the courts before being brought to bear through statute, especially where the actions involved were obviously capable of being interpreted differently in the light of prevailing legislation and practice (see the text box about the *Royal Mail* case for instance). The issue of disguised returns of capital was such a matter.

Disguised returns of capital

Although there is no rule that directors' fees – or employees' wages – have to be paid out of profits rather than available cash, creditors (and shareholders too in certain circumstances) may be defrauded if the capital base of the company is eroded by such

---

[11] Cheffin, *Corporate Ownership*, p. 231

activities. Accordingly, shareholder-directors may be guilty of a disguised return of capital if they pay themselves for work not genuinely done or engage in transactions which solely result in payments to them. To avoid similar problems in the opposite direction, there may be no payment to shareholders in the form of a fee or by way of an undervalued sale. The determination of these provisions was decided in three cases (*Trevor* v. *Whitworth* (1887) 12 App Cas 409; *Re Halt Garage* [1982] 3 All ER 1016 and *Aveling Barford* v. *Perion Ltd* [1989] BCLC 626) which led to changes in statute law.

Trevor v. *Whitworth* (1887) 12 App Cas 409

This case, heard in 1887 by the Court of Appeal, established the rule that a company may not re-purchase its own shares since to do so would be a return of capital. During the 1970s the rule was subject to some relaxation as its application in the UK courts was found to be stricter than in other jurisdictions. This principle is now found specifically in s. 658 of the Companies Act 2006.

Re Halt Garage [1982] 3 All ER 1016

The liquidator of a failed company sought to recover money paid to directors in previous years – 1967/68 to 1970/71 – when they had been paid in cash. For some of these years the company had no profits but did have distributable reserves. As losses continued in the later years it had no distributable reserves. It was held that payments in excess of distributable profits exceeded reasonable remuneration and the liquidator was entitled to recover them

Aveling Barford v. *Perion Ltd* [1989] BCLC 626

Two companies both controlled by the same shareholder sold assets between them at undervaluation in order to allow one to pay a dividend to the controlling shareholder. The asset – some building land – was subsequently sold on for nearly five times the price at which it had been conveyed. The company which had originally owned it failed and the liquidator sued the purchasing company as a constructive trustee to the proceeds of the sale and that the transaction was a disguised return of capital.

Circumstances in which capital may be returned to shareholders

1. Where the company has surplus capital in excess of its needs.
2. Where the company has a dividend block – when the company has lots of cash but no distributable reserves.
3. Where the company needs to create a distributable reserve to finance a redemption of shares.
4. Where the company wants to make a non-distributable reserve (like a share premium account) distributable.
5. Where a company wishes to cancel an unpaid amount on partly paid shares.
6. Where a court-sanctioned scheme of arrangement is taking place.

While these are technically possible, directors must ensure that they do not prejudice class rights in the mechanism of effecting a reduction of capital.

As a further protection against fraud, subsidiary companies may not own shares in their own holding companies, since to do so would involve a looping arrangement that would give a small minority of shareholders a lock on control and also open the way for misbehaviour over cash remittances up and down the chain of control of the company. This would allow dividends to be paid when there would be no real supporting reserves from which to pay them.

The 2nd Single Market Directive of the European Union required the specific provision of protections in respect of use of capital and payment of dividends. Most of these were already incorporated in UK legislation – or more particularly in the common law. However as a result of some of the provisions of the Companies Act 2006, English statutory provisions went further than the Directive required – a condition known as 'super-equivalence'.

Mention was made above of the secondary initial purpose of capital in acting as a protection for creditors. Obviously very small amounts of capital of the amounts often found in private companies offer very little protection. In public companies however, the directors have an obligation to call the attention of the shareholders to significant declines in the value of the company's assets (once the asset value of the company has fallen to half or below half that of the value of the share capital) and this is designed to offer some protection (see also Chapter 16). (Prior to the enactment of the Companies Act 2006 companies were required to state their issued share capital in the Memorandum of Association but that obligation was abolished with the relegation of the Memorandum to a very subordinate document by the provisions of the Act.) The protection of creditors is accomplished mostly by insolvency legislation – the Insolvency Act 1986 – which protects creditors and not shareholders by virtue of the residual rights argument. However, insolvency is an after-the-event remedy rather than a preventative (at least usually). The law expects creditors to exercise appropriate commercial judgement in trading with companies.

It is of course entirely possible for mistakes to be made by those in charge of companies – the directors – which are not intended to be fraudulent but which may, through some form of oversight or sloppiness, occasion loss to shareholders. The law protects shareholders' interest in capital in this regard too.

If, for instance, directors make an improper payment of dividends to shareholders through some accounting fault they are required to compensate the company personally and may not expect shareholders to rectify a faulty declaration of dividend by reimbursement or waiver (CA 2006, s. 847) – unless of course the shareholder knew the distribution to be faulty (and therefore unlawful). Shareholders are not required to assure themselves of the correctness of a dividend distribution – since that is what they have elected the directors to do on their behalf – but if they do become aware of such they are under an obligation to the rest of the shareholders to make it known widely.[12] In this respect directors must ensure that the payment of any dividend is only from profits available for the purpose, and not from some undistributable profit. Directors must also ensure that they do not prejudice class rights when declaring (and paying) dividends to shareholders – if they do then once again they are liable to make good the loss to shareholders.

Multiple voting rights

In listed companies – the ones with which this book is mostly concerned – shares issued in a flotation must be ordinary shares with limited characteristics, as already described; any existing preferential capital rights must be eliminated.

But that is not necessarily the case in private companies where shares may have very many additional rights or none in respect of voting – except, under the English system, multiple voting rights are not allowed; other jurisdictions used to allow the use of multiple voting rights attached to a small number of shares to effect control. This is no longer possible under the blanket provisions of the 2nd Single Market Directive of the European Union (although certain long-standing exceptions are still allowed even so).

If that characteristic is required in a UK company it is dealt with by a different mechanism involving creating more shares for one class of shareholder on the crystallisation of some significant event. This is a mechanism often found in venture backed companies where venture investors effectively take over control

---

[12] Companies Act 2006, s. 847.

of the company by using convertible shares which balloon into a larger proportion of the total issued capital if some unfortunate event occurs. Such rights have to be written into the Articles of Association and may not be retrospectively incorporated.

Additional rights for non-quoted company shares may typically include:

- The right to have the waiver for auditing and accounts disapplied in any given year on application to the company.
- The right to protection of minority rights ('oppression of a minority').
- The right to apply for winding up –
  - if the company cannot pay its debts (as they fall due);
  - if the number of shareholders has fallen below two in a public company;
  - on any other just or equitable reason.
- The right to appoint a proxy to attend a meeting and vote in the member's place either on his instructions or as agent.

Classes of shares

There are no fixed formulas for share types or definitions (they will be defined by the Articles of each company). Consequently not all shares are equal (or some are more equal than others!) but in the absence of any other guide all shares of the same class rank equally. But broadly the classifications are as follows:

Ordinary shares – sometimes known simply as 'equity'; usually carrying one vote per share.

Preference shares – entitled to a prior call on any funds available for dividends (sometimes at a fixed rate); often also a prior right to the return of capital.

Deferred shares – rare and archaic, now used only for tax avoidance; not permissible for plcs.

Redeemable shares – these will be bought back at some fixed point in time for a specified sum; they will usually be traded at a discount. A company's share capital cannot be formed entirely of redeemable shares.

Convertible – these are only found in private companies. They change their character and rights on some event – for instance a takeover; or failure to achieve some pre-determined target of profitability or turnover. They are highly flexible ways of altering the apparent value of a company (which can be of great value in re-investing or in meeting expectations of an existing management when a new investor puts money into a company or of incentivising managers of a company). They are thus much used in companies which are backed by venture capitalists.

Because of Stock Exchange rules the following types of share are *never* found in UK listed companies:

Cumulative – these shares have rights to missed dividends before any other payments are made to other shares.

Participating – these shares have some fixed percentage of available profits which are taken out before any other distribution and are often fixed at a 'preferred' level.

Non-voting shares – used to restrict control of the company; there may also be limited or enhanced voting right shares – but not multiple votes – to effect the same purpose.

These may be found occasionally:

Employees shares – which will usually have the same rights as ordinary shares ('*pari passu*') if issued as part of a share scheme but will have the rights of ownership and employment by the company directly linked.

Warrant – a document entitling the holder to subscribe for equity capital (shares) of a company at some future date(s) at a price determined at the time the warrant is issued. Some warrants can still be traded on the London Stock Exchange.

Shareholders collectively (2): protecting value and power

One of the theoretical problems that shareholders face in committing money to a company is that they may think that they have bought a certain proportion of the company's shares, only to find that the company has sold more shares to someone else and that the value of their shares has diminished. Apart from the issue of having a much smaller stake in the company in terms of value, an ability to swamp the existing voting value of shares by creating more shares (to be sold to different shareholders) might be manipulated by unscrupulous managers to dilute the voting power of 'difficult' shareholders. This would enable the managers to run the company according to their own views, backed up by the votes of placemen. To protect against this, companies are required to include *pre-emption rights* in their Articles of Association.

Pre-emption rights (CA 2006, ss. 560–77) require a company to offer any new issues of shares to existing shareholders in proportion to their existing holdings. This enables shareholders to preserve their proportionate interest in the company without fear of having that interest diluted by action they have not approved. However, while the statutory right must be included it may be disapplied, waived or modified by virtue of the phrasing in the articles of the company (which of course requires the consent of the shareholders either acting to agree the articles originally or subsequently).

Pre-emption comes into effect most usually where the company needs to increase its capital base substantially and therefore wishes to raise money from shareholders. Existing shareholders, if the disapplication of pre-emption has not been applied, must be offered the shares first. This is the legal and practical basis for 'rights issues': shareholders have the rights to subscribe for shares in proportion to their existing holdings of shares with the shares being issued at discount to their prevailing price to compensate for the lower return likely to each share in participating (immediately) in profits and dividends.

Issues of shares subject to pre-emption rights

Any new issue of shares of the same class or having substantially similar rights to a pre-existing class.

Rights issue – An offer of new shares to existing shareholders in proportion to their existing shareholdings.

For example a '2 for 1 Rights Issue' would give a shareholder the (contractual) right (by virtue of the Articles of Association) to purchase two new shares for every share already held. Companies use them to obtain additional funding from the company's shareholders, rather than obtain working capital by borrowing from banks or other financial institutions. If a company is listed it may be required by the Prospectus Rules to issue a prospectus in relation to the rights issue. Rights can be sold on to others 'nil paid' in which case the new acquirer is liable to pay the cost of the subscription (as well of course as the price demanded by the owner of the rights); can be taken up (in which case the existing shareholder is responsible for paying for the new share) or may be ignored.

Bonus issue – fully paid shares of the same class are issued free of charge to existing shareholders in proportion with their existing holding. Also referred to as a capitalisation issue. No new capital is raised by the company and holders can keep or sell all or part of their allotment. A bonus issue is often perceived as a sign of confidence in the company's strong financial position.

Open offers – existing shareholders may be invited to subscribe for securities but the benefit of the right cannot be sold or assigned.

Exchanges and conversions – new shares may be issued as a result of existing shares being exchanged for, or converted into, new shares.

Shareholders collectively (3): shareholder meetings and votes

Shareholders, once they have committed their money to the company, achieve the protection of limited liability. But in return for this give up much direct access to the company. They are no longer entitled to intervene in the formulation of the company's strategic development or have access to the assets which the company purchases (with the money that they have provided) to bring the strategy to fruition. It now becomes the directors' function to control the strategic development of the company and the deployment of the assets. The directors may, if they wish, consult with shareholders about some of this – or they may not. Shareholders are not entitled to see the minutes of directors' meetings nor to see detailed information about the company's progress during the financial year (with the exceptions that private companies may choose to do more or less what they like about revealing information to shareholders – provided that all shareholders are treated equally; and that listed companies release interim results every six months as an obligation of listing).

Shareholders are entitled to a report at the end of each year about the performance of the company and have the right at that point to question the directors and to vote on a few other matters (the value of these meetings and the voting powers for listed companies will be dealt with in Chapter 9). For private limited companies the powers can be both very powerful or almost worthless depending on the structure of the company's shareholdings and the permissions granted by the Articles of Association. The Companies Act 2006 removed the obligation on private companies (because it was seen as a burden to the majority) to hold annual general meetings and so took some of the power away from shareholders in these companies who may now be largely reduced to the passive role of mere providers of capital.

Shareholders collectively (4): shareholders' remedies

It will be apparent from what has been said to this point that the remedies available to shareholders once they have committed their money into a company are largely formulaic, governed either by the procedures protected by law or by the articles of association of the company if these are (allowably) different. The procedural aspect of governance serves to constrain available actions to shareholders as well as to protect overall positions: the bargain of limited liability is bought at the expense of freedom of action.

Actions which the shareholder can take in respect of their 'rights' are therefore restricted to certain procedures – especially if it is a private company: an incoming shareholder, unless in a very special position, cannot expect the articles to be re-written solely to accommodate their own particular requirements.

In summary, therefore, shareholders can seek redress for what they regard as some form of mismanagement only in a limited number of ways. Their routes to redress are limited to the following.

Redress via the Articles

If they believe that something has been done or is about to be done which runs contrary to the initial contract then shareholders can employ the provisions of the articles to protect or deflect such activity. If they are correct then the company is bound to observe the contract between itself and them. In this respect, the company (or probably more accurately the company secretary) sometimes acts as the arbiter between shareholders who dispute each other's positions. Matters which cannot be resolved this way have to move to legal disentanglement of course.

Court resolution

In the event of some procedural defect which cannot otherwise be resolved through negotiation or because the position is legally ambiguous the shareholders may approach the High Court for a resolution of their dispute (which may be with the company or with each other). Such issues may not always signal hostilities between shareholders or between the company but may require some form of legal ruling to resolve an issue amicably which is not otherwise soluble, because of some defect in the original phrasing of the Articles of Association or some fault in subsequent administration.

Removal of directors

If the shareholders perceive that the directors are not performing their duties satisfactorily, then they have the right to remove the directors. The right to do this is fundamental to the arrangement between the company, the shareholders and the directors and may not be abridged by the company's Articles of Association. Removal of a director (or directors) can be effected by failing to re-elect if there is a regular rotation of directors' positions; or by failing to renew a fixed term contract; or by voting a director off the board (CA 2006, ss. 168–9). This last action can only be achieved if a sufficient fraction of the total shareholding can be mobilised to agree that a special notice should be presented to the company requiring a meeting and that a resolution should be placed on the agenda of that meeting. A simple majority of shareholders is sufficient to eject a director.

Derivative actions

The Companies Act 2006 introduced the principle of derivative action, whereby shareholders can take legal action on behalf of the company against directors who are believed not to have acquitted their obligations. This is necessary because it may well be the case in such circumstances that the directors as a board are unwilling to take action against themselves. The way in which derivative actions may be used is dealt with at greater length in the next chapter.

Oppression of minorities

Events which result in some minority of the shareholders being treated contrary to natural justice, or contrary to the provisions of the Articles for the apparent benefit of another set of shareholders can be dealt with by recourse to the courts in respect of 'oppression of minorities' (CA 2006, s. 994). This route for remedy of an injustice was first introduced by the 1948 Companies Act. Strictly speaking, the term 'minorities' is now redundant to the basis of the action since the 2006 Act refers to acts that are prejudicial to the members generally; to a proportion of the members or to an individual member. The act(s) complained of can be either actual or proposed; so it is unnecessary to wait until something has been done (and which may then be more difficult to unravel) before taking action.

Winding up

In the event that some serious action has occurred which has resulted in the effective irreparable breakdown of the trust between the company and the shareholders then they have the right to apply for a winding up of the company under instruction of the High Court. This is an extremely unusual event, obviously.

Shareholders also have recourse to the courts in respect of claims under the Insolvency Act 1986. It is normally creditors who take such action, but occasionally shareholders may be creditors and *vice versa*.

The company and the law

The vast bulk of the Companies Act 2006 is taken up with detailing a company's essential procedural governance mechanisms: the Articles; constitutional matters; a company's legal capacity; the registered office; the register of members; the rights of members; appointment and removal of directors; duties of directors; resolutions at meetings; accounts; provisions concerning the audit of companies' accounts; share capital matters; distributions; mergers and division of companies; fraudulent trading – and so on for forty-seven parts, all divided into multiple chapters, and sixteen schedules. And this is only for the Companies Act, there are many other pieces of legislation – the Insolvency Act 1986; the Financial Services and Markets Act 2000; the Enterprise Act 2002; the Corporate Manslaughter and Corporate

Homicide Act 2007 to name just four of the more significant ones – which impact on matters of procedural governance (and as will be shown matters of structural governance too, in terms of more recent legislation). The law obviously takes basic procedural governance very seriously.

The massive amount of effort employed in detailing the mechanics of procedural governance is necessary since the law's primary impact is to create a new legal personality when a company is incorporated by its shareholders. This legal personality will expect, and be entitled to, the protection of the laws. If shareholders were to be left entirely to themselves in determining how companies should be organised and the relationships between them, then the State would be forever expending vast sums in maintaining legal processes to disentangle the messes that shareholders got themselves into. This is aside from any considerations of how the State would deal with the numerous issues of regulation that it has to organise for taxation purposes and other social regulation, if no basic procedural framework were laid down.

But the State, through the pronouncements of the law, under the British system of corporate governance by principle, concerns itself only with what it regards as the essentials to maintain justice and broadly equitable balance between the power of the market and the protection of the individual. The rest is left to the companies to sort out themselves, together with other agencies such as Stock Exchanges in the case of listed companies. The attitude that the law adopts is a bit like ensuring that a human being is fully-fashioned in physical form – and totally neglected emotionally and mentally. This emotional and mental aspect is the stuff of behavioural governance – it is not the concern of the law and so the law leaves it for other parties to determine.

The company is a creature of the law, endowed by the law with personality – and also gifted by the law with rights that human beings do not possess. For instance, no company can be imprisoned for committing a breach of the law as real persons are – even a crime which takes someone's life; and no person escapes paying their taxes because of an excess of expenditure over income, which companies frequently do. Some commentators [Bakan][13] go so far as to say that humans would be labelled as pathological if they displayed the same characteristics as those routinely displayed by some companies. The further development of this argument will have to wait until Chapter 15, which deals with counter-governance, but it is sufficient to note at this point that the procedural aspects of governance only operate to produce the framework around which the rest of the governance mechanism has to fit.

---

[13] Bakan, *The Corporation.*

Summary and conclusion

The law, in the form of the Companies Act 2006 and associated legislation, produces a basic but extensive framework of rules which governs the operation of the company in respect of shareholders and their relations with each other. For the vast majority of companies – which are private – this legal framework is, when supplemented with the original contract of the Articles of Association, their corporate governance framework too.

Statute law – through its prescriptions on how capital is to be dealt with; how shareholders rights are to be protected; how meetings are to held and run and what remedies are available to shareholders who feel their rights have been infringed – deals largely with issues of *procedure*. So at the basic level, much of corporate governance is also procedural in nature.

Until the middle of the twentieth century, the law concerned itself mostly with the development and extension of such procedural matters – protecting shareholders' capital especially in a variety of ways.

By the middle of the twentieth century, however, the development of the law had begun to move into different areas – affecting economic behaviour in terms of issues such as the collapse of companies (the Insolvency Act 1985); the abuse of share markets (the Theft Acts; the Financial Services and Markets Act 2000); liability for injury done to members of the public (the Corporate Manslaughter and Corporate Homicide Act 2007); and most recently the conduct of business between companies and other companies and public bodies (the Bribery Act 2010). By putting the force of law behind the arrangements between listed companies and the Stock Exchange the law also bolstered the contract between the Exchange and listed companies that is represented by the UK Corporate Governance Code. The law thus moved strongly into dictating the context of *behavioural governance* – the way in which companies are run, over and above mere procedural matters.

The way in which the law has changed and developed has affected the context of the traditionalist theories of governance, since the company is now required to comply with a set of legal rules that the traditionalist theories have barely begun to take account of – for instance, the concept of legal personality has been extended dramatically (in governance terms) by the introduction of the Corporate Manslaughter and Corporate Homicide Act 2007 and the Bribery Act 2010. Even the requirements laid upon directors to behave in a certain way by the Companies Act 2006 have altered the relationship of the company to shareholders and stakeholders.

Further investigation of the impact of the law in these specific instances, and how the law and traditionalist theories of corporate governance consequently interact, is the subject of the next chapter.

CHAPTER 5

Critical governance law

This chapter will consider recent developments in the law affecting the corporate governance of companies through the prism of three specific statutes:

- The provisions in the UK Companies Act 2006 affecting the obligations of directors; the provisions enabling derivative actions; with a brief comment on the Act itself.
- The Corporate Manslaughter and Corporate Homicide Act 2007, which improves the legal delineation of the corporate entity's responsibilities.
- The Bribery Act 2010 – which is the most far-reaching piece of legislation for many years and, this chapter contends, will have a profound cultural impact on corporate governance in the UK.

Introduction

Taking the pieces of legislation listed above collectively, the conclusion of this chapter is that recent legislative developments have begun to form a legislative framework for some areas of corporate governance which reflects more accurately the real world than conventional or traditionalist descriptions of governance used in the UK Corporate Governance Code.

In the order in which they are dealt with in the text, these Acts affect behavioural governance (directors' obligations – CA 2006); the behavioural governance of a company as a legal person, further distinguished from shareholders and management (Corporate Manslaughter and Corporate Homicide Act 2007); and the control of risk – again a behavioural issue (Bribery Act 2010). The behaviour of the company in the marketplace, which is affected by legal constraints and is matter of systemic governance (through the Financial Services and Markets Act 2000) will be looked at briefly below – but more closely in Chapter 9.

Market regulation

The regulation of listed companies' market activities is mostly dealt with through adherence to the continuing obligations of the listing rules that are policed by the Stock Exchange. These are embodied in the UK Corporate Governance Code which effectively forms part of a contract which listing companies agree with the Stock Exchange when their shares are listed.

The companies agree to adhere to the listing rules – especially the operation of the 'comply or explain' regime – in return for the Exchange accepting their shares for trading. Because of the powers given to the FSA under the Financial Services and Markets Act of 2001 (which it is assumed will be effectively carried over into the new regulatory arrangements involving the Prudential Regulatory Authority and the Consumer Protection and Markets Authority – see Chapter 11), these effectively have the weight of legal obligations. In addition, some company activities are subject to the strictures of the Enterprise Act 2002 which affects competition policy and insolvency arrangements

There is, of course, in addition to the statutes listed above and the reference to the contractual nature of the listing agreement, a huge body of law which deals with the specifics of mercantile contracts; trading; employment; health and safety regulation; intellectual property; real property and so on, which – although it may impact upon corporate governance in the widest sense – is too voluminous to be touched on here. A comprehensive review is beyond the scope of this book and would require a book in itself.

The argument will be advanced that legal change is taking place of a substantial nature which extends across large areas of governance, using the evidence of the legislation referred to above. In short, the beginnings of a legislative framework for the control and support of (particularly) behavioural governance activity is developing in the UK, with the law becoming more sympathetic in its effect to some of the issues that have been raised in previous chapters concerning the actual relationships (rather than theoretical ones described in the conventional theories) between shareholders and the company; shareholders and directors; and directors and the company. While there does not appear to be a co-ordinated or strategic pattern behind recent changes, the overall effect is to bring many law and real-world governance issues into a position of support with one another – which is obviously desirable – in a form of 'incremental coherence' rather than co-ordinated overhaul. And also to further distance the descriptions offered by the conventional theories of governance from the real world.

Directors' responsibilities: the Companies Act 2006

The main stated purpose of the Companies Act 2006 was to simplify the regulation of private companies ('limiteds') in comparison with companies which owe some form of obligation to the public (plcs or, more likely, listed companies). However, as part of this the government also took the opportunity to make some additional changes to the legal obligations that companies face. The effects of some of these have been dealt with earlier in terms of the retrograde step of eliminating the obligation to hold annual shareholders' meetings for private companies. (There is of course no obligation *not* to hold such meetings; the law is permissive in this respect and companies are at liberty to continue with the practice, if they wish.)

More radical than this, however, was the first formal statement of the obligations of directors that the law will hold them to, which is set out in ss. 171–7 of the Act.

These obligations (see text box) bring company law closer to the thrust of development of the law affecting trustees. They mirror the obligations placed on trustees in respect of their obligations to the assets which they look after (see second text box). Thus the latest comprehensive manifestation of company law begins to establish a description of the activities of company directors in terms of a form of stewardship for the benefit of stakeholders (which is what trustees do when they look after a trust), rather than the supposed agency relationship of the traditionalist governance theories. Presumably this change potentially allows the directors to be pursued, as trustees may be pursued, for negligence involving pure economic loss. Section 170 of the Act also states very plainly that the general duties specified in ss. 171–7 are owed by the director of a company to a company.

Directors' obligations under the Companies Act 2006

There are four **specific issues** in the 2006 Act:
- Directors must act within powers granted to them by the articles of the company and any statutory authority [s. 171]; any acts outside these powers are ultra vires and directors may become personally liable for them.
- They must act in such a way as to promote the success of the company [s. 172] (see below).
- They must exercise independent judgement in the execution of their duties [s. 173].
- They must apply reasonable care, skill and diligence to their tasks [s. 174] – a form of wording based on the Insolvency Act 1986.

The definition of success in s. 172 is taken to be a long-term increase in the value of the company and has to take into account:
1. long-term implications for the company
2. the interests of employees
3. business relationships
4. the community and the environment
5. a necessary reputation for high business standards.

This list constitutes the concept of 'enlightened shareholder value'.

The need to act fairly between shareholders [s. 172] can be over-ridden in the case where the directors employ the provisions of s. 247 of the Act to provide benefits for employees on cessation of the whole or part of the business or when the business is transferred to another set of shareholders.

There are in addition to the four principal provisions three further consequential provisions:

- a duty to avoid conflicts of interest [s. 175] – which can be resolved by other directors giving authority to the director operating under a potential conflict, in a quorate meeting
- a duty not to accept benefits from third parties [s. 176]
- and a duty to declare an interest in proposed transactions [s. 177] if one exists. Once the declaration is made it does not need to be repeated if the transaction becomes actual.

Trustees' responsibilities

Charity trustees may also be known as trustees, directors, board members, governors or committee members. The principles which they adhere to and their main duties are the same in all cases.

Trustees have ultimate responsibility for directing the affairs of a charity, and ensuring that it is solvent, well-run, and achieving the purposes for which it was set up.

Trustees must:

- Ensure that the charity complies with charity law, and with the requirements of the Charity Commission as regulator; in particular ensure that the charity prepares reports on what it has achieved and Annual Returns and accounts as required by law.
- Ensure that the charity does not breach any of the requirements or rules set out in its governing document and that it remains true to the charitable purpose and objects set out there.
- Comply with the requirements of other legislation and other regulators (if any) which govern the activities of the charity.
- Act with integrity, and avoid any personal conflicts of interest or misuse of charity funds or assets.

Trustees have a duty of prudence which they discharge by:

- Ensuring that the charity is and will remain solvent.
- Using charitable funds and assets reasonably, and only in furtherance of the charity's objects.
- Avoiding undertaking activities that might place the charity's endowment, funds, assets or reputation at undue risk.
- Taking special care when investing the funds of the charity, or borrowing funds for the charity to use.

They also have a duty of care which means that they must
 – Use reasonable care and skill in their work as trustees, using their personal skills
   and experience as needed to ensure that the charity is well-run and efficient.
 – Consider getting external professional advice on all matters where there may
   be material risk to the charity, or where the trustees may be in breach of their
   duties.
 – The similarities between these obligations and those of company directors
   under ss. 171–7 of the Companies Act 2006 are plain.

Source: adapted from the Charity Commission website, www.charitycommission.gov.uk/
publications/cc3.aspx

The wording and underlying principles of ss. 171–7 effectively distance the directors'
obligations from any form of direct obligation to shareholders such as that described
by the traditionalist theories of governance; its meaning is made plain by s. 170: the
directors clearly owe their obligations to the company – the wording in the Act is
essentially a reiteration of the fiduciary duty they owe established by common law.

Shareholders are not mentioned specifically except in the context of 'enlightened
shareholder value', which is clearly a reference to taking note of stakeholder interests;
employees – a stakeholder group – are given one specific mention – or two if the override that is available to directors where the company is sold on to another set of
shareholders or even ceases to exist is taken into account. Stewardship of the assets
of the company for the long term and for a constituency that extends beyond the
shareholders is therefore a fundamental obligation of directors' behaviour under
the 2006 Act. The law recognises the obligations of directors go much wider
than simply the link which traditionalist theories mistakenly describe as the 'agency
relationship'.

Derivative actions

The 2006 Act also simplified the process by which shareholders could initiate 'derivative
actions' – an action undertaken against a director by a shareholder. This type of action
had been available before the introduction of the 2006 Act but although frequently
threatened was rarely initiated. Consequently when the process of simplification was
raised there was some concern among directors, with advice coming from several large
firms of City solicitors.[1] Yet from the standpoint of those who had feared that such
stiffening of the law in favour of shareholders might have brought about better

---

[1] Freshfields and Radcliffe Chambers both produced balanced notes.

governance, early legal tests suggest that directors had little to fear.[2] If the intention of the legal draftsmen and Parliament was to provide a route for more vigorous action by shareholders, then the reforms have failed.

Any action still faces a series of very difficult gateways to pass through – even though the process has been simplified. In particular, a judge hearing the case is required to consider from the outset whether a hypothetical new director would consider it worthwhile to pursue the action, on behalf of the company, against the director or directors who have been challenged. In one case, heard in 2007 just after the Act came into force – *Stimpson & Others* v. *Southern Landlords Association* [2009] EWHC 2072 (Ch) – the judge gave a long list of reasons for rejection on the hypothetical director test and also remarked that if he was wrong on that reason there were plenty of others why the application should fail.

One of the reasons is probably that of pinning blame on directors for actions that have been shrouded in collective responsibility and cloaked with advice from professional advisers – which probably explains why none of the directors of any of the major banks in the UK have been the targets of derivative actions for neglect of their obligations under s. 172 (although the failure of the FSA to pin blame for a lapse of directorial obligation, after an extensive investigation, may also have something to do with it).

The court will refuse permission under s. 263(2) of the Act if:

- a claim does not promote the success of the company; or
- the act or omission was authorised; or
- the act or omission has been or is likely to be ratified by the company.

The financial collapse of 2007–8 has seen no attempts to use the same provisions for the pursuit of the directors of the banks who could surely – morally and practically at least – have been held to have transgressed their obligations under ss. 172–4 of the Act. It would be difficult, for instance, to think of more blatant instances of neglect for the long-term interests of the company than the pursuit of ABN by RBS – but they will clearly have fallen into the 'reasons for refusal' under s. 263. Even taking this case aside, the failure of a route to pursue action in the three or four cases that have been brought to the courts under the new provisions of the Act since 2007 suggests, at the very least, that the obligations placed on directors are either not working effectively or the legal authorities see no sense in encouraging the pursuit. So, it has to be asked – from a governance point of view at least – what is the sense of having such provisions?

---

[2] At the time of writing only three cases had reached the courts and these were related to private companies on technical issues.

Other actions

Although it is notoriously difficult for public prosecutors to devote sufficient resources to secure a conviction for fraud, in the event that this is not regarded as a likely outcome under criminal law, the obligations now placed on directors open the way for civil actions (with an obviously lesser burden of proof) to be mounted for dereliction of their obligations to shareholders. This has already been done in the case of the collapsed hedge fund Weavering Capital, where liquidators of the fund have mounted a civil action against the directors after it folded with over £300 million of losses when it was unable to met investors' demands for withdrawal.[3]

The Companies Act 2006

Aside from the issues noted above, there must be general questions raised about the value of the Companies Act 2006. It was the largest piece of legislation ever to pass through Parliament and one of the longest in its gestation and implementation (it might really have been called the Companies Act 2006–2010, since it was not until the later date that all the provisions were operative). Its provisions, now fully implemented, have met with a mixed response.

A third-party study commissioned by BIS[4] reported in April 2011 that:

> On the whole the changes are not seen as overly burdensome by companies and in particular key deregulatory measures such as the removal of the requirement for private companies to hold AGMs and the greater use of written resolutions have been particularly welcomed by companies and stakeholders, and seen as increasing flexibility …

> Stakeholders in particular noted a number of positives resulting from the Act including a reduction in bureaucracy, greater privacy for directors and shareholders, greater clarity on directors' duties and greater engagement with shareholders.

But a paper by a leading academic concluded differently:

> Firstly, what is good in the CA 2006 (i.e. most suitable or right for a particular purpose) is trivial and, at parts, quite bad (i.e. having negative and undesirable qualities). Secondly, what is bad is very bad for business, and quite ugly (i.e. likely to cause trouble, and threatening or ominous) too. And thirdly, the ugly truth is that reform has made

---

[3] L. Armitstead, 'Serious Fraud Office criticised for closing Weavering Capital investigation', *Daily Telegraph*, 9 September 2011.

[4] *Evaluation of the Companies Act 2006*, BIS December 2011.

very little difference (the CA 2006 is not 'fit for purpose') and has failed to focus on the real important challenges.[5]

While the intention of reducing the burden of administration on companies is to be applauded, as has been noted earlier, some of the changes have been retrograde (the abolition of certain protections for shareholders in private companies) and some have been merely cosmetic (removing the obligation to appoint a company secretary does not remove the obligations to fulfill the functions of the company secretary). If the reception from 'stakeholders' has been lukewarm (the BIS report) and the conclusion of at least one authority is that the Act is poor and if it failed its first big test in making the obligations of directors' duties to the companies they are appointed to more rigorous, then again, the value of the Act has to be questioned: 47 parts with 1,300 sections and 16 schedules and a further 70 statutory instruments made under the Act seems an awful lot of Parliamentary time to have produced no significant effective result.

The Corporate Manslaughter and Corporate Homicide Act 2007

In the concluding decades of the twentieth century a spate of transport disasters involving substantial loss of life – the *Herald of Free Enterprise* disaster; the King's Cross fire; the sinking of the *Marchioness* pleasure cruiser; the Hatfield and Paddington rail crashes – brought about calls (particularly from the Press) for a revision of the law involving the responsibility of companies and company managers for the deaths of others brought about by their companies' actions or negligence.

Part of the momentum for change may have been due to a desire to exact some form of retribution – a feeling that some individuals drawing fat salaries were 'getting away with' avoiding their responsibilities. The case of the *Herald of Free Enterprise* in 1987 was a particularly stark example of this, with poor safety practices, inadequate seamanship and malfunctioning equipment all contributing to the ship sinking with the loss of 193 lives – yet no one suffering any criminal penalties. A condemnatory report by a public Court of Inquiry concluded that there was 'negligence at every level of the company's hierarchy and that 'a disease of sloppiness pervaded the organisation'.[6] Nor were the circumstances which brought about the sinking of the Herald unique, in that it was not the first instance of sloppy practices at Townsend Thoresen – the company which owned three ships of the same design

---

[5] A. Reisberg, 'Corporate law in the UK after recent reforms', *Current Legal Problems*, 63 (2010), 315–74.

[6] DoT, *Report of Court of Enquiry 8074 under the Merchant Shipping Act 1894; mv Herald of Free Enterprise* (Norwich: HMSO, 1987).

on the same (Dover-Zeebrugge) route. Similar events which had happened in some of their sailings had not brought similar results only by good fortune.[7]

Yet the operation of the law as it stood was such as to prevent more than minor reprimands being imposed on directors, sailors and managers. Judges were very reluctant to assign blame, finding it impossible to allocate certain responsibility to the standard required for a conviction and reluctant to pursue some of those accused while letting others go. Public opinion was inflamed and subsequent disasters (King's Cross, also 1987; the *Marchioness* in 1989; Paddington in 1999; Hatfield in 2000) did nothing to improve the situation.

There was a perception that the legal machinery was unable to bring about any form of action – not retributive, since it had manifestly failed to bring about either deterrence (because penalties were toothless) or even an educative effect (because profit was more important). In the case of the Hatfield disaster, the immediate response of the company was to effectively paralyse the rail network for weeks until the entire rail system could be checked: trains were forbidden to operate at normal speed because of the risk of similar accidents occurring brought about by (undiscovered) instances of poor maintenance. The financial consequences of this were that the company had to ask the Government for a loan to keep operating – which it then ineptly paid immediately to shareholders to try to preserve its credit lines.[8] To the public's sense of injury and injustice was added gross inconvenience and a feeling of having been duped – an unstoppable compound force.

It was out of this stew of events that the Corporate Manslaughter and Corporate Homicide Act 2007 (CMCHA) was born (the addition of the 'corporate homicide' clause to the long title is because Scots law does not recognise an offence of manslaughter). Prior to the introduction of the Act, while it was possible for a company to be prosecuted for the common law offence of gross negligence manslaughter, in order for the company to be found guilty it was necessary for a senior individual who could be said to embody the company (also known as a 'controlling mind') to be found guilty of the same offence. The law required this because of the operation of the legal entity principle which held that while the company was an independent legal entity it could not commit acts of its own volition but had to have human intervention to perform them. It had no independent mind and therefore 'the identification principle' had to operate where one person's actions and those of the company were identical. This bedevilled the achievement of convictions in most cases – not least because of the problem of identifying who was being punished.

The intention of the new offence created by the Act – corporate manslaughter – was to provide a means of enforcing accountability for very serious management failings across the organisation by not falling into the problem of having to identify which

---

[7] Evidence to Lord Justice Sheen, as above.

[8] G. Trefgarne, 'Railtrack told to freeze final dividend', *Daily Telegraph*, 21 May 2001.

individual in the organisation was specifically to blame. To assist overcoming the problems at common law of 'identification', the new law allowed the prosecution to aggregate the failings of a number of individuals in the same organisation to prove the existence of an endemic culture of sloppiness such as that complained of by the *Herald of Free Enterprise* court of inquiry.

The offence of manslaughter under the CMCHA 2007

An organisation is guilty of an offence if the way in which its activities are managed or organised:
– causes a person's death; and
– amounts to a gross breach of a relevant duty of care owed by the organisation to the deceased.
An organisation is guilty of an offence … only if the way in which its activities are managed or organised by its senior management is a substantial element in the breach referred to in subsection (1).

This offence is indictable only (in other words it must be tried in a Crown Court) and on conviction the judge may impose an unlimited fine.

Governance effect

In governance terms, the effects of the legislation are threefold. The first effect is to remove another of the planks to the legal construct that the company lives its legal life only through the directors and shareholders; and that the directors are the agents of the shareholders. By virtue of the impact of the Act it is the company which owes the duty of care and it is not a necessary consequence that directors, because of their role, owe a similar duty to others who may be also affected by the actions or omissions of the company. In legal terms, this simplifies the issue of assigning responsibility. Second, as a consequence of the issue of responsibility, the company's wider obligations to a whole constituency of stakeholders (rather than the narrow duties to shareholders) are much more obvious. Finally, the Act's emphasis on unlimited consequences in the event of guilt being proved should reinforce the behavioural obligations of the directors in terms of governance: the removal of the barrier to pursuing the company for actions undertaken in its name emphasises that governance is involved with risk management.

However, the disadvantage of this is that it may punish the shareholders of the company who are innocent of and distanced from the events which brought the prosecution. In one case involving the death of a worker after a trench collapsed on him, the judge specifically said that it was likely that the punitive fines placed on the

Table 5.1 Fatal injuries in the Waste Disposal industry in the UK 2009/10–2010/11					
	2009/2010		2010/2011p		
	Incidence	Rate per 100,000	Incidence	Rate per 100,000	All industry rate per 100,000	Comparison between W&R and all industry rates
Fatal injuries	3	2.3	10	8.4	0.5	× 16.8
Major injuries	511	390	483	405	99	× 4.1
Over 3-day injuries	2089	1595	1954	1637	363	× 4.5
All injuries	2603	1988	2447	2050	462	× 4.4

Source: HSE website, www.hse.gov.uk/waste/statistics.htm

company would bring about its extinction as a business.[9] The balance of the governance effects in favour of imposing obligations on directors then, will only be restored if shareholders decide to punish directors who have brought the company to this position by removing them from office or failing to re-elect them – and then the action must occur before the likelihood of any event that might result in the company being extinguished by fines. Active shareholders, in combination with the law's prospective effects, then might bring about a cultural change.

To date (December 2011) successful prosecutions under the Act have been directed at prosecuting small companies for deaths of their employees. While there are a number of possible reasons for this, two in particular stand out: first, the line of control is more easily traceable in smaller companies, making prosecution easier; and second, many large companies are organised operationally into groups with smaller operating subsidiaries. The record of the *group* may therefore be poor – the waste disposal business has seen several fatalities for instance across the UK over the past few years (see Table 5.1) – but the offences may have been committed by individual subsidiaries, which happen to be members of a larger group, and so considerations of aggregated liability cannot be brought into play.

The Bribery Act 2010

As with the point mentioned above in connection with the CMCHA 2007 the punishment available to the courts for offences caught by the Bribery Act 2010 are such as to potentially extinguish a transgressing company. This once more then underlines the need for shareholders to take their obligations seriously in electing and re-electing directors who are competent and for directors to take their obligations seriously in respect of protecting the assets of the company for the benefit of all stakeholders.

---

[9] CPS Press Release, 15 February 2011 and Lord Judge's comments on appeal.

The Bribery Act 2010 signalled a new departure in UK law in two respects: it created a new corporate offence and it introduced the concept of extra-territoriality in terms of UK regulation (while States have often enacted laws which purport to impact upon economic actors outside their boundaries this has often been strongly resisted by other States leading to a body of study concerned with the so-called 'conflict of laws').

The Act arose out of the obligations assumed by the UK's subscription to the OECD Convention on anti-corruption of 1997 (officially titled Convention on Combating Bribery of Foreign Public Officials in International Business Transactions). After a slow start – and formal international exhortations to speed up legislative progress after visits from OECD inspectors – the law was enacted as the last legislative action of the outgoing Labour Government. It supersedes a number of previous pieces of legislation dating from the late nineteenth century and early twentieth century and brings UK legislation fully into line with EU directives concerning disbarment from public contracts for companies found to be guilty of corrupt behaviour. The Act creates two new offences, using principles borrowed from the Convention: it makes it illegal to bribe 'foreign public officials' and it creates a corporate offence of 'failure to prevent'.

Definition of a bribe under the Bribery Act 2010

The Act replaces the common law offence under Acts of 1889, 1906 and 1916 with 2 offences:

a. Offering, promising or giving an advantage to another person intending to induce another person to do something improper or to reward someone for behaving improperly; or knowing or believing that the acceptance of the advantage would itself constitute the improper performance of a relevant function or activity

b. requesting, agreeing to receive or accepting an advantage, intending that a relevant function should be performed improperly or in anticipation or as a reward for the improper performance; or where the request, agreement, or acceptance is itself improper.

Foreign public officials

A Foreign Public Official is a legislative, administrative or judicial position of any kind outside the UK; anyone exercising a public function of a non-UK country (or part of); a public agency or enterprise or an official or agent of an international organisation ... not permitted or required by written law to be influenced by the offer promise or gift.

The corporate offence: 'failure to prevent'

The creation of the new offence effectively renders the parent liable for any bribery-related activity committed by anyone – legal or human – connected with the company and influential in determining the gaining of business. Its scope is very wide-ranging:

- it applies to any business which carries on business (esentially an undefined term although the Department of Justice has offered guidance on its website) in the UK;
- it applies to any agent who performs services for or on behalf of the principal (even if the principal has no direct knowledge of the agent's actions);
- a 'reasonable belief' that the payment is lawful or even supporting legal advice are not defences;
- it expressly precludes 'local custom' as being a defence against prosecution; and
- it extends to UK nationals working for foreign organisations.

In addition, it provides no specific requirement that the bribe relates to that part of the business resident in the UK – so any company with any activity located in the UK may be pursued by UK authorities for suspected bribery that occurs within any part of its operations worldwide. This is obviously a potentially huge regulatory burden in terms of resources.

For those companies which are accused of an offence under the Act – which also criminalises so-called 'facilitation payments' and may even extend to ransoms – there are only two defences. The first option is to challenge the factual accuracy of the case and the second is to prove the existence of an 'adequate procedures regime' which states clearly that the organisation refuses to countenance bribery as a method of transacting business (see text box).

Principles of operation – the Bribery Act 2010 'adequate procedures' regime

- Top down operation – a formal statement of policy approved, reviewed and monitored by the board of the organisation
- appropriate safeguards in place at all levels – for instance no one person signs off company payments
- evidence of 'zero tolerance' of bribery
- evidence of due diligence procedures before specific transactions
- evidence of clear policies and procedures
- regular board review
- appropriate decision points involving the acceptance of tenders and bids and payments at all levels of the organisation

- a public statement of company policy prominently displayed and communicated
- a dynamic policy of enforcement which is prioritised; fact-based and actively pursued.

This regime has to be supported by specific policies:

- appropriate training
- encouragement of self-reporting by staff including a whistle-blowing procedure
- appropriate guidance for staff on the organisation's policy and its implementation.

In the event that a prosecution succeeds, the penalties are very significant and apply to both individuals and to organisations. Individuals may be imprisoned for up to ten years; companies may be subject to an unlimited fine which, like the penalties for corporate manslaughter, may be sufficient to extinguish the company (although informally the penalties tariff has been suggested at 10 per cent of turnover). In either case the traceable proceeds of the act of bribery may be subject to confiscation under the Proceeds of Crime Act 2002. Most significantly for many companies, a conviction under the Act will result in mandatory exclusion from public contracts. Organisations which report themselves as having infringed the act will be subject to lesser – civil – penalties which will not result in exclusion.

The governance consequences of the act are very significant. Like the CMCHA 2007 it emphasises the role of the company as a separate body which has its own responsibilities – and is not merely a collection of legal rights but an entity which has to be held accountable for its actions. Thus it consolidates further the view that the company is not merely the vehicle for shareholders to combine in a state of limited liability with their interests projected by the agency of the directors; it supports the stakeholder concept with a view of shared obligations and duties and erodes further the concept of the company as an entity operating in a world of atomised relationships.

Importantly it gives teeth to an aspiration that other pieces of legislation have not yet been able to consummate: it will require a culture change in the attitudes of organisations to bring continual monitoring of their activities to the fore. Failure to do this actively, in a fashion based on fact and with appropriate gateways to be passed through before actions can be approved, will result in penalties that may extinguish the organisation. The cultural change that will be required therefore is very significant as a contribution to making all organisations – not just companies – think more seriously of governance as a means of controlling risk and not in a detached fashion isolated from external issues but within an ethical framework. As such, the Act will contribute to the strengthening of the structural dimension of governance, the glue that holds the organisation's other dimensions of governance together (which is considered more extensively in the chapters on counter-governance).

There is a dark side to this, too, in much the same way that the CMCHA 2007 has a dark side which operates to counter the beneficial governance effects in the area of corporate manslaughter. The successful prosecution of financially-based criminal cases is a trade-off between their complexity and the amount of resources that can be devoted to them. The authorities are often anxious to limit the amount of money spent on building cases in the knowledge that juries may be unable to absorb the complexity of the case and therefore acquit the accused.

It has been the practice of US prosecutors for many years to enter into 'deferred prosecutions' where companies are effectively able to place themselves 'on probation' after payment of large fines.[10] The fines are supposed to guarantee the company's good behaviour against similar infractions since they remain at risk for full prosecution for a determined period. But the payments of such fines also enable the companies – and their directors – to avoid criminal sanctions. The cost of the behaviour which prompted the prosecution is therefore passed on to the shareholders – which simply negates the intended effect of the law in attempting to bring about a cultural change. It allows companies to buy themselves resolution to a criminal prosecution in a way which is open to no other legal person – i.e. humans accused of crimes – and merely contributes to the coffers of the State without, again, prompting cultural change.

An examination of the record of the major financial institutions in the USA in paying such fines supports the contention that no fundamental cultural change takes place in the attitude of companies to the risk of prosecution when measured against the reward of profit.[11] At the time of writing, American financial institutions had made over $1 billion in such payments collectively – to bring about cessation of investigations for fraud – yet no criminal blame had been attached to their actions nor had any senior manager or director been prosecuted or been sent to jail. In Germany, however, where the concept of deferred prosecution is unknown and plea bargaining is not permitted, there has been a criminal conviction of a banker resulting from his directorial actions prior to the collapse of the bank of which he was chief executive.[12]

In addition, if the alleged offences took place across international boundaries, avenues to prosecution in one jurisdiction may be shut off if legal treaties exist between countries where the offences are supposed to have taken place, to avoid the consequences of the accused being subject to double jeopardy.

---

[10] As an example American Express entered such an agreement in August 2007 – prior to the financial crisis – and paid a sum of $55 million in respect of bank secrecy infringements.

[11] P. Spivack and S. Raman, 'Regulating the "new regulators": current trends in deferred prosecution agreements', *American Criminal Law Review*, 45 (2008).

[12] J. Wilson, 'Ex-IKB chief guilty of market manipulation', *Financial Times*, 14 July 2010.

A consequence of this – and the issue of limited prosecutorial resources – has been the development of 'plea bargaining' and charge reduction where the prosecutors swap the uncertainty of a criminal prosecution for a more serious charge in return for the company accepting guilt for a lower level of offence. The notorious Tanzanian bribery case involving BAE Systems cost the company a £30 million fine for corruptly obtaining a major air traffic control system contract (which was also vastly above Tanzania's requirements). The company pleaded guilty to a lesser offence in the UK, of not maintaining proper books of account – which is not an offence which would exclude it from public contracts under European Community law.

Summary and conclusion

The admittedly selective review above of recent legislation suggests that English law is developing a view of the company that, *in governance terms*, is very different from that of regulators and the authors of the documents which have coalesced to form the UK Corporate Governance Code.

The three pieces of legislation selected – all enacted within the past decade and all the result of pressure for change after periods of extended review – have produced an image of the company, *for the purposes of governance*, which therefore runs at odds with the direction of traditional regulatory activity.

The image produced by the legislation shows the company – listed or unlisted – to be not merely the creature of the shareholders but with a series of obligations of its own separate from the contractual obligations which it undertakes and which have previously defined it, as far as theorists of governance are concerned.

Under the terms of the new legislation, the law recognises and defines that directors are responsible to a much wider constituency of stakeholders than the shareholders alone; that they have an obligation to the continuing well-being of the company which goes beyond the traditionalist view of governance that they are simply the agents of the shareholders. These are all reinforcements of the dimensions of behavioural and structural governance. A further consequence of the statutes is that the company must behave in a way levelled by the claims of some commentators: that it is effectively no more than a licensed psychopath.

In its most extreme form this last view suggests that because of the lack of self-constraint that it has been legally endowed with, company directors have been able to use the company for activities that would result in the company's imprisonment if it were a human being. By virtue of climbing into the protective suit offered by the company's privileged legal status, the argument runs, directors can enrich themselves and the company's shareholders at the expense of the rest of society with substantial legal impunity.

The three pieces of legislation reviewed above contain the mechanisms to prevent that happening if they are enforced. However there are flaws. As legal commentators have pointed out in respect of the Companies Act 2006, the Corporate Manslaughter and Corporate Homicide Act 2007 and the Bribery Act 2010,[13] the laws are far from being perfect in terms of their impact scope or even the powers of enforcement they contain. Nor are they perfect in conceptualisation and they have yet to fully demonstrate their ability to bring about the results that they were intended to secure.

The derivative actions provisions of the Companies Act 2006 were bewailed by critics who foresaw a wave of activist shareholders making life hell for the inhabitants of boardrooms. They have not been used to effect as yet. The Companies Act 2006 is regarded by many as being unfit for purpose in so many respects because it has not solved the problems it set out to remedy and has even made some of them worse. And it also failed its first major test of efficacy by providing no platform for holding to account the directors of failed financial institutions after the collapse of 2007. By contrast, German prosecutors were able to use their laws to convict the chief executive of one failed bank (Stefan Ortseifen of IKB) and hold him to account for misleading investors.

Previous firm proponents of the Corporate Manslaughter and Corporate Homicide Act 2007 changed horses in mid-stream. Jack Straw, a lawyer himself, completely reversed his position from when he was in opposition and as a Government Minister strongly contested the sense of introducing the legislation. Prosecutions taken under the Act have been limited to pursuit of small companies or companies have been pursued with charges for lesser offences brought under pre-existing health and safety legislation.

The Bribery Bill was hotly contested as it went through its final stages with critics complaining that it would catch the most trivial of offences while doing little to resolve the problem of proving to a jury that an offence had been committed.[14] Its first successful prosecution was for a minor public official convicted of accepting money to pervert the course of justice[15] – an offence which would have been picked up by the legislation that the Act superseded. (Though the Japanese Olympus Scandal of 2011 – see Chapters 15 and 16 – might never have been as thoroughly aired as it was without the Bribery Act 2010 being in place, since the British managing director was covered by the provisions of the Act.)

So all three laws which have been reviewed are flawed and have serious implementational problems. But they still move the argument – *in governance terms* – on from

---

[13] J. Gobert, 'The Corporate Manslaughter and Corporate Homicide Act 2007 – thirteen years in the making but was it worth the wait?', *Modern Law Review*, May 2008.

[14] J. Croft, 'Clerk first to be prosecuted under Bribery Act', *Financial Times*, 31 August 2011.

[15] J. Kirkup, 'Bribery Act to be reviewed after business fears', *Daily Telegraph*, 14 January 2011.

the stance which the traditional theories have adopted by opening a gap in the supposedly close link between shareholders and the company.

What it now requires if the change is to be exploited to the purpose of better governance is cultural changes to follow in the wake of these laws. This will mean that there will have to be changes to other regulations for shareholders to be given *effective* powers to hold directors more strictly to account (changes to derivative action gateways for instance and to votes on remuneration reports) and equally importantly to use those powers.

PART 3

GOVERNANCE AND THE LISTED COMPANY

CHAPTER 6

The development of governance – the Governance Codes

This chapter:

- reviews the origins, history and development of the UK Corporate Governance Code;
- looks at the corporate governance processes in listed companies;
- considers one of the key mechanisms of governance – the operation of committees of the board in listed companies;
- evaluates the operation of the code, processes and committees in terms of traditionalist theories of governance and real world operations.

Introduction

The first two sections of this book dealt with the traditionalist/legalist approaches to corporate governance; offered some challenges to those interpretations by using illustrations from the real world and by examining the real role of the principal actors in the governance process. The way that the law interacts with governance has also been reviewed, in both general and specific terms, to illustrate ways in which protections to stakeholders and approaches to corporate governance have been based on specific theoretical premises, some of which do accord with real life and some of which do not.

This section of the book now deals with the corporate governance of listed companies – both internally, through the application of the protections that are supposed to be afforded stakeholders by the operation of the governance codes, and through the impact of listing itself.

Listed company governance is subject to the full weight of the UK Corporate Governance Code.[1] This occurs through the contractual obligations which companies assume when they agree to the continuing obligations regime of the listing agreement. The State imposes additional obligations through the regulatory structure and through the operation of primary and secondary legislation. As such, listed company corporate

---

[1] The UK Corporate Governance Code is the consolidated series of recommendations from the various reports that was known as the Combined Code until 2010.

governance might be regarded as the pinnacle of corporate governance – where the State (in its broadest sense) has recognised the significance and value of effective corporate governance in companies that are publicly traded and has put in place steps – formal or informal, through agents or directly – to bring about its implementation.

It might also be said that rather than demand that certain mechanisms be implemented legally, the State has attempted to identify those structures and behaviours which bring about 'good' corporate governance (as distinct from effective corporate governance) and encourage their adoption through exhortation and (non-statutory) enforcement. This is a result of the chosen mechanisms for UK corporate governance being principle-based and not rule-based. The measures which are identified and propounded in this way are therefore attempts at behavioural modification – influencing behavioural governance – as distinct from the mandatory obligations of procedural governance.

Ideal listed company governance structure in the UK

A listed company in the UK must conform to a certain governance structure in order to comply with the UK Corporate Governance Code. The ideal listed[2] (main market) company would look broadly like this:

- A board of directors (the size of the board is discretionary) with a preponderance of non-executive directors, none of whom has a contract in excess of twelve months and all of whom are subject to retirement (and re-election if appropriate) by rotation on a three year cycle.
- A separate chairman and chief executive.
- At least four committees of the board – nomination; remuneration; audit; risk – the remuneration committee being composed entirely of non-executives, the remainder with a majority of non-executive directors; (some companies might choose not to appoint a risk committee and incorporate it into the audit committee but an ideal company would have one).
- Each committee to have separate written terms of reference and a budget allowing access to external advisers if required.
- A qualified company secretary – ideally a chartered secretary but possibly a lawyer or an accountant; (note that there is no obligation to have a finance director, or any other specified directorial post for that matter, nor is there any stipulation about what the professional qualifications of the finance director should be, if one is appointed).

---

[2] This ideal model includes all the recommended, but not obligatory, provisions of the UKCGC and the Stock Exchange Listing Rules.

- Regular board meetings.
- A written, published schedule of matters which the board alone is competent to deal with.
- Committee meetings of the nominations committee as required; the others to meet 'regularly'.
- A senior non-executive director who takes principal responsibility for liaison with institutional investors.
- A formal induction and annual evaluation process for all directors.
- Unqualified accounts[3] filed for at least three years prior to coming to the market.
- Revenue earning at the time of listing.
- A continuity of senior personnel between the time when it was private and the time of listing.
- Independence of any controlling shareholder.
- Free transferability of fully-paid shares in the company (except in respect of any suspected illegality).
- The first issue of shares on to the market will have been at least £700,000 in value.
- A minimum of 25 per cent of the company's shares will have been in public hands on completion of listing (but this is a condition that may be relaxed by the Listing Authority and when it has there have been adverse results – see Chapter 9).
- The company will abide by the Continuing Obligations regime of the London Stock Exchange which provides for information to be released immediately in respect of:
  1. Any information which could lead to substantial movement in price (the catch-all clause).
  2. Alterations to capital.
  3. Changes in class rights.
  4. Redemption of securities.
  5. Information relating to major interests.
  6. Board decisions on dividends.
  7. All notices and circulars other than those of a routine nature.
  8. Any change in directors.
  9. Issue of half-yearly and annual results and accounts.
  10. Details of significant contracts.
  11. Preliminary profits statements.

---

[3] Unqualified accounts are those which have not been subject to some audit qualification regarding their completeness, accuracy or value and do not indicate some frailty as to the company's trading position.

Furthermore the company must:

1. provide that an open offer for shares must not allow directors to purchase the shares;
2. ensure that directors do not trade shares during a closed period;
3. maintain a register of Persons Exercising Significant Influence which is lodged with the FSA, and up-dated as required;
4. issue annual accounts within six months of a year end;
5. publish half-yearly accounts within 90 days with policies consistent with those at the last year end;
6. hold any meeting at which non-routine business is to be transacted only after an explanatory circular has been issued;
7. ensure the directors issue a recommendation, at any meeting where shareholders are entitled to vote, on which policies are in their view in the best interests of the company as a whole;
8. issue two-way proxies for all votes of shareholders.

This very extensive list of characteristics is a mix of legal controls and behavioural obligations which come from the Companies Act 2006 and, more particularly, from the series of corporate governance reports stemming from the Cadbury Report in 1992 and which are now collected under the UK Corporate Governance Code.

The mixed (procedural/legally required and behavioural/quasi-voluntary) list might be thought sufficiently detailed to ensure that companies behave themselves. Yet corporate governance failures still occur in the UK – and, as the introduction to this book suggested, seem to be happening with greater frequency and greater impact.

This chapter will argue that one of the reasons that this occurs is because the history of developments in corporate governance over the past twenty years can be interpreted as an attempt to get back to a pre-lapsarian state, a time before managerial behaviour began to go sour and require greater supervision (to impute an opinion to the policy-makers behind the Code). While the traditionalist view would hold that the elements of the Code are consistent with shareholder primacy and use that to promote the interests of shareholders, a more radical view would be that in historical terms the conditions policy-makers were (and are) probably thinking of have not existed since, at least, the early 1970s. As with all attempts to revert to an ideal state, the conditions that controlled and influenced the pre-1970s economy no longer exist (or we wouldn't be trying to revert).

Attempts to alter corporate governance behaviour by appealing to some imaginary conditions which no longer exist and which are no longer appropriate are bound to fail. This chapter will look at the economic and commercial conditions which prompted reviews (and minor reforms) and then consider the reports that were produced both in the light of their effectiveness and in relationship to traditionalist corporate governance theories and to the conditions of the real world.

The development of the Corporate Governance Codes in the UK

The historical and economic background

The de-nationalisations, or privatisations, undertaken by the Thatcher Government in the 1980s – British Gas, British Telecom, the electricity industry, the water industry, British Airways and others – mark a watershed in British industrial history. Born of an ideological intention to restructure the social and economic landscape, whatever the economic and social benefits they brought, the denationalisations also produced or contributed to a number of issues – perceived excessive remuneration for directors; outright fraud perpetrated on shareholders and stakeholders; variable standards of transparency and truthfulness on the part of directors – which roused both popular and political disquiet.

Out of this came calls for changes in behaviour which prompted four major reviews, in one decade, of the way that listed companies were governed and for whose benefit they were operated: these were the Cadbury Committee Report (1992), the Greenbury Committee Report (1995), the Hampel Committee Report (1998) and the Turnbull Report (1999). Those four reports and the two major reports that occurred just into the new century – the Myners Committee Report of 2001 and the Higgs Committee Report of 2003 (which was the lead report in a trio, the other two of which – the Smith Report and the Tyson Report – are mostly forgotten except for technical changes to audit committee operation) – were all responses to developments that had started in the 1970s and 1980s and which were considered sufficiently important to warrant the time, expense and visibility of non-State bodies expending money on quasi-public investigation. In order to understand how those trends originated and how they developed it is necessary to review briefly the economic background to those decades.

The governance effects of the structure of the British economy

The seminal work on analysing the British economy was completed by Andrew Shonfield in 1965 in his book *Modern Capitalism: the changing balance of public and private power*.[4] In the book Shonfield described the British economy as being rooted in pre-war industrial practices and attempted to identify agents of change in order to bring about improvements in economic performance (similar later analyses which echoed the findings were produced by Anthony Sampson[5] and

---

[4] A. Shonfield, *Modern Capitalism: the changing balance of public and private power* (RIIA/Oxford University Press, 1965).

[5] A. Sampson, *Who Runs This Place?: The Anatomy of Britain in the 21st Century* (London: John Murray, 2005).

later by Robert Peston[6]). Shonfield had been a senior journalist at the *Observer* and the *Financial Times* and was employed at the Royal Institute of International Affairs when he wrote his book. His conclusion was that bankers and policy planners were among the best placed to effect change through their impact (then) on the industrial structure. Along with the ideas of rising politicians like Anthony Crosland (see *The Future of Socialism*[7]), Shonfield's ideas began to be taken up in the policies of the Labour party.

At the end of the Second World War, Britain was essentially a command economy. Large sections of the economy had been nationalised during wartime or just prior to it, during the great depression of the 1930s. Industrial capacity had been harnessed to the demands of wartime production of armaments and the prosecution of the war, resulting in State domination of major sectors of the economy: coal; steel; shipbuilding; utilities and transport. Furthermore, those sectors of the economy that were not owned by the State were often either dependent on it for maintaining their order-books or for sponsoring innovation – the aviation industry for instance – or affected by residual controls or spending restrictions: textiles,[8] food[9] and pharmaceuticals.[10] Industrial production during wartime had been increased by stupendous efforts using capital equipment that had not been replaced or even redesigned for perhaps three or four decades because of war or the industrial depression that had blighted those years. In sum, the British industrial structure was tired, worn-out, starved of resources for growth and heavily dependent upon government economic policy for future development.[11]

The shape and nature of the British economy were changing with the release of pressures brought about by peace. Prior to the Second World War, the economy had resembled what economists describe as a liberal market economy (LME[12]) based on the supremacy of private contracts; typified by high levels of shareholder involvement in governance and the potential use (or threat) of litigation as a means of enforcement of shareholder wishes.

---

[6] R. Peston, *Who Runs Britain?: and Who's to Blame for the Economic Mess We're in?* (London: Hodder, 2008).

[7] A. Crosland, *The Future of Socialism* (London: Robinson, 2006).

[8] See G. Owen, *The Rise and Fall of Great Companies: Courtaulds and the Reshaping of the Man-Made Fibres Industry* (Oxford University Press/Pasold, 2010).

[9] I. Zweiniger-Bargielowska, *Austerity in Britain: Rationing, Controls, and Consumption, 1939–1955* (Oxford University Press, 2002).

[10] E. Jones, *The Business of Medicine: A History of Glaxo* (London: Profile Books, 2001).

[11] S. Broadberry and N. Crafts, 'British economic policy and industrial performance in the early post-War period', *Business History*, 38(4) (1996).

[12] P. Hall and D. Soskice, *Varieties of Capitalism* (Oxford University Press, 2001).

During the Second World War it had effectively become a co-ordinated market economy (CME[13]) based on the presumption that the State is a major stakeholder and plays a significant part in allocating resources.

CMEs and LMEs: dense and diffuse economic network arrangements

One way that markets are classified by economists – in addition to the CME and LME distinction – is to divide them into 'dense' and 'diffuse' networks.

Dense networks

- Typified by insider type governance systems – the so-called Rhenish type prevalent in Europe or the Asian family-type.
- Companies often have two tier boards with supervisory arrangements.
- European companies often have 'hausbank' arrangements; banks as investors *and* financiers, privy to policy and confidential information not available to other investors.
- Shareholders and stakeholders both contribute to policy.
- Different worker-manager relationships from diffuse type of network consequentially (see below).
- Employees often act in semi-autonomous fashion in interpreting company policy – since the workers are often highly educated and socialised in the company's culture.
- Such industrial arrangements may require officially-organised training mediators to prevent poaching of talented staff between companies; Britain had these briefly in the Industrial Training Councils.
- These characteristics affect the operation and context of both employment and contract law.
- The overall effect is to have companies look to medium to long-term – less affected by short-term profitability considerations.

Diffuse networks

- Companies have sharply distinguished stakeholder and shareholder sets.
- Single board structures are more common.
- Managerial power, strategic policy and operational decision-making are all concentrated in one board.

---

[13] *Ibid.*

- No unique funding arrangements in respect of dedicated banking or special banking relationships.
- Highly regulated release of information to market to ensure 'fairness'.
- Firms look to arms-length market mechanisms to resolve market co-ordination and procedural problems between collaborators in projects.
- Consequential impact on the context of contract law and employment law.
- Investment decisions by outsiders are determined by reference to earnings (or profitability).
- Remuneration arrangements are often typified by managerial incentivisation in the form of options.
- Regulatory regimes are tolerant of hostile takeovers as a market mechanism.
- Consequently companies become highly defensive of earnings and short-termist in outlook.
- Employees exhibit little employer-loyalty and regard their individual careers as the focus of their ambition rather than their advancement with one employer.
- Lower overall levels of employee education are likely since power is concentrated and company-specific skills are not cultivated. Much work is de-skilled to enable companies to take advantage of larger labour pools.

CME and LME characteristics compared

These characteristics then give rise to a number of additional characteristics:
- LMEs better suited to fast-moving and changing consumer goods and service businesses.
- CMEs better suited to incremental change in 'heavy' goods.
- Unions more powerful in CME – less overtly so however in recent years.
- LME companies are highly dependent on macro policy and market mechanisms to control wages and inflation.
- LMEs encourage individuals to invest in general skills.
- CMEs encourage companies to invest in workforce development.
- LME labour markets are usually held to be fluid.
- Education standards stress 'certification' for general applicability.
- This tends to emphasise service industry structures which are not application specific.
- Inter-company relationships in LMEs are based on formal contract.
- This further reinforces short-termism as an attitude.

- So such knowledge transfer as does take place is outside inter-company relationships – academic research; employee defection (often with obstruction) or franchising/licensing – especially in bio-tech and electronics sectors.
- Market standards are then set not by rational allocation but by market superiority or domination – as an example when video recording systems first arose Betamax was a superior recording system to VHS but VHS won because of faster entry to the market and more company support.
- LMEs concentrate power in top management who are able to control resource allocation.
- In CMEs, companies' access to finance and technological collaboration is seen through the filter of their reputation – which is not entirely dependent on top management.
- The European-type CME and the Asian-type CME are dissimilar.
- European structures are usually dependent on sectoral or industrial types of collaboration; Asian types are more dependent on family arrangements.
- Asian types: employees skills are both firm and family specific – even more socialisation of employees – requiring even greater levels of investment by both individual and company.
- Can lead to very nimble corporate strategy as all the resources for change are immediately available with no worker feeling threatened.
- In Europe – especially France – many managers are the product of elite State administrative schools – leading to a potentially greater loyalty to the State than to the company.

The type of businesses which tend to prosper in these conditions can be divided into 'radical' and 'incremental' changers.

Radical:
1. biotech
2. electronics
3. telecoms
4. airlines
5. advertising
6. sophisticated financial services
7. entertainment.

Incremental:
1. consumer durables
2. capital goods
3. specialised transport
4. intermediate industrial goods.

Radical innovation tends to produce:

- top-driven management and governance structures;
- fluid personnel policies;
- minimal specific skills in the workforce.

To summarise:

CMEs often have:

- Product differentiation rather than intense competition (supported by evidence from Patent Office applications across different economies).
- Varying effectiveness of industrial control – often dependent on geographic dispersion (for instance in France where Paris dominates and its initiatives are often viewed with hostility and suspicion regionally).
- Political power structures which strongly influence the economic structure.

LMEs often have:

- Fluid job markets.
- Dispersed equity markets.
- Weak but proliferative trade or employment associations – for instance 'The Institute of Image Consulting'.
- Government unable to influence detailed industrial policy.
- Strongly developed venture capital functions.

Thus at the end of the 1980s, the British economy, with its framework of State controls being dismantled or close to abolition, was in transition from a dense-network semi-CME into a structure more like a diffuse-network, semi-LME.

With the end of hostilities, there was no need for the structures of the command economy to be retained in the long term: the Labour Government elected in 1945 subscribed to a return to a position closer to that which had existed before the War rather than to entrenching State control.[14] Once economic growth had brought the UK once more within shouting distance of faster-growing European neighbours, by the end of the 1960s, changes in the economic structure moved faster still.[15]

A policy of neo-corporatism developed in the 1960s in the UK with government and industry becoming increasingly intertwined as the State released direct control but took it upon itself to organise industrial policy, promote innovation and resolve conflicts over wages by becoming involved in bargaining and industrial

---

[14] D. Kynaston, *Austerity Britain, 1945–1951* (London: Bloomsbury, 2008).
[15] J. Hennessey, *Economic Miracles* (London: IEA/Andre Deutsch, 1964).

disputes.[16] This manifested itself through state-sponsored agents of change such as industrial planning agreements; industrial/sectoral wages councils and training boards and industrial funding agencies such as the Industrial and Commercial Finance Corporation and Finance For Industry (which much later merged to become 3i[17]), the National Research and Development Corporation and the National Enterprise Board (later the British Technology Group). The Advisory Conciliation and Arbitration Service was created and a new industrial relations policy 'In Place of Strife' was proposed. These bodies and policies all had a profound, but at the time unrecognised, impact on the development of the context of corporate governance, preparing the way for industrial change and altering perceptions of the industrial future.

But the 1970s were marked by widespread unrest and turbulence in industry; in the early part of the decade, after a period of sustained stable economic activity, the prevailing economic concern was inflation and then 'stagflation' – a pernicious combination of slack growth and rising prices. The secondary banking crisis[18] that followed the 'Barber boom' revealed the absence of appropriate controls in board-rooms and the weakness of regulatory controls supporting policy.

With the arrival of the Thatcher Government in 1979, after a timid start, much of the public-industrial governance structure developed to that time was dismantled and industrial/commercial problems were once more left to the market to sort out.

'The Mayfair Set'

Staid relationships continued to dominate the City, which was regarded as a club and regulated itself like one,[19] an approach which will be reviewed again in considering the systemic dimension of corporate governance in Chapter 7. While takeovers using the mechanisms of the market were nothing new (the so-called Aluminium Wars of the late 1950s for instance), successive governments had shied away from the full consequences of imposing more distanced regulation.[20] The first overtly hostile UK takeover might be traced to 1972 when Beecham mounted a bid for Glaxo and Boots acted as 'white knight'. Until then takeovers had been more in the nature

---

[16] A. Campbell et al. (eds), *The Post-war Compromise: British Trade Unions and Industrial Politics 1945–64* (London: Merlin, 2007).

[17] R. Coopey and D. Clarke, *3i: Fifty Years Investing in Industry* (Oxford University Press, 1995).

[18] M. Reid, *The Secondary Banking Crisis, 1973–75: Its Causes and Course* (London: Palgrave Macmillan, 1982).

[19] M. Moran, *The British Regulatory State: High Modernism and Hyper-Innovation* (Oxford University Press, 2007); D. Kynaston, *The City of London* (London: Chatto, 2003), vol. IV.

[20] Moran, *The Regulatory State*.

of amalgamations, negotiated between managements behind closed doors without polling of any more than a very few 'influential' shareholders – still less any stakeholder consideration. With the deregulation of the UK Stock Market in 1986 ('Big Bang') the artificial distinction between stock market operators (brokers and jobbers) was removed and foreign banks were able to enter the City as both market-makers in shares and traders of shares. This then reinforced the trends towards active management of assets, which had begun in the 1970s with the arrival of a younger set of entrepreneurs who had seen what was happening in the USA and were prepared to emulate the techniques they had been watching. James Hanson and Gordon White, Jim Slater, Peter Walker, James Goldsmith and Roland 'Tiny' Rowland – the so-called 'Mayfair Set'[21] – were concerned with making money rather than making products, and their activities prompted changes in perceptions of what companies were in business for and re-defined what shareholders could expect from the companies in which they held shares.

These men – almost all accountants or with a financial rather than industrial background – were concerned with squeezing money out of the assets they had purchased rather than the long-term consequences for the companies that they took over. They perceived most of British industry to be inadequate in its management of physical assets, producing only modest returns which could be dwarfed by the returns made in selling those assets to someone else, perhaps for a more profitable use. The process of buying companies which underutilised their assets and selling them on to other operators who believed they could make the assets produce more was at the base of the reorganisation of the UK's industrial structure. Their apparent lack of concern for the workforce or customers or suppliers associated with those businesses led to the term 'asset-strippers' being applied to them collectively.[22] 'Asset stripping' produced quick returns if the targets were properly chosen, levering out self-contented managers and squeezing out costs (which usually meant labour costs) so that stripped-down businesses could be forced to make higher returns or be sold on to others who believed that they could do the same, bringing very quick returns to the managers of the takeover vehicles and their shareholders. (There is an irony in this: corporate governance changes made by the Cadbury Committee and subsequent reviews can be interpreted as attempts to reconcile managerial strategies of pursuing 'increasing shareholder value' which were prompted generally by the asset-strippers, with public expectations of fairness and equitable behaviour.)

The process represented the zenith of the conglomerate structure: the individual asset-strippers turned their individual acquisitions into diversified groups like Hanson

---

[21] A. Curtis, *The Mayfair Set*, BBC video, first broadcast 1999.
[22] C. Raw, *Slater Walker* (London: Andre Deutsch, 1977).

Trust, Cavenham, Lonrho or Slater Walker Group. They and the imitators that they spawned like Tomkins or even Polly Peck, became conglomerates as much as anything else for the structural purpose of pipelining the buying and then selling of assets, not for any sustained interest in industrial stewardship or cultivating the products that the assets could be used to produce. Since this process of buying, stripping out costs and then selling on was inherently unstable and limited, this was a transient phenomenon that would naturally expire once the rest of the management of public companies woke up to the need to think differently about the furtherance of the interest of their shareholders and use the assets they possessed more effectively.

Thus the conglomerates became conglomerates not because they wanted to *sustain* themselves in that form but rather because they were in the process of *disposing* of the conglomerate style and at the same time using that particular structure to do it. This obviously throws up particular difficulties for the conventional concept of shareholders as stewards (which was admittedly articulated more fully later) – since the issue of sustainability is reduced to one of 'creative destruction' in the Schumpeterian style.[23] Professional investors recognised this and saw the conglomerates as useful ways of boosting their own returns on a temporary basis, recognising that the timing of getting in and coming out would be crucial. Private investors just saw sky-rocketing share prices and piled in.

The shareholders of the asset-strippers were speculators (to use a term that now has a certain amount of opprobrium attached to it) rather than investors, who bought into the conglomerates not for any long-term concept of ownership but merely for the brief ride to higher profits, higher P/E valuations and capital growth. These are all of course entirely legitimate objectives, In fact, for certain investors – e.g. trustees of pensions funds – they are legally required objectives.

The large UK pension funds – as the dominant owners of shares in industry and acolytes of the cult of equity[24] – had originally collaborated with the new style of dispassionate industrial entrepreneurs, focused on profit alone, to shake up complacent companies. Now they were forced by the nature of their legal obligations to their beneficiaries to continue to support radical change which increased earnings (and hence share prices) and dividends. This meant abandoning holdings in slower-performing investments and concentrating on profit growth as much as dividend yield, precipitating a cultural change in both investment practices and in industrial behaviour. This trend raised the pressure on all boards of directors to produce

---

[23] J. Schumpeter, *Capitalism, Socialism and Democracy* (Basingstoke: Routledge 2010).
[24] The 'cult of equity' was the term given to the change prompted by George Ross Goobey, an eminent fund manager who persuaded Imperial Tobacco trustees to move out of bonds and into equities in the early 1950s. See Y. Avrahampour, 'George Ross Goobey and the cult of equity', *Professional Pensions* (2005).

increasing profits and maximise dividends progressively, utilising the same asset-squeezing tactics of the raiders, or risk being taken over. The pressures came about despite the logical conclusion that increases in profit and earnings growth and the dividends generated by short-term actions would be unsustainable in the long term, and the actions taken to bring about the financial improvements might be at the expense of the interests of other stakeholders.

The largest cost component of most businesses is the cost of labour and so much of the attention of the cost-cutters focused on reducing labour costs. The move towards reducing labour costs occurred at the same time – was inextricably linked to – the fact that by that time union membership in the UK had reached its peak and industrial relations were beginning to worsen, as the industrial compact of the post-war years dissolved.

As managements became alert to this change in environment they adopted a number of postures. Some of those who had been watching the growth of the personal wealth of the entrepreneurial asset-strippers wanted to emulate it for themselves;[25] some decided that they had to take more risks than they had been accustomed to doing, in order to maintain the impression of coherence with the financial markets' perceptions of the imperative about 'increasing shareholder value';[26] some decided that the time was right to take advantage of sentiment that rewarded the adventurous who could apparently produce 'increasing shareholder value' as if by magic without the hard work that normally has to go into it.

The results of the adoption of these attitudes were increases in the pay of directors who suddenly 'bench-marked' their own pay and abilities against the levels of inflated income achieved by a few (British Gas); increases in prices, which were used to generate inflated levels of turnover (many of the privatised utility companies) without any real external cause; manipulation to support share prices to enable takeovers to be effected (the Guinness Scandal[27] and Blue Arrow[28] affairs); and, occasionally, as in the cases of BCCI, Polly Peck[29] and the Mirror Group, outright fraud.

[25] There were distinct waves of conglomerate development, with several smaller companies like Tomkins and Williams Holdings following on behind the leaders.
[26] Popularised by Jack Welch, the CEO of the American company General Electric between 1981 and 2001.
[27] The Guinness scandal involved an attempt in 1986 to maintain the share price of Guinness to allow it to purchase Distillers plc. Several prominent businessmen including Ernest Saunders and Gerald Ronson were convicted and imprisoned.
[28] The Blue Arrow scandal involved an attempt to conceal a failed rights issue to enable the Blue Arrow employment agency to take over a much larger American competitor. The case against the stockbrokers involved eventually failed through misdirection by the judge among other factors.
[29] Polly Peck was a company under the control of Asil Nadir which grew very rapidly in the 1980s on the back of acquisitions which were largely phantom in their value.

Public disquiet and change

It was against this background and as a consequence of the last two cases, the most recent in a string of frauds that had occurred during the 1970s and 1980s,[30] that public disquiet came to the pitch where calls for review and (possible) overhauls of the ways that the system worked could no longer be overlooked. (This is in itself somewhat perverse since whereas the British Gas 'fat cats' furore and the Guinness and Blue Arrow share price manipulations had been attempts to manipulate the operation of the system, the last two cases were acts of outright criminality, the circumstances of which were not really related to the poor governance of companies at all.) As a response to the clamour the London Stock Exchange and the Institute of Chartered Accountants decided to establish a review committee to investigate existing corporate governance practices. It was from this series of events that the Cadbury Committee was set up and the discipline of corporate governance came to be – in the UK at least – with a rolling programme of reviews at intervals of roughly three years.

The Cadbury Committee Report (1992)

The Committee was set up on the presumption that what existed in corporate governance was operating effectively and that if any corrections were needed they were probably going to be minor. And although it had been constituted because of public pressure, support for the Committee among City institutions was far from being universal: at least one co-opted member had had initial doubts about its value which had only been 'partially modified' several months into the life of the Committee (Cadbury papers).[31] The terms of reference of the committee were therefore set quite tight both to ensure as much common ground as possible from existing City institution viewpoints and to avoid too much novelty creeping in to the investigation and the recommendations.

Not surprisingly, therefore, the report concentrated very much on 'what was' rather than 'what could be' in the light of the changes in the industrial/commercial landscape in recent years. The Committee produced a Code of Best Practice and a series of recommendations supporting it.

Even allowing for the familiarity brought by hindsight and twenty years of operation the conclusions and summary are hardly radical. They amount to the repetition of an existing catechism rather than a fresh look at what might be done – in other words entirely in keeping with the circumscribed remit afforded to the Committee. But shrouded in the undergrowth of 'what should be is what is'

[30] See the list in the Introduction.   [31] This was Mike Sandland, Cadbury Archives.

there were a few recommendations which offered some prospect of reform that would work in shareholders' favour:

- the distinction of the roles of chairman and chief executive;
- the audit committee suggestion; and
- the 'comply or explain' requirement that was recommended as mandatory for all listed companies.

The first two of these were obviously tactical responses to the scandals that had brought about the review. There was a threefold purpose to the specific recommendations: first, to avoid problems of domination of the board by one strong character – in the mould of a Robert Maxwell or an Asil Nadir at Polly Peck; second, to eliminate the problem of potential concealment of inappropriate activity (again as in the case of the Mirror Group and Robert Maxwell) by allowing two crucial governance roles to exist in one person which operated to frustrate organisational checks and balances; and, third, to enable succession planning to be carried out objectively.

But beyond this the Committee's Report was both looking in the wrong direction and blinkered: it looked back to a time when the British economy was more in the nature of a dense network/CME economy at exactly the moment when it was moving to a diffuse network/LME structure and, crucially, it ignored the increasing power of the stakeholder.

Cadbury's recommendations were adopted by the 'Yellow Book' of the Stock Exchange which required all companies seeking or maintaining a listing to comply with them. This then formed the basis for the UK's 'comply or explain' regime of governance, which once more looked backward to a set of economic conditions whose time was passing rather than to the future and the problems that might arise as the structure of the economy changed. Nowhere was this more significant than in the issue of what proportions of the increasing wealth generated by changing industrial structures should go to which parts of the economy. Who should take the first bite of the surplus: the directors, the shareholders or the workforce?

The Greenbury Committee Report (1995)

The 'Fat Cat' report was prompted largely by the activities of the directors of British Gas and their Managing Director, Cedric Brown.[32] Shareholders became incensed with the behaviour of the board of the newly-privatised company – who suddenly as in Brown's case, after forty-four years working for the same employer, became 'world-class' managers – who had awarded themselves higher and higher salaries. Some British Gas shareholders bought a pig, christened it Cedric and brought it along to

---

[32] 'Who pays for unions?', *The Economist*, 9 July 1998.

an AGM, where it snuffled in the gutter outside the meeting, to signify their views. The Greenbury Committee was set up by the CBI specifically in response to these concerns, as the preface to the Report makes plain.

Like the Cadbury Committee's terms, the remit for the Greenbury Committee had been predicated on a justification of the status quo. The terms of reference were commendably short – 'to identify best practice in determining directors' remuneration and prepare a code for such practice for use by UK PLCs'. There was no instruction to contemplate what might be – merely to filter existing practice to find the best currently available. The effect of these limited instructions was therefore to pickle existing 'best' practices and to justify them in the immediate context of what was happening then. There was no attempt to consider whether a better system or more sensible, safer or workable system might be considered or to see the existing practices worked in the interests of shareholders *and* stakeholders. Like the Cadbury Report it merely looked at the existing position and made no attempt to consider whether anything else might be appropriate. As with Cadbury the underlying presumption was that 'what should be is what is'.

£5 million pension for Cedric Brown

BRITISH GAS chief executive Cedric Brown could receive a pension worth a total of £5.5m after a secretive deal which will raise his annual entitlement to £316,000 on retirement. David Jefferies, chairman of the National Grid, could get a total of £2.9m.

Yesterday Shadow Chancellor Gordon Brown said he intended to raise the 'appalling' sums due to the privatised industry bosses with John Major when the Prime Minister returns from the Madrid summit.

Details of the multi-million pound deals were revealed by Mr Brown's Shadow Treasury team yesterday. The estimates were based on the calculating procedures of leading actuaries.

Labour claims that industry and government have been trying to wriggle out of the requirement that companies disclose the full cost of pensions, which was the most radical suggestion in this year's Greenbury report on executive pay, which was meant to dampen down the 'fat cat' scandal.

Huge pay rises for industrialists have led to correspondingly enormous increases in their pension entitlements. The extra benefit will be met from company pension funds, parts of which have been built up by the contributions of low-paid employees and workers sacked by utilities directors. Cedric Brown has presided over the loss of 30,000 jobs at British Gas. Last year he received a 75 per cent pay rise, which took his salary from £270,000 to £475,000.

Mr Brown, 60, is entitled to a pension of two-thirds of his final salary when he retires. The hike in his pay means that his annual pension will be £316,000 instead of £180,000. The estimated cost to the fund of his retirement, based on standard pension industry calculations and assumptions, has risen from about £3.5m to £5.5m, Labour says. The £2m increase is so large that it cannot be met by Mr Brown's contributions to the fund, which at present stand at £19,000 a year.

A British Gas spokeswoman said that the rules that applied to Mr Brown were the same as applied to any other employee with 40 years service. A spokesman for the National Grid said the company did not comment on its employees' pensions. But he said it disclosed all forms of remuneration to directors in its prospectus.

Gordon Brown said he would demand to know why 'these extraordinarily generous pensions' had not been disclosed after the Greenbury report.

'The country will be rightly appalled by the fact that the privatised utility bosses continue to pay themselves huge pensions, while the general public still has no right to know how much they are giving themselves,' he said.

Labour said that of the 24 private utilities in the top 250 companies, only one had implemented the full Greenbury recommendations.

Source: N. Cohen and P. Routledge, *The Independent on Sunday*, 17 December 1995

One of the prime recommendations of the Cadbury Report had been that the roles of chief executive and chairman of the board of directors should be clearly distinguished. During his chairmanship of the Committee, Sir Richard Greenbury held the combined positions of chairman and chief executive of Marks and Spencer, in clear contravention of the Cadbury recommendations. The wisdom of the Cadbury proposals became clear a few years later when Greenbury's position and attitudes damaged Marks and Spencer, although at the time it appeared that the Committee's chairman might almost have been chosen as a snub.

Sir Richard Greenbury, the chairman and chief executive of Marks and Spencer, has discovered how much corporate governance matters when things go wrong

As British institutions go, Marks and Spencer is almost as venerated as the royal family. It supplies Britons with a quarter of their suits, almost all their bras and a third of their sandwiches. In recent years the clothing chain has burrowed into the nation's psyche by introducing a country raised on soggy veg to such delicacies as smoked salmon stuffed with trout mousse. Investors have been impressed. The firm's shares have long been as safe a buy as its clothes, outperforming the market for the past 30 years. Ruling the M&S kingdom is Sir Richard Greenbury, a brilliant retailer who joined the firm 45 years ago, aged 17.

But Sir Richard's crown has slipped. The immediate difficulty is a power struggle over when he should step down as chief executive and who should be his heir apparent. Keith Oates, the group's deputy chairman, has made a bid to be either chairman or chief executive, appealing directly to M&S's non-executive directors. Mr Oates, a finance man and still seen as an outsider by the board after 14 years' service, was miffed that he might be passed over for the more reserved Peter Salsbury who is, like Sir Richard, an M&S lifer and a born retailer. This unseemly spat came just after a shock profits warning from M&S on November 3rd, the first in its 30-year history as a public firm, and a share slide.

Behind it all lurks Sir Richard's tendency towards absolutism. He has ruled the firm unquestioned, feared as much as revered. This sits oddly next to the Cadbury-Greenbury reforms to British corporate governance. Although the eponymous Sir Richard was concerned chiefly with executive pay, the Cadbury committee also recommended that firms should split the roles of chairman and chief executive. As the head of Britain's most admired company, you might think Sir Richard would embody best corporate governance practice. But he has belligerently refused to give up either of the top jobs. And now he is in a pickle.

The sight of M&S riven by infighting is as shocking as coming across a rotten tomato in its immaculate food hall. 'This is unthinkable,' said one investor of 20 years. Most outraged of all is Sir Richard, who last week hurried back from India to gag his firm. If nothing else, Sir Richard seems to have grasped that he is struggling to preserve his legacy.

M&S's history reflects Sir Richard's strengths. In the past 40 years it has been one of the world's most profitable retailers, with a strong brand that has dominated the British high street. Much of that is due to the sober attention to detail that Sir Richard has demanded.

However, the modern M&S is also a measure of his weaknesses. There is more than a hint of complacency. It had an early lead in selling up-market ready-made meals; now Britain's big supermarkets, Tesco and Sainsbury, are catching up. There has also been an arrogant reluctance to change. M&S's determination to buy almost all of its clothes from domestic suppliers is causing problems. With a fifth of the British clothes market, M&S is increasingly seen as a commodity retailer; yet rivals, importing more cheaply, can be keener on price. John Richards, retail analyst at BT Alex Brown, a broker, puts the tired look of some M&S ranges down to a lack of new ideas from British suppliers, many of whom depend on M&S for most of their business. Clothes sold in its overseas stores are often too expensive, because they have the final buttons stitched on in Britain.

Worst of all is the parochialism. Although M&S has had some success with the remarkable ambition of persuading Parisians to buy English food and English clothes, growth in Europe has been too slow. Brooks Brothers, acquired in America, has lost money. Last year, just when consumer demand in Britain looked uncertain and Asia slumped, Sir Richard announced a £2.2 billion ($3.7 billion) global expansion plan, updating technology and dramatically expanding floor-space worldwide. After the latest poor results (half-year profits fell by 23%, the first decline in six years), the mighty M&S is retrenching, raising doubts about its commitment to growth.

A people problem

The nub of the problem is the company's inward-looking culture. The group has been held back by Sir Richard's failure to take competitors seriously enough and by his resistance to criticism: stitched on to a cushion in his office are the words, 'I have many faults, but being wrong is not one of them' – a joke perhaps, but close to the bone all the same. Taking their lead from Sir Richard himself, M&S executives have failed to understand much of what is happening outside their green-and-white shop window, let alone Britain's borders.

In the end corporate governance is at fault. The firm has few outsiders to provide dissent or new insights. At the top is a board made up of no fewer than 16 executive directors, most of whom have spent most of their careers at M&S. Of the six non-executives, one is a former executive and member of the founding family. With M&S now selling financial services and going overseas, the narrowness of experience of M&S's senior managers and board directors is a weakness. Given the firm's difficulties, a big competitor with global distribution – Wal-Mart, say – might be tempted to bid for such a strong British brand.

Without either a chairman or an independent-minded board to harry him, Sir Richard has mismanaged what is probably any boss's most important task – to provide for his own succession. While M&S was thriving, Sir Richard could afford to be disdainful of the norms of corporate governance. Now that it is in trouble, M&S finds itself without the machinery to put things right.

Source: *The Economist*, 19 November 1998

The Greenbury Report strove to establish a link between directors' salaries and their performance so as to – supposedly – align the interests of managers of companies with those of the shareholders. The Report gave rise to a multiple component structure for pay to directors and senior managers – basic pay, performance-related pay, and bonus – which like the Cadbury recommendations became enshrined in the Listing Requirements of the Stock Exchange so that all companies which listed had to employ those strategies or explain why they had departed from the recommended procedures. Bonuses thus became an inbuilt part of the standard pay policies of listed companies. This readiness to accept the status quo and set up the playing field on the foundation of what already existed took no account of some of the systemic problems that would arise from doing so (see Chapter 14).

For instance, the Report recommended that there should be 'no potential conflicts of interest arising from cross-directorships in respect of the remuneration committees deliberations' yet given the very limited pool from which non-executive directors were drawn, some form of relationship between individuals was almost unavoidable.

Similarly, the report recommended that 'the [remuneration] committee's annual report to shareholders should **not** be a standard item in the AGM' (why not?) but later that in an apparent conflict of advice, 'the remuneration committee should make a report each year to the shareholders on behalf of the Board'. But there was no suggestion that shareholders might be allowed a vote which might have teeth. Remuneration committees were instead enjoined to show that 'the committee has given full consideration to the best practice provisions' – which were universally protected from shareholder sanction if no effective rejection by shareholders would be allowed.

Much of the rest of the report was a recitation of provisions that already existed:

> The amounts received by, and commitments made to, each Director should be subject to audit ... Shareholdings and other relevant business interests and activities of the Directors should continue to be disclosed as required in the Companies Acts and London Stock Exchange Listing Rules ... Shareholders should be invited specifically to approve all new long-term incentive schemes (including share option schemes) ... Executive share options should never be issued at a discount.

All of these issues being matters of then-existing law.

It was only when the committee began to consider the nub of personal interest that it began to become prescriptive about obligations:

> Remuneration committees must provide the packages needed to attract, retain and motivate Directors of the quality required [with the modest proviso tacked on the end that they] should avoid paying more than is necessary for this purpose.

Other aspects of the Committee's Report can only be judged to have been blithely ignored in subsequent behaviour: the Committee enjoined companies to remember that 'Remuneration committees should be sensitive to the wider scene, including pay and employment conditions elsewhere in the company, especially when determining annual salary increases'. This was a call to think about the effects of directorial pay on the future of companies as vehicles for shareholder and stakeholder interests. Yet since the report, both stakeholders' and shareholders' returns have not kept pace with the increase in directorial remuneration: between 1998 and 2010 the multiple of average salaries represented by chief executives' pay in the FTSE 100 rose from 45 to 120 times.[33]

But it was the consequences of the recommendations about bonuses, and more particularly share options, that have been the most damaging to the interests of shareholders and stakeholders since the time the report was published. The bulk of the increase in rewards for senior managers has come through the operation of bonuses not from increases in base pay and has not borne a relation to contemporary shareholder returns: from the trend cited above about the multiple of earnings, in just one year alone (2010) the median salaries of executives in companies in the FTSE 100 rose by 32 per cent while the value of the same share index rose by only 7 per cent (and during this period, aggregate employee pay in the same companies rose by only 2 per cent).[34] The idea that 'performance-related elements of remuneration should be designed to align the interests of Directors and shareholders' is facile at best (the damaging effects of bonuses and option arrangements will be considered further in Chapter 14). And the purpose of providing 'Directors [with] keen incentives to perform at the highest levels' is unclear – mostly because it is unnecessary, even in the terms of the traditionalists' view of the world. If the traditionalist theory of governance holds, then the directors are supposed to be the agents of the shareholders; that means that they are subject to the operation of the doctrine of utmost good faith – legally, morally, ethically and practically. They don't need to be offered additional incentives to make them perform in the interest of their principals – anything less is a dereliction of their obligations. And if the traditionalist theory doesn't hold then falsely directed incentives are going to produce perverse effects, because the directors are not under an obligation of utmost faith to shareholders.

The Hampel Committee Report (1998)

The Cadbury Committee had not seen its work as a one-off: the final comments in the Report had suggested that the task of developing effective corporate governance was a continuing one and that a successor body should continue to review matters. It had specifically suggested that the issue of pay was one that should be looked at again in a few years time – as it was, by Greenbury.

---

[33] B. Groom, 'Executive pay: the trickle-up effect', *Financial Times*, 28 July 2011.
[34] B. Groom, 'UK directors' earnings doubled in 10 years', *Financial Times*, 5 September 2011.

The review function was not performed by a standing body but by ad hoc committees: presumably it was regarded as inappropriate for the State to dictate what might happen in the field of behavioural activity, which it had not entered – perhaps it was thought it had enough to look after in the prescriptive procedural area.

So after a lapse of a further three years the Hampel Committee was formed in November 1995 under the chairmanship of the then chairman of ICI, Sir Ronald Hampel. Initiated by the Financial Reporting Council, its sponsors were the London Stock Exchange, the Confederation of British Industry, the Institute of Directors, the Consultative Committee of Accountancy Bodies, the National Association of Pension Funds and the Association of British Insurers. Its remit was to review the workings of corporate governance in the following terms:

> The committee will seek to promote high standards of corporate governance in the interests of investor protection and in order to preserve and enhance the standing of companies listed on the Stock Exchange. The committee's remit will extend to listed companies only.
>
> Against this background the committee will:
> (a) conduct a review of the Cadbury code and its implementation to ensure that the original purpose is being achieved, proposing amendments to and deletions from the code as necessary;
> (b) keep under review the role of directors, executive and non-executive, recognising the need for board cohesion and the common legal responsibilities of all directors;
> (c) be prepared to pursue any relevant matters arising from the report of the Study Group on Directors' Remuneration chaired by Sir Richard Greenbury;
> (d) address as necessary the role of shareholders in corporate governance issues;
> (e) address as necessary the role of auditors in corporate governance issues; and
> (f) deal with any other relevant matters.
> Without impairing investor protection the committee will always keep in mind the need to restrict the regulatory burden on companies, e.g. by substituting principles for detail wherever possible.

It was fairly clear from the remit that the sponsors and initiators wanted to see no more of this new-fangled corporate governance malarkey interfering with the business of making money. Stakeholders were once again prominent by their absence in consideration; shareholders were only to be considered as necessary, and auditors – the shareholders' watchdogs – were similarly relegated.

With such a loaded remit it is not surprising that the Committee produced a very backward-looking report – which then got roundly criticised from all quarters as not having gone far enough. The recommendations made by the committee amounted to over sixty points but the vast majority of these were of the 'no change required' pattern or supportive of what had been deliberated before.

The thinking behind some of the conclusions and recommendations in the Report appeared at times to be complacent. The role of auditors was seen in Goldilocks terms: 'We do not recommend any additional requirements on auditors to report on governance issues, nor the removal of any existing prescribed requirements' – not too hot, not too cold, just right. Yet auditing is an inexact practice, whose characteristic feature is uncertainty (see Chapter 13). The report also wanted the word 'effectiveness' removed from the corporate governance disclosure made by directors that was recommended by Cadbury and wanted discussions about internal controls to be conducted in private between directors and auditors; they also considered that 'companies which do not already have a separate internal audit function should *from time to time* review the need for one'.

On matters of communication with shareholders the Report appeared to ignore the law, or common sense, or verge on the trivial. The Report recommended that 'companies should be ready, where practicable, to enter into a dialogue with institutional shareholders based on the mutual understanding of objectives' which, apart from being so bland as to be meaningless, courts the problem of insider dealing (a trap fallen into by the Walker Review, see below). Companies were encouraged to establish nomination committees for new directors, to make the nomination process transparent, 'unless the board is small'; yet no attempt was made to define what constitutes a 'small' board (which could equally apply to a very large company with only a few directors) and 'companies whose AGMs are well attended should consider providing a business presentation at the AGM, with a question and answer session'.

Yet some of the comments that the Report made were perceptive – 'We urge caution in the use of inter-company comparisons and remuneration surveys in setting levels of directors' remuneration' and 'We … urge remuneration committees to use their judgement in devising schemes appropriate for the specific circumstances of the company. Total rewards from such schemes should not be excessive' – presumably because the committee saw the possibility of the continual upward creep in inter-company comparisons.

They also defended the rights of shareholders to review the business properly – '[w]e consider that shareholders should be able to vote separately on each substantially separate issue; and that the practice of "bundling" unrelated proposals in a single resolution should cease' – but fell short of recommending a vote on the remuneration policy.

Despite its shortcomings the recommendations of the Hampel Committee can be seen in some ways as being more realistic in its world view than those of its predecessors. It provided the trigger to amalgamate the Cadbury and Greenbury recommendations into the Combined Code on Corporate Governance which became the governance guidelines for UK listed companies and emphasised the poverty of the box-ticking approach which the comply or explain system is prone to. It can be interpreted as not pandering to the traditionalist view of shareholders of listed companies as owners of the companies; it recognises in some respects the real world of disinterested holders of shares who look primarily for progressive capital appreciation and dividend returns while expecting directors to direct, and discounting the price of the company if they don't.

Immediately after the Hampel Committee reported, the Government launched a review of company governance including, specifically, reviews of executive salary formulations and the role of shareholders. The Secretary of State for Industry, Margaret Beckett announced the review by saying that it was now time for companies 'to show leadership in delivering best practice on the basis of that structure (the UK Governance Code)' and that they must 'think more deeply about how they can be transparent and accountable to all those with an interest in their business'. One of the directors of PIRC (Pension and Investment Research Consultants) speaking in 1997 at the time of the announcement of the Department of Trade and industry Review said: 'Sir Ronald Hampel wanted a line drawn under corporate governance and Margaret Beckett has very politely rubbed the line out'.[35]

The Turnbull Committee Report (1999)

Almost as a rebuttal to the views of the Hampel Committee, within a year another Report appeared which took a contrary view about the significance of audit and internal control. Supported by the Financial Reporting Council and the Institute of Chartered Accountants the Turnbull Committee,[36] chaired by the finance director of the Rank Group, produced recommendations that took into account the details surrounding the failure of Barings Bank and the obvious shortcomings of that company's internal control systems. It also dealt four-square with the responsibility of the auditors, as the adviser to shareholders, for the probity and integrity of the accounts. Building on the preliminary work of the Treadway Commission Report[37] in the USA over a decade earlier it attempted to establish transparency of information and effective internal control as the fundamentals of effective corporate governance, mostly through considering technical issues rather than matters of principle.

The Report went well beyond the limited aspirations for internal audit of the Hampel Committee by recommending that the directors of companies should

---

[35] 'Boardroom practices under the microscope', *BBC website* (archived), 4 March 1998.
[36] ICAEW, *Internal Control: Guidance for Directors on the Combined Code* (London: ICAEW, 1999).
[37] A. P. Brief et al., 'What's wrong with the Treadway Commission report?', *Journal of Business Ethics*, 15(2) (1996), 183–98.

conduct regular reviews of the effectiveness of their internal control systems. The report established a conceptual framework for internal control, divided into a number of stages, that allowed directors to implement self-reinforcing control structures. It therefore neatly squared the principled overview with a detailed prescriptive approach to the problems of control, transparency and disclosure. It also moved away from a strictly traditionalist view of governance, dealing with issues of managerial control by a technocratic approach. The original report was later (2005) strengthened by amendments to include the recommendation that directors report on the findings of their review of internal controls to shareholders, although again without being prescriptive – a nod towards a combined traditionalist/nexus viewpoint.

The Higgs Report (2003)

Following the collapse of Enron[38] in the USA (2001) and the Parmalat[39] and Royal Ahold[40] scandals in Europe (2003) attention turned to the role of non-executive directors in supposedly acting as check on the executive directors and their independent role in the stewardship of the company. The Higgs Report was part of a suite of three reports – Higgs, Tyson and Smith – but the significance of the other two was largely swamped by the closeness of the timing of publication. The Tyson Report looked into the recruitment and development of non-executive directors, while the Smith Report dealt with the relationship between companies and their external auditors. Neither made much impact and Smith was criticised for both the limited range of the review undertaken and modesty of the proposals.

That the failures of Enron and Parmalat were in part due to the ineffectiveness of their non-executive directors seemed clear. Not that these individuals had lacked ability: in Enron's case one of the non-executives on the audit committee was a distinguished professor of accounting and former dean at Stanford Business School.[41] But after evaluating submissions of evidence, the conclusions of the Higgs Report were that there should be at least a numerical balance between executive and non-executive directors on the boards of listed companies; that there should be a greater degree of contact between the non-executives and the company's institutional shareholders; and in particular one non-executive should be identified as senior to the others and act as the principal point of contact for shareholders.

---

[38] Enron collapsed in 2001 and was to that date the largest corporate collapse in American history; see B. Cruver, *Enron: The Anatomy of Greed* (London: Arrow, 2003).
[39] Parmalat was the European Enron; see M. Jones, *Creative Accounting* (Chichester: Wiley, 2010).
[40] See Jones, *Creative Accounting.*   [41] 'Enron's board of directors', *Guardian*, 1 February 2002.

The argument of sheer numbers carries little validity and quite why it should be thought important is unclear – especially in terms of the traditionalist theory, which it will be remembered correctly recognises that the law stipulates that all directors are equal and owe a responsibility of good faith to the company (although it then gets muddled about agency issues). There should obviously be sufficient non-executive directors to serve on committees of the board, but good boards reach decisions by the power of argument and *not* by immediate resort to voting on issues, where the simple power of numbers would count. It is of course always easier to argue a case against a colleague, who is presumably better equipped with information (as an executive director should be), with moral support from fellow-directors. But numbers alone do not guarantee that there will be a supportive colleague (unless very large numbers are proposed). Enron and Parmalat also showed that formal, expert qualifications for non-executive directors are not a sufficient safeguard to against executive director misbehaviour. There could be few individuals better qualified, on paper at least, than Robert Jaedicke (the professor of accounting at Stanford) to sit on the Enron audit committee. Who wouldn't have felt safe with his name on the company letterhead? But simple expertise was not in play in Enron, other cultural (structural governance) issues were – just as they are in all companies.

The necessity for a senior non-executive director (or SIND as it has come to be known) is also a little hard to comprehend. If the chairman is not an executive – as he or she should not be under the Cadbury proposals – why should there be another director set up to act as a counter-balance, as a second locus of power? Was the Higgs Committee saying that chairmen could universally *not* be relied upon to be fair and unbiased in their dealings with shareholders, or other non-executives? And what implications does that have for governance, if so? Are all directors to be regarded as potentially unreliable in their ability to deal with shareholders impartially, if the Higgs proposals are taken at face value? And if that is the case why should the senior non-executive be any different?

There is a further objection to this position. At what point do SINDs decide they do not hold the confidence of those whose interests they are supposed to be stewarding? In the summer of 2011, the senior independent director of BP, Sir William Castell, faced calls for his resignation and votes were cast against his re-election at the AGM[42] (as they were for the chairman (Carl-Henric Svanberg)). There were comments in the Press that he did not retain the confidence of the shareholders as a whole in the performance of his job – yet he remained in his position. There is of course a judgement to be made about how many votes constitutes a signal about an absence of confidence rather than a simple protest. But without a firm policy – either specific

---

[42] 'BP faces storms of protest at annual meeting', *The Guardian*, 14 April 2011.

to each company or through regulation – it is possible that a SIND could retain his position until fully a majority of shareholders decide that they wanted to turf him out. By that time who knows what damage would have been done to the company?

Similarly, there is little sense to the Higgs recommendations in issues of principle. Calls for larger numbers of non-executives and for alternative focuses of power miss the essential point of the major corporate collapses they were set up in the wake of – the executive directors of Enron, Parmalat, Royal Ahold, World Crossing, Worldcom, ADT and all the rest told lies in the pursuit of their own interests. The culture of the company (its structural governance) was rotten in all those cases. Numbers of non-executive directors can have little effect where the culture of the company is fundamentally flawed (and in this respect it should be noted that some of the non-executive directors of Enron were sued by investors in the company and paid $13 million personally, out of a final settlement of $168 million, against claims of insider dealing).[43]

As to the point about greater degrees of contact between institutional shareholders and the company, this flies in the face of a number of critical, central tenets about the fair and legal operation of markets. Are institutional shareholders with access to companies for 'dialogue' to be privy to information in excess of, and before, that given to 'ordinary' shareholders? Are institutional shareholders thus to be made insiders and neutered in their capacity to deal on information which could be of vital importance to the value of the pensions and savings funds of their policy-holders? Should large institutional shareholders assume the rights and responsibilities of stewards of the company when, as has been shown, all that 'shareholding' confers in the modern environment is the right to a dividend; the right to trade the share unfettered; and the possibility of capital appreciation, with some limited and backward-looking approval rights in general meetings? And in the absence of being treated to an in-depth appreciation of the companies that they are talking to, what is the purpose of this dialogue – since it will be at a very superficial level unless the companies take investors into their confidence? These issues are perennial – exactly the same points were raised six years later when the Walker Review produced a Stewardship Code which proposed similar behaviour on the part of institutional shareholders (see next chapter).

The Myners Report (2001)

The Myners Report[44] was undertaken at the request of the Treasury. In March 2000, the Chancellor of the Exchequer commissioned Paul Myners, then chairman of Gartmore plc (a firm of fund managers) to conduct a review of institutional investment in the UK. Myners concluded that there were a number of areas where change would result in

---

[43] 'In brief', *The Guardian*, 10 January 2005.   [44] Myners, *Institutional Investment*.

improved investment decision-making. In his Report, which was published in March 2001, he recommended that pension fund trustees voluntarily adopt, on a 'comply or explain' basis, a series of principles codifying best practice for investment decision-making. The Myners Report was a pre-cursor of the Stewardship Code suggested by Sir David Walker almost a decade later after the financial sector collapse. It looked to the models operated in the USA where voting of pension fund holdings is compulsory.

The Government accepted Myners' recommendation, as well his further recommendation that it should review after two years the extent to which the principles had been effective in bringing about behavioural change.[45]

Conclusion

The eleven years between 1992 and 2003 saw much effort and much money expended on eight major governance reviews (including the largely-forgotten Tyson and Smith reviews) and much more money expended by companies to implement their recommendations. Yet their impact has been very mixed: only three can be considered to have made any substantial beneficial impact on governance from the shareholders' point of view (Cadbury, Turnbull and Myners) and there is evidence now of some diminishing returns and further extension of regulation might produce governance fatigue.

Despite the criticism of the Cadbury Report in the first chapter of this book, it can probably be regarded as a success in that it identified the bulk of the problem, it made a definition of it (which is still the basis for most subsequent work), and its recommendations are still largely in place. The Turnbull Report's recommendations have now probably been absorbed into the culture of most large and/or listed companies regardless of any stipulation by the UK Corporate Governance Code (although an exception might be drawn for News International), so it too can be considered to be a success.

The other successful report is the Myners Report which, largely forgotten in terms of detail, established a threshold for investment management activity. It encouraged a more professional approach to fund management governance and helped to shine a spotlight on the costs of trading, while encouraging institutional shareholders to be more diligent in the exercise of their responsibilities. Ironically in terms of what it was supposed to do – apocryphally its genesis was as the result of a senior government adviser's trip to California, which resulted in him coming back fired up to get British pension funds to invest in venture capital – it might be considered a failure. But by

---

[45] S. Horack, J. Leston and M. Watmough, 'The Myners principles and occupational pension schemes, Volume 1 of 2, Findings from case study research', DWP Research Report No. 195 (London: HMSO, 2004).

some lights, given the poor returns of the venture capital industry in the UK,[46] even that 'failure' might be considered a success.

The other three reports produced little real benefit to shareholders – as opposed to the regulatory industry (broadly defined). The Greenbury Report may be argued to have reversed the progress of good governance, from the shareholders' point of view, by embedding the pernicious effects of bonuses in managerial remuneration. The Hampel Report almost certainly intended to retard it if not to actually reverse it – although it might be conceded that Hampel correctly recognised the possibility of rapidly diminishing returns from investment in the superstructures of governance. The effects of the Smith and Tyson Committee Reports are largely lost to history.

The Cadbury Report 'succeeded' because it was the first report on the subject at a time when public interest was hooked by the misbehaviour that had occurred. It came up with a reasonably concise and catchy definition that, if not inspected too closely, appeared to make sense. But it predetermined the course of all subsequent investigations – UK ones at least – which resolutely refused to revise the definition to take account of what Cadbury had neglected. In this sense, Cadbury is at the root of all the subsequent failures of governance reports and policies since it failed to identify the right levers to pull in a changed economy.

Greenbury failed because it was quite simply determined to continue to pull on the wrong levers, by regarding the issue of remuneration – *as it then stood* – as the primary issue.

Turnbull succeeded because it adopted a technocratic approach to the issue of risk which it would be difficult to disagree with from any standpoint – even though the initial instance was dismissive of transparency and openness towards shareholders.

The sum of all these then is that the UK Corporate Governance Code is an amalgam of policies and procedures which are mostly unsuited to what they are trying to do – principally because they have chosen the wrong things to try to influence. The most successful implements for producing good governance appear to be the procedural ones – which cannot be easily evaded – or the technocratic ones which commend themselves to managers because they assist them to do what they want to do. It is after all in no-one's interest to be involved with a company that is in continual danger of collapse because of some managerial flaw. But that is what happened in the biggest of all the governance scares so far – the financial collapse of 2008 which was entirely due to a failure of governance and which will be considered in the next chapter.

---

[46] J. Hurley, 'Venture capital "gap" between US and UK closes', *Daily Telegraph*, 1 June 2011.

CHAPTER 7

The 2007–8 financial crisis: the failure of systemic governance

This chapter will:

- consider the long-term causes of the financial crisis of 2007/8/9 as an introduction to the *systemic* issues of corporate governance;
- track the precursors to the 2007–8 collapse;
- review some of the governance issues involved in the collapse;
- consider the significance of risk issues in precipitating the collapse.

Introduction

So far the issues of corporate governance that have been dealt with in previous chapters have been essentially those related to the company and its immediate constellation of interested parties. Detailed attention has been paid to its stakeholders (which include its shareholders) and the legal context in which the company operates. Mention has also been made of the context of corporate governance in terms of the historical development – the 'geological' aspect outlined in the Introduction – all with a view to examining if the descriptions of corporate governance and how it works in the UK environment are accurate.

This chapter will introduce an examination of another dimension of governance, described in the introduction, to join the procedural behavioural and structural dimensions already dealt with. This is the *systemic dimension* of governance: it refers to the interlinking relationships between separate companies that form an economic or sectoral structure.

Systemic governance therefore describes the way that entire system of governance works and reflects the significance of the inter-relationship and the impact that good or bad governance can have on all parts of the economy. Collectively, effective systemic governance is nearly as important for all companies and for all shareholders as is the proper procedural and behavioural governance of any single company, since if the systemic part refuses to function properly – or is impaired in its performance – then the behavioural aspects which are supposed to reinforce the effects of the procedural systems cannot support the load and the system effectively breaks down. This variant of governance is especially important in one particular area of the economies of the Western world – the financial sector, where the individual products of companies in the sector are largely indistinguishable from each other except in small detail, and the influence of the sector is pervasive.

This vulnerability to collective breakdown is compounded by the economic significance of the sector. In the Western world over the past fifty years or so the financial sector has grown to be the most significant sector in terms of its political power, if not its contribution to the economy. Banks (in their various guises), pension funds, hedge funds, institutional investors and so on have become pivotal in terms of the attention paid to them – mostly because of the reliance of the rest of the economy of the financial sector to mobilise money as one of the factors of production. A large part of this chapter is therefore concerned with a summary of some of the significant events of the last thirty years or so that have contributed to this position.

In the years immediately preceding the 2007 collapse, the financial sector accounted for 40 per cent of the profits made in the American economy[1] and about 20 per cent of the profits of the UK economy.[2] This was the result of a sustained movement out of the primary and secondary stages of economic development into the tertiary stage in the economies of the West; in terms of the composition of the economy the provision of services has assumed greater importance than the production of goods. Consequently, governance failures in this sector have had repercussions vastly out of proportion to their individual weight. In 2007–8 the financial system of the Western world suffered a paralysis from which it is not yet fully recovered, when the systemic governance of the sector failed.[3]

In 2007–8 the financial system was so badly shaken that it almost failed completely, and exposed the glaring weaknesses of corporate governance structures in the financial sector. It was only saved when stakeholders' money was drafted in to fill the gaps in the banks' balance sheets that the shareholders had been unwilling to plug. To be fair to the banks' shareholders they were unaware of what was happening, first because of the obscurity of the banks' accounts and second, because those in charge of the banks did not themselves know what was going on.[4] Nor did the stakeholders have much choice in the matter, since they were taxpayers whose wealth was pledged by governments. But the result of the near-collapse and the nick-of-time rescue was a

---

[1] Statistics published by US Department of Commerce, Bureau of Economic Analysis.
[2] Statistics published by Office of National Statistics.
[3] C. M. Rheinhart and K. Rogoff, *This Time is Different* (Princeton University Press, 2011).
[4] A. Darling, *Back from the Brink* (London: Atlantic 2011).

topsy-turvy solution of stakeholders bearing losses while (some of) the shareholders (the managers) held on to their profits: to repeat a phrase in use at the time but now left behind in the attempt to return to business as usual, losses were socialised while profits were privatised.

Fifty years ago, Kenneth Boulding, the economic adviser to President Kennedy said that only an economist or a madman could believe in infinite economic growth on a finite planet. The economic system of the Western world has been founded on that predicate, however, and – regardless of Boulding's perception – continues to be regarded as the best way of advancing the interests of shareholders, and stakeholders too, for that matter. This partly accounts for the growth of the financial sector in the Western world – younger populated and less developed economies have been able to produce manufactured goods more cheaply and so, since the end of the Second World War the economies of the West have increasingly moved into the production of intangible goods – financial services in particular – as a defensive strategy.[5] The policy of stimulating development of the financial sector was built on pre-existing strengths in the case of the UK, the harnessing of massive potential in the USA, a race to achieve the type of perceived material opulence achieved by the Americans on the part of other European economies, and a need to push employment as high as possible in the face of sustained competition from lower-cost manufacturing economies in the East.[6] In an attempt to maintain overall growth and individual expansion, the participants in the financial products marketplace have developed ever more elaborate products to sell to each other and to the richer members of the developing world.

Near misses

The 2007–8 financial crisis has been the worst so far but there have been several near-misses, as far as corporate governance failures are concerned, across the whole financial system in the past forty years. The secondary banking crisis in the UK in the early 1970s; the collapse of Long Term Capital Management in 1998 (of which, more later) and the dot com bust of the early years of the century all came close to pushing economies over the brink.[7] But despite these, the sector has generally been allowed freedom to regulate itself in conformity with political preferences supported by economic theories which were being developed in the 1960s and 1970s – notably the Efficient Market Hypothesis and the Capital Asset Pricing Model. In addition, in the 1980s, under the banner of abolishing restrictive practices which were held to constrain competition, the UK financial sector was progressively de-regulated and

---

[5] Hall and Soskice, *Varieties*.   [6] *Ibid.*   [7] See J. Cassidy, *dot.con* (London: Penguin, 2002).

controls were relaxed, removed or made remote, on the basis that risk was being progressively better understood and that the previous market structures could be dismantled – despite some warnings to the contrary.

The Efficient Market Hypothesis

Mostly associated with Eugene Fama of the University of Chicago, who developed the theory from his PhD thesis, EMH suggests that the prices of shares reflect all information available at any given time in the marketplace. There are two 'forms' of the EMH – the strong form and the weak form; a third version suggests that share prices also reflect information that is not publicly available.

The implications of the hypothesis are first, that markets are 'informationally perfect' and, consequently, that activities of regulators can only distort this situation and will interfere detrimentally with market processes.

The Capital Asset Pricing Model

A contributory technique to 'Modern Portfolio Theory', CAPM considers the implications on share prices of systematic risk (market risk) and unsystematic risk – which is also known as idiosyncratic or diversifiable risk, the risk unique to an individual asset. It uses mathematical formulae to arrive at a suggestion of whether the price of an individual asset is greater than or less than the market risk and assigns a value to it – a beta value, which therefore describes the returns from the asset in relation to the returns achievable from the market as a whole. It is effectively a measure of an asset's value-volatility. The implications of the model are derived from its assumptions – that the past history of the movements in the price of a share is a good indicator of its future volatility.

The corporate governance structures required of companies listed on the UK Stock Exchange – especially the procedural ones – were developed during a period when the power of the financial sector as a dominant component of the economy, although nascent, had not yet fully developed. Even so, it had long been recognised that the governance procedures required of financial businesses, because of their unique nature, are of a different order from those of other businesses – the stakeholder–shareholder balance is very different. Everyone is a consumer and user of money and therefore has an interest in the proper working of the financial system, which makes large financial businesses – the components of the financial system – different from, say, large construction companies, where the number of stakeholders is limited.

In addition to this, the complex nature of banking since the de-regulation of the financial services industry in the UK in 1986 means that a considerable variety of activities are often sheltered under one corporate roof in this sector. Some of these activities are very mundane (but still mechanically complicated) like deposit-taking; some are very risky, like arbitrage and proprietary share-dealing. The belief among regulators and industry alike is that the comply or explain regime – coupled with the support of the regulatory system and founded on the traditionalist view of governance – is supposed to deal with this wide spread of activity through the procedural and behavioural mechanisms of corporate governance.

Yet the blanket nature of the comply or explain policy makes no distinction between either the significance of certain economic sectors or the significance of certain companies within those sectors and their importance to the economy. The principle of 'comply or explain' applies to the very last company in the FTSE 100 as much to the one at the very top. The indiscriminate imposition of blanket expectations opened up an immediate yawning gap in the efficiency of the coverage of the governance regime, explained away by its proponents as a procedure of levelling up (rather than a more accurate assessment which might suggest that it was one of temporary patchy coverage to cover the least effective governance systems). The usual phrase employed was that 'a rising tide lifts all boats'. In other words, the expectation was that the best companies would – probably and in the majority – adhere to the principles set out in the Code and the others would – gradually and over time – follow their example, if any improvement was required. The unspoken assumption of this description of what should happen was that the 'best' companies in governance terms would be at the top (in terms of size and importance to the economy) and that the others would gradually rise to meet their standards.

Practice, as so often, did not follow theory

The financial sector had been a significant – although not dominant – part of the British economy, since before the First World War. Its particular nature – the greater potential for damage occasioned by the misuse of other people's money – prompted special oversight. Although the generic nature of the Factory Acts,[8] which regulated all manufacturing activity and the surge of enabling railways acts in the middle of the nineteenth century, meant that much legislation had been concerned with regulating manufacturing, banking was the only sector of the economy to have its own unique regulator (the Bank of England) until late into the twentieth century.

After the 'Big Bang' in 1986, when de-regulation took effect, the special over-sight was composed of a mix of regulation by government (in various agencies)

---

[8] The first Factory Act in the UK was passed in 1802.

and self-regulation, which gradually became increasingly 'light touch'. With occasional set-backs and scandals marring its progress (for two examples see the text boxes) the financial sector became extremely successful in the benign economic conditions of the 1990s and early years of the twenty-first century. The justification for the regulatory regime becoming increasingly 'light touch' was that since it was generating jobs, wealth and foreign currency revenues the golden goose should be left alone to lay its eggs.

Until 1997 banks in the UK were regulated by the Bank of England through the Board of Banking Supervision, which oversaw, in particular, their capital positions. But this regulatory structure was largely based on a form of 'club regulation' where individuals knew each other[9] and trusted their contacts, rather than on the basis of hard facts about information not immediately available from basic banking statistics. The holes in this form of regulation resulted in the collapse of Barings in 1995.

As a sector, the banking business had been used to requiring others to explain themselves rather than justifying themselves to the public – except when a scandal broke – and even these occasions were dealt with mostly by 'the club'. (To date the Bank of England remains the only one of the major UK policy-makers not to have published a report into its actions during the financial crisis.) The introduction of the wider requirements of the comply or explain regime was sufficiently gradual not to disturb the residual of the club form of regulation and thus a sector which was an instigator of the need for reform rather than a recipient of the reforms, was left to itself to comply – or explain – without particular intrusion into its affairs. Two cases – that of Barlow Clowes and the collapse of the Lloyd's insurance market – illustrate the dominant style of regulatory oversight in the sector.

The Barlow Clowes affair

In 2011, twenty-three years after the conclusion of a court case and an ombudsman's inquiry, the Treasury was finally able to close the accounts on the Barlow Clowes case after having recovered four-fifths of the £153 million it paid out in compensation to 14,250 victims of the swindler Peter Clowes.

The insurance broking company owned by Clowes collapsed in 1988. The resulting investigation resulted in a ten-year sentence for Clowes who was found guilty of using investors' money, which he had promised them was going into gilts, to manufacture tax avoidance schemes and thereby boost returns illegally.

---

[9] See Kynaston, *City of London*; Moran, *The Regulatory State*; see also H. Davies and D. Green, *Global Financial Regulation* (London: Polity, 2008).

The compensation arose because of lax supervision by the Department of Trade and Industry, which allowed the fraud to go on longer than it would otherwise.

Clowes had organised a web of companies through which he channelled clients' money, managing to provide himself with a yacht, four personal jets, a helicopter, a chateau in France and a farm in the Peak District as it passed through his hands.

Clowes was released from jail in 1996 after serving less than half his sentence. He was later jailed again for a benefits fraud while working as a computer programmer.

The Lloyd's insurance market failure

During the 1980s, the capacity of the Lloyd's insurance market grew rapidly, as did the number of its members – yet the global insurance and reinsurance industry did not achieve the same level of growth.

We soon discovered a fundamental flaw with the market: there was not enough business to underwrite in order to satisfy the demand created by the increasing numbers of Lloyd's members. It became necessary to invent new ways of trading and specialist syndicates developed, which reinsured other syndicates. So long as there were no underlying losses, these new syndicates showed good profits and they attracted more capital. The market grew yet further.

However, in reality the market wasn't growing, it was simply inventing ways of recycling the excess capital. When underlying losses did develop they were funnelled into the new reinsurance syndicates – and we had what became known as the LMX spiral (London Market Excess of Loss spiral).

The consequence with the excess capital was that underlying risks could be underpriced as they were being passed on to the new specialist reinsurance syndicates. In turn, they could not measure the correct pricing as they appeared to be hugely profitable.

So, when the underlying losses did occur, there was systemic collapse of the Lloyd's market not just because the losses went around in an impossibly complicated spiral, but because many members of Lloyd's were also members of other reinsurance syndicates and the losses came back to them in another cycle of contracts.

Our current financial predicament has also been caused by an oversupply of capital and lack of transparency. The oversupply was generated by new instruments of debt such as the Credit Default Swap and Collateralised Debt Obligation markets. These were unnecessary because the capacity was not actually needed and was clearly growing at a pace well beyond the growth of the real economy. These instruments were not transparent, which is why no-one could calculate where capital was being employed. The Lloyd's market crisis has many parallels with the current crisis.

In essence, the Lloyd's solution was to centralise liabilities and discount them by creating Equitas, a form of bad bank. This enabled three key components. Firstly, a consolidation of management costs. Secondly, the ability to negotiate down and mitigate the potential liabilities to counter-parties. Thirdly, the tools to discount the estimated liabilities to allow for time. These three components would give the UK a more powerful hand in countering the current threat to our banking system than the arrangements being mooted by the Government would allow.

The case for creating a bad bank to purchase the tail liabilities depends upon whether the Government has the right strategy in place to manage it, but it appears to have absolutely no idea.

The alternative is to insure the UK banks against these liabilities, but this leaves the culprits in charge of an uncoordinated run-off with little moral hazard or incentive to reduce the original liabilities.

Is there a hybrid – a bad bank, which is insured by the UK Government? This would have the advantages of the bad bank solution, which consolidates the problem, but by using a Government reinsurance arrangement (similar to Pool Re for terrorist cover) it would not be necessary to capitalise the bad bank. The banks ceding their CDO portfolios could pay a premium/value to be rid of the liability based upon a prospective adjustment, with the Government taking a charge over their equity until the bond is released, rather than argue about price now.

The hybrid solution brings with it some familiar features. The most fundamental of which is the compulsory transfer of all 2008 and prior liabilities – good and bad – from any bank regulated in the UK in respect of CDO and other derivative liabilities. Once under the single wholesale management of the UK bad bank it would then be in a position aggressively to negotiate down the liabilities against counter-parties (mostly in the USA). And once those liabilities are established, they can then be discounted within the bad bank on book values to allow for time, rather than 'marked to market'.

In this way, the UK taxpayer need only inject the minimum capital into the bad bank and the counter-parties should accept the Government reinsurance security in respect of its obligations.

The ongoing clean banks will, initially, transfer these contracts to the bad bank at a modest premium to be negotiated, but each of these banks will also be liable to pay an additional premium to the bad bank until such time as the final liabilities are ascertained, but with a cap so that the markets can value the entities and evaluate counter-party risk and borrowing.

Ultimately, the bad bank could be sold as a run-off opportunity or just wound up. Meanwhile, the taxpayer's equity in the current banks could be offered back to the markets without delay.

The mainstream economic recession is only just commencing. Lloyd's survived and learnt how to thrive on better managed risk, a lower cost base and a drive for more business. Fundamental to this was cash flow – and this is where the Conservative Party has it right in promoting its plan for a National Loan Guarantee Scheme for business loans via the banking system. Cash Flow is king. The core principles need to be policies supportive of private sector survival and an environment under which they can recover and thrive. From this, all else flows – learn this from the near death experience of Lloyd's.

So in drawing lessons from the painful 13-year Lloyd's experience, the pointers for the UK Economy might be summarised as needing a long-term plan which embraces a sense of society but which also comes together to reduce its cost to taxpayers. It must also ensure that it is competitive and entrepreneurial in order to generate commercial income from the global economy – and that involves low taxation, higher income generation based upon real business and services.

Source: M. Wade, 'Lloyd's of London's collapse has lessons for today's crisis', *Daily Telegraph*, 13 February 2009. Michael Wade was a Member of the Council of Lloyd's and of the McKinsey & Co Taskforce commissioned to address the issues facing Lloyd's in the 1990s

Not that the financial scandals of the 1990s would not necessarily have been caught by the comply or explain provisions: the insurance broker Barlow Clowes and the Lloyd's insurance market were both excluded, for instance – one as a private company the other as an exempt corporation. However, one instance of scandal – that of the collapse of Barings Bank (even though it was not a listed company) could have provided some material that might have assisted in developing a more appropriate and stringent governance regime for large financial businesses, if the lessons had been learnt. And interestingly, these lessons were not simply not learned by regulators in the UK: at almost the same time that Barings was brought down by Nick Leeson, the American firm of Merrill Lynch was nearly fatally crippled by the losses incurred by one dealer who was trading in the newly-invented collaterised mortgage obligations (CMOs), the precursor of the collateralised debt obligations (CDOs) that disembowelled the financial markets twenty years later.[10]

The collapse of Barings Bank

In 1995 Barings Bank collapsed having suffered losses of over £820 million because of the unauthorised trading activities of Nick Leeson in its Singapore office. Barings – a private company – was the oldest of the London merchant banks that had risen to prominence in the Victorian and Edwardian era.

The bank's activities in Singapore were concentrated on trying to make profit from arbitrage (taking advantage of minor variations caused by timing and currency in the price of stocks) on different Asian exchanges. The losses had arisen because Leeson had concealed initial minor losses after an unsuccessful trade.

Because of the rapid expansion of the Singapore office (which led to insufficient numbers of staff being recruited to fill posts) and his own trading record, Leeson had risen rapidly and was given increasing amounts of responsibility. He eventually ended up as both chief trader and a head of settlements in Singapore – a clear conflict of responsibilities since it allowed him to conceal his losses, unsupervised, in a special account, the now-notorious five-eights (88888) account. These losses escalated to the point where they could no longer be concealed after the Kobe earthquake caused massive reversals in Asian exchanges.

Following the collapse the Board of Banking Supervision of the Bank of England launched an investigation. Their report was released on 18 July 1995, just over five months after the collapse. Its conclusions and evidence were strongly attacked at the time, even though it reported that:

'Barings' collapse was due to the unauthorised and ultimately catastrophic activities of, it appears, one individual (Leeson) that went undetected as a consequence of a failure of management and other internal controls of the most basic kind'.

The corporate governance structures that were put in place by the Cadbury Report and its successors were intended to act mostly on industrial businesses rather than financial ones – since that is where problems of governance were perceived to be at the time the reports were commissioned – another indication of the out-dated perceptions that structured the recommendations. The perception was that it was the excesses of the wholesale restructuring of the British economy which needed to be regulated and shareholders – which of course included banks, insurance companies and pensions funds, through their investment arms – which needed to be protected.

---

[10] M. Lewis, *Liar's Poker* (London: Hodder, 2006).

The banks were not seen as part of the structure that required regulation in this way. The Bank of England had responsibility for banking supervision and the British experience had been that rather than in the banks, financial scandals mostly occurred in the broking and professional areas; the strictures of comply and explain were not intended to, and did not, fully reach these areas.

Although the deposit-taking activities of UK banks were regulated by the Bank of England, when banks sold investment services they were at the time supervised in that area by a Self Regulating Organisation (SRO), the Securities and Investment Board (SIB). This division of responsibilities was altered by the Bank of England Act 1998, which transferred the regulation of deposit-taking by banks to the direct successor of the SIB, the FSA.

At this time too, the Bank of England was stripped of its powers for banking oversight and these were given to the FSA – the reason being that in the rapid expansion of the large banks into broking, share-trading and market-making after the de-regulation of 1986, the market came to be dominated by these players and they had expressed fears about the cost of being overseen by two or more regulators. By this time the clearing functions of banks had become subordinate partners in banking empires to the investment businesses.

The regulatory system set up by the Financial Services Act 1986 had been subject to persistent criticism since it first came into operation.[11] Those in the financial sector were critical of the costs it imposed on the industry, and found the changing regulations expensive to comply with. Outside critics felt that the self-regulatory structure appeared to favour the industry rather than the investors, and that while the system was expensive, its costs were not proportionate to the degree of investor protection which it provided. Yet the individual experience of the regulatory agencies which amalgamated to form the FSA was not, by and large, in dealing with very large companies or businesses of the nature of the banks. They had been used to dealing with a multiplicity of small(ish) organisations and with people who were often known to each other through shared backgrounds (the club form of regulation again). This then placed strains on the regulators who, having come from one form of regulatory environment, which they understood and were not too far behind the players in so doing (see the phenomenon of regulatory lag discussed in Chapter 12), were increasingly required to supervise an ever-widening and more complex market where the accelerating initiative for market development had passed firmly to the players.

In 1992, when the Financial Services Act regime had been in operation for four years, the then Chairman of the SIB, Andrew Large, was asked by the Chancellor of the

---

[11] P. Ashall, 'The new settlement under the Financial Services Act 1986', *Journal of Financial Regulation and Compliance*, 1(1) (1992), 47–55.

Exchequer to carry out a review of the effectiveness of SIB's regulatory role. The review was prompted by the theft of assets from company pension funds in the Maxwell empire, and the subsequent criticism of the way that IMRO (the SRO for the investment management sector) had discharged its regulatory responsibilities. Large conducted what he described as a 'personal review' – the SIB had already conducted its own investigation into the performance of IMRO in the Maxwell affair (as had IMRO) – and the results were not made public. The regulators had already concluded that IMRO's monitoring had been too mechanistic and that it had treated information uncritically which it received about potential problems.

But the regulatory/supervisory structure persisted and developed along the lines of comply or explain since it was both familiar and comfortable to British custom and procedure.[12] The gap between the supposed efficiency of comply or explain as a mechanism for controlling corporate governance and the reality of operations in the market was supposed to be filled by the investigatory and monitoring activities of the regulatory superstructure. In addition, the vogue for 'light touch' regulation – a recognition that the regulators were lagging behind the banks anyway and could not hope to keep up except on an exceptions basis (see Chapter 8) – meant that the banks were expected to be regulated by diligent non-executive directors, under the comply or explain structure, with the more detailed regulatory structure of the Financial Services Act 1986 filling in the gaps (through monitoring procedural, behavioural and structural governance issues).

The flaw here is obvious – the regulatory superstructure was still based on the supposed effectiveness of the 'comply' part of the comply or explain behavioural dimension (since the two were supposed to work in tandem). Yet the mechanisms did not exist at the top of these very complicated organisations for comply or explain to flush out all the problems; as will be shown later they were simply too big to audit effectively. The collapse of Barings had already shown what happened when these mechanisms failed.

The lessons of the Barings collapse were also the subject of study by the Turnbull Committee and technical recommendations resulted – which, because they appealed and spoke to technocrats, have probably been the most successfully implemented of all the governance reports. But overall no special recommendations were made – at least publicly – about the circumstances of the Barings collapse (although one senior official of the Bank of England resigned) and the serious failures of organisation caused by over-extension, nor was any detailed attention given to the specific role of the Bank's auditors in the collapse (who later successfully defended a legal action in respect of their conduct[13]) or the even more significant role of what might have happened had

[12] Moran, *The Regulatory State*.
[13] Staff Reporters, 'Coopers and Deloitte face Barings suit', *The Independent*, 8 June 1996.

the Bank had effective non-executive directors. The comply or explain regime was crucially dependent on the effectiveness of both auditors and non-executive directors in the expanding banks. Leeson had provided figures to line management which suggested a profit of £102 million from Singapore; his actual losses by the time of the collapse were about £200 million – a difference of over £300 million. It might be thought this was sufficiently large to merit some attention: the basic alarms should have been rung if the triangle of cash, profit and loss statement and balance sheet did not agree, but the systems in the bank and the auditors all failed to pick this up. Barings was, of course, exempt from the comply or explain regime since it was a private company.

In that sense defenders of the effectiveness of the comply or explain regime might choose to point out that the regime did not apply to Barings, so criticism of it not working is unfounded, because it wasn't supposed to apply. It might also be concluded that the governance regime inside Barings was less strong for this reason. But this is to discount the fact that the recommended systems of corporate governance had never been identified on what was the best, merely what was 'best available' practice. But in the case of Barings much might have been learned that could have been applied to the necessity of strengthening oversight in the listed banks – and the potential weakness of a comply or explain structure which relied solely on the competence and ability of the company's directors to stay abreast of the rapid development of the market place. This was particularly important as the marketplace was producing increasingly technical products to mop up the excess liquidity that was swilling around in the West's financial system.

These lessons, together with those that should have been learned from an event three years later, if they had been heeded, might have helped prevent the financial crisis of 2008 – the worst economic reversal since the depression of the 1930s. The repercussions of the 2008 collapse will be felt for a couple of generations in terms of reduced economic opportunities and blighted well-being.[14] But significantly in the collapse of a major investment fund called Long-Term Capital Management (LTCM) there had been a dress rehearsal of the events of 2008, which might have produced a prophylactic change in regulation and supervision if the root cause had been recognised and dealt with.

The cause of the collapse of LTCM[15] could have produced changes in the way that the governance problems of the financial sector were dealt with if the cause of the

---

[14] While estimates of recovery vary, the world has not yet recovered in output terms from the damage done half a decade ago; assuming output recovers to pre-2007 levels by 2017, there will have been ten lost years of activity – broadly one economic generation.

[15] R. Lowenstein, *When Genius Failed* (London: Fourth Estate, 2002).

problems – that there existed an arrogant assumption among market operators *that risk could be driven out of the system* – had been understood and absorbed. But the problem was patched over with sticking plaster and the lessons never learned (or wilfully disregarded) by the authorities.

The collapse of Long-Term Capital Management

In 1994 John Meriwether, a highly-regarded bond trader from the firm of Salomon Brothers in the USA, set up a new investment fund, Long-Term Capital Management (LTCM), using so called 'quant' (quantitative) methods that he promised could largely remove risk by judicious balancing of investments – a practice known as hedging. Eighty investors, mostly banks, were persuaded to contribute a minimum of $10 million each to establish the fund, giving it an initial capitalisation of $13 billion. The fund had two Nobel-prize winning economists as advisers who had developed the Black-Scholes equation (which supposedly can be applied to reduce risk in investment strategies and was the basis of the risk-reduction claim). LTCM boasted that it had eliminated risk from investment management by hedging against individual positions and would use its capital to effect arbitrage (the taking into account of minute differences in the prices of assets in different markets to make a profit). This involved taking positions in 'linked' stocks that were perceived to be too expensive or too cheap relative to the market, using so-called convergence trades – taking long positions in the cheap stocks and short positions in the over-priced ones.

By 1997 LTCM had control of funds of well over $100 billion, while net asset value stood at some $4 billion; its position in the swaps market (another sophisticated financial instrument) was valued at some $1.25 trillion, equal to 5 per cent of the entire global market. It had become a major supplier of index volatility instruments to investment banks, was active in investing packages of mortgage-backed securities and was dabbling in investing in emerging markets such as Russia.

In the middle of 1998 Russia devalued the rouble because of political problems and declared a moratorium on 281 billion roubles ($13.5 billion) of its sovereign debt. This resulted in a massive 'flight to quality', with investors flooding out of any remotely risky market and into the most secure instruments within the already 'risk-free' government bond market. World-wide, the effect of this was a liquidity crisis of enormous proportions, placing LTCM's portfolio under severe pressure.

By the following month LTCM's equity had dropped to $2.3 billion. Meriwether circulated a letter which disclosed the massive loss. Existing investors were told that they would not be allowed to withdraw more than 12 per cent of their investment, and then not until December of 1998. By the end of the month, the value of LTCM's equity had dropped to $600 million. Since in terms of numbers of shares held the portfolio had not shrunk significantly, its gearing was even higher. Banks with investments in the fund began to doubt the fund's ability to meet its margin calls (the means by which the arbitrage profits are supposedly realised) but were unable to move themselves to liquidate their own holdings for fear of precipitating the very thing they feared most – a crisis that would cause huge losses among the fund's counterparties and potentially lead to a systemic crisis.

On 23 September 1998 Goldman Sachs, AIG and Warren Buffett offered to buy out LTCM's partners for $250 million, to inject $4 billion into the ailing fund and run it as part of Goldman's proprietary trading operation. The offer was refused. That afternoon, the chairman of the Federal Reserve Bank of New York, William McDonough, acting to prevent a potential systemic meltdown, called all the major investment banks into the Federal Reserve's offices and organised a rescue package (by refusing to let them leave until a deal had been done). A consortium of leading investment and commercial banks, including LTCM's major creditors, injected $3.5 billion into the fund and assumed management, in exchange for 90 per cent of LTCM's equity. (The only New York bank not to participate was Bear Stearns – a position that would not be forgotten ten years later when Bear Stearns became one of the first casualties of the 2008 crisis as other banks refused to support it.)

Though this stabilised LTCM, many banks suffered a substantial write-off as a result of losses on their investments – UBS lost $700 million, Dresdner Bank AG $145 million, and Credit Suisse $55 million.

LTCM's managers had believed it had hedged its position in Russian government bonds by holding contracts to sell roubles. The risk of the Russian government defaulting was recognised and the managers believed that if Russia did default, then the value of its currency would collapse and a profit could be made in the foreign exchange market that would offset the loss on the bonds.

What happened though was that the counter-party banks guaranteeing the rouble hedge shut down completely when the Russian currency collapsed, and the Russian government prevented further trading in its currency. This occasioned substantial losses but still not bad enough to shut the fund down. What really affected LTCM was its inability to predict the size of the flight to liquidity which meant that it could not liquidate its own holdings fast enough to cover its short positions and faced a classic liquidity squeeze as a consequence.

LTCM's operations were based on claims that their investment operations were based on financial algorithms developed from theories, developed by Nobel prize-winners, that had seemingly conquered the malevolence of risk. That intelligent and sophisticated individuals should be duped by the fatuousness of this claim is difficult to understand. And not only market operators but regulators too. It is a further piece of evidence in the case against an unsophisticated view of the efficacy of regulation – considered later in Chapter 13. (Unfortunately much of the same is *still* peddled in advanced finance courses at some business schools which should know better. So because they were too busy wiping the sweat of relief off their brows, the lesson of this crisis was never properly absorbed by regulators or the markets.)

LTCM was a failure of two aspects of the governance system – the non-executive directors apparently parked their common-sense at the doors of the boardroom of LTCM and the regulators abandoned the argument about detailed regulation in awe of crack-brained theories of risk elimination (although in partial excuse, as a hedge fund LTCM was not subject to the same kind of regulation as a broker or a bank).

The success of the New York Federal Reserve meeting, and the cool nerves of some of those engaged in arranging the rescue, produced a conclusion that the failure of LTCM and its products had been a blip. Consequently, no fundamental reform needed to be undertaken: a sticking plaster would do, couched in terms of a bail-out.

The disturbed waters were smoothed over and business resumed largely as before, but at greater volume, in what were subsequently called 'weapons of mass financial destruction' – the sliced and diced packages of debt based on loans which many of the debtors could not afford to repay, the CDO. It was these financial instruments, which were the proximate cause of the 2007 financial collapse.[16]

The use of unregulated debt as a cause of the collapse

Much ink has already been used up in elaborating the causes of the 2007–8 collapse. A book by Howard Davies, the former chairman of the UK regulatory body, the FSA, identifies thirty-eight potential suspects – but not one absolute culprit.[17] Maybe Macavity did it – the financial equivalent of T. S. Eliot's cat who was never there when the evidence of a crime was found. The dominant cause was poor corporate governance – incarnated in several forms – with multiple failings in behavioural and systemic dimensions and possibly some procedural failings too.

But it is indisputable that one of the contributory factors to the paralysis which affected the banking sector was the widespread problem of the opacity of the financial

[16] See P. Augar, *Chasing Alpha* (London: Bodley Head, 2009).
[17] H. Davies, *The Financial Crisis: Who is to Blame?* (London: Polity, 2010).

instruments – the CDOs, CDO2s, other 'synthetic' debt instruments and default insurances – which were developed in the last part of the twentieth century in America and which extended across the whole of the Western banking system by the turn of the new millennium. For a fuller exposition of how this happened the reader is referred to the numerous accounts noted in the bibliography – although most of these fit in the geographical rather than geological category of explanation.

Some of the detail of these has already been touched upon in relation to failings of the systemic aspect of corporate governance. But since the potentially most pointed investigations into corporate governance in the UK occurred in the aftermath of the financial collapse then it is worthwhile looking in more (but brief) detail at this particular issue of the mechanics of the failure.

The ancestors of CDOs (collateralised debt obligations) were invented as CMOs (collateralised mortgage obligations) and first developed into a marketable instrument by the Wall Street firm of Salomon Brothers in the 1970s.[18] After a slow start and significant occasional losses (see above in respect of Merrill Lynch) the market grew very rapidly because of the massive profits which could be generated by amalgamating lots of debt into pools and thereby eliminating the major objection to taking mortgages into a portfolio of tradable debt: that the redemption period (and thus the yield on the debt) was indeterminate.

As the market expanded in terms of the numbers of brokers and banks participating, so fees from the trade diminished for individual brokers. This led brokers to develop ever-more exotic variants and exploit ever-more risky marketplaces. Coupled with political moves in America[19] which supported the extension of debt (on the grounds of social inclusion and the expansion of home-ownership) more and more fragile debt was incorporated into the blended debt instruments – both in quality and in quantity.

The problems that this gave ratings agencies have already been touched on. The shock to the system which pulled down the whole edifice came on 9 July 2007 when BNP Paribas froze redemptions from three of its investment funds specialising in CDOs as a consequence of increased levels of default caused by rising interest rates in the USA. American and German funds had already been experiencing reductions in earnings or problems 'rolling over' debts and in September of that year the first run on a UK bank for over 150 years[20] took place when Northern Rock's problems in securing short-term funds from the wholesale money market were leaked[21] and depositors queued outside the bank's branches to redeem their deposits. The Government was forced into guaranteeing deposits in UK banks (but not to the disastrous level later

---

[18] Lewis, *Liar's Poker*.
[19] 'The National Homeownership Strategy: Partners in the American Dream', US Dept of Housing and Urban Development (1995).
[20] Overend Gurney in 1866.   [21] To Robert Peston of the BBC.

guaranteed by the Irish Government[22]) and the contagion then spread back across the Atlantic as brokers and banks took fright, causing the collapse of Bear Stearns and its rescue for a nominal sum by J.P. Morgan.[23] The refusal of the Federal Government to rescue Lehman Brothers, in the face of intransigence on the part of other banks to support a rescue, precipitated a widespread paralysis of the Western banking system. The whole system froze with, by all accounts, the imminent possibility within hours of High Street cash-points snapping shut and refusing to disgorge cash.[24]

The problem was further exacerbated by the supposed 'insurance' against defaults which had been written, particularly, by one (London-based) unit of the huge insurance company AIG (American International Group) and which the banks then took comfort from. In believing that risk had been squeezed out of their individual positions by taking on board pooled debt and insuring those instruments against default with insurance policies, each individual trader confused localised positions with the market position overall. Risk had not disappeared from the system at all – the insurance market had merely temporarily absorbed the risk and carried it around like a huge rain cloud waiting to dump its load when it could absorb no more. Behavioural governance and systemic governance reached incipient collapse at this point, merely waiting for a trigger.

The individual governance systems failed because no one inside the big banks was asking questions which mattered and the systemic dimension was close to failing because the regulators did not know which questions to ask.[25] The trigger came when individual banks and investors became anxious about the true security of loans to each other based on the CDO 'asset'.

Rumours began to circulate that the pooled loans were often contaminated with debts of very poor quality and worth very little as investments and certainly not what the rating agencies had rated them as. The rumours were well-founded: in America a process of mortgage redemption became so common – dropping the keys to a property through the letterbox of the bank when the loan could no longer be serviced and walking away from the debt – that it became known as 'redemption by post'. Apocryphally, on subsequent investigation, such non-recourse loans had been made to individuals who often signed themselves as M. Mouse or D. Duck on the bottom of the self-certificated mortgage papers[26] which were then duly processed and accepted.

---

[22] See M. Lewis, *Boomerang; the Meltdown Tour* (London: Allen Lane, 2011).

[23] The company could not be saved and was sold to J.P. Morgan Chase for $10 per share, a price far below its pre-crisis 52-week high of $133.20 per share.

[24] Darling, *Brink.*   [25] *Ibid.*, Davies, *Financial crisis.*

[26] One of the features of the extension of homeownership in the USA was the self-verification mortgage where borrowers attested to their income without any form of evidence or scrutiny of their ability to pay. Similar practices were introduced into the UK by at least five mortgage lenders. As of April 2012, they were still available from some lenders.

Summary

The financial collapse of 2007–8 had its roots well beyond the excesses of the 1990s which have been blamed by many commentators. From the end of the Second World War there was a sustained shift from one type of economy to another in the Western world, but particularly in the UK. Making changes that were in response to events and reactive rather than anticipatory, the regulatory system which was devised – the comply or explain system – while appearing to have sympathetic structural virtues, was relying on an economic arrangement which was in transition. Coupled with this was the aggressive development of financial products which outstripped the ability of regulators to control (or understand) and a development of techniques among market operators which gave a spurious impression of having conquered the single most powerful factor which drove the market – risk.

All this was compounded by the continual search for extra profit from financial products which were poorly-understood by the vendors or the customers and also by the directors of the businesses in which they originated. These products offended all the three major dimensions of internal corporate governance: they were procedurally corrupt (self certification to customers who had no capacity to service their debts, but they appeared to satisfy box-ticking obligations); they were behaviourally perverse (they could not produce the results expected of them over the long run); and they were ethically deficient (the likelihood of them failing over the medium term was well appreciated by many vendors). In addition, they were systemically dangerous – yet this was largely unremarked by regulators.

Such lessons as could have been learned were ignored as a consequence of an inadequate amount of will on the part of regulatory policy makers who preferred to concentrate on the short-term gains of income and an ill-founded economic growth, while being oblivious to the longer term consequences. The irony is that the factor which the market of the late 1990s was supposed to have subordinated – risk – came back to bite it so hard that it – briefly – threatened the entire structure. That is until policy-makers once more closed their eyes, turned private losses into public debt and determined that what was as a regulatory structure was good enough to continue to serve almost untouched, as we shall see in the next chapter.

CHAPTER 8

Systemic governance: the Turner Review, the Walker Review and the Vickers Commission

This chapter will examine:

- the scrutiny of corporate governance after the financial collapse through the Turner and Walker Reviews;
- what the Reviews revealed about corporate governance in the financial sector prior to the collapse;
- whether the conclusions the reviews arrived at were borne out by events.

Following the financial collapse of 2007–8 and the huge public sums invested in shoring up the financial system – and especially the banks – there was, unsurprisingly, a clamour to find out what had gone wrong. The British Government in particular had said that they would 'do anything it takes' during the crisis to maintain the structure of the financial system and prevent any UK bank collapsing. In an effort to re-assure the tax-paying, riding-to-the-rescue electorate who now found themselves in possession (if not ownership) of all but two of the UK's major banks (the exceptions being Barclays and HSBC, both of which still accepted money to bolster their resources through the electronic 'quantitative easing' scheme), at least five separate reviews were set in train: a review of the activities of the FSA by its chairman Lord Turner; a review of the response of the Treasury (which reported in March 2012); the Walker Review; the Future of Banking Commission established by a consumer group; and the Independent Banking Commission (the Vickers Commission). Alone of the major policy-makers no review was carried out by the Bank of England.

Issues of detailed corporate governance were understandably subordinated during the crisis to the necessity to preserve the fabric of the financial system. But an absence of full comprehension of what had gone wrong, required an examination of the post-collapse situation – to see if, in corporate governance terms, it was wreckage held together only by the taxpayers' support and in need of fundamental overhaul, or merely a bruised system that would heal if left alone.

Unfortunately, the conclusion appears to have been that sticking plaster could be applied to the shortcomings of the system exposed by the 2008 collapse. By the time that the rescue had been put in place a few significant individuals had been forced out of office as a token price for rescue and a few egregious words of apology had been voiced – but the pre-existing structures of behavioural and systemic corporate governance remained. It appeared as if a few of the chairs had been removed when the music stopped but the game remained as before.

In particular, the collective conclusion of the reviews of the corporate governance structures and procedures that existed immediately before the financial collapse in the UK (and which therefore might be construed to have played some part) broadly concluded that there was and is nothing wanting in the theoretical underpinning of the corporate governance system. Both reviews – the Turner Review and the Walker Review – conceded that the structure had been given a nasty shake by the financial collapse of 2008 but neither report carried any suggestion that the more generalised system of corporate governance in the financial sector required any form of overhaul, nor that the financial system might require special provisions because of its centrality to the well-being of the country.

There has been much more concern with the regulatory implications of what went wrong rather than the issues of governance internal to each financial institution. The FSA's own review of what happened in RBS[1] – seen by many commentators as a significant precipitator of the collapse – was originally supposed to be kept confidential (allegedly because of legal manoeuvring), then when released was found to be anodyne. Other criticism[2] focused on the 'light-touch regulation' which had been the hallmark of the previous decade – but aside from a couple of references by Turner (and more muted ones from Walker) there has been no sustained suggestion that there might need to be a more considered overhaul of corporate governance of the crucially significant finance sector.

Similarly, the Vickers Report published in September 2011 represents another impeccable analysis without a logically consistent follow-through. The 360-plus page report assembled analysis that was overwhelmingly – conclusively – in favour of substantial reconstruction of the banking sector to ensure that the damage done by the collapse of 2007–8 could not be repeated by further lapses of good governance. Yet the recommendations which followed this analysis delayed any substantive reconstruction of the sector until 2019 – eight years into the future and with probably time to fit in at least one more substantial financial crisis. Sir John Vickers had obviously never read Macbeth – 'if it were done, when 'tis done then 'twere well it were done quickly' – nor Machiavelli – 'If a prince is too compassionate, and does not adequately punish disloyal subjects, he creates an atmosphere of disorder, since his subjects take the liberty to do what they please'.

---

[1] FSA, *The Failure of the Royal Bank of Scotland* (London: HM Treasury, 2011).
[2] M. Moran, 'The rise of the regulatory state in Britain', *Parliamentary Affairs*, 54(1) (2001).

The Turner Review (2009)

Adair Turner explained his remit in the introduction to his report:

> The Chancellor of the Exchequer asked me in October 2008 to review the causes of
> the current crisis, and to make recommendations on the changes in regulation and
> supervisory approach needed to create a more robust banking system for the future.[3]

The Review focused on fundamental and long-term questions in relation to banking
and bank-like institutions, and not on other areas of the financial services industry.

The Turner Review was published six months after the collapse of Lehman Brothers in
March 2009. It was concerned principally with regulatory issues rather than shareholder
or governance matters, as part of the self-examination conducted by the FSA of its
effectiveness in regulating the sector. However, the governance issues could not be ignored
and its 17th conclusion stated that: 'remuneration policies should be designed to avoid
incentives for undue risk-taking; risk management considerations should be closely
integrated into remuneration decisions. This should be achieved through the development
and enforcement of UK and global codes'. The 23rd recommendation went on to say that:

> the Walker review should consider in particular whether changes in governance
> structure are required to increase the independence of risk management functions. [and
> also] the skill level and time commitment required for non-executive directors of
> large complex banks to perform effective oversight of risks and provide challenge to
> executive strategies.

However, the invitation which it offered to Sir David Walker to make recommendations about the governance of the banking sector in his review, was declined. Walker's
Review was brought out just over a year after the collapse of Lehman Brothers and he
had the benefit of being able to review the conclusions of the Turner Review before
drafting his own.

The Walker Review (2009)

The review conducted by Sir David Walker[4] had the following terms of reference:

> To examine corporate governance in the UK banking industry and make
> recommendations, including in the following areas:
> • the effectiveness of risk management at board level, including the incentives in
>   remuneration policy to manage risk effectively;

---

[3] FSA, *The Turner Review: A regulatory response to the global banking crisis* (March 2009).
[4] Walker, *Review of Corporate Governance.*

- the balance of skills, experience and independence required on the boards of UK banking institutions;
- the effectiveness of board practices and the performance of audit, risk, remuneration and nomination committees;
- the role of institutional shareholders in engaging effectively with companies and monitoring of boards;
- and whether the UK approach is consistent with international practice and how national and international best practice can be promulgated.

The terms of reference were subsequently extended so that the Review included other financial institutions.

The Walker Review concluded that the basic form of the UK Corporate Governance Code was 'fit for purpose' and that as far as the BoFIs (Banks and Other Financial Institutions) were concerned the structures were likely to remain fit for purpose.

The Review's conclusions were as follows:

- First, the UK unitary board structure and the Combined Code of the FRC [which later became the UK Corporate Governance Code] remain fit for purpose.
- Second, principal deficiencies in BOFI boards related much more to patterns of behaviour than to organization.
- Third [there should be] a dedicated NED focus on high-level risk issues.
- Fourth, there is need for better engagement between fund managers acting on behalf of their clients as beneficial owners and the boards of investee companies.
- Fifth, against a background of inadequate control … Substantial enhancement is needed in board level oversight of remuneration policies.

This is essentially a clean bill of health – bar a few minor blemishes – for the UK Corporate Governance Code's relevance to the financial sector. In total the review offered very little more than a warming over of supporting comment for provisions that already existed in the Code. Yet the opening sentences of the review sit oddly with the conclusions – 'serious deficiencies in prudential oversight and financial regulation in the period before the crisis were accompanied by major governance failures within banks … these contributed materially to the breadth and depth of the crisis' and later 'improvement in corporate governance will require behavioural change' – which might have led an innocent reader to conclude that there would be some hard-hitting criticism in the review of the way that the financial sector's governance systems had failed.

Walker identified early on in the review that it was behavioural problems in the operation of the BoFIs' boards which were at least partly to blame for the problems of the financial sector, which then shock-waved through the rest of the economy. It is the behavioural issues of governance which are at the heart of the UK Corporate Governance Code, since the procedural elements are dealt with by statutory provision.

So the Walker Review recognised that behavioural issues were to blame (that the Code had not worked properly) and then ducked the issue by concluding that there was no pressing need for any form of revision to accommodate change – despite the clear cue given by the Turner Review. The Walker Review's view can be summarised as one of being satisfied that the corporate governance of the banks was handled competently, on the basis of contrary evidence, and that the only adjustments which were needed were to ensure that the provisions of the code were observed:

> A BoFI board should provide thematic business awareness sessions on a regular basis and each NED should be provided with a substantive personalised approach to induction, training and development ...

> A BoFI board should provide for dedicated support for NEDs on any matter relevant to the business on which they require advice

and so on for a total of thirty-plus recommendations.

The discrepancy between the fighting talk of the preamble and the meekness of the conclusions is soon revealed when the report offers some information about the evidence that it received from interested parties:

> concerns were expressed that the UK should not move significantly ahead of or out of line with relevant policy developments elsewhere, in particular in the United States and elsewhere in the European Union. Such concerns were largely associated with the recommendations on remuneration.

The point of the remit concerning making a review and suggestions about remuneration practice was thus kicked into touch very early on.

The Vickers Commission Report (2011)

The Independent Commission on Banking[5] was established in 2009, not long after the Walker Review was published, to 'consider the structure of the UK banking sector; and look at structural and non-structural measures to reform the banking system and promote competition'. It was to formulate suggestions to:
- reduce systemic risk in the banking sector, by exploring the risk posed by banks of different size, scale and function;
- mitigate moral hazard in the banking system;
- reduce both the likelihood and impact of firm failure; and
- promote competition in both retail and investment banking.

---

[5] Sir J. Vickers, *Report of the Independent Commission on Banking* (London: HM Treasury, 2011).

It was also to consider the extent to which large banks gain competitive advantage from being perceived as 'too big to fail'.

The Commission was charged then with making recommendations covering both:

- Structural measures to reform the banking system and promote stability and competition,
- Related non-structural measures to promote stability and competition in banking for the benefit of consumers and businesses

while having regard to the legal and operational requirements of implementing the options.

The Commission was also enjoined to have 'regard to the competitiveness of the UK financial and professional services sectors and the wider UK economy' which suggests that, converting bureaucratic-speak to English, it was not supposed to paddle in the waters of governance – procedural, behavioural or systemic. In fact the only specific reference to governance in the remit was the detail of to whom the commission should report.

The big let-out clause was that:

> The Commission 'will also take into account the findings of ongoing EU and international work, and inform the UK Government's approach to international discussions on the financial system'.

In the event, after much lobbying from the bankers – 'the new trade unionists' as some commentators labelled them – who attempted to conflate structural reform with the disturbances in the financial markets at the time the report was being finalised and provoke concerns about their ability to lend to small businesses under a different structural arrangement – most of the Commission's punches were pulled. In particular, and most significantly, the need to effect reforms was postponed for eight years from the date of the report.

The Commission believed that 'banks should be strongly encouraged to implement any operational changes as soon as possible'. But because of the additional capital (balance sheet) requirements that their proposals would require 'an extended implementation would be appropriate for what amounts to fundamental and far-reaching reforms'. That would then nicely tie in with the implementation of Basel III reforms, thereby neatly complying with the stricture to take into account 'the findings of on-going EU and international work'.

By the time that those proposed changes are effected therefore, two parliaments will have passed – certainly time enough to fit in another crisis. In addition, by that time, eight of the current thirteen members of the board of RBS; six of the current ten members of the Barclays board; seven of the current twelve members of the

Lloyd's board and eleven of the seventeen current members of the HSBC board will be eligible for their old-age pensions.[6]

The changes that would have to be effected if the Vickers reforms were immediately implemented were estimated at £7 billion (or roughly half the amount that the banks paid out in bonuses in the third year of their nestling under the wing of the taxpayer).[7] Bank complaints that the ringfence changes required by the commission would greatly increase the cost of their capital seemed to relate principally to the cost of the capital that they played with in their investment arms rather than to the cost of capital that they could lend on to small businesses.

The word 'governance' occurs twenty-seven times in a report close on 180,000 words long (about the same length as this book). True, the report was not supposed specifically to look at the governance of the banks but since that is where the problem lay – see Turner and Walker – one might have expected that the proposals for the new structures might be better tied up with the problems that caused the need for a review of the old structures.

The 'bonus culture'

Few major events are mono-causal. The search for a single cause – someone or something to blame – is likely to be wrong in conception, wrong in method and wrong in conclusion. But running through all three of the reports – Turner, Walker and Vickers – is a common thread (even if only incidental in the IBC's work) that one significant problem that contributed to the collapse of the financial sector in 2007–8 was excessive levels of risk being accepted by banks in their investment dealings. This was partially brought about by linking the financial rewards available to certain sections of the bank's staff with bonus payments which encouraged reckless behaviour in respect of the valuation of assets and the calculation of profits. It is important to recognise that the banks were doing nothing intrinsically wrong in either regard. The integral use of bonuses had been established as a component of directorial pay in the UK by the Greenbury Report of 1995 and international accounting standards required the use of certain protocols – see Chapter 13 – when valuing financial assets, which in an attempt to produce clarity, produced a paradoxical decline in usefulness.

However, none of these considerations precluded a root-and-branch review of the fundamentals of corporate governance as applied to the financial sector by any of the three major reports.

Turner had implied in clear terms, and journalistic and popular comment asserted, that the issue of remuneration – the 'bonus culture' – had been at the origin

---

[6] Board members as at April 2012.

[7] M. Murphy, 'Compensation ratios become latest jargon', *Financial Times*, 12 February 2010.

of the problems of the financial sector. But Greenbury's Report of a decade-and-a-half before had locked bonuses into the structure of UK corporate governance and Walker obviously felt unable to try to unlock it or even to recommend that it might be an unsuitable way of rewarding employees in a tertiary sector industry. Vickers simply ignored it. It was outside the remit of the Independent Banking Commission since the ground had already been trawled over by Walker who – because the boxes were being ticked in appropriate fashion – found no reason to complain about the usefulness of the exercise. But as Chapter 14 will show, issues of reward and culture go to the very heart of efficient and effective corporate governance and more importantly, can drive out good governance (as Chapters 15 and 16 show).

The impact on traditionalist views of governance

That Walker did not wish to follow through on his initial premise, the need for changes to the behavioural components of governance behaviour, throws the standing of the traditionalist viewpoint of corporate governance further into shadow. The traditionalist view holds first, that the directors are the agents of the shareholders and second, that the directors are bound to act in the best interests of the shareholders. Yet here are two reports identifying significant problems in corporate governance – within the province of the directors to control – in major listed companies, problems which caused huge wreckage in the world economy, refusing to make adjustments to the structure of corporate governance for fear of upsetting the balance of reward between shareholder and employee.

To put it more starkly, the Walker Review effectively says that the rewards which must be given to directors and managers to ensure 'competitiveness' in the short term are more important than securing the long-term interest of shareholders by ensuring governance is effective. Brutally, the interests of the managers – directors and senior employees – triumphed over the interest of the shareholders and nor was this simply in the short term. In August 2011, the London Stock Market experienced a huge reversal in value – it entered 'correction territory' in the jargon of the market[8] with £125 billion being wiped off share values in London in five days. Financial shares were particularly badly hit in this correction in value as they issued results which had been adversely affected both by write-downs on loans to some European economies and compensation for mis-selling insurance to customers (a practice undertaken to inflate profits to reap rewards in bonuses, see Chapter 15). Yet the *Financial Times* reported[9] that bonuses to bank staff in the first half of the calendar

---

[8] M. Hunter, 'FTSE 100 enters correction territory', *Financial Times*, 4 August 2011.
[9] J. Treanor, 'Are banks heeding King's bonus call?', *Guardian*, 5 December 2011.

year 2011 amounted to £14 billion, a transfer of wealth from the shareholders to the agents, which the former are unlikely to have volunteered.

Perhaps by suggesting in the opening paragraphs of the review that 'major governance failures [occurred] within banks' Walker was referring to the errors of judgement of the disgraced directors whose departures from office followed the rescue by the taxpayer; and that the problems were therefore related to individual personalities rather than to any more deep-seated problems. If this is what he did mean, then presumably he concludes that the departures satisfy the solution to the problem since the individuals who committed such egregious errors are no longer in place and the survivors will have learned the lessons. This will also have satisfied the precepts of the traditionalist theories of governance: bad agents were displaced. If that is indeed the substance of the case then that argument does not hold water.

First, the decisions of boards of directors are collective so it is not possible to split out degrees of culpability (which, as will be seen in the chapter dealing with corporate criminality, makes problems for the law courts). So there is no guarantee that those who went were the 'guilty parties' nor that those who are left are any less guilty of poor decision-making.

Second, particular failures of corporate governance *systems* cannot be vested in individuals – the decision-making mechanisms of boards require discussion, persuasion, argument, factual information and proper deliberative processes engaging those facts. This is therefore a *group* behavioural problem: the directors collectively made bad decisions or else boards of directors were dominated by the personalities of one or two among their number and herded or persuaded (bullied?) into making wrong decisions. In which case it was a failure of governance of a different type – the wrong people had been picked by the system to engage in corporate governance both to challenge and to lead the process. (At the time of its collapse Lehman had ten independent directors: nine were otherwise retired; four were over seventy-five years of age; one of those was a theatre producer who sat on both the Audit committee and the Finance and Risk Committee; one was a former Admiral of the US Navy, who had been a specialist in education and personnel; only two had ever worked in the financial field.)

Or, to be charitable, as a third option, rather than individual bombast or overweening arrogance on the part of the executives coupled with group-think among non-executives, perhaps it was a problem caused by a disconnect between the corporate governance structures that were supposed to control the banks and other financial institutions and what was actually going on inside the fabric of those companies. Again, this cannot be a problem of individual responsibility but is an indication of what is supposed to be an effective governance structure pulling on the wrong levers.

Finally, no shareholder votes were ever held to remove disgraced directors – part of the price for rescue was the resignation of some of the more incompetent individuals, but this is hardly a valid vindication of market theory.

The systemic governance issues – the subordinate cause

Walker's view of the effectiveness of corporate governance systems was not shared by others. Alan Greenspan, the arch champion of the efficiency of the market, had professed to be 'in a state of shocked disbelief' about the failures of 'self-interest of lending institutions to protect shareholders' equity' when he gave evidence to a Congressional Committee which also grilled the heads of the major Wall Street banks.[10] The Treasury Committee of the House of Commons wrung a collective apology out of the banks' chairmen in February 2009 and said in its report:

> the current financial crisis has exposed serious flaws and shortcomings in the system of non-executive oversight of bank executives in the banking sector. Too often eminent and highly-regarded individuals failed to act as an effective check on executive managers, instead operating as members of a cosy club.[11]

The OECD waded in with criticism of the corporate governance arrangements 'which did not serve their purpose to safeguard against excessive risk-taking'.[12] The International Corporate Governance Network said that 'boards fail to understand and manage risk'.[13]

All these indicate a problem caused not by procedural failings – possibly not even behavioural failings (since the obligations of the Corporate Code were largely followed in their form) – but of *structural* and *systemic* failings in that the systems on which the procedural and behavioural aspects depended for their effective functioning also failed.

Pursuing the line about structural problems in individual companies, corporate governance may not work internally for a number of reasons – among these are first that the form may be followed correctly but the policies that are put in place are either wrong or ignored by those supposed to execute them (structural and behavioural problems); second, that the information coming up from the organisation may not show a proper picture. As a variant on this, if information is correct the obscurity and complexity of the information may be such that the individuals who are engaged in governance are unable to grasp its significance.

---

[10] K. Scannell and S. Reddy, 'Greenspan Admits Errors to Hostile House Panel', *Wall Street Journal*, 24 October 2008.

[11] Treasury Select Committee Report, *The Banking Crisis: reforming corporate governance and pay in the City* (May 2009).

[12] OECD, *Corporate Governance: Lessons from the Financial Crisis* (Paris: OECD, 2009).

[13] ICGN, *Second Statement on the Global Financial Crisis* (London: ICGN, 2009).

There are other variations on these possibilities of course but, provided the procedural and behavioural structures of governance are in place, then the principal causes of governance failure almost certainly have to be from one of these two avenues of policy-and-form disjuncture or complex information of obscure significance. In the case of the banks and financial institutions it seems likely that it was the second reason. The directors were unable to grasp the significance of the information being thrown up by the internal management systems. It was beyond their ability to grasp what was going on because it was beyond their experience and their understanding in its ramifications. As a consequence of this the basic requirement of a corporate governance system – that it cope with risk management – was not met.

Not too big to fail ... too big to audit – the contributory cause

To be fair to the non-executive directors, during a period when the share prices of companies in the financial sector were sky-rocketing on the basis of strong earnings growth (even though those earnings were illusory), it would have required exemplary strength of character, extreme percipience and substantial independence of spirit to stand up in a boardroom and question the entire basis on which record levels of profit were being made and record share prices were based – and then to bring your fellow directors along with the argument.

However, to be completely even-handed, those are the very characteristics non-executives are supposed to possess in some measure – and they are employed to act as a check on the executives, not simply absorb what is said and nod in agreement. But, just like the case of the Emperor's new clothes, the record shows that they were all prepared to go along with group think.

No non-executive director resigned from the boards of the financial institutions before the collapse and wrote about why he or she did so, in order to sound some sort of warning – because none of them appreciated the nature of the problems that were being built up inside the companies individually and across the system. Why should they have done so? After all, the information that they were receiving from very well-qualified financial directors and advisers, from the financial press and from stockbroker reports was pretty much uniform in endorsing the development of 'sophisticated' financial instruments that generated massive profits for the financial sector. In short they all saw what they wanted to see (or perhaps, what the executive directors of the boards wanted them to see).

This illustrates a factor that has probably been underplayed in the examination of what went wrong with the corporate governance of the banks in the years between the dot.com bust and the fall of Lehman Brothers – it wasn't so much that the companies were too big to fail as that they were *too big to audit* (see also the concluding remarks in the summary chapter). The complexities of highly imaginative parcels of fragile debt being moved around, packaged, re-packaged and passed on and their impact on the balance sheets and profit and loss accounts of the banks were too difficult for auditors to properly assess. It is manifest that audit certificates were issued which should not have been issued, certifying that all was well when it was obviously not, given what happened only weeks later in some cases.

In some respects the banks had become federations of individual business units which reported to a controlling board. They are controlled as individual units of the federation by powerful and ambitious individuals who guard their own power-bases.[14] The size of these individual units dwarfs that of many other businesses in terms of transaction volumes and operational scope rendering it extremely difficult to understand the effectiveness of managerial oversight. The governance of such organisations may have to be recognised as of a different nature from more unified businesses with more recognisable common characteristics and smaller transaction volumes

Inadequate regulation – the visible cause

The avalanche of information that has been forthcoming since the 2007–8 collapse suggests that the factors of the problem were known and were being publicised, examined and analysed:[15] the fundamental seeds of the later blow-up were appreciated – at least by some. Some market players were in fact apparently constructing vehicles which would enable them to profit from the collapse of other investment vehicles that they knew to be unsafe (see the Goldman Sachs case below). This gives a clue to the fourth reason for the collapse – lack of effective regulatory oversight.

If, as is noted above, there is evidence that some alert commentators were indicating problems that were approaching inexorably, the question arises of why the regulators did not take notice of the imminence of the problem and adapt their regulatory stance. Justifications in terms of 'light touch' regulation are inadequate – as are claims that the collapse, when it came, was too swift for action to be taken.[16]

The problem with the regulators appears to be that they were doing what they so often exhort others *not* to do – regarding governance and regulation as box-ticking exercises that were mechanistic and backwards-looking in nature, rather than anticipatory and flexible. This is the problem of regulatory lag (which will be dealt with further in Chapter 12), long-recognised as being one of the inhibiting issues to effective regulation in dynamic markets. Turner came close to admitting the problem in his review.

---

[14] On the succession struggle inside HSBC, see J. Treanor, 'HSBC chief Mike Geoghegan ousted after brutal boardroom battle', *Guardian*, 23 September 2010.
[15] See Table 11.1 in Chapter 11.   [16] Darling, *Brink*.

But the regulators were not alone in looking backwards and behaving mechanistic-ally. The non-executives of the major banks chose not to act as a brake on the activities of the companies that they were stewards of. They chose rather to ignore the obvious problems with the concept of self-certification mortgages feeding into their asset bases. They were supported by the ratings agencies that certificated all mortgage debt as AAA[17] and by insurance companies that defied the logic of actuarial calculations and said that everyone could be insured against everything and the insurance company could still make a profit.[18] The bank directors thus did what they saw as the minimum required: they followed the form of the corporate governance codes – regular board meetings; nomination committees; remuneration committees; audit committees; the continuing obligations regime – and when the market crumbled, watched the companies they stewarded paralysed one after the other because of the diet of poor quality assets that they had all feasted on and exchanged between them.

In that sense Walker was right – the corporate governance system did work properly if evaluated solely in terms of its form. What he neglected to say was that it worked to no effect whatsoever, because the individual governance procedures, although they may have been dutifully carried out, ignored the fundamental *that risk cannot be eradicated from the system as a whole*. After all, the elimination of risk argument had been discredited in the LTCM collapse and simply passing the parcel of risk is *not* risk elimination. The lesson which Walker failed to point out was that if corporate governance activities are limited to mere supervision of procedural and behavioural structures internal to each company, the system will continue to fail. There must be structural and systemic support to pin all the dimensions together.

The paralysis of the banking system that followed the failure of Lehman Brothers in 2008 occurred because at some level each financial organisation involved was corporately aware that the parcels of debt which it was busily engaged in moving around the system to other banks were of substandard quality as assets[19] and offended sound banking principles for the system as a whole. Somewhere in each organisation, managers had deliberately chosen to ignore – in a mind-set that developed over a period of time – the problems that would arise if the packages of debt were scrutinised in greater detail. The ratings agencies were apparently willing to certify packets of CDOs as being of investment grade without any detailed evaluation (quite simply because that would have been impossible given the absence of proper initial information and the subsequent packaging and re-packaging

---

[17] A. van Duyn, 'CDO fees flow to ratings agencies', *Financial Times*, 29 April 2010.

[18] J. Sterngold, 'AIG Writedowns May Rise $30 Billion on European Swaps', *Bloomberg.com*, 17 December 2008.

[19] T. Braithwaite, K. Scannell and C. Bryant, 'BofA and JPMorgan sued over securities', *Financial Times*, 30 September 2011.

of the debts) and because of the way in which the defaults affected different investors at different times in terms of recognising loss.

Some traders knew that they were engaged in trading financial instruments which operated against the interest of their clients (the notorious Abacus fund for instance).[20] In a legal action commenced in August 2011 by AIG against Bank of America,[21] as part of its evidence for commencing the $10.5 billion suit, AIG alleged that they had evidence that a trader in BoA said that 'he did not care about debt to income ratios as we [BoA] can sell the loans on to whoever'. If the case is proven BoA will, therefore, be guilty of having derived, developed and sold a financial product while knowing that it had failed to properly represent the underlying quality of the mortgages and the inherent riskiness of the debts it had packaged up. So in that sense, corporate governance definitely failed – and the failure was structural (it had spread throughout the organisation) and was not confined to the top of the organisation or beyond the reach of change.

Goldman Sachs, Fabrice Tourre and the complex abacus of toxic mortgages

On January 23, 2007, Fabrice Tourre sat down to write what is likely to go down in the annals of the financial crisis as one of the most memorable emails to have found its way out of Wall Street.

Typing in French and in English to a friend who may never be named, the Goldman Sachs banker shared his apparently true feelings on the state of the US housing market: 'More and more leverage in the system. The whole building is about to collapse anytime now ... Only potential survivor, the fabulous Fab[rice Tourre] ... standing in the middle of all these complex, highly leveraged, exotic trades he created without necessarily understanding all of the implication of those monstruosities [sic]!!!'

But a month later, on February 26, French-born Tourre produced another document, a 65-page 'flip book' that contained details of a $1bn investment fund, designed to be given to potential investors.

The fund was no ordinary fund, however, but a synthetic collateralised debt obligation (CDO) – a parcel of sub-prime mortgages – to be called Abacus 2007-AC1.

In other words, it was jam-packed with the types of 'highly leveraged, exotic trades' he had previously criticised.

Tourre's role in Goldman Sachs' scandal – which yesterday saw the bank and Tourre charged with two civil counts of securities fraud – is central to

[20] T. Alloway, 'Goldman's Tourre says show me the inexperience!', *Financial Times*, 1 February 2011.
[21] T. Braithwaite and B. Masters, 'AIG set to sue BofA for $10.5bn', *Financial Times*, 8 August 2011.

understanding what exactly happened in the marketing of the Abacus fund, and why the world's biggest bank is now effectively on public trial.

The Securities and Exchange Commission's 22-page court filing details what it portrays as an orchestrated attempt by Goldman and its junior employee to allegedly deceive clients in order to profit twice – once from structuring the Abacus fund, for which it earned $15m, and once from Paulson & Co, the New York based hedge fund run by John Paulson, for which its profits are not known.

Under the SEC's version of events, Paulson came to Goldman in January 2007, asking it to help buy protection against what it believed would be a fall in US residential mortgage-backed securities, and then 'discussed with Goldman possible transactions in which counterparties to its short position might be found.' Those counterparties were to be 'found' in Abacus 2007 AC-1 – a new CDO which was part of a wider programme of CDOs structured by Goldman.

Unlike other CDOs, however, the SEC allege that this one had been constructed under the influence of Paulson – which is not itself accused of any wrongdoing.

Having decided to create a CDO to allow investors to invest in a potential increase in the value of sub-prime mortgages – which Paulson would then short – Goldman needed independent validation that what it was selling was kosher. Step forward ACA Management, a specialist in analysing credit risk owned by ABN Amro, the Dutch investment bank.

But although ACA was recruited as the ultimate 'portfolio selection agent' of the mortgages within the Abacus derivative for its 'credibility', unbeknown to it – or future investors – Paulson is alleged by the SEC to have initially handed Goldman a list of 123 residential mortgage-backed securities (RMBS) to be considered for inclusion.

The 123 RMBS were based on Paulson's selection criteria of those most likely to default – and so included mortgages from borrowers with low credit scores, and from states which had seen high rates of house price appreciation, states like Arizona and Florida which have since seen high repossession levels.

After discussion with ACA, the SEC alleges that ACA and Paulson together selected 90 RMBS in which Abacus would invest, but only after Paulson allegedly 'kicked out' a number of Wells Fargo mortgages which were 'generally perceived' to be of higher quality.

Paulson, in a statement, points out that ACA had 'sole authority' over the selection of RMBS in the CDO, and stresses that it did not market Abacus to investors.

Of course, once Abacus had been constructed, it was up to Tourre to market the issue, and market he did.

The SEC alleges Tourre misled ACA into believing Paulson invested up to $200m in the equity of Abacus, and told IKB, the German bank which invested $150m, that the mortgages were selected by ACA, as the bank had previously informed Goldman it was not interested in investing in CDOs that hadn't been selected by a third party.

But Tourre also allegedly misled investors by not telling them – either verbally or in the CDO's marketing documents – that Paulson was all the while shorting the RMBS within Abacus.

Goldman for its part categorically denies any wrongdoing, pointing out that it lost more than $90m in Abacus, that investors knew the risks, and that it did 'not structure a portfolio that was designed to lose money.'

Some six months after Abacus's fundraising closed on April 26, 83pc of the mortgages within had been downgraded.

On January 29 – a year and six days after Tourre wrote his original prescient email, and ten days after his 29th birthday – 99pc of the portfolio had been downgraded, leading investors to lose more than $1bn, and Goldman – and Tourre's – reputation to be left open to question.

Source: J. Quinn, *The Daily Telegraph*, 16 April 2010

While the case in question, between BoA and AIG, involves American financial companies, the activity in buying and selling such instruments was not confined to America. European companies performed the same trades.[22] The British banking system seized up partly because none of the banks were willing to lend to each other and accept potentially worthless debt as collateral – because at some level they all knew the nature of the assets they had been trading between themselves. In Germany, for instance, the country's fourth largest bank – Hypo Bank – had to be rescued twice within 48 hours[23] because the management were unable the first time round to accurately assess the hole in their balance sheet caused by the sudden write-down of what were held to be worthless debts. To suggest that bankers in England and Germany were not aware of the nature of the assets and simply sleep-walked into buying sub-standard assets from the wily Americans is a ludicrous position to argue from and anyway does nothing to protect those financial institutions from the charge that their corporate governance systems failed – 'sleep-walking' is not 'exercising good governance'.

[22] S. Jones, 'Synthetic eurotrash', *Financial TImes*, 22 January 2009.
[23] J. Wilson and B. Benoit, 'Berlin agrees second package to save Hypo', *Financial Times*, 6 October 2008.

But the banks were not alone in this culpability. One of the features of the systemic governance failure of 2007–8 is that other components of the system – apart from the regulators dealt with above – which are supposed to act as a check on the activities of the primary actors in the financial system, also failed.

The other guilty parties

Reputational intermediaries, collectively

Financial companies by their very nature, in dealing with intangible movements of money between customers, ought to be belt and braces operations, with a second line of safety if the first line fails for some reason. But it was not simply the internal mechanisms that gave way in the financial companies. There were supposed to be systemic mechanisms outside the individual organisations that were external to each bank and linked in to them, to prevent failure. These external mechanisms should have operated like the system's braces, operating with the internal structures of governance in each company, ready to keep the system's trousers up if an individual belt gave way. In the event, the braces failed, the belts weren't there and taxpayers, and some shareholders, lost their shirts – as well as their trousers.

Shareholders have developed these external systems in other situations to protect themselves and had every reason to expect them to be there in the case of the financial institutions – in fact the financial sector should be, and is, subject to more sets of checks than almost any other sector. Not only are there are auditors and stockbrokers (collectively sometimes called 'reputational intermediaries') but also ratings agencies and financial regulators and financial journalists. The levels of supervision or oversight should have been many-layered: the directors should have been looking after the shareholders' interests, the auditors should have been helping them and the shareholders by independently verifying information, the stockbrokers should have been making judgements about the products that the banks were developing and evaluating each bank's worth, the journalists should have been commenting on the brokers' evaluations. The regulators should have been looking over the whole picture: accountancy regulators in the form of professional bodies for the auditors, the Stock Exchange for the analysts, and the FSA with umbrella oversight for them all and in particular for the banks. Beyond the FSA was the IMF.

British banks have a poor record in terms of corporate management and adventuring; the history of British banking over the past fifty years is littered with the wrecks of corporate ambitions, especially in the USA (and all carefully air-brushed from their corporate-history websites): Crocker (Midland); First Jersey National (NatWest); Barclays home-grown retail banking network in the USA; and Household (HSBC). This is not to mention, of course, AMRO Bank – the deal that eventually sunk NatWest as an independent company but which Barclays had been interested in too. So, if anything, the reputational intermediaries and the regulators ought to be have been very careful with scrutinising the activities of these clients. Yet they all failed.

The problems of audit are dealt with in a separate chapter but the problems encountered by the others need to be reviewed to cast light on the central issue of this book – how corporate governance works in practice against the 'received wisdom' of current theory.

Stockbrokers

Stockbrokers employ analysts to review the companies in each sector and produce research which should enable clients to make informed judgements about the economy and the value of companies – whether to make an investment, hold it or dispose of it. Their work is often derided – Nigel Lawson, the Chancellor of the Exchequer under Mrs Thatcher, called them 'teenage scribblers' – but the market depends to a large extent on the work of these individuals as a conduit for its basic information in valuing shares. It is thus important to their clients that they get things, collectively, broadly right and are able to produce considered information. Companies recognise this and the finance directors of companies spend time and effort cultivating the analysts to make sure – within the rules of insider information and market abuse – that they have a reasonable idea of the operations of the businesses that they follow. But many of the analysts work for firms which depend for fees on the operational activities of the banks and they are naturally reluctant to be too hostile in respect of their potential clients' reputations – let alone the problem of cutting themselves off from future channels of information by being too critical of senior City figures.[24] Unfortunately, like the non-executive directors of the banks, most of them were probably unable to appreciate the complexity of the products that the banks were dealing in; certainly none ever said that things were getting too complicated and the banks should pull back. When the collapse came it came to a bank in the UK – Northern Rock – that had been praised by analysts for its rapid growth[25] to stand as the fifth largest lender since the time of its de-mutualisation eight years previously. These analysts had applauded Northern Rock's use of the wholesale money market to fuel its growth.

---

[24] T. Mokoaleli-Mokoteli et al., 'Behavioural Bias and Conflicts of Interest in Analyst Stock Recommendations', *Journal of Business Finance & Accounting*, 36 (2009); and K. Brown, 'FSA issues further reprimand to analysts', *Financial Times*, 13 August 2004.

[25] See Augar, *Chasing Alpha*, Chapter 9.

Journalists

The Stock Exchange places a very high value on the rapid and efficient publication of information to shareholders, and the market as a whole relies on journalists to absorb, interpret and comment on this information. The free flow and transfer of information to and between shareholders is a fundamental plank of efficient and effective corporate governance. Although they are not crucial to the internal governance process itself they have a valuable role to play in systemic governance in disseminating the information provided by analysts to a wider public and conducting their own commentaries on economic and commercial matters.

But much newspaper copy on companies and the City is simply that: copy. Press releases which originate from company PR departments are the basic material for most newspaper reports.[26] Newspaper journalists are mostly dependent upon the reception of information since they usually originate little – although they can be far from powerless: the fall of Enron, for instance, can be traced back to articles in *Fortune* magazine casting doubt on the figures reported by the company.

Ratings agencies

Investors, pension funds, company treasuries – and even nations – depend on the ratings agencies to evaluate the debt which they issue. The ratings agencies used to charge the users of their information for their services, but a change in policy in the 1990s meant that they charged the issuers of debt to evaluate it – a clear conflict of interest, which was cultivated by American legislation which required investment banks and broker-dealers to use recognised agencies for the rating of debt. In consequence there are now only three agencies of standing – Standard & Poor's, Moody's (both American-owned) and Fitch, which has a French parent.

Criticisms of ratings agencies

- **Slowness to react:** Enron's investment rating remained at investment grade until four days before the company went bankrupt; Moody's continued to give the American mortgage corporation Freddie Mac, the highest rating until the American investor Warren Buffet criticised the company – at which point it reduced the rating to one level above 'junk'.
- **Too familiar a relationship with company management:** no 'distance' and dependent on the companies who issue debt for their income.

---

[26] D. Tambini, 'What is financial journalism for?', POLIS (LSE, 2008); N. Davies, *Flat Earth News* (Chatto & Windus, 2008).

- **Narrow range of variables:** analytical myopia; after the downgrading of American sovereign debt, some small companies in Asia had higher ratings than the US Treasury.
- **Easy attitude to newcomers:** to solicit business. For instance, Moody's published an 'unsolicited' rating of Hannover Re, a German re-insurance company, with a subsequent letter to the insurance firm indicating that 'it looked forward to the day Hannover would be willing to pay'. When Hannover management refused, Moody's continued to give Hannover Re ratings, which were downgraded over successive years, while continuing to make payment requests.
- **Herd mentality:** ratings agencies tend to move together and re-adjust their ratings only after one moves, since the integrity of their data and judgements immediately becomes questionable if they stand out.
- **Lack of discriminative ability:** sub-prime mortgages rated at BBB became investment grade when aggregated into CDOs issued by major investment banks like Goldman Sachs, with whom the agencies had a cosy relationship.
- **Inaccuracy:** the downgrading of US Treasury debt by S&P in August 2011 was based on a forecast made by S&P analysts which had an error of $2 trillion compared to the US government's own data.

The failure of the intermediaries in the 2007/8/9 crisis underlines the major failing – that the directors of the finance companies involved had no handle on the risks that the businesses they were entrusted with were running. Turner's Review concluded that the 'complexity of the measures used to manage and determine risk … made it increasingly difficult for top management and boards to assess and exercise judgement over the risks being taken'.

In a book published in 2010,[27] based on a series of lectures he gave to students at the London School of Economics, Howard Davies, a former chairman of the FSA during the heyday of bank growth at the beginning of the century, identified thirty-eight possible causes of the failure. He was unable to conclude which of the thirty-eight (which ranged from 'auditors' at one end of the alphabet to the effect of 'video games' at the other) were responsible for the problem. But he did have this to say about corporate governance and the non-executive directors of the banks and financial institutions:

> it is difficult to see a justification for placing much greater reliance on boards primarily composed of part-time independent directors in bolstering defences against future bouts of severe financial instability.

---

[27] Davies, *Financial Crisis.*

Boards of directors, and the non-executives who sit on them, are the first bulwark in the traditionalist view of corporate governance. With criticism like that, the obvious question becomes 'Then what purpose do they serve?'.

Walker's reforms suggested switching responsibility away from the boards of directors and encouraging institutional shareholders to reassert their involvement through a 'stewardship code'. This proposal, although adopted and promoted by the government, gives rise to considerable problems of insider information and conflict of interest. To take just one illustration of the conflict, how should a major investment fund react to fresh inside information in a 'stewardship conversation' with senior directors that an investee company is going through bad times that were previously unknown by the market? If it sells its investments in pursuit of its obligations to maximise the return on money investors have paid in insurance premiums, endowment premiums, pension contributions, ISAs, bonds and so on, it will be breaking the law. And on the other hand, conducting conversations where the information is not detailed, focused and pertinent will be a waste of time.

The case for ringfencing

Of course it's right to ringfence rogue universals

Ringfencing is relevant, however, because it addresses what is now the biggest danger of all: rogue universal banks. In the FT's round-table on the report this week, the finance director of RBS stated that: 'If you look at who failed in the crisis it wasn't the broad, universal banks – there's a diversification benefit of having a full range of products and services. [T]he ringfence will potentially cause a loss of some of those benefits. If this was really making the system safer and sounder, then why are the rating agencies putting the banks on notice of potential downgrade actions?'

In the real world, three universal banks failed – Citigroup, UBS and RBS itself. But they did not collapse, as Lehman did. This was only because policymakers did not dare to let them do so. They were 'too big to fail'. If banks with combined balance sheets ten times those of Lehman had collapsed, we would now be in another great depression.

Again, the main reason why UK banks risk 'potential downgrade' is that they might be resolved without taxpayer support. It is because the provision of retail banking cannot be interrupted without causing gigantic damage, while global universal banks are too complex to resolve swiftly, that taxpayers remain on the hook. This must end. The combination of the measures in the report, with steps taken elsewhere, will move us a long way in this direction, though yet more capital would help, as well.

Now turn to the view that the proposals are damaging. Much attention was attracted by the report's estimate that the costs to banks might be £4bn–£7bn a year. But at least half of this (probably much more) is due to the withdrawal of implicit fiscal guarantees – or subsidies – principally from investment banking. Who argues that taxpayers should subsidise these activities? Some will bleat about 'level playing fields'. My response is that if France wishes to put French taxpayers at risk, that is its folly. Again, some argue that the ringfence will damage the City. As the ICB's Interim Report showed, the role of British banks in the City is quite modest. The City is an entrepot, not an arena for national champions.

A more significant, though mistaken, argument is that the higher costs imperil the economy. To this there are three answers. First, lending to business or even the domestic non-financial economy, is a small part of the banks' balance sheets: subsidising the whole, in fond hope of favouring the part, is folly. Second, the connection between credit expansion and sustainable economic growth is, as we can all see, not close. Third, ringfencing will create entities that have to focus on the UK economy, as critics want.

The third line of objection is that these recommendations are toothless. I disagree. The ringfence is not a feeble compromise. It combines the benefits of separation with the benefits of a universal bank.

Full separation suffers from two objections. First, non-financial corporations need the services of both retail and investment banks. This makes a big overlap inevitable. Second, while diversification's benefits can be exaggerated, the investment bank will sometimes rescue a failed retail bank. This advantage ought to be retained.

Three years ago on Thursday, Lehman collapsed. The lesson taken was that no systemically important bank should fail – one applied to the giant universal banks. That is intolerable. Banks must be able to lose vast sums and, if they still fail, be resolved smoothly. This is impossible for an internally undivided universal bank. The ringfence should transform this, so imposing market disciplines. That must be right.

Source: M. Wolf, *Financial Times*, 15 September 2011

The case against ringfencing

Taming the banks: long overdue or utter folly?

The Vickers report is elegantly argued, long and detailed. It has been welcomed in official quarters. But its proposals risk damaging a vital sector of the UK's economy, hitting tax revenue and employment. Moreover, it does not achieve total bank safety. Its main target is the universal bank model, the combination of commercial and investment banking. But a well managed universal bank can be perfectly safe – something that is not fully recognised – and while the commission recommends increased regulation, relying on regulation without good management does not guarantee safe banking.

The report does not address the serious worries now besetting the European financial sector, which result not from mistakes by bankers so much as blunders by European Union governments in the management of the euro. Its remit is the more remote future.

The report is sound when dealing with competition. As to the rest I remain sceptical. The ringfencing proposal involves much detailed regulation. But there is an inherent problem with this approach. When governments decide that retail depositors must not lose money and that some banks are too big to be allowed to fail, regulation becomes essential, and the importance of sound management is diminished.

When regulation governs conduct it is this that sets the limits of behaviour, rather than reliance on prudent commercial judgment. It follows that when the regulations prove defective, as in 2007, trouble arises. I had hoped the report would prioritise the need for a serious incentive for prudent management. The ringfenced part will remain subject to commercial risk, it is true, but this goes only part of the way.

The change to ringfenced retail (or 'commercial', which is a better description) bank subsidiaries will be expensive. Much more capital will be required and banks will have to pay more for deposits overall, which is not good news for the economy. The new rules will also prevent banks from providing a convenient and economic service to many companies. Imagine a company has won a five year contract requiring the purchase of US components. To eliminate the exchange risk it needs to purchase dollars at a fixed rate for gradual drawdown over the period. A transaction to provide this seems to be prohibited within the ringfence. The same is the case where a company wants the bank to issue to investors, on its behalf, a five-year US dollar note with an option to repay earlier, to run alongside its borrowings from the bank.

The report aims to keep retail banking safe within the ringfence. But even retail banking involves risk. Deposits must be lent out if the bank is to earn the margin needed to sustain the operation, and some loans may go wrong. Not so long ago, crises that had nothing to do with investment banking engulfed whole elements of the sector. The US thrift industry in the 1980s and the Secondary Banking crisis of the 1970s in Britain are examples. The idea that ringfencing provides total safety is an illusion.

The proposals will damage London's competitive position. They will be expensive and they are not likely to be followed elsewhere. There must be universal bankers in Frankfurt rubbing their hands.

Commentators speak loosely about going back to Glass-Steagall. But the Glass-Steagall Act was introduced to deal with a problem that no longer exists: the distribution of fraudulent securities to uninformed customers. It was abolished because customers wanted the services universal banks can provide. This is to be reversed.

The government's commitment to legislate in this parliament is unfortunate: though the changes lie far ahead, it has instantly altered the international view of London's attractions. Maybe the authorities want to make the banking sector a smaller proportion of the economy; if so, they should take the long haul of boosting the rest of the economy.

Source: M. Jacomb, *The Financial Times*, 13 September 2011

Conclusions

In most situations systemic governance acts as the safety-net for deficiencies in the other forms of governance situated internally in companies. Appropriate procedural measures, mandated by the law, form the foundation for behavioural governance, which can be policed, to some extent, by activist shareholders. Structural governance – company culture – should ensure that procedural and behavioural governance are effectively secured to each other. The auditors, brokers, journalists and regulators are there to catch instances of when such primary dimensions of governance fail, and bring to the attention of shareholders the prospects of misbehaviour of some sort.

In the case of the financial system, the systemic dimension of governance assumes much greater importance because of the pervasive characteristics of the financial system in respect of the wider economy.

In the 2007–8 financial crisis it was not just the internal governance of the financial institutions which failed – mostly the behavioural elements but also in some measure the procedural and structural dimensions too – but the entire systemic structure of governance. The need to review the three elements of governance in the financial sector was accepted as soon as the huge amounts of funding were poured into the banks in immediate rescue funds and the succession of 'Quantitative Easings' that followed. Politicians, the public and the regulators all agreed that the same thing must never be allowed to happen again.

The Turner Review paved the way for a consideration of fundamental reform which the Walker Review failed to pursue. The Walker Review must be regarded, therefore, as an example of a crisis having gone to waste. The IBC's recommendations were exactly right in calling for a ringfence around the 'retail' elements of the banks. The unassailable logic of this recommendation (see text box containing Martin Wolf's justification of the report's recommendations) was amply demonstrated only three days after the publication of the report when UBS announced that 'unauthorised trades' on its Delta One desk (the part of the bank which trades in derivatives where the price of the original asset and the derived asset are in lock step, with very limited optionality) had brought about a €2 billion loss in the third quarter of its year.[28] The circumstances of the loss appeared to be almost identical to those which cost SocGen €4.9 billion in 2008[29] and undisclosed losses at Nomura bank in 1997[30] and similar to those experienced by Barings in 1995. It will be remembered that the losses which Leeson incurred in bringing down Barings were much smaller: the scale of the UBS loss was roughly a third of the total cost alleged to be the price for *all* the UK-based 'universal' banks moving to a ringfenced structure.

These unauthorised trades are therefore not isolated incidents and their continued appearance indicates that the governance structures – procedural, behavioural and structural – of the banks are far from watertight. Senior managers and directors can have little understanding of the theory of such operations, and still less of the detail of individual positions in respect of the exposure of their banks. One commentator, Terry Smith, the chairman of Tullett Prebon (an independent broker), remarked on the UBS fraud that 'Management doesn't understand what's going on in the Delta One desks. If you sat down with a bank CEO and asked them to explain to what happens ... they couldn't give you an accurate answer because they don't understand.'[31] If the procedural, behavioural and structural elements of governance in the financial sector are inadequate then the systemic dimension must be strong enough to take the strain. It was not in 2007–8, and little appears to have been done to strengthen it (with one major exception – see below).

Yet the IBC's recommendations were couched in an eight-year horizon of change – allowing plenty of space for many more of the type of losses recorded at UBS and rendering stakeholders – the taxpayer – at risk for, at least, that period.

---

[28] T. Alloway and I. Kaminska, 'UBS loss throws light on "synthetic" problem', *Financial Times*, 4 October 2011.

[29] S. Daneshkhu, 'Kerviel found guilty in SocGen scandal', *Financial Times*, 5 October 2010.

[30] 'Familiar sins', *The Economist*, 13 March 1997.

[31] M. Murphy, K. Burgess and S. Jones, 'UBS trader held over $2bn loss', *Financial Times*, 15 September 2011; Terry Smith had been sacked in 1992 by his then employer UBS for writing a report critical of listed companies' accounting practices.

The conclusion must be that the systemic aspects of the governance of the financial sector – which trades in a single, overwhelmingly homogenous, commodity distinguished only by the smallest of individual characteristics and on which we are all dependent – have not yet been adequately addressed in the three reviews that have taken place.

But if the reviews leave much to be desired then there is still some hope through one of the less-heralded structural changes in the machinery of regulation that has already taken place. The changes that have been introduced in the UK with the break up of the FSA into two parts – one of which will be absorbed by the Bank of England – may go some way to overcoming the problem of 'regulatory lag'.

The creation of a Financial Policy Committee (FPC) (a sub-committee of the Court of Governors of the Bank of England) is a significant strategic step in the long and quiet struggle for power over economic regulation waged between the Treasury and the Bank.

The FPC's remit – contained in *The Blueprint for Financial Regulation Reform* published in the summer of 2011 – may well attack some of the institutional blind-spots that allowed the FSA to plough on with its pre-existing stance until it got hit head-on by the collapsing banks.

The new FPC will, if the final structure remains as the published proposals, use policy levers and regulatory tools to manage systemic risks in order to influence, recommend and direct activity. It may do this by a number of measures which may include any of the following:

a.   Creating a counter-cyclical capital buffer in firm's balance sheets, that may exceed the Basel or Solvency obligations.

b.   Varying risk weightings applied to a firm's asset exposures.

c.   Limiting operational gearing in individual cases.

d.   Enhancing liquidity requirements.

e.   Requiring firms to provide against prospective future lending losses.

f.   Increasing collateral requirements.

g.   Adding to disclosure requirements.

h.   Requiring stress tests to be conducted.

The FPC's role is therefore forward-looking and anticipatory and may go some way to providing the horizon-scanning function that the FSA so obviously lacked in terms of the stance of its response to the crisis.

PART 4

GOVERNANCE AND REGULATION

CHAPTER 9

The company and the stock market

This chapter will consider the following issues:

- how well stock exchanges actually acquit their primary function of mobilising the financial resources of many small savers to supply large amounts of capital for industry and commerce;
- how shareholders are then treated – in terms of corporate governance issues raised by traditionalist theories of governance;
- whether the market mechanisms founded on the traditionalist theories acquit their supposed functions in terms of efficiency of resource allocation.

Introduction

As with other aspects of the traditionalist theories of governance in previous chapters, this chapter will contend that the traditionalist, conventional theoretical descriptions of what markets do and how they support procedural, behavioural and structural governance are different from how stock markets work in practice. This is mostly because the traditionalist view starts from the assumption of two problematic positions: first, it employs the conceit that the financial market is close to 'perfection' in the economic sense and second, it assumes that all trades are undertaken by potential long-term holders of shares – in other words that all shareholders are investors, in the sense that they have some concept of stewardship at heart based on the privileges of ownership. We have already seen that the concept of the share in a listed company conferring what would normally be recognised as 'ownership' is a specious one: possession of a share in a listed company is effectively a limited ticket to participate in some uncertain financial benefits with extremely limited associated rights to receipt of backward-looking information. Stock markets conflate the very different attitudes of both trader and investor and try to impose obligations on the resulting composite which simply do not fit the reality of the market.

The last two chapters have concentrated on the problems of inadequate governance of the financial sector and their consequences and built on the argument of previous chapters in suggesting that existing descriptions of how corporate governance works are flawed. The financial sector's collective collapse is probably the most egregious example of the failings of corporate governance in the last fifty years and the starkness of its effects has been used, in the last two chapters, to illuminate the problems of inadequate governance – partly brought about by an inadequate theoretical underpinning of governance concepts.

Given the size and effect of the financial sector's failings it is impossible to disregard the financial sector in discussing the current state of corporate governance, since it exemplifies in exaggerated form much of the failure of corporate governance overall – and in particular the gap between how traditionalist theories hold how governance should work and what actually happens. Some aspects of governance across the entirety of the economy are illuminated by the experience of the financial sector (the problems of payment by bonus, cultural failings, structural governance weaknesses operating down through organisations, behavioural governance failings). Some issues perhaps are less marked in the non-financial sector (the issue of individual directorial competence, certain over-arching systemic issues), but highlighting the failures of the financial sector should not allow general issues of corporate governance failings, which affect all sectors of the listed market, to be eclipsed.

But while some of these failings are the consequence of flaws in governance in the procedural and behavioural dynamics of individual companies, some are also due to the problems of systemic shortcomings in the process by which shareholders can exercise their (supposed) power. This power has three variants, typified by the title of a book written over twenty years ago by Albert Hirschman,[1] discussing how individuals respond to institutional decline. Shareholders can 'voice' their concerns in the hope of effecting change – indicate satisfaction with the situation of their investments in companies by exhibiting 'loyalty' or indicate unhappiness by making for the 'exit' and selling their shares to another party.

Once companies are listed on the main market their behaviour is a matter for the consciences of the directors and four other factors: the strength of their own systems of procedural, behavioural and structural governance; the sanctions that shareholders may be able to impose through the articles; the protections to shareholders offered by the market regulations and the law – the systemic dimension of governance; and the dynamics of the sale and purchase of shares.

This would seem to be enough. Certainly some companies appear to find the burden of such regulations insupportable and leave the market: the total number of companies whose shares are listed on AIM, for instance, has fallen for each of the past four years (after reaching a high point of 1,694 companies in 2007) and not all of these losses are due to transfer to the main market or as a result of takeover by other companies.

---

[1] A. Hirschman, *Exit, Voice and Loyalty: Responses to Decline in Firms, Organizations and States* (Cambridge, MA: Harvard University Press, 1990).

Many companies have left claiming that the benefits of listing were not worth the cost.[2] But there are numerous instances in listed companies (some of these are used as examples in this chapter) where the combined weight of all the regulatory factors is unable to prevent either open abuse or behaviour that fits merely the letter of the law or severe disadvantage to a group (as opposed to a formal *class*) of shareholders.

This is partly because the governance mechanisms, law and regulation in combination are not directed towards the right ends because the theoretical issues which underpin them are incorrect or inadequate. Every company that has its shares listed on a public Stock Exchange is subject to the practical effect of the impact of the traditionalist theories of governance that are embedded in corporate governance codes (the vast majority of 'unlisted', smaller, companies are not so affected since their governance is a matter of private rather than public concern). Consequently, if there are shortcomings in the traditionalist theories they will affect the interests of shareholders and the behaviour of companies across *the entire range* of Stock Exchange listings. It is therefore incumbent on any discussion of corporate governance operations to examine how these theories hold when applied to the operations of listed companies in terms of their activities on Stock Exchanges and whether the mechanisms of corporate governance that are founded on relationships described by the traditionalist theories, including the economic purpose of stock markets, work properly.

This then resolves into three considerations. First, how well Stock Exchanges actually acquit their primary function of mobilising the financial resources of many small savers to supply large amounts of capital for industry and commerce. Second, how those shareholders are then treated – in governance terms – even at the remove of simple possession of an insurance policy or contribution to a pension fund. Third, whether the market mechanisms founded on the traditionalist theories acquit their supposed functions in enabling shareholders to achieve an efficient economic allocation of resources.

Wrapped around all these considerations is the concept of shareholder value which expresses itself partly through the market for corporate control – enabling the effective mobilisation of shareholder voice and/or loyalty and the possibility of effective shareholder exit.

The purposes of stock markets

There are two purposes of a stock market under traditionalist theories of governance: first, to permit companies to raise fresh capital (for a variety of purposes, not simply for growth or expansion); and second, to provide a potential market in the shares

---

[2] M. Stothard, 'Delisted Aim groups cite financial stress', *Financial Times*, 2 January 2012; and K. Burgess, 'Pond life', *Financial Times*, 24 July 2012.

of those companies for investors. The implications of these purposes are themselves threefold: first, markets are available for existing investors to trade shares between themselves, depending on their perceptions of value; second, new purchasers are able to enter the market by buying shares from existing owners; and third, those shareholders who wish to sell are able to thereby reduce their holdings easily or even exit the market place completely.

Markets can then be categorised as either 'primary markets' where new shares are available for the first time, sold on the expectation of some combination of capital growth or yield, or 'secondary markets' describing markets for *all* other transactions, where the movement up or down of individual and collective share prices is subject to the impact of perceptions of anticipated value. Regardless of the type of market in which transactions take place, shareholders measure the attractiveness of their investments relative to other companies and to other methods of investing, using earnings per share information (for capital growth) and dividend yield (for income) as primary methods of evaluation inside a given risk profile. The normal stock market is therefore a combination of both functions; it is both a primary and a secondary market. Different markets may cater for different types of investor in terms of offering shares that exhibit mostly growth prospects or income prospects, since incoming shareholders are usually attracted to buying shares in individual companies by the prospect of either capital growth or a dividend – or some traded-off combination of both.

The achievement of the objectives of the individual shareholder – to maximise his or her wealth by accurate valuation of risk and asset value – are wholly dependent upon two things: valid possession of the shares and the fulfilment of financial anticipations, with the latter being brought about (mostly) by appropriate procedural governance in the companies. The fulfilment of these conditions therefore requires an ordered market (to validate possession), operated in an honest and transparent fashion, with costs of dealing that are not disproportionate to the market value; and also requires shareholders to be provided with accurate and reliable information on a frequent basis, to enable assessments of value of sufficient utility to enable trading between parties. These are obviously issues of *procedural* governance.

For these conditions to fully operate a further set of characteristics is required to ensure that the market operates effectively once the framework requirements have been set. These are: *liquidity* – the existence of willing buyers and willing sellers to engage in trade at some price which matches their individual current expectations of value; *trust* – the belief that valid ownership can be achieved as a result of a transaction between buyer and seller mediated by another party; and *confidence* – the understanding that the market is run in a clean fashion for the benefit of those entering the market to trade and not for the benefit of market operators. Again, these last three conditions approximate to the core characteristics of efficient *procedural* governance.

From this recitation of characteristics it can be seen that many of the procedural and behavioural elements of corporate governance are intimately bound up with the existence of a sophisticated stock market. This is of course hardly surprising at one level. But it also goes some way to explain why corporate governance codes have been developed in the context of the structures of listed companies, and why the British approach to corporate governance has been one of 'principle' rather than 'rule'. It fits better with the cultural, legal and historical operation of the stock market in the UK, where governance processes were those of the club variant rather than the legalistic.[3]

The physical structure and dynamics of the market are neutral to the market outcomes under such 'perfect' conditions: details of the market's precise form diminish into insignificance if the perfect conditions are obtained. Or rather, if the complete conditions of the perfect market existed, the dynamics of the market *would be* neutral and its physical structure *would be* irrelevant. But since no perfect market has ever existed or is ever likely to exist (outside the minds of economic theorists), markets require regulation if the conditions that approximate to 'perfection' in the economic sense are to be even approached and maintained. If not, the interests of the many will be subordinated to those of the few – those who have the power to manipulate the marketplace. This necessity to regulate the market makes it intrusive as a factor in the market's operation: instead of acting as a neutral background to trading it becomes part of the structure of trading, whose characteristics must be taken into account.

However, at the same time as this happens, the existence of the rules which a well-regulated, and liquid, market requires, also promotes the development of more sophisticated share ownership strategies beyond simple buying and selling. Sophisticated market operators move beyond simple possession for the long-term financial benefits of ownership into areas where short-horizon trading becomes the primary method of making profit.

Without attempting to be exhaustive, these types of activity include:
- using the market merely as a vehicle for reaping capital growth by dodging in and out of shares as they rise and fall;
- buying shares for streams of income (dividend) alone;
- or taking advantage of wrinkles in the real-world imperfection of markets through the mechanisms of arbitrage and short-selling.

The common factor between all these forms of trade is that there is no direct interest on the part of the trader involved, in long-term ownership of shares in the companies they trade in – and no interest in how well the companies are run over the long or medium term. In short, issues of agency, shareholder involvement and good stewardship are irrelevant to the trader. In fact, as far as one particular and very

---

[3] Moran, *The Regulatory State*; Kynaston, *City of London*.

specialised group of traders are concerned – the short-sellers – issues of good stewardship are positive obstructions to their business of making money, since they want the market to realise that there is some issue – some failing – which detracts from the value of an individual company's shares as currently perceived by the market. (The market of course is neutral in this regard and the existence of a regulated market implies no concept of particular trading behaviour – nor equally of any concept of stewardship.)

Taken to its ultimate level of objectivity, one investment strategy – that of using companies as temporary vehicles for generating wealth by trading in shares on a purely short-term basis – becomes similar to backing horses at a race-course. The trader (as opposed to the investor) uses 'form' (historical record) as a guide but is always subject to the vagaries of individual race (economic) conditions, the 'going' (market sentiment), the skill of the jockey (management) and the comparative strengths of the competition (other, faster horses or better jumpers on the day). The amount of information available for analysis is probably greater for the share trader than for the punter but the fact remains that the outcomes are still uncertain – if they were not then no-one would ever lose money in investing in the stock market (and so the impact of risk becomes evidently significant again as a factor in governance).

As noted above, the point about all these strategies are that they do not necessarily conform with the traditionalist view of the stock market's purpose – that unstated but crucial assumption that the stock market investor is *not* solely interested in making rapid returns over the short term but also has a long-term interest in the fortunes of one particular company or a set of companies. Traditionalist theories implicitly assume that the shareholder is an investor for the long term and largely disregards the short-term prospect of often moving into another more attractive investment proposition *as an investment strategy in itself*. There is even a distinction – a rather pejorative one – in the names given to the two types of shareholder. The *investor* holds for the long term; the *trader* or *speculator's* horizons are short. The investor might well be concerned with the long-term stewardship of the companies he or she invests in and the *probity of the companies*. For the trader this is a subordinate consideration, taking second place to the *probity of the market*.

Efficient procedural governance is far more important to the trader than behavioural issues: he wants to make sure that stock is registered efficiently and quickly and that settlement and dividend payment systems work as they should. Whether there is an effective nomination committee, or a Senior Independent Non-Executive Director, or the gender balance of the board conforms to good practice in the companies which he trades in and out of is largely irrelevant as a first-order issue. This is a different order of the values of the market from those held by the investor.

The situation of the short-term trader in respect of good corporate governance is akin to the lighthouse problem in economic theory.[4]

The first issue – mobilising capital

Against these general issues then, how well do Stock Exchanges actually acquit their primary function of mobilising the financial resources of many small savers to supply large amounts of capital for industry and commerce?

As has already been alluded to, the primary market function of stock markets is the sale of a company's shares for the first time. This can itself be split into two sub-divisions: the first is raising money for companies coming on to the market for the first time; the second is raising money for existing companies whose shares have already been traded through the sale of new, *additional* shares.

Premium and standard listings

Premium listing

A premium listing is only available to equity shares issued by trading companies and closed and open-ended investment entities such as unit trusts and REITs (real estate investment trusts). Issuers with a premium listing are required to meet the UK's 'super-equivalent' rules.

Standard listing

Standard listings cover issuance of company shares, Global Depositary Receipts (GDRs), debt and securitised derivatives that are required to comply with EU minimum requirements. A standard listing allows issuers to access the Main Market by meeting EU harmonised standards only rather than the UK 'super-equivalent' requirements.

Prior to October 2009 when the FSA introduced new rules, only companies incorporated outside the UK were eligible for a standard listing. Now standard listings are open to all companies regardless of domicile.

Super equivalent obligations

A premium listing of equity demonstrates that the company meets London's standard of regulation based on the requirements of the UK Listing Authority

---

[4] R. H. Coase, 'The lighthouse in economics', *Journal of Law and Economics*, 17(2) (1974).

(UKLA) and often referred to as a 'super-equivalent' standard in that it meets or exceeds the requirements of other EU listing authorities, by virtue of the obligation to adhere to the UK Corporate Governance Code; Model Code on Directors Dealings; pre-emption obligations; and stated course of business. The EU MiFID directive of 2008 (2008/10/EU) required that super-equivalence be phased out to produce a level playing field in listing requirements

Under the Listing Rules, prior shareholder approval or notice is required for Premium listed companies to enter into a transaction outside the ordinary course of business and with certain 'related parties'. The class tests are used to compare the size of the listed company with the size of the transaction in question. The results of the class tests are expressed as percentage ratios that are then used to categorise the transaction in accordance with Chapters 10 and 11 of the Listing Rules as a Class 1, Class 2, or Class 3 transaction, a reverse takeover or a related party transaction.

The class tests are:
1.   The assets test.
2.   The profits test.
3.   The consideration to market capital test.
4.   The gross capital test.

Transaction classes

For **Class 1 transactions**, which produce a result of 25 per cent under any of the class tests, the Listing Rules require an announcement to a regulatory information service, an explanatory circular (known as a Class 1 circular) and shareholder approval of the transaction.

For **Class 2 transactions**, which result in a percentage ratio of 5 per cent or more, but less than 25 per cent under any one of the class tests, the Listing Rules require notification to a regulatory information service of prescribed details of the transaction without delay after the terms of the transaction are agreed.

A **Class 3 transaction**, the size of which results in a percentage ratio of less than 5 per cent, does not require announcement to a regulatory information service unless the company releases any details to the public or, in the case of an acquisition, the consideration includes the issue of shares which will be listed.

The distinction between standard and premium listings is to allow companies originally listed with exchanges in the EU the right to 'passport' their listings directly, as required under the Market Directive, at the governance level to which they originally subscribed – that is, below the super-equivalence level which UK listed companies have ordinarily had to meet.

The distinction is significant because one of the major functions – possibly the primary economic function – of a stock market in advanced economies, as noted already, is the collective mobilisation of funds from modest individual savings to supply businesses with the cash resources they require in order to grow. If the health of the economy is to be maintained, there has to be a constant flow of new companies with new products addressing new markets. Consequently, there has to be a mechanism for directing finance to those companies to enable them to develop – as well as access to new funds for companies with existing listings, which prove themselves to be able to validate the expectations of their shareholders. The Stock Exchanges in the UK have been declining in their ability over a long period of time to do this.[5] For most companies, retained earnings have been and remain a much more significant way of generating investment capital, thereby undercutting some of the rationale for claiming that there is a direct link between resource allocation and shareholder primacy[6] and, since the issues of corporate governance are founded on quoted company characteristics, this has profound implications for the structures of corporate governance.

Over time the increasing levels of stringency required in the preparation of information to enable new or young companies to list their shares – stringency required partly to ensure good governance in itself and partly to ensure that the market's reputation is maintained – have reduced the flow of businesses using the market to access this form of funding. The latest edition of the Listing Rules of the London Stock Exchange (now published by the FSA) runs to many hundreds of paragraphs on its website, with further hundreds of paragraphs in other supporting documents which cover the Model Code on Directors' Dealings, Continuing Obligations and the UK Corporate Governance Code. Listing a company's shares is now a very complicated, and costly, process.

The difficulties experienced by young companies, seeking to raise capital for expansion, in coping with the expensive and burdensome burgeoning regulations of listing their shares on a public market were recognised formally over three decades ago in 1980, when to help reduce the cost and effort of listing – and to capture income for its member firms from a part of the market which was being developed by over-the-counter/matched-bargain specialists – the Stock Exchange created the Unlisted Securities Market (this was superseded by the Alternative Investment Market (AIM) in 1996).

Over the past forty to fifty years the development of this thicket of regulation has choked off applications to the market. The pattern of entrants to the main market over the thirteen years 1998 to 2011 is shown in Table 9.1.

---

[5] LSE Statistics for new issues, Main Market and AIM, www.londonstockexchange.com/statistics/markets/markets.htm.

[6] Cheffin, *Corporate Ownership*, Chapter 3.

Table 9.1	Numbers of companies on the Alternative Investment Market 1995–2011		
Year	Admissions	Total companies	Of which UK based
95	120	121	118
96	131	252	235
97	100	308	286
98	68	312	291
99	96	347	325
2000	265	524	493
2001	162	629	587
2002	147	704	654
2003	146	754	694
2004	294	1024	905
2005	399	1379	1179
2006	338	1634	1330
2007	197	1694	1347
2008	87	1550	1233
2009	30	1293	1052
2010	76	1195	966
2011	67	1143	918

Source: London Stock Exchange website, www.londonstockexchange.com/statistics/markets/markets.htm

On AIM net numbers have consistently fallen as companies have left the Market, some citing costs and procedures that are too burdensome for the benefit accruing. By the end of 2011[7] the junior market had raised less than £4.3 billion during the year for both its new *and* existing members – a lower figure than even that recorded during the 2008 credit crunch. There were at the end of 2011 about 1,150 companies with their shares listed on AIM, down from the peak of almost 1,700 recorded in 2007. But what is worse than all this is that the index of share value – the FTSE AIM share index – which started life at 1,000 in 1996 had declined to 678 by the end of 2011, having touched 3,000 at the height of the boom in dot.com shares in 2000.[8] With over 50 per cent of the shares of AIM companies now in institutional hands the market is atrophying, and possibly dying. It is certainly not fulfilling its primary economic purpose.

But even before this, the record of the UK exchanges (before 1965 there were separate regional exchanges and the London Stock Exchange, all operating under different regulations), in respect of their supposed primary economic function, had been poor for many years previously. *The Economist* reported in 1953 that 'in the last five years there has been no net personal investment on the Stock Exchange'.[9] Occasioned by the effects of their own regulatory structures, national tax regimes

---

[7] LSE Statistics for new issues.   [8] *Ibid.*
[9] J. Kay and M. King, *The British Tax System* (Oxford University Press, 1978), p. 375.

and government policy in respect of the priority given to national debt over company funding, the small company and the start-up had found it difficult to raise capital for thirty years before the formal creation of a 'junior' stock market, with easier and less costly access to a listing and lighter regulatory requirements in terms of continuing obligations to the Stock Exchange's rules.

During the Second World War, priority had been given to the State's needs for funds to finance the war effort, so the Treasury had effectively vetoed company cash calls, partly accounting for the worn-out nature of British capital stock post-War. In 1947, the London Stock Exchange (LSE) had begun to require auditors to report on ten years worth of profit statements, effectively discouraging applications that had a shorter span of information available. It will be remembered (from Chapter 3) that it was not until the passing of the Companies Act 1947 that the use of secret reserve accounting was made illegal (and that this was largely as a result of the Royal Mail Line case of sixteen years previously).

After the war, the need to rebuild State finances, the imposition of consequent taxation regimes and other austerity measures meant that the private investor diminished in importance as a source of funding, being supplanted by institutional investors who collected the savings of the many through tax-efficient assurance and pension funds and then re-invested them. According to evidence given to the Wilson Committee in 1977 by the London Stock Exchange, 'The personal sector has been, for over twenty years, a consistent net seller of securities at a fairly constant rate in constant price terms'.[10]

Supplanting the private investor with the massive funding firepower of the institutions collecting insurance premiums and pension fund contributions then gave rise to another problem – that of the 'Wall of Money'. Institutions were collecting so much money – over a million pounds a day in 1959 (a huge sum in terms of the value of the currency of the time)[11] – because consecutive tax regimes promoted *personal* thrift through concessions on *institutional* saving. There was little in the way of consumer goods for people to spend money on until the domestic boom of the 1960s and exchange controls bottled up free cash that might have been used abroad. As a result, the institutions had difficulty in getting rid of their inflow on a selective basis into investment assets. As one senior fund manager recounted, they were 'not always in a position to implement what might be described as a theoretical investment policy. Their decisions were governed to some extent by what investments were available'.[12] Pension funds had only begun to embrace wholeheartedly the use of equities in the 1950s[13] when the rise of inflation and the static

---

[10] Cheffin, *Corporate Ownership*, p. 343.   [11] Cheffin, *Corporate Ownership*, p. 349.   [12] *Ibid.*
[13] The policy of using equities instead of gilts was developed by George Ross Goobey as noted earlier.

nature of yields on gilts offered negative rates of return. Consequently, with the sheer volume of money that had to be invested, the market for shares became introverted in that increases in value in shares were prompted by the rising supply of money rather than the rising value of returns from companies, as investors bid against themselves for a limited pool of assets. As a consequence of this, coupled with the prevailing attitudes to the respective roles of investment managers and industrial managers in the corporate governance dance – very different to those that exist now – there was a lack of any interest in enforcing good governance in investments. Even by the time that the Wilson Committee reported in 1980, it felt able to excuse the institutional lethargy over intervention by saying that 'they [the investment houses] were still feeling their way, which may inhibit them intervening at an early stage'.[14]

However, even though the prevailing culture and social attitudes to the accretion of personal wealth were very different then, plenty of instances of poor behaviour among company managers can be adduced – as the list of corporate scandals in the preface shows.

So a paradox existed (and continues). There was plenty of money available for investment but regulatory considerations, inert attitudes among investment professionals and social/cultural *mores* stifled the operation of the market. The market turned in on itself and became an investment outlet in its own right with the companies whose shares it represented supplying information on which investment judgements were made, but with company fortunes effectively being a secondary exercise to that of seeing which shares would go up and which would go down by the sheer weight of speculation.

The second issue – treating shareholders equally

The record of the stock market mobilising cash to feed growing businesses is apparently not good then. Could this be linked to the issues of corporate governance shortcomings? Once a company's shares have been listed how are shareholders then treated in terms of the corporate governance issues raised by traditionalist theories of governance?

In the market and economic environment of the 1950s, 1960s and 1970s, somnolent institutional shareholders deferred to industrial managers and then when changes were introduced of necessity, to prevent gross abuse, the sudden (supposed) increase in regulatory cost was criticised by industrial managers as being burdensome. Industry wanted the City's (public's) money but didn't want the (protective) costs associated with it.[15]

---

[14] Cheffin, *Corporate Ownership*.
[15] Staff Reporters, 'Fund managers should stay out of boardrooms', *The Independent*, 2 March 2004.

At the outset, as noted above, the large investment institutions were largely inert – more concerned with investing than enforcing standards of governance or goading industrial managers to produce better returns for the companies' nominal owners. (There were of course occasional exceptions, e.g. the removal of Lord (and Lady) Docker from BSA by the other directors of the company with the assistance of the Prudential Assurance as noted in Chapter 1, and the intervention of investment companies during the 'Aluminium Wars'.)

The Aluminium Wars of the 1950s

The phrase 'Aluminium Wars' has usually referred, in recent years, to the murky transfer of State assets to a few rapacious Russian oligarchs. But long before the Soviet Union broke up and the oligarchs fought over the spoils of State industry there were the British Aluminium Wars, fought in the late 1950s over one of the weakened components of the British metal industry. The affair is credited by some observers (Kynaston and Ferguson, for instance) with prompting change in popular and political attitudes towards 'the City' that eventually resulted in the major structural changes of the 1980s.

By the end of the 1950s, the relaxation of the tight grip of monetary policy in the UK allowed the beginnings of a takeover boom in British industry. Sir Charles Clore, the financier and owner of Sears Holdings, in a magazine interview in 1957, remarked that 'the profits earned show that existing assets are not being employed in the fullest capacity. I maintain that neither this country nor any business can afford to have its resources remain stagnant'.

One of the companies that became the target of takeover speculation was British Aluminium. With little investment since before the war years, the company was short of both smelting capacity and cash and led by a board out of touch with change. The chairman of the company was Lord Portal, previously Marshal of the RAF, a brave man and distinguished aviator, but with a patrician view of life; its managing director, Geoffrey Cunliffe was the son of a previous (highly conservative) Governor of the Bank of England. As a defensive move, with its advisers Lazards and Hambros, the company approached ALCOA to talk about partnership, since it became clear that Reynolds Metals, another American company was interested in acquisition, in combination with the British company, Tube Investments which had been brought in as a partner to provide a domestic dimension. Reynolds was advised by Warburgs while TI was advised by Schroders. The two industrial partners made a bid at 78 shillings a share after building up a 10 per cent stake in BA during the summer of 1958.

The BA board responded by announcing that it had already signed a deal with ALCOA for a sale of new shares to ALCOA representing one-third of the increased issued capital of BA, at a price of 60s per share. The deal would therefore take precedence over the bid, according to the company's board.

The City did not think so, however, and a nasty row developed between the major pension funds, which had just begun to take major stakes in industrial companies as a result of the shift to equities; the Bank of England; the respective sets of advisers; and the Treasury. Official (but not political) involvement was significant in a way that would be unthinkable now, with regular meetings of Bank and Treasury officials with both sides to the bid.

An increase in the offer from Reynolds and TI resulted in the first defensive newspaper advertisement against a bid in the UK, but it was so badly handled that it got the board of BA into even more trouble: at one stage Portal dismissively described shareholders as 'people unaware of the mysteries of negotiations between great companies'. The bid proceeded to a full, and unpleasant, fight.

On 12 January 1959, a column appeared in the *Financial Times* (in response to a letter the previous day to *The Times* which had criticised the temerity of newspaper editors in pronouncing on the merits of the bid). The author of the column was the renowned financial journalist Harold Wincott, who took the board of BA to task for their remoteness towards the 'man-in-the-street share-holder' who was 'being pushed around without being told the reason why'. The response of the City to Wincott's broadside was largely dismissive and attracted adverse political comment.

The Reynolds/TI consortium eventually won control but only after a serious amount of damage was done to the reputations of some City banks and the superior attitudes of some British industrialists towards their shareholders.

But by and large the insurance companies arranged their investments in such a way as to avoid a semi-proprietorial role.[16] And in its 1980 report, the Wilson Committee suggested – well before Lord Myners or Derek Higgs – that the investing institutions should bestir themselves and take action against under-performing managements. (Not until the same year was there any general statutory protection against incumbent managers selling shares at different prices to new investors without the agreement of existing shareholders.) Despite such exhortations, it was left to the Mayfair Set – Slater Walker, Hanson, Goldsmith and their protégés – to effect major change in the attitudes of many managers in respect of their own corporate obligations.

[16] Cheffin, *Corporate Ownership*, pp. 347–9.

But by the early 1990s, with the arrival of the committee reports looking into the worst excesses of the corporate culture and after the highwater mark of the lead set by the Mayfair men, the institutions began to exercise their strength. But only for those companies where they perceived there to be some general issue and where principle was also backed by expedience in the higher reaches of the FTSE listings. Sainsbury, Granada and Carlton Communications, and Glaxo Smith Kline (all in 2003) suffered major defeats in terms of their plans, after shareholders balked at nodding through changes to nominations, remuneration or even amalgamation. Each of the events was greeted by the Press as being 'a watershed' in investor-company relationships.[17]

Yet the realities of shareholder-company engagement and the power of shareholders in respect of having their preferences observed collectively are far from ever having tipped over some sort of watershed as more recent events may illustrate, on a number of counts.

First, there is the matter of the relative power of the position of the institutional investors and that of small investors. There is, in law, no distinction between shareholders in a company just as there are no distinctions between directors of a company. Yet, not surprisingly, the power of numbers is significant. Institutional investors holding many thousands or millions of shares will be accorded preferential rights of access to a company's management to discuss the affairs of the company (subject of course to the law regarding insider dealing). The small shareholder has to be content – for the most part – with a brush-off answer from the chairman at the AGM after a glass of warm wine and a curly sandwich. It would be very unlikely that a request from even a party of small shareholders to meet with the finance director or chairman would be sympathetically entertained, as are the requests received from individual institutional investors.

The UK Corporate Governance Code sponsors this type of distinction by actively encouraging the concept of stewardship by large investors, which excludes small shareholders. Regular meetings between institutional shareholders and senior members of the company management are supposed to produce conversations, understandings and actions, the effect of which will then trickle down – supposedly – to the benefit of all shareholders. Except that it does not.

The conversations between institutional investors and company management will remain guarded and private since, at root, institutional investors are concerned only with their own individual investment positions and not with those of all shareholders. Their operating positions are entirely rational – they are making money themselves on the basis of their (superior) investment record, fuelled in part by superior access to information (which they cloak as superior perception and investment ability). The net effect, however, is to create distinctions between shareholders: between those who

---

[17] Cheffin, *Corporate Ownership*, p. 383.

have access to good market and company information and can deal quickly at superior, bulk rates (the institutions) – and the rest.

Ironically, the wilting AIM contains a system which potentially works much more cleanly in terms of attempting to treat all shareholders alike. Under the AIM rule the sponsoring broker – the Nominated Adviser or 'Nomad' – acts as the regulatory agent for the company with money at risk, in terms of fines, if the company does not behave itself by observing the rules and the continuing obligations of listing. Although some of the blur that exists between the undefined functions of broker and market-maker in the senior market exists in greater degree under this arrangement, the shareholders' interests are protected by a resident policeman who can legitimately act as a proxy for their interest – and with some clout, since the Nomad can refuse to sanction a course of action or can resign and effectively take the company's listing with it if it does so. Shareholders on the main market have no such recourse, with only ritualistic and ossified structures of public governance to fall back on.

Much of the cause of the differential treatment of shareholders occasioned by current governance structures is because of the devalued status of the AGM. The Annual General Meeting of public limited companies is supposed to be the forum at which ordinary shareholders can voice their opinions, air their concerns and ask questions of the directors of 'their' companies. The Companies Act 2006 reinforced the significance of an annual general meeting for plcs, even though it was dispensed with for smaller companies. Yet, as anyone who has ever attended a plc general meeting will be aware, they are very heavily stage-managed events, the organisation of the day is designed principally to prevent any form of embarrassment to the board of directors, rather than expose the company's business to shareholder scrutiny. No business is truly conducted at the AGM, they are merely empty formalities where the motions of governance are traipsed through.

This is not surprising, since the whole foundation of the concept of stewardship, as discussed above, is to nip in the bud any form of divergence between the views of institutional investors and incumbent management about the direction of the company. Only foolish or very headstrong management get themselves into trouble at AGMs. The chairman will know before he even enters the meeting that the votes cast by institutional investors will be in favour of the company's (that is, incumbent management) proposals; he will know that he can hide behind all sorts of legal prevarication about revealing valuable detail about the company's activities and that all that he really has to contend with is scrutiny of backward-looking information and formalistic points of procedure which most private shareholders will not have the knowledge, skill or experience to challenge. He (at the time of writing there is no female chairperson of a quoted company) may also have to contend with one or two eccentric shareholders concerned about arcane matters of share registration or customer service, and politely listen to them before he can either shut them up for occupying too much time – or have them ejected from the meeting.

Most small shareholders conspire in this dance: they are not really interested in – or capable of – detailed objective scrutiny and are happy for the chance of a day out. Grasping the complexity of most large companies is well beyond the ability of any but those with large amounts of time at their disposal and substantial knowledge gathered by regular contact with management, which is, of course, why institutional investors employ full-time, highly-qualified staff to research companies in detail.

(In this sense, the reforms of the Companies Act 2006 were directed at exactly the wrong target. By eliminating AGMs for non-plcs – where shareholders usually have much more experience and knowledge about the business and can subject directors to effective scrutiny – shareholder power was eliminated in practice in the vast numerical majority of companies, to join the emasculated shareholder 'power' which still survived in theory, but not in practice, in the quoted company.)

The chairman will also know that if it comes to a showdown about matters like pay, then again, all the aces are held by management. The remuneration report is toothless, subject only to an advisory vote (although this may change during the life of the current Parliament which runs until 2015). If there is sustained complaint the responsibility can be shuffled off on to the backs of the remuneration committee or professional advisers and, if all else fails, the deal is done anyway. Remuneration reports, like all company information presented at the AGM, deal with past matters, the unravelling of which would be very difficult. Once more, this is not a recent development. In 1934, in a judgement in respect of a scheme of arrangement for a bankrupt company (*Re Dorman Long & Co Ltd*), Justice Maugham[18] observed, as an aside, that:

> in the great majority of cases, the proxies given to the directors before the meeting have in effect settled the question of the voting once for all.

There may be occasional exceptions to this pattern of course, the AGMs of smaller companies may well produce embarrassment for the incumbent management (a small property company listed on AIM called Conygar suffered an embarrassing reversal in early 2012 when neither the chairman nor the FD could explain the operation of a generous bonus scheme to shareholders at the AGM).[19] But even the opprobrium generated by remuneration arrangements which attract substantial adverse votes can be ridden through by determined boards – witness the Thomas Cook 'volcanic ash' vote in 2010, where the arrangements were revised to make it easier for the

---

[18] *Re Dorman Long & Co Ltd* [1934] Ch 365 (Chancery Division).
[19] N. Fletcher, 'Shareholder group attacks bonus payments at property group Conygar', *The Guardian*, 5 January 2012.

management to scoop up their bonuses even though targets had not been met,[20] or the political storm over the bonuses awarded to RBS's directors in 2012[21] when the company was cutting staff numbers in its divisions and flying in the face of popular and political sentiment – despite being 83 per cent owned by the State.

Third, there are instances outside the formal arrangements of meetings and discussions where shareholders may find themselves disadvantaged by the actions of a small number of powerful or wealthy or influential shareholders or by the actions of the directors. Just three recent examples of such influence and the consequences for other shareholders are given in the text box below.

Mitchells and Butlers

Mitchells and Butlers was created in 2003 out of the splitting of the previously unified components of the brewer Bass plc into a hotels group and a separate brewing and restaurants company – both then listed.

In 2008 shareholders of Mitchells and Butlers saw nearly £300 million of the asset value of the company wiped off its balance sheet after a disastrous speculation over the group's property assets by the then finance director, Karim Naffah – sanctioned of course by the board – in combination with the property speculator Robert Tchenguiz. The chairman, Sir Roger Carr, resigned as did Naffah. (Carr went on to the chairmanship of Cadbury which was sold to Kraft in 2010 and also to become the President of the CBI; Naffah became managing director of the Rocco Forte Collection group of hotels in 2010.)

In its weakened financial state, but with a substantial property portfolio, the company became a takeover target and three multi-millionaires – Joe Magnier, J. P. McManus and Derrick Smith – took a combined 24 per cent stake in the business. Under the effective control of these investors, the board of the company has been subjected to a merry-go-round of new directors with three chairmen leaving within an eighteen month span. They were later joined as substantial shareholders by Joe Lewis, a currency trader with a colourful past. (Lewis grew up in comparative poverty in London's East End; has a fortune that places him in the top 400 wealthiest people globally; travels the world in his private yacht which houses his £200 million art collection and narrowly escaped death in 1999 when his private helicopter blew up while lifting off, seconds after he disembarked from it.)

---

[20] S. Bowers, 'Thomas Cook investors express anger at high levels of executive pay', *The Guardian*, 8 February 2012.

[21] J. Treanor and H. Stewart, 'Anger at further RBS bonus payouts', *The Guardian*, 28 January 2012.

In the summer of 2011 Lewis made a so-called 'low-ball' (nil-premium) bid, making an offer for the company below the then share price – but this was rejected by the company's board. The share price languished for many months as the company drifted strategically, which share analysts ascribed to the managerial problems. The Stock Exchange sought assurances from the individuals involved that they were not acting in concert but took no further action since it maintained that no rules were broken or obligations to other shareholders infringed.

Mouchel

Mouchel, a consulting engineering company, can date its history back to 1897. In the early years of this millennium it expanded rapidly, acquiring businesses and merging its interest with other smaller operations. The board of directors turned down approaches from Costain, Investec and VT – the last in 2009 which offered 294p per share for the company. However, as an infrastructure contractor to the public sector it was potentially badly hit by the prospect of substantial reductions in public sector spending following the election in 2010, although this did not appear to dent the optimism of the board. By the middle of 2011 the company was beset by public problems however: an 'accounting problem' in respect of an acquisition wiped out the banking covenants; the company took an 'impairment' charge of £41 million against past acquisitions and it became evident that internal spending on accounting systems and property was out of control. The chairman resigned; his successor stayed just four days, having been unable to secure the approval of the banks – and the company effectively put itself up for sale. The share price by this time had declined to less than 15p.

Cadbury

By the end of the twentieth century Cadbury was much more than a confectionery company, with the share price wallowing in the absence of any firm strategic direction and the management lacking any credibility with the City. The company's share register had become very diverse as a result of acquisitions and divestments and the separate floating off of its US beverage interests. In 2008 the company's plan to acquire Wrigley's Gum was frustrated when Mars purchased that company, leaving Cadbury even more strategically vulnerable. In 2009, the chief executive of Kraft foods, Irene Rosenfeld approached informally the chairman of Cadbury, Roger Carr (previously the chairman of M&B among other posts), to discuss a bid and was rebuffed by Carr without the possibility of the offer being discussed with the shareholders of Cadbury.[22] A formal, hostile offer was then made and after a long and acrimonious battle the company was eventually taken into the ownership of Kraft. Kraft then reneged upon assurances which it had given to the Takeover Panel in respect of the maintenance of production of chocolate in the UK.

It would of course be unreasonable to expect that all companies would always be run in a completely uncontentious way and that there would never be any form of controversy over occasional aspects of the behaviour of directors and individual shareholders. Nor is it reasonable to expect standards of behaviour or intelligence in the boards of public companies that are any different from those of society as a whole. If that were the case then the subject of corporate governance would be redundant and the commercial courts would have atrophied long ago.

But the issue is not one of occasional lapses. As the quotation from Justice Maugham in *Re Dorman Long*, which was made over eighty years ago, shows, the effective substance of corporate management, developed from the theory that underlay law and regulation, did not then and does not now accord with the real world. Thus, when the levers based on the theory are pulled to try to effect change, nothing happens because they are not properly connected to the mechanisms of the real world.

The final issue – effective allocation of resources

Regardless of how effectively the Stock Market works overall to mobilise the collective funds of society, or how well it treats the shareholders thereby created, it could still theoretically provide an efficient allocation of resources within its own limitations. So the final question that remains is to ask whether the market mechanisms founded on the traditionalist theories that underpin corporate governance, all dependent upon the shareholder seen as owner, acquit their supposed functions in terms of efficiency of resource allocation.

The focus of the traditionalist theories is on the investor – using the term to indicate a long-term holder of shares. But the operation of the modern market favours the short attention span of the trader over the patient, distant-horizon view of the investor, both in operational and technological senses. The market is therefore trying continually to reconcile a number of different motivations and contain those within a paradigm that is predicated on one type of investment behaviour.

---

[22] J. Wiggins, 'The inside story of the Cadbury takeover', *Financial Times*, 12 March 2012.

Operationally, those with money to place are constantly scanning the market for better opportunities to enhance their return. (In fact, some classes of shareholder – trustees – are legally required to do so and fail in their obligations if they do not.) Fund managers are subject to increasing scrutiny on the basis of performance league tables; internally to their organisations they may be subject to even more short-term review than the information which is published to potential customers. Companies report on tighter and tighter schedules and against stricter and stricter rules, to satisfy the supposed desire of investors to know more and more about company business more and more frequently. This is presumably in order for potential investors to make better judgements about whether to continue with an investment in a company or to terminate it and seek a better return elsewhere. This is, of course, not to imply that the pursuit of a better return is not both economically rational and socially desirable. Better information is an unequivocal good thing in terms of *quality* of information, but a shorter and shorter horizon may not produce higher quality information, it may merely produce *more* information – which is quite a different thing.

But regardless of whether the information is of higher quality, rather than simply greater in volume, it cannot go hand in hand with an obligation on the recipient shareholder to sit tight and try to sort out bad governance, while other shareholders trade their shares into holdings in other, better-run businesses. In simple terms, an obligation on shareholders to shoulder the burdens of stewardship and an obligation (either self-imposed or externally mandated) to maximise short-term returns, are not compatible. In this sense urging institutional investors to engage and interact with companies is a push in the direction of inefficient allocation of resources.

Technologically, the rapid development of virtual trading markets – electronic markets – using powerful computers to replace physical trading, has produced sophis-ticated trading strategies, with traders trying to reduce the impact of risk – *for themselves* – in ever-more sophisticated ways which completely sever the link with issues of stewardship. (This apparent shuffling off of risk is limited to the individual trade. Part of the cause of the financial collapse in 2007–8 was an apparently wide-spread belief that individuals could somehow bet against risk *conclusively*. In other words, by appearing to have shuffled off risk for their own portfolios they believed they had somehow eliminated risk altogether. But it should have been evident that the amount of risk in the system overall cannot fall below a certain level and actions designed to remove risk for individuals merely push the risk into a different place, to the potential detriment of others and into places where it may then become a systemic problem, rebounding on those who have supposedly made themselves risk-free.) These techniques include algorithm-based hedging strategies[23] and the development of High

---

[23] P. Gomber et al., 'High-Frequency Trading' (2011), available at http://ssrn.com/abstract=1858626.

Frequency Trading (HFT)[24] – a technique which takes into account minute variations in prices across currency boundaries or the particular nature of momentary price differentials between individual market-makers.

The growth of electronic markets developed particularly rapidly after the Big Bang in the London Stock Market in 1986, and the development of fierce competition between brokers then stimulated the development of short-term performance measures in both fund management and company performance as an indication of ability to generate profit for clients. The UK followed the lead of the American market as it accepted large American broking firms into trading in the UK Stock Market, through their ownership of UK brokers.

The problems that these sometimes pose came together in the worldwide Stock Market crash of 1987 ('Black Monday') which indicated for the first time how the development of machine-driven trading could produce unintended consequences in the behaviour of markets at the same time as perfectly properly acquitting the (limited) procedural obligations of good governance. While no single cause can be isolated for the crash, 'programme trading' – where computers buy and sell shares according to pre-determined instructions about short-term price movement – was identified as a major factor.[25] Since the 1987 crash, the programmes used have become more conceptually sophisticated and algorithmic trading is now a backbone of many hedge funds and specialised funds. In 2001 researchers from IBM presented a paper[26] to the International Joint Conference on Artificial Intelligence which showed that machine-based trading systems could consistently beat human traders under laboratory conditions, using systems that had been developed fifteen years earlier. The potential value of this superiority was estimated at billions of dollars annually. Such systems take advantage of what are essentially static markets from the point of view of new information, driven by changes mostly in individual preferences for assets rather than perceptions derived from external influences like 'new' information about a company. Issues of good governance – and consequently involved stewardship – have nothing at all to do with such highly-temporary possession.

In the traditionalist view of governance and the macro economic view of the stock market, individual perceptions and risk appetites coalesce to form a supposedly efficient allocation of resources overall: attractive shares are bought and held; unattractive investments are sold to other shareholders with different risk appetites

---

[24] M. Avallaneda and S. Stoikov, 'High-frequency trading in a limit order book', *Quantitative Finance*, 8(3) (2008).

[25] Securities and Exchange Commission, *The October 1987 Market Break* (Washington DC: SEC, 1988).

[26] R. Das et al., 'Agent-human interactions in the continuous double auction', *Proceedings of the IJCAI* (2001).

who may exercise their proprietorial rights to change managers, perhaps. Resources (in the form of what can be bought with the money contributed by new shareholders in the primary market for shares) are available to companies that exhibit an ability to make efficient use of them. They are denied to those that do not, as the share prices of those companies drop to a point where they are either unable to raise fresh capital for expansion – or even recovery – or are bought out by other better managed companies. The information to enable assessments to be made which underpin such transactions is provided by the companies; the assumption of investors is that the information is provided in good faith; and that it is accurate and reliable. These characteristics are obviously closely associated with elements of *behavioural* governance.

If all these conditions are met then the traditionalist theory goes on to hold that the market will value assets efficiently – in the sense that appropriate risk will be recognised in the value of each asset; and also, consequently, that the price of each asset will reflect its true value.

In short, the conditions required for an effective and sustainable stock market are not far from those suggested by economists in describing a 'perfect market' – minimal barriers to entry; 'frictionless' trading; 'perfect' information (immediately and uniformly distributed); willing buyers and willing sellers; voluntary contractual observance. This apparent similarity has led economists to develop theoretical devices such as the Efficient Market Hypothesis (EMH) and the Capital Asset Pricing Model (CAPM) which supposedly help to organise investors' risk. Although empirically based, neither theory is accepted wholeheartedly and, to make a crude distinction, the theories generally have more support among academics and less support among market operators. What can be agreed upon is that they require – broadly – that the strictures of the perfect market be maintained in order to hold good.

The EMH in particular holds that it is impossible to 'beat the market' because all that is known about an individual share is reflected all the time in its price: prices will go up and down as new information reaches the market but, accordingly, investors can only make super-normal gains by investing in different grades of risk. The CAPM, by contrast, assigns a value to each share which correlates its price volatility with that of the volatility of the market; riskier shares are more volatile. Taken together these two devices have influenced the investment behaviour of institutional investors for the past thirty years. (They were also contributory to the investment strategies that brought about the failure of Long-Term Capital Management – which was based upon a purportedly provable contention that investment risk could be eliminated by appropriate strategies.)

It is at this point that the first cracks in the edifice are detected by the detractors of the theories. The Stock Market may appear to possess the characteristics of a perfect market but in truth its actual nature is very different. The most immediately obvious concerns are those of the imperfections of the information available to investors and the freedom of access to trade of all participants in the market.

Without going into great detail there are a number of significant practical concerns to doubt the applicability of both the EMH and the CAPM. Roger Lowenstein's book[27] on the failure of Long-Term Capital Management described the CAPM thus:

> it is one of the oldest canards in finance ... intellectually it has no merit and in practical terms it has been discredited by numerous academic studies

which he then went on to list.

What is intuitively obvious is that, other than in a 'perfect' market, not all investors know simultaneously all the information that is available about a share and equally that not all the information that does exist is completely reflected in the price. Aside from issues of the speed at which information travels inside companies enabling them to make announcements about events (which means that some individuals will know about a significant event before the market does), the market regulations are also structured in such a way – by punishing the use of 'insider information' – to attempt to *prevent* certain information getting to the market (at least in a certain way). However, the application of certain rules may be taken to produce exactly the opposite effect in a perverse illustration of the law of unintended consequences – to act in the interests of insiders while disadvantaging ordinary shareholders as the case of the disposal of directors' shares occasionally demonstrates.

Tesco: director's share sales 2011

On 12 January 2012, Tesco – the largest of the four major UK supermarket chains – announced that Christmas trading had been the worst for many years and that the company would see minimal profits growth for the year as a whole. The Stock Market reacted badly and £4 billion was wiped off the company's market capitalisation.

The following weekend it became clear that Noel Robbins, Tesco's UK Chief Operating Officer, had sold 50,000 shares at 404.5p on 4 January, a week before the company publicly announced the sales slump. By selling in advance of the announcement he had thereby achieved a sale value a little over £50,000 greater than he would have managed after the precipitate fall in the price.

Robbins was selling in the period allowed directors – outside the so-called 'closed period' dictated by the Model Code on Directors' Dealings that is part of the UK Corporate Governance Code – and had broken no formal rules. The

---

[27] Lowenstein, *Genius*.

company maintained that he was not privy to confidential information, despite the fact that as part of his everyday responsibilities he saw turnover figures for all UK stores.

Even when new information becomes known about a company, share prices may remain unmoved while the market digests the implications, leading to unperceived (and unacted-upon) changes in the inherent riskiness of the share – which violates the precepts of the theories.

The question of frictionless dealing follows along close behind in casting doubt on issues of market efficiency. Although the supposed conditions of the perfect market mean that there are no costs to dealing, in the real world there are numerous charges to be borne – dealing fees, taxes on dealing, taxes on capital gains and so on. These will all have the effect of distorting the rate of return that individual shareholders receive. Academic studies have often concluded that while some analysts may make a good job of selecting stocks, in order for their recommendations to have effect investors would have to trade so often and incur such large costs that even an out-performing portfolio composed of analysts' recommendations would be reduced to no better than an indexed performance because of transaction costs.[28]

Nor are these transaction charges the same for all shareholders or all entrants to the market: institutional shareholders will pay a different series of transaction prices to 'retail' investors. Even among institutional investors there may be different fees depending on whether they are able to trade for themselves or are using clients' money; different volumes of trade will attract different prices for the bargains for the shares being traded in. There is not, therefore, one price for a transaction in any given share but many. In addition to this thicket of different prices for what is effectively the same commodity, some investors will have difficulty in effecting transactions in any given time because of physical constraints on their ability to arrange a deal. Further, while the price ruling in the market for any given share is an indication of its valuation by the market it is only representative of the *last* price at which a bargain was struck. Consequently an ability to deal instantaneously may produce a shift in the price that renders the deal unattractive to an individual shareholder or potential shareholder. And the last price may itself be the result of a highly biased transaction: some share prices respond only to very large amounts of shares changing hands or may be very 'sticky' in the sense that there is shareholder inertia (which may be for a whole variety of reasons); or the market for the shares may be very 'thin' prompting very large changes in share prices for relatively small volumes of shares traded.

---

[28] B. Barber et al., 'Can investors profit from the prophets? Security analyst recommendations and stock returns', *The Journal of Finance,* 56 (2002), 531–63.

Of course when similar *types* of shareholder are compared the position is less dramatically unfair: all private shareholders operate under roughly the same constraints; all institutional investors do, too; all traders need – and for the most part receive – a procedurally largely efficient market.

The problems therefore arise when the superficialities of a blanket approach to governance theorising are applied to all shareholders in all conditions. Traditionalist theories are largely blind to this since they concentrate on the 'perfection' of the market and the supposed attributes of ownership. Just as much as there are differences between procedural, behavioural, structural and systemic aspects of governance so there are different considerations which have to be applied *in market terms* to the way that markets apply and respond to issues of all three types of governance.

The starkest difference between the capacities of different types of shareholder to deal are between the retail investor and the High Frequency Trader. Ironically, the conditions under which HFT is conducted are closer to the conditions of the perfect market – for those participants able to use it – except in one respect. The market is formed of 'dark pools' where the identity of buyer and seller are unknown as are the amounts that they may wish to trade – unlike the 'bright light' market of the traditional exchange. Like icebergs, much of the quantity of a potential trade may remain hidden beneath the surface.

However, even in this method of trading, specific stratagems have been developed to attempt to give an advantage in terms of the information available to one of the parties by whom the trade will be effected. So-called generic 'sniffer' or 'pinging' strategies are designed to tempt other parties to reveal prices and then take advantage of minute differences in price in order to effect an arbitrage. Mathematically-based, proprietorial techniques are used to try to identify trends in share price movements correlated with esoteric variables (many of the strategies have militaristic names like 'Stealth', 'Dagger', 'Sniper', or 'Guerilla' – and the term 'pinging' is an allusion to the noise made by sonar, the system used to detect submarines). Whatever the title or the purpose, more and more competition to skim off profit from market variances, using more and more subtle (and fragile) mathematics, produces smaller and smaller returns. In an effort to achieve even the smallest advantage HFT traders are now co-locating their computers with those of the exchanges to give them miniscule temporal advantages over competitors: these gains are limited by the laws of physics to about 3.3 milliseconds per 1000 kilometres of cable, but may be the difference between making a profit and making a loss.[29]

For the purposes of the retail investor, HFT is almost like a virtual market running parallel to the real market. Its impact on prices is lightning fast and may leave real market prices virtually unmoved even while many thousands of trades have been

---

[29] M. MacKenzie and J. Grant, 'The dash to flash', *Financial Times*, 5 August 2009.

accomplished at tiny currency fractions (a move from one-sixteenth of a dollar to one-hundredth of a cent in the USA as the minimum market price quote was allowed for this reason in 2000). Problems for the entire market arise however, because of the potential destabilising influence of the increased liquidity required by this reduction in the calculable size of bargains.

Evidence collected by different market regulators points to different conclusions in this respect: regulators from Sweden, Italy and France have all come to different conclusions.[30] The Swedish regulatory body Finansinspektionen concludes in a report published in February 2012[31] that HFT 'contributes to – but is not responsible for – changes in trading' and warned that there was 'considerable concern that the market will be subject to greater abuse'. The Italian regulator Consob announced in the same month that it had decided it was necessary to put 'blocks' on the system 'to slow down' HFT transactions in an effort to achieve some stability in the markets.[32] In December 2011, the French AMF (Autorite de Marche Financiers) said national regulators across Europe should 'have the possibility' of imposing a speed limit 'to ensure that the market share of HFT is at a point where the risks are reduced in the system and where all other kinds of investors will not be discouraged to use the markets, since they feel there is no level playing field'.[33] The French wanted the proposal already being considered as part of the new MiFID regime to be strengthened. But at roughly the same time the chief executive of the Malaysian Stock Exchange, the Bursa Malaysia, said to local newspapers 'Markets are about liquidity. As they say, liquidity begets liquidity. And these [high frequency traders] are providers of liquidity' – indicating in the interview that the Malay exchange would allow HFT later in 2012.[34]

Regardless of the detail of the issues about how HFT affects either liquidity or market fairness, it should be evident that the real market and the ideal market operate in very different ways. It becomes very difficult, as a consequence, to talk about an economic allocation of resources or about economically-driven participants in the real marketplace as if it were acting in accord with issues of the traditionalist view to bring about 'good' governance while the concepts are founded on the perfect market construct.

Part of this disconnection problem is the changes that occurred at the time of the de-regulation of the London Stock Exchange in 1986.

---

[30] J. Grant, 'UK study questions liquidity claims of HFT', *Financial Times*, 29 February 2012.
[31] P. Stafford, 'Sweden finds HFT effects "limited"', *Financial Times*, 21 February 2012.
[32] J. Grant and R. Sanderson, 'Italy to limit high-frequency orders', *Financial Times*, 20 February 2012.
[33] J. Grant and P. Stafford, 'France wants tougher HFT regulation', *Financial Times*, 19 December 2011.
[34] J. Grant and T. Demos, 'Superfast traders feel heat as bourses act', *Financial Times*, 5 March 2012.

Prior to the 'Big Bang', the functions of market maker and broker had been separated so that clients dealt with brokers for the execution of their orders and the market in stocks was made by specialists. After the de-regulation of the market the distinction between the two separate functions became redundant; the terms 'buy-side' and 'sell-side' replaced the old terms, with the possibility that both sides could be incorporated in one firm. While the authorities were keen to proclaim that this would only make a positive difference to the client (by abolishing old embedded fee structures and an artificial distinction of role) the reality has been something different. The changes effectively allowed one firm to set a price, make a market at that price and then collect fees for so doing. Numerous authors have demonstrated how the odds are stacked against the shareholder because of this.[35] The division of responsibilities between the functions of making a market and acting for the client which had kept both sides of the trade (reasonably) honest were swept away.

In 1940, at possibly the blackest time of the twentieth century, a book was published in America by a failed stockbroker (but clever humourist) called Fred Schwed.[36] Quoting a joke which was old even when Schwed wrote his book, the title – *Where Are the Customers' Yachts?* – refers to the fact that the benefits of trade in shares appear to accrue mostly to other parties to the trade in shares, rather than the end customers, who become 'owners' of the companies that the brokers deal in. Events of the last two decades will have done nothing to reverse that imbalance in respective rewards between the two parties.

Part of the reason for the disparity between cash input and cash returns by small shareholders is due to disconnects between theoretical constructs and real world structures in the fields of corporate governance, which do little to support the theoretical position that all shareholders are created equal and even less to balance the unequal power of the professional shareholder against the small investor. Governance theories are based on the supposition that the playing field is flat when in actual fact it is curved and lopsided. The true nature of the stock market is less an adjudicated investment platform and more of a betting shop or, as has become fashionable to describe it, 'a casino' populated by an elite who gamble with other people's money.

Conclusion

As this chapter has demonstrated, shareholders in listed companies are not always treated equally as they might presume they should be. In matters of stewardship, as nurtured by the UK Corporate Governance Code, there is a positive discrimination

---

[35] P. Augar, *The Greed Merchants: How the Investment Banks Played the Free Market Game* (London: Penguin, 2006).

[36] F. Schwed, *Where are the Customers' Yachts?* (New York, NY: Wiley, 2006).

against small shareholders and a (legally unfounded) presumption in favour of the large shareholder. In matters of canvassing opinions, small shareholders are fobbed off with the strictly and rigidly procedural theatre of the AGM, while large shareholders are in comfortable conjunction with the boards of directors. If the shareholders and/or the companies are large enough then the directors take to the limit the discretion afforded to them by the Articles of Association, the principles of law and the conventions of listing.

Developments in trading technology beyond the reach of all but the very wealthy funds render the concept of stewardship increasingly obsolete for many major market operators, pursuing profit with no concern for the corporate vehicle through which this is effected.

CHAPTER 10

Non-shareholder regulation of companies

This chapter will consider:

- the regulation of companies in markets – characteristics, structural considerations;
- the regulation of markets – characteristics, structural considerations, regulation of the market by the market, international issues;
- unregulated markets;
- illustrations of the impact of regulation: short-selling, insider dealing, the control of takeovers and mergers.

Introduction

This chapter will move from consideration of issues of governance in companies and of companies to a consideration of issues of regulation and, in particular, of the regulation of certain stock market activities. The previous chapter introduced some of the issues involved, which centred principally around shareholder-orientated controls. It provided a conceptual stepping stone between those aspects of governance where the shareholder – or a set of shareholders – is closely engaged in the activity; and regulation where the shareholder is more often the passive recipient of consequences brought about by some external agent, often a stakeholder.

Regulation is almost exclusively a State-dominated activity – either through direct action or some form of delegated power given to bodies which act on behalf of the consumer or the State, or under the authority of the State. It carries in attenuated form one of the fundamental characteristics of the State (under a Weberian definition) – the monopoly of violence – into the (normally) peaceable realm of commerce. Participants in commercial activities are required to submit to some form of state intervention through the medium of regulation and effectively accept that intervention (and the costs associated – levies, financial solvency obligations, fines and so on) as a part of the price of a licence to trade. If they do not accept, or infringe, these conditions then the State will do them some violence – usually this involves some form of additional cost, such as increased staffing; or some form of physical restitution or, more likely, a fine; possibly even imprisonment. To do this, however, the State has to occupy a position where it is able to conduct activity which defines another primary characteristic of the State – this time as defined by Giddens (in *A Contemporary Critique of Historical Materialism*[1]) – which is 'the reflexive monitoring of aspects of the reproduction of the social systems subject to the rule of the State'.

A definition of regulation

An intervention, usually by a public or quasi-public agency, to bring about some change in behaviour in a market or potential market, and therefore usually having an economic component. The intervention can be:

- in a variety of forms ranging through persuasive to mandatory;
- at a micro or macro level or incorporating elements of both;
- for a variety of reasons which are usually reflections of the priorities of the political structure of the society.

From the definition suggested in the text box above it follows that distinctions between procedural, behavioural, structural and systemic approaches to governance which are all designed to directly affect shareholders, are consequently of less than central importance in any consideration of regulation. This is because one of the significant characteristics of regulation – of corporate entities at least – is that it impacts (or perhaps more correctly, should impact) on all shareholders equally and without any decision-making contribution from them. So while issues of procedure are important in regulatory conformity these are essentially consequential aspects of administration and not concerned, from the origin, with the interests of shareholders *per se*.

It is of course possible that the degree of regulatory involvement the State imposes may stipulate that certain forms of governance are to be maintained which benefit shareholders but these are for the purposes of the State primarily, with the shareholder being in the position of a subordinate beneficiary. The State may undertake such regulation either for the purposes of extracting some form of rent or for the purposes of minimising what are otherwise external costs which will have to be borne by society as a whole. These might be costs associated with the legal machinery for untangling contractual disputes, for instance.

Where companies are concerned, the degree of precision required by regulation will often be determined by the nature of the activity being undertaken rather

---

[1] A. Giddens, *A Contemporary Critique of Historical Materialism* (Basingstoke: Palgrave, 1981).

than in any absolute form. For instance in the UK, the Companies Acts have long required that companies keep records and books of account but the Acts do not stipulate the detail in which those books should be maintained. This procedural element of control is enforced by reference to other institutional bodies – in this case, the international bodies which set accounting regulations; professional standards organisations; and in the case of listed companies, the Stock Exchange.

But as part of this process – an externally imposed exercise to which the trader must submit if it wishes to trade – the stakeholder becomes a much more important actor than the shareholder. The stakeholder becomes a primary actor (even though it may be reactive rather than initiating) while the shareholder's position becomes relegated to one of recipient of the consequences of the action, rather than a partner in originating the action. Effectively, for some purposes, the consequence of this is that the stakeholder supplants the shareholder in terms of the stewardship of the organisation. This gives rise to a paradox – at least in terms of established ideas about the respective roles of managers and shareholders. In an environment where shareholder primacy is the foundation of corporate govern-ance, because of increasing amounts of regulation, the controls over management that are most potent are often those exercised by stakeholders – or, at least, a certain set of stakeholders.

The links between governance and regulation

Shareholders' powers are limited, as has been demonstrated, to actions that depend upon historic information, subjected to a heavy asymmetry in favour of managers. By contrast, the regulatory agents operate in an environment which is often close to real time, in that their presence is constant and pressing, dictating the actions of managers in terms of planning, executing and reporting.

However, useful illumination of the style of corporate governance can be obtained by overlaying the style of regulatory control adopted by the State against some of the theoretical issues of corporate governance. To this end the chapter will introduce a further classificatory device in the form of a spectrum of regulatory styles – 'the regulatory spectrum' – which helps to illustrate the inter-relationships between regu-lation, social organisation and governance.

The axes of the spectrum can be labelled variously. Limiting the range of some form of capitalist/civil society arrangement produces a continuum shown in the text box below. These labels are not exclusive of others, of course, nor exhaustive in themselves.

The regulatory spectrum

Using a continuum based on the social arrangement theories of John Rawls (as expounded in the *Theory of Justice*[2]) and Robert Nozick (from *Anarchy, State and Utopia*[3]) produces a conceptual range where the type of state foreseen by Rawls – heavily biased towards consensus; egalitarian and interventionist – might be positioned on the left of the spectrum while the minimalist night watchman state of Nozick – with its absence of anything more than basic systems to uphold contract and enforce territorial integrity – would be on the right.

Stage 1

   Rawls←--→Nozick

   This might then be elaborated by positioning 'spontaneous governance' mechanisms described by Oliver Williamson[4] at the same end of the spectrum as Nozick's social organisations while Williamson's 'intentional governance' mechanisms are co-located with Rawls' ideas.

Stage 2

   Rawls←--→Nozick

   Intentional governance←-----------------→Spontaneous governance

   Intentional governance requires the application of rules and regulations while spontaneous governance is autonomic – without regulation – giving another layer to the arrangement, involving regulatory characteristics.

Stage 3

   Rawls←--→Nozick

   Intentional governance←-----------------→Spontaneous governance

   High levels of regulation←----------------→Low levels of effective regulation

   Overlaying this arrangement it is possible to locate issues of shareholder interest against stakeholder interest, since the rule-giver is effectively the stakeholder:

Stage 4

   Rawls←--→Nozick

   Intentional governance←------------------------→Spontaneous governance

   High levels of regulation←------------------→Low levels of effective regulation

   Stakeholder interests←----------------------------→Shareholder interests

---

[2] J. Rawls, *A Theory of Justice* (Cambridge, MA: Harvard University Press, 1999).

[3] R. Nozick, *Anarchy, State and Utopia* (New Jersey: Wiley-Blackwell, 2001).

[4] Williamson, *Mechanisms*.

And finally, additional intervals can be added to the spectrum which indicate broadly the style of compliance adopted with regard to regulatory norms:

Stage 5

Rawls←--→Nozick

Intentional governance←------------------------→Spontaneous governance

High levels of regulation←------------------→Low levels of effective regulation

Stakeholder interests←------------------------------→Shareholder interests

High Compliance – Aspirational Compliance – Utility Compliance – Casual Compliance

Where 'High Compliance' indicates an intention to comply to the maximum extent possible with regulatory procedures; 'Aspirational Compliance' indicates an intention to comply with the regulatory impositions where possible without undue dislocation of the organisation; 'Utility Compliance' indicates that the organisation complies with the essentials of regulatory impositions sufficient to avoid becoming obviously delinquent and therefore targeted by the regulators; and 'Casual Compliance' indicates that the organisation adheres only to basic contractual obligations or succumbs to regulation only when it is in its own (incidental) interest to do so, for reasons of competition or market-positioning for instance.

The spectrum then provides a possible template for indicating consequent regulatory styles and structures.

However, some interesting anomalies to the predictive ability of this arrangement can be illustrated. For instance, the far ends of the spectrum may well produce aberrations from expected outcomes. Under certain circumstances stakeholders may become more powerful than the template may suggest as the right-hand side of the spectrum is approached; for instance, after a point the control exerted by financial stakeholders may begin to exceed that of shareholders under conditions of formal (State) regulatory powerlessness. At the left end of the spectrum, tightly-organised block-holders with stakes in several significant companies may well be able to fend off interference by (non-State) stakeholders by arranging that the levels of compliance are maintained at the level of 'principle' rather than 'rule' or using cross-holdings as defensive devices.

As the box shows, regulation usually tends to have greater impact on corporate activity at the end of the spectrum where stakeholder power is more significant than shareholder power. From this it seems then that stakeholder power is significant in terms of regulatory involvement and that with corporations continually being subjected to increasing amounts of regulation, the importance of the stakeholder is in the ascendant.

The consequences of regulatory increase on shareholders

Detailed regulation of companies is mostly confined to matters of operation rather than areas which affect the fundamentals of relationships between shareholders, as a review of the most recent significant legislation will support (see Chapters 4 and 5). Stakeholders are in the driving seat as far as influencing the detail of operations of companies is concerned: by contrast shareholders have little ability to influence operational events – either in law, or through the procedures open to them by the Articles of Association. This is despite what traditionalist theory might appear to suggest they should have if they truly are owners of the business; it may well operate in private companies but does not hold for listed businesses.

Furthermore, as Chapters 4 and 5 showed, some of the changes demanded by stakeholders – the reforms made by the Corporate Manslaughter and Corporate Homicide Act 2007 and the Bribery Act 2010 – have both fundamentally altered the way that companies have to behave in terms of structural governance, with significant implications for the positions of shareholders. But apart from a proposal which has been made by the UK Government, at the time of writing, to give minority shareholders more power – a path blazed by the introduction of derivative actions in the 2006 Companies Act – the legislation which is focussed on the behaviour of companies has been at the instigation of, and is pointed towards, the interests of stakeholders.

The suggestions made by the Coalition Government in the UK to give shareholders compulsory powers in respect of directorial remuneration were met with a very cool reception in 2012.[5] City shareholder pressure groups largely appeared to reject any further burden on their responsibilities, characterising the proposals as an attempt to push shareholders into micro-management of companies – a function for which they maintained that they employed the companies' directors.

Shareholders in listed companies are therefore left in the position of passengers rather than occupying any position of influence, with the effective power of stakeholders, over the long run, being of greater significance to the way that companies are able to operate – especially if the managers are included as a stakeholder group.

The impact of the detailed regulation of stock markets on the position of shareholders is of potentially still greater significance. This is particularly marked in four areas: first, in the way that the markets regulate themselves; second, in the regulation of the use of information that, it is claimed, would produce an unfair advantage by insider dealing (briefly touched on in Chapter 9); third, in the regulation of short-selling; and last, the regulation of takeovers and mergers. It is in these areas that the interests of shareholders are usually

---

[5] K. Burgess, 'Cable outlines plans on executive pay', *Financial Times*, 23 January 2012.

dominated by rules made by stakeholders – because the largest stakeholder of all is the State and it is the State which passes legislation.

Regulation of the market by the market

The UK Stock Market until 1986 was a self-regulating organisation based on precepts of 'club regulation' (Moran[6]) and run for the benefit of its member firms. It could afford to be so since it had no outside shareholders to consider who might be anxious for growth of regular increases in dividend yield. After 'Big Bang' it became possible for outsiders to own member companies, which brought both improvements in market liquidity and different styles of trading particularly in the shift from 'open-outcry' to electronic trading that the changed structure of the market prompted.

The commercial pressure to become a different type of organisation, able to tap outside funding and to compete in a different way from that chosen historically, built steadily in the decade and a half after the Big Bang. In 2000 the members of the Stock Exchange voted to become a public limited company. The role that the Exchange had previously occupied as the UK's listing authority was transferred to the FSA. The Stock Exchange's role thus became somewhat anomalous – as a plc it was both an instrument of government (and EU) regulatory policy and also a profit-seeking, commercial operation that was in competition with other bourses in Europe and the USA to attract customers to itself in order to swell its revenue and generate profit for its shareholders – this resulted in competition and re-positioning.

As part of the process of expansion in 2007, the London Stock Exchange Group bought the major Italian exchange – the Borsa Italiano in Milan – for €2 billion to secure a position as an international business. Heavy capital investment is required of Stock Exchanges to provide continually evolving trading mechanisms – the rapid development of HFT and competition from other multi-lateral trading facilities (MTFs) such as Chi-X and Turquoise (now absorbed into the LSE). This made small bourses a threatened breed and in the case of the London Exchange required the LSE to concentrate strongly on profitability. Proposals for international links between exchanges still continue as individual exchanges seek to consolidate their positions (see the proposed merger of the NYSE Euronext and the Deutsche Börse blocked by Brussels, in February 2012).[7]

Such competition has meant that standards of regulatory oversight exercised by the LSE's listing committee have been relaxed, according to critics.[8] This is held to have

---

[6] Moran, *The Regulatory State.*
[7] J. Grant, 'D Börse to sue Brussels over NYSE block', *Financial Times*, 20 March 2012.
[8] R. Gribben, 'FSA wants reform of listings rules', *Daily Telegraph*, 15 January 2008.

occurred through one of two routes. First, in recent years large companies from economies where they would swamp their home exchanges if they listed there (if indeed such exchanges existed), have been keen to allow their existing shareholders to reap the benefits of globalised markets by selling shares.[9]

Given their size and economic importance they have been able to select from a variety of exchanges with the potential to act as listing host. Some of these newly-listed companies are often grappling with the nuances of the concepts and regulations of Western-based corporate governance for the first time. Second, in some cases – like that of Glencore plc floated in May 2011– the free float requirements were relaxed because of the size of the offering (Glencore floated 20 per cent of the company on to the market instead of the usual 25 per cent).[10] There were few detractors among the banks and professional firms to this relaxation; the flotation was the largest ever for the London market and the sheer size of the flotation was used as the justification for the normal rules being flexed. But one of the consequences of this huge valuation was that Glencore entered the FTSE 100 on the day it was listed, requiring an immediate holding for most pension and insurance funds. The advisers to the issue were estimated to have reaped over £240 million in fees[11] with only one major bank, J.P. Morgan, being excluded from the flotation because of a long-standing link with Xstrata plc – a link up with which had once been seen as an alternative to the flotation.

Exchanges have been anxious to secure these large companies as clients, since they represented an initial increase in market fees and then secure continuing revenue. In this scramble to bag new clients, the LSE's reputation as the toughest regulated market with the highest established standards for listing has not always been the best selling point. The London Stock Exchange found itself in the position of having to negotiate away some of the most stringent listing requirements, as a consequence of commercial pressure to attract listings. The development of premium and standard listings, following a review of the listing regime conducted by the FSA in 2008–10,[12] was partly an 'official' response to this problem, supposed to give investors 'greater clarity' according to the FSA[13] (the prime benefit of a premium listing for many companies was that it acted as a passport into the FTSE indices with consequent substantial benefit to demand for the company's shares).

[9] R. Wigglesworth, 'Listings: gold standards', *Financial Times*, 6 December 2011.
[10] P. Stafford, 'LSE calls for smaller IPO syndicates', *Financial Times*, 8 December 2011.
[11] J. Blas and S. Kerr, 'IPO values Glencore at $48bn–$58bn', *Financial Times*, 4 May 2011.
[12] FSA Press release, 'FSA fines stockbroker £250,000 for using high pressure sales tactics', 14 January 2008 (FSA/PN/002/2008), available at www.fsa.gov.uk/library/communication/pr/2008/002.shtml.
[13] FSA Press release, 'FSA consults on changes to the Listing Rules', 26 January 2012 (FSA/PN/006/2012), available at www.fsa.gov.uk/library/communication/pr/2012/006.shtml.

Decisions made to relax the free-float obligation and the purity of some corporate governance arrangements in some large companies (some of which were represented in listing terms by remotely-controlled businesses – SPACs or special purpose acquisition companies – set up specifically for the purpose but effectively controlled by a few significant individuals) were criticised as a consequence of problematic behaviour following the listing. Among these were Bumi plc, a Malaysian natural resources company (brought to the market by the financier Nathaniel Rothschild as Valler plc and later renamed Bumi), effectively controlled by the Bakrie family, who later (February 2012) tried to displace him from the board;[14] Eurasian Natural Resources Corporation plc, with a secondary listing on the Kazakhstan Stock Exchange, and dominated by three Kazakh investors;[15] and Vallares plc (a fund managed by Tony Hayward the ex-CEO of BP and merged with a business 44 per cent controlled by Mehmet Sepil,[16] who had been the recipient of the largest fine levied by the FSA for insider dealing until the fine levied in the Einhorn case; see p 255).[17]

London's experience was not unique. Instances of failure of regulation of stock markets can be adduced from nearly every country with a large operative stock market (further details of some major scandals are carried on the website that accompanies this book). Inevitably, in the larger markets the problems have been commensurately larger and a few cases illustrate the range of the problem.

Serious concern was expressed in late 2010[18] by Canadian and American investors about the influx of Chinese-based companies which had sought listings on relaxed requirements. The most prominent of these cases was Sino-Forest Inc, a forestry resources company quoted on the Toronto Stock Exchange since 1996 when it reversed into an existing listed company. Sino-Forest is supposedly asset-rich, with a market capitalisation that peaked in 2010 at C\$6.2 billion. However, allegations of fraud 'on a stratospheric scale' were made by Muddy Waters LLC, a research house/short seller, prompting an investigation into the company.[19]

Despite the investigation, the relationships of the backers, suppliers and management of this company are obscured by deliberate action by some of the parties and its earnings base – even the physical existence of its assets – is disputed. And perhaps what is most worrying about the allegations against this company is that concerns about its probity

[14] J. Aglionby, 'Bumi governance problems "put to bed"', *Financial Times*, 27 March 2012.
[15] W. MacNamara and P. Jenkins, 'Third independent director to quit ENRC board', *Financial Times*, 9 June 2011.
[16] Staff reporter, 'Former BP chief explores the final oil frontier', *Financial Times*, 7 December 2011.
[17] B. Masters and S. Jones, 'Einhorn and Greenlight fined £7.2m', *Financial Times*, 25 January 2012.
[18] K. Burgess, 'FTSE considers tougher listing rules', *Financial Times*, 1 November 2011.
[19] R. Cookson, 'Sino-Forest suffers another blow', *Financial Times*, 6 April 2012.

arose from investigations from investors and not from the supposed due diligence conducted by the exchange, as the guardian of shareholders' overall interests.

Extracts from the Report of the Independent Committee set up to review Sino-Forest (released 1 February 2012)

'While many answers and explanations have been obtained, the IC [Independent Committee] believes that they are not yet sufficient to allow it to fully understand the nature and scope of the relationship between SF and Yuda Wood. Accordingly, based on the information it has obtained, the IC is still unable to independently verify that the relationship of Yuda Wood is at arm's length to SF. It is to be noted that Management is of the view that Yuda Wood is unrelated to SF for accounting purposes. The IC remains satisfied that Yuda is not a subsidiary of SF. Management continues to undertake work related to Yuda Wood, including seeking documentation from third parties and responding to e-mails where the responses are not yet complete or prepared. Management has provided certain banking records to the Audit Committee that the Audit Committee advises support Management's position that SF did not capitalize Yuda Wood (but that review is not yet completed). The IC anticipates that Management will continue to work with the Audit Committee, Company counsel and E&Y [Ernst and Young] on these issues.'

'And later ... in respect of a report prepared by Kaitong the legal advisers to Sino-Forest which they supplied to the Independent committee'.

'The Kaitong Report stresses the importance of "Guanxi" [which can be loosely translated as 'face'] in Chinese business, but is not specific as to particular benefits and why these particular relationships are important. The Kaitong Report contains little information to validate the political or business connections of such backers, or the nature of the relationship between the backers and the Suppliers or AIs [authorised intermediaries – the brokers that Sino-Forest used to buy and sell forests]. There is no documentary evidence of the nature of their support for their respective Suppliers or AIs nor the consideration (if any) received by the backers for their support of the Suppliers or AIs. The Kaitong Report suggests that such backers may provide resources that are important in China such as introductions, endorsements and connections.'

It is perhaps pertinent to point out that the 'Independent Committee' was composed of the (Canadian) chairman of Sino-Forest, one of its current board members and a board member who had resigned (for undisclosed reasons) the previous month.

As an aside to the Sino-Forest affair, on 9 February 2011 the Toronto Exchange announced[20] that it was merging with the London Stock Exchange in an 'all-share merger of equals'. The merger failed in June 2011, when Toronto Exchange shareholders refused to back it.

Sino-Forest is not the only listed company to have a murky set of accounts, despite what the regulations require, as the revelations of fraud in 2011[21] at the Japanese camera maker Olympus show. It is not unknown, either, for political issues also to impinge on matters of strict regulatory concern. For instance, in 2012 the South Korean company Hanwha, which specialises in chemical and explosives manufacture, was threatened with de-listing by the Seoul exchange after government prosecutors sought a period of imprisonment for its chairman, and ten other executives of the company, on charges of embezzlement.[22] The chairman had previously received a jail sentence in 2007 for abduction and grievous bodily harm but had received a presidential pardon and had been officially involved in the Korean campaign for the 2008 winter Olympics. In January 2012, the chairman of the third biggest Chaebol was also accused of embezzlement.[23] He had been convicted in 2003 of a $1.2 billion accounting fraud and served time in jail before receiving a pardon and acting as a business ambassador at the Group of 20 summit in Seoul in 2010.

Olympus Camera – retaining a listing

On 10 November 2011, the company admitted hiding losses of more than Y135 billion – about $1.7 billion – over a ten year period as a result of speculative investments it had made during the 1980s boom. The losses had come to light after a new managing director had questioned the huge amounts of money being paid to 'advisers' who had been involved in more recent acquisitions. It transpired, after much investigation, that these were supposedly being used to camouflage the original losses.

On 20 January 2012 the Tokyo Stock Exchange announced that it would be allowing the company to retain its listing but would instead be levying a fine of Y10 million on the company for its misdemeanours (10 million of any currency is pretty insignificant against 135 billion but it still means that the shareholders who were bilked of huge amounts of money they had

---

[20] Lex Column, *Financial Times*, 23 June 2011.
[21] M. Nakamoto, 'Olympus is litmus test on governance', *Financial Times*, 22 February 2012.
[22] S. Jung-a, 'Hanwha chairman sentence suspended', *Financial Times*, 11 September 2007.
[23] S. Jung-a, 'S Korea: the tiny roar of the NPS', *Financial Times*, 14 February 2012.

invested – the share price fell to about a sixth of its pre-scandal value at its lowest point – were the ones who would be hit again).

The previous managing director, who had uncovered the problem, and the Asian Corporate Governance Association had both urged that the listing be maintained to protect the interests of employees, suppliers and other stakeholders. The formal investigation conducted by the Tokyo Stock Exchange concluded that the company's core manufacturing base had not been compromised by the huge losses and that consequently, since there had been no effect on sales or operating profit, 'investor judgement had not been distorted to the extent of warranting de-listing'.

The influence of the Bribery Act 2010 was central to this case: Michael Woodward, the managing director was covered by the provisions of the Act as British citizen and therefore had a legal duty to report the problems – which could have resulted in serious legal penalties if he had not done so.

Sino-Forest and Olympus are not the only companies to be tainted in this way. The same research house, Muddy Waters LLC (which is also a short seller, see below), that accused Sino-Forest has also claimed that the Chinese advertising agency Focus Media has been producing fraudulent sets of accounts.[24] Research conducted by Muddy Waters calculated that Focus Media has written down $1.1 billion out of $1.6 billion in acquisitions since 2005, an amount equivalent to one-third of its enterprise value at the time that the report was released in November 2011. The firm suggested that the overpayment was a signal that Focus Media hid losses through its overpayments, or pushed acquisitions costs back into its turnover or that its capital expenditures were being misappropriated – a sequence of accounting tricks very similar to those used by Olympus.

Investment capital is now very mobile internationally and very willing to move to chase fractions of a per cent of profit. Managers of the large pension funds and insurance companies trade on an international basis and probably cannot hope to achieve returns that are adequate to the expectations placed on them by their clients unless they trade internationally. Consequently it is not possible – or desirable – to take a narrow view of the probity of one particular exchange and be content with that. Of the ten largest all-time flotations, three are accounted for by Chinese banks, two by Asian telecoms businesses and one by an Asian insurance group.[25] They have been floated in markets – Tokyo, Hong Kong and Shanghai – very keen to compete with established exchanges and which have offered terms for potential listings which have driven down

---

[24] E. Boyde, 'Fund file: a Chinese opacity problem', *Financial Times*, 28 November 2011.
[25] Staff Reporters, 'The 10 biggest IPOs in history', *Daily Telegraph*, 14 May 2011.

the regulatory thresholds of older, established exchanges which previously boasted of their regulatory rigour and the discipline of their listing requirements.

'Passporting' and the international regulation of markets

The increasing pressure for exchanges to integrate under common ownership or to adhere to transnational rules of listing requirements has also contributed to a decline in the protection afforded to innocent third parties, which further nibbles away at the integrity of the traditionalist view of governance through market dynamics. These issues contribute to the disjuncture between the reinforcing elements of procedural, behavioural, structural and systemic governance and probably represent the point where governance becomes most fractured in coverage.

Potential foreign investors in Sino-Forest were presumably reassured by the firm's listing on the foremost Canadian exchange and the fact that it had resided there for more than a decade. The procedural governance aspects of the listing were supported by the integrity of the Toronto Exchange's procedures to ensure that shareholders' buy and sell orders were properly executed; the longevity of the listing would give comfort in structural and systemic terms – although this can be regarded as superficial until such time as a problem is revealed. The linking aspects of behavioural governance and the structural governance which should have been guaranteed by the obligations that the Exchange put on Sino-Forest as a company, were simply absent. Shareholders in Sino-Forest thus found themselves properly-attributed owners (through efficient procedural governance) of shares in a company in a closely-supervised market which were largely worthless (the failure of the behavioural aspect) because of the lack of structural and systemic governance (inadequate market policing by the market authorities).

At a different level, a similar issue might be held to arise through the London Stock Exchange Group's ownership of the Borsa Italiana. If the London market's rules of corporate governance are held to be the standard to which others aspire – the commonly trumpeted claim of the FSA and the LSE – then this might be thought to give some comfort to foreign investors in Italian companies; common ownership of the exchanges might be thought to equate to common standards of systemic govern-ance for the markets – even though behavioural issues for companies would still be governed by national codes and laws. Yet the line between the two is not so easily drawn: standards of managerial or behavioural governance acceptable under the Italian governance codes (in terms of control of companies) have long been tolerated which would be the cause of political and financial scandals under the behavioural governance standards included in the codes and rules operative in the UK and these impinge on issues of systemic governance for the Italian stock market.

Under Italian regulations, cross-holdings in companies are permissible to an extent which allows firms which would otherwise be bankrupt to continue to operate. For instance, the holding company Premafin, owned by Salvatore Ligresti, controls Fondiaria-SAI, a listed insurer. The Ligresti family interests also own a sufficiently significant stake in Mediobanca, one of Italy's major banks. Premafin is able to skim along just the right side of insolvency thanks to loans provided by Mediobanca and the large Italian bank, UniCredit. Mediobanca owns 13 per cent of the Italian assurance company Generali and 7 per cent of UniCredit via a structured finance deal. UniCredit owns 9 per cent of Mediobanca. It was Unicredit which, in 2011, put forward a plan for a complicated merger of Premafin and Unipol (which finances student accommodation throughout Europe) which would have effectively bailed out the Ligresti family from their debt-laden vehicle – to the detriment of minority share-holders. The deal was barred by regulators and substituted with one which will 'involve a cascade of rights issues'[26] and may be even more unbalanced as far as minority holders of Premafin are concerned.

The outcome of that relationship and the associated manoeuverings demonstrates that the two issues of behavioural and systemic governance are not distinct and separable; they cannot operate independently and they impact on each other to marked effect.

In February 2012, the UK's FSA announced[27] that it had secured the recovery of €77,000 for victims of a fraudulent 'boiler room scheme' established to sell non-existent shares to individuals in the UK, from a company called Monobank plc, which had secured a listing on the Frankfurt First Quotations Board – the broad equivalent (without the regulatory rigour) in terms of its purpose and intent to the UK's Alternative Investment Market. The First Quotations Board is designed to allow access to public equity markets for finance for growing companies and is managed by the Frankfurt Stock Exchange which is itself regulated by BaFIn, the Federal Financial Supervisory Authority of Germany – equivalent broadly to the FSA. Companies achieving a listing under the rules of any approved European exchange – with a level of disclosure initially in excess of that required by the First Quotations Exchange admittedly – are permitted to carry their listings over to other European markets with minimal further scrutiny. This process is called 'passporting'. Passporting of listings between junior markets is not permitted but the principle of transferability of listings is implicit in the European market, as the 'business case' behind Monobank demonstrates.

---

[26] R. Sanderson, 'Machiavellian corporate princes resist Monti reforms', *Financial Times*, 17 February 2012.
[27] C. Newlands, 'Crime and the City', *Financial Times*, 30 March 2012.

FSA secures €77,000 for victims of boiler room fraud

The Financial Services Authority (FSA) has obtained a court order against Mono-bank Plc (Monobank) which paves the way for €77,000 (approximately £64,000) of redress to be paid to victims of a boiler room scam.

Monobank, a UK incorporated firm, provided promotional literature stating that it was in the final stages of setting up a prepaid credit card service in the UK and Europe and had entered into commercial agreements to that effect. However, the FSA found no evidence to suggest that any of this was true. Despite this, Monobank still managed to obtain a quotation on the Frankfurt Stock Exchange's First Quotation Board.

At a case heard in the High Court in London, Mr Justice Peter Smith ruled that Monobank was complicit in offshore boiler rooms cold calling UK consumers and offering them shares in the firm. Some of the boiler rooms selling the worthless shares were: Ellis Capital Management; Fallon Brookes; Morgan Stern; Rothmans Capital; and International Consulting Services.

The FSA first took action against Monobank in August 2011 when it took steps to freeze its assets by obtaining an injunction from the High Court.

Source: FSA Press Release, 17 February 2012

The significance of all the activities related above is that they effectively produce a market regime which is not as well-regulated as existing shareholders may believe it to be. The importance of this becomes apparent when companies which are introduced into the market automatically assume positions in major stock market indices, resulting in an obligatory holding for funds which track the index or have a market-weighting in shares, as in the cases of Bumi or ENRC or Vallares for the London market. (This means most pension funds will have a holding in such companies.) Since these companies – despite their size and position in the major indices – are usually accorded a 'governance discount', it means that they tend to be more volatile than other shares in the large indices (they have a higher beta value[28]) and consequently when the market moves they move by a greater amount – the movements are usually exaggerated downwards. There is thus an unavoidable misallocation of resources since investors have no option, because of their size, to avoid them as index components. As the *Financial Times* pointed out in January 2012 there is an old stock market adage to the effect that the further away from the market the higher has to be the premium

---

[28] 'Beta' is a measure of a share's volatility against an index of shares.

to attract investors. This is to say nothing of the discounting effects of the compromised governance arrangements of the exchanges themselves.

The exchanges should primarily act as a buttress against frauds on the buyers of shares for which they operate a market – that much is contained in the charter of the UK Listing Authority (the FSA with another hat on) to which the London Stock Exchange is responsible and all exchanges proclaim their standards of probity in similar ways. Yet proclamation and process are not always the same as the experiences illustrated above indicate. In early 2012 both the FSA and the US SEC moved to tighten the regulations over the listing of companies (see above) – the SEC directly and the FSA after consultation.[29] But the FSA's proposed consultation almost ignores the Alternative Investment Market – the market to which new companies – supposedly less tried and tested – are supposed to turn if they need development capital and where regulation is through brokers. As alluded to above, brokers have a financial risk at stake if their supervised companies misbehave but if a Nomad walks away from his charges then that leaves the shareholders unrepresented. The regulatory authorities, at least in the UK, have a schizophrenic stance – brought about to some extent by the differing purposes of the main market and AIM – but which from the outside at least seems more conditioned by a desire to avoid blame than to effect proper regulatory control to protect shareholders.

Unregulated markets

If the regulatory coverage of the market as a whole is inadequate then it makes little difference how well-policed individual elements are; the outcome of a failure of the poorly-regulated element is still likely to be systemically damaging. This was essentially the problem in 2007–8.

There are three highly volatile components of financial markets which are essentially unregulated nationally and internationally – the over-the-counter market; the hedge funds and the shadow banking sector. In 2007–8, when the unregulated parts of the market (derivatives and inter-bank transactions) brought about problems in a lightly regulated part (the insurers who dealt in market-risk) some hedge fund activity had actively contributed to the problem by making certain financial instruments very volatile and obscuring their nature (the Abacus example, see below). Hedge fund apologists would say that the actions of the hedge funds brought liquidity into the market but this is not supported by the opinions of all observers.[30]

---

[29] FSA, 'FSA consults on changes to the Listing Rules', available at www.fsa.gov.uk/library/ communication/pr/2012/006.shtml.

[30] P. Lysandrou, 'The real role of hedge funds in the crisis', *Financial Times*, 1 April 2012.

Hedge funds – which are effectively giant shorting machines – are not entirely unregulated of course: in the UK they are required to nominate individuals as regulated persons to the FSA. However, they are not subject to the detailed regulatory control in respect of capital and transaction reporting which other financial institutions are subject to. In November 2010 the European Union passed a draft regulation[31] under the Lamfalussy procedure – which approves the principles of legislation and works out the detail later – which will bring hedge funds under a European regulatory umbrella, but this is likely to take several years to implement.

The Solvency Regulations[32] – the latest iteration of which is Solvency 2 – are a fundamental review of the capital adequacy regime for the European insurance industry which aim to establish a revised set of EU-wide capital requirements and risk management standards that will replace the current solvency requirements. They will also affect pension schemes – in an example apparently of the effect of unforeseen consequences – and thus risk falling under their own cumbersomeness. When the extension of the regulatory umbrella to hedge funds is linked with the far-reaching changes in Solvency 2 and the substantial changes required of the Basel III procedure, the regulatory net will affect many of the current poorly-covered areas of the financial markets.

However, there are as yet (early 2012) no plans to catch the shadow banking sector (shades of the causes of the UK's secondary banking crisis in 1972 from which much damage flowed but few policy lessons were learned). In addition to this gaping hole, the strength and effectiveness of the revised and extended regulatory coverage will only be tested *in extremis* – and all the while markets will be actively moving into areas which are unregulated, since this is what they always do.[33]

Regulatory lag

Markets and market operators innovate; regulators (usually) respond to innovations and changes – and usually after some time, once the concept and particulars of the products being offered have been absorbed into the market-place. The concept of regulatory lag applies specifically to reviews of rate changes in regulated organisations – for instance in most utilities some form of price control is

---

[31] A. Barker, 'European rules alarm fund managers', *Financial Times*, 1 April 2012.
[32] A. Gray, 'Insurance body cautious on solvency deal', *Financial Times*, 21 March 2012.
[33] This is a phenomenon known as Goodhart's Law, after its originator Charles Goodhart who was an economist at the Bank of England. See C. Goodhart, *Monetary Theory and Practice* (Basingstoke: Palgrave, 1983), p. 96. The proposition is expressed as 'Any observed statistical regularity will tend to collapse once pressure is placed upon it for control purposes'.

standard in view of their central importance – where often the change has to be announced and then implemented before the regulator responds.

However, the concept can also be extended to instances where companies have to issue innovative products in highly-competitive markets in order to maintain some form of unique identity. The financial sector is a prime example of this, with constant new variations of existing products being offered to consumers, many of which it is difficult for regulators to keep up with.[34]

Regulatory coverage always lags behind the market's innovative capacity – hence one of the other abiding characteristics of regulation: that it is always trying hard to catch up with the realities of the marketplace. In few areas is this better illustrated than in the practice of short-selling.

Regulation of short-selling

Selling short is the practice of selling a share, without having physical ownership, with the intention of being able to take advantage of a dip in price. The principle is based on the difference between transaction and settlement dates – a difference of three days in most markets. This means that sellers can agree to sell and then take advantage of falling prices to buy shares at a lower price than the original transaction, with which they can physically settle the trade – with a consequent profit. The type of transaction described above is called 'naked short-selling'; some markets (the US markets for instance) ban such transactions – principally because of the risk of the selling party defaulting if the price moves adversely (that is, rises) between the times of transaction and settlement, leaving an unconsummated trade which has to be disentangled at cost and trouble. However, most jurisdictions allow 'covered short selling' where shares are effectively borrowed from another shareholder (at a fee) and returned once the transaction has been settled.[35]

Short-selling has a very mixed reputation and is one of those activities that carries a whiff of the black sheep. A bit like the mad relative locked in an upstairs room in a Victorian novel, among 'ordinary' investors it is thought to be something admitted to only under duress. Fred Schwed, whose book has been quoted before, was far from being hostile to the practice but said that it seemed to run counter to the nature of most investors to trade in something with the express intention of watching it lose value: 'Occasionally a customer is persuaded to try his hand at it. Immediately he

---

[34] The concept of 'regulatory lag'.

[35] J. Chapman, 'The truth behind short selling's public face', *Financial Times*, 24 April 2011.

makes his sale he becomes so wretched and stays that way until he has covered, whether at a profit or a loss'.[36]

As a consequence of the profits to be gained from the practice, most listed companies have a proportion of their shares which are typically subject to shorting as some share-holders allow other funds to use part of their holdings to speculate, while they make money through cover fees. In the UK, market regulations policed by the FSA require short-sellers to report net positions of stocks they have shorted at the end of each trading day (but not during the day); so many, many transactions can take place in a volatile market as traders take a different view of the prospects for share prices over very small intervals of time, while a smaller summary report is made at the end of the day. This is also of course the principle under which High Frequency Traders operate. Consequently, short-selling activity is confined mostly to banks' own, proprietary traders and – crucially – to hedge funds because of the risk involved and the large amounts of liquidity required. The money that the proprietary traders play with is the property of the banks because of the legal nicety that money deposited with a bank does not belong to the depositor but becomes the possession of the bank (clearing up the debris of Lehman Brothers after the financial collapse of 2007–8 provided endless argument for lawyers over this issue). Hedge funds can be thought of in one sense therefore as little more than short-selling machines.

DSL faces court case over Simon Cawkwell's gains from short-selling Northern Rock and Eurotunnel

Britain's most outspoken short-seller Simon 'Evil Knievil' Cawkwell has filed a legal claim against his stockbroker after being unable to collect or verify what he alleges are legitimate profits from bets that the share prices of Northern Rock and Eurotunnel would fall.

Cawkwell, who calls himself 'Britain's most feared bear-raider', boasted in early 2008 that he had made more than £500,000 from short trades in Northern Rock as the Treasury frantically – and fruitlessly – searched for a 'white knight' bidder.

Claiming the credit crunch had triggered huge gains on his short positions in several businesses, Cawkwell said at the time: 'It has proved a ripe old harvest.' Northern Rock was nationalised days later.

However, Cawkwell's windfall might not be as large as he had hoped. Direct Sharedeal Limited (DSL) has vowed to defend itself against the claim. Cawkwell says he has been unable to verify his DSL account details, which he believes should show gains from more than £660,000 of short bets on Northern Rock made between October 2007 and the end of January 2008.

---

[36] Schwed, *Where are the Customers' Yachts?*

When shares are delisted from the stock market it is difficult for traders who have taken a 'short' bet – that shares will decline in value – to complete the transaction. Determining the final value of delisted shares can take a long time and closing out short positions can be troublesome.

Separately, DSL's auditors have for two years raised concerns about risks, albeit remote, to the broker's financial health. DSL faces a potential legal claim in relation to a penny share mis-selling scandal involving DSL's 'appointed representative', a firm called First Colonial Investments, which went bust in 2009. DSL was fined £101,500, but its auditors say this may not be the end of matter and could 'in extreme circumstances cast doubt about the company's ability to continue as a going concern'.

There is no suggestion DSL's attitude to Cawkwell's claim is influenced by its own financial concerns.

Cawkwell made his name short-selling Maxwell Communications and Polly Peck International. He has resorted to the courts, he says, after fruitless attempts to seek assurance that proceeds he believes will be due to him from the Northern Rock short trade – and from a separate £111,000 short trade in Eurotunnel – are securely ring-fenced within DSL.

A DSL spokesman said: 'We will be defending the claim but have no further comment.'

Source: S. Bowers, *The Observer*, 30 January 2011

But short-sellers are also credited – or blamed – with pitching markets in individual shares into more and more volatile movements. During the time of the financial crisis in 2008, Lord Dennis Stevenson – the Chairman of HBOS (Halifax/Bank of Scotland) – made a fuss about the activities of short-sellers pushing the price of HBOS down while it was attempting to float a rights issue to rebuild its balance sheet. The FSA felt compelled to investigate but terminated the investigation fruitlessly after five months because it was impossible to accumulate evidence that the short-selling had been accompanied by any illegal behaviour (but see the point about Morgan Stanley below). While short-selling is not illegal – either naked or covered in the UK – it is illegal to spread rumours that act in such a way as to affect a share price. This behaviour is known as 'trash and cash'; such activity was what Stevenson suspected and why he demanded an investigation.

Short-selling and the collapse of Northern Rock

The spate of short-selling that accompanied the demise of Northern Rock after its problems were leaked to the BBC is estimated to have made speculators as much as £1 billion in one week.

More than half the bank's shares were loaned out to speculators which allowed them to sell the shares at higher prices, which prevailed as the shares fell, and then buy them back in the market at a lower price, to return them to the original owners, paying the 'rent' on the borrowed stock out of the profit made.

One particular hedge fund, Lansdowne Partners, was believed to have been heavily involved in short-selling having been shorting Northern Rock consistently for four years because of concerns over the bank's method of sourcing capital from the wholesale markets.

Because of the precipitate fall in the price of Northern Rock's shares it was believed that a significant number of short-sellers were running 'naked' or uncovered short positions, which tend to have the effect of precipitating falls even further.

One company, RAB Capital, took advantage of this to buy up the shares which were being offered in the expectation that what it believed to be the company's underlying worth would prompt a reversal. When the bank was eventually nationalised to quell the first run on a British bank in 150 years, RAB sued the Government for the expropriation of its asset. Other investors had already lost large amounts of money with one Scottish fund which had been the largest single investor with 7 per cent of the company suffering multi-million pound losses, as did Lloyd's fund management arm and that of Deutsche Bank.

The differing attitudes to short-sellers can be gauged from the stories in the text boxes above; in the opinion of its defenders, short-selling is a legitimate market activity; in the eyes of its detractors (those usually on the wrong end of share price movements) it is a cause of potential destabilisation.

Mostly though, the activities of short-sellers are not sufficient to drive prices dramatically and there is academic evidence[37] to suggest what market operators (see Schwed again) have long held to be the case – that short-sellers perform a useful market function by increasing liquidity in the market and providing a catalyst for revealing information (see the case of Sino-Forest and Muddy Waters above).

However all such market activities provide potential problems once they become either, first disproportionate or, second inappropriate.

---

[37] S. J. Randall Woolridge and A. Dickinson, 'Short selling and common stock prices', *Financial Analysts Journal*, 50(1) (1994), 20–28.

Disproportionate activity

In most cases the amounts of profit made on short-selling trades are tiny and require vast resources to bring about. This characteristic is one of the reasons why hedge fund managers appropriate such huge salaries from their activities. Aside from the issue of the supposed limited availability of talent, the hedge fund owners are unable to sell their businesses on to other buyers with a valuation based on a consideration of the value of a continuing stream of earnings, since it is not possible to predict how consistently such profits can be made. Profits depend very much on the availability of large amounts of cash and the activities of individual traders – who may, of course, run out of luck. This explains why hedge funds guard their proprietary trading models so jealously[38] – they are the totems that they use to fend off the inevitable turn of bad luck by deriving what they believe to be long-term statistical relationships between the history of past trades and current pricing anomalies.

However with the growth of the volume of money moving into hedge funds and the similar increase in the volume of HFT the significance of shorting becomes magnified and without proper controls on the operation of the market – controls which do not normally keep pace with the development of trading technology – the entire market becomes jeopardised.

This is what happened in the 'flash crash' of 6 May 2010 when the activities of HFT houses pushed the US stock market into temporary free fall. Although there is some controversy over the exact sequence and the precise contribution made by HFT traders, both regulators' investigations and advanced computer modelling point to the multiplier effects of HFT activity.[39] The market lost 1014.5 basis points in the space of minutes and recovered almost as quickly – or to put it another way, over $1 trillion of value disappeared (and mostly reappeared) in a blink of the market's eye. Some traders will obviously have lost and some will have won during this period – but it cannot in any rational sense be described as an efficient allocation of resources. Trading 'circuit breakers' have since been put in place in the trade matching mechanism of the US exchanges, which are supposed to prevent a re-occurrence of such events.

---

[38] S. Jones, 'Cypriot court rules for Martin Coward', *Financial Times*, 22 March 2012.
[39] Bethel et al., 'Federal market information technology in the post flash crash era: roles for supercomputing', Lawrence Berkeley National Laboratory, Proceedings of the fourth workshop on High performance computational finance (2011), pp. 23–30, available at www.lbl.gov/cs/html/CIFT-LBL-report.pdf.

Inappropriate activity

While the concept of disproportion is easily understood in terms of market activity, the concept of 'inappropriate activity' requires clarification. The Oxford English Dictionary defines inappropriate as *'not suitable to the case; unfitting; improper'*. It is this concept of impropriety which characterises short-selling which is damaging. It usually involves some form of betrayal of trust – which in a commercial sense is often linked to some failing of the fiduciary relationship between principal and agent. It may also of course shade into the use of information not known generally to the market and therefore approach the legal definition of insider dealing.

In July 2008 it emerged that Morgan Stanley – one of the two merchant banks helping HBOS to raise funds in the UK through its rights issue by acting as underwriter – had also been shorting the shares during the same period.[40] The value of this is difficult for an outsider to assess since as underwriters to the issue Morgan Stanley would have been left with shares in HBOS worth less than they otherwise would have been as the share price fell – a fall caused by its own actions. Without proof, such actions are legally unpursuable even though they may be morally distasteful – and they were quite possibly the source of the rumours that drove the HBOS share price down and down, resulting in billions in losses for other shareholders.

Such trading also comes perilously close to being a signal that someone has succumbed to temptation in breaching the supposed Chinese Walls that are erected to protect activity in one part of a City trading house from being affected by what is going on in another part of the same institution. They may have used insider information to effect a market advantage.

Insider dealing and market abuse

Insider dealing – using information that is not in the general possession of the marketplace to effect an advantage in dealing in shares – is considered a crime in most jurisdictions. The usual reasons for outlawing insider trading are fourfold: first, on a moral plane that it offends a sense of justice about the treatment of shareholders who are not in possession of the information; and, second, from a more practical point of view, that it may increase the cost of capital to companies, as shareholders require higher levels of return in order to be tempted into the ownership of a more volatile asset which they may find moving for reasons they may never know. Third, one step beyond these concerns, is the acute (as opposed to chronic) problem of market manipulation by parties in possession of information to gain market advantage to

[40] 'Morgan Stanley in hot water over HBOS short', *The Independent*, 23 July 2008.

swindle shareholders. Fourth, one step beyond that is the continual, chronic spectre of sustained exploitation of information asymmetry which nips at the heels of the relationships between managers and shareholders. Within this conceptual framework however are very different views, with the actual impact of specific laws being calibrated differently.

Corporate governance reforms in Germany, France and Italy all followed privatisation programmes or were the consequence of reforms intended to respond to the mobility of international investment capital. There are marked variations in the way that different jurisdictions – the USA, UK and the European Union for instance – treat the abuse of market rules.

The European Union's transnational controls centre around the application of Markets in Financial Instruments Directives (MiFIDs) – which tend to concentrate on issues of transparency in formal dealing in individual markets rather than issues of insider trading, and the Market Abuse Directive (MAD) – first implemented in 2005, which deals with more specific infractions of fair trading. The UK's laws had 'super-equivalence' over MAD (that is, they were more stringent than the EU's recommendations in all respects) until the so-called sunset clauses of the FSMA took effect at the end of 2011.

The differences in definition and calibration between jurisdictions can sometimes produce anomalies, and apparent injustice, depending on which side of the jurisdiction investors and traders stand. For instance, while the USA's laws against insider dealing (SEC Regulations 10b.5 *et seq* and The Securities Act of 1933 and The Securities Exchange Act of 1934) are generally held to be the strictest they are interpreted narrowly with heavy enforcement activity – often involving telephone taps and extended surveillance of individuals. This occasionally produces dramatic results as in the case of the Galleon Fund (see text box, p. 256). The UK's laws by contrast are drafted more loosely but are widely interpreted and actions may be pursued under two pieces of legislation – the Criminal Justice Act 1993 and the Financial Services and Markets Act 2000 – although generally enforcement has not been vigorous, with the first effective prosecutions for blatant abuse occurring only in 2008.

The American system includes some specific issues regarding market operations, on which the laws and regulations are based. American law allows legitimate insider dealing under the Securities Exchange Act of 1934, s. 16, which is similar in concept to the UK's Model Code on Directors' Dealings, but also allows for the continuation of trades under a pre-existing contract. There is also the concept of 'misappropriation' which includes the use of information obtained in the course of employment. Although the legal theory took some time to evolve after a deadlocked case ten years earlier (US Supreme Court, *Carpenter* v. *United States*, 484 U.S. 19 (1987)) it was finally decided in the case of *United States* v. *O'Hagan*, 521 U.S. 642, 655 in 1997 that someone who came into possession of confidential information through his employment would become an insider if he dealt on it and would then be subject to legal penalty, even though he owed no fiduciary duty to the company in which he dealt.

The UK definition of insider dealing

The civil offence, as defined in the FSMA, s. 118, can be any of seven types of behaviour:

- Insider dealing – when an insider deals, or tries to deal, on the basis of inside information.
- Improper disclosure – where an insider improperly discloses inside information to another person.
- Misuse of information – behaviour based on information that is not generally available but would affect an investor's decision about the terms on which to deal.
- Manipulating transactions – trading, or placing orders to trade, that gives a false or misleading impression of the supply of, or demand for, one or more investments, raising the price of the investment to an abnormal or artificial level.
- Manipulating devices – trading, or placing orders to trade, which employs fictitious devices or any other form of deception or contrivance.
- Dissemination – giving out information that conveys a false or misleading impression about an investment or the issuer of an investment where the person doing this knows the information to be false or misleading.
- Distortion and misleading behaviour – behaviour that gives a false or misleading impression of either the supply of, or demand for, an investment; or behaviour that otherwise distorts the market in an investment.

The relevant test takes the following form:

An 'insider' is any person who has inside information:

- as a result of their membership of the administrative, management or supervisory body of an issuer of qualifying investments;
- as a result of holding capital of an issuer of prescribed investments;
- as a result of having access to the information through their employment, profession or duties;
- as a result of criminal activities; or
- which they have obtained by other means, e.g. a tip-off from a friend, and which they know, or could be reasonably expected to know, is inside information.

Insider dealing has occurred where an individual is:

- Knowingly dealing in securities on the basis of inside information.
- Encouraging another to engage in such dealing.
- Disclosing inside information other than in the proper performance of one's duties, office or profession.

'Inside information' is information relating to particular issues of or particular issuers of securities that would be likely if made public to have a significant effect on the price of the securities concerned. To be guilty of an offence the information must have been obtained from a director, employee or shareholder of the company concerned and directly or indirectly from such a person (who must have also known it was inside information).

The American Rules

The regulations provide that when an issuer, or person acting on its behalf, discloses material non-public information to certain enumerated persons (in general, securities market professionals and holders of the issuer's securities who may well trade on the basis of the information), it must make public disclosure of that information. The timing of the required public disclosure depends on whether the selective disclosure was intentional or non-intentional; for an intentional selective disclosure, the issuer must make public disclosure simultaneously; for a non-intentional disclosure, the issuer must make public disclosure promptly. Under the regulation, the required public disclosure may be made by methods that are reasonably designed to effect broad, non-exclusionary distribution of the information to the public.

Rule 10b5–1 addresses the issue of when insider trading liability arises in connection with a trader's 'use' or 'knowing possession' of material non-public information. This rule provides that a person trades 'on the basis of' material non-public information when the person purchases or sells securities while aware of the information. However, the rule also sets forth several affirmative defences, to permit persons to trade in certain circumstances where it is clear that the information was not a factor in the decision to trade. This is the misappropriation issue.

Rule 10b5–2 addresses the issue of when a breach of a family or other non-business relationship may give rise to liability under the misappropriation theory of insider trading. The rule sets forth three non-exclusive bases for determining that a duty of trust or confidence was owed by a person receiving information.

As an example of the different stances adopted by the regulatory authorities, there is the prosecution of David Einhorn and Greenlight Capital in the UK in early 2012 (for selling shares in Punch Taverns, in which Mr Einhorn was a substantial shareholder) after having been told of a potential emergency fund-raising by the company's broker, which would not have occurred in the USA. Einhorn had taken steps which he believed put him in the clear in respect of being informed of sensitive information.

The UK authority's view was different – that Mr Einhorn should have appreciated the difference between the application of the law in the UK and the USA given his position as an experienced investor. The broker had contacted Mr Einhorn to enlist his support as substantial shareholder for the forthcoming rights issue. The positional outcome (as opposed to the legal outcome) of this case was that the Americans could not understand why Mr Einhorn was being prosecuted and the FSA appeared to have pursued a broker (since he was also fined) who was compromised by his client's actions for doing his job in enlisting the support of a major shareholder.

After the fines had been levied on both Mr Einhorn and Andrew Osborne, the broker who spoke to him, controversy rumbled on with both men claiming that they had been unfairly treated in the light of the different laws that existed in the USA and the UK and with the introduction of the concept of 'fine by association' (in the case of Mr Osborne). Having been for many years – in the words of the *Financial Times* Lex Column[41]– like PC Plod, the FSA was now coming down on miscreants like Judge Dredd, turfing out any concept of balanced stewardship in its zeal to demonstrate its toughness; the FSA's behaviour could be regarded as turning the concept of steward-ship upside down. For it now becomes difficult to see how a major shareholder's support can be enlisted for a rights issue, if he cannot be informed of it happening in advance. To try to reduce the inflammation, the FSA took the very unusual step of releasing transcripts of the phone calls between Mr Einhorn and Mr Osborne – 'to let the market decide' – but with little effect since it merely further entrenched views on each side of the Atlantic.

A similar case is that involving the financier Ian Hannam[42] who was acting under instructions of client and apparently self-declared the issue to the FSA. Bad laws make hard cases. But sometimes the issues are clearer.

Insider dealing: the difference in scope

The Galleon Fund insider dealing scandal

In the early summer of 2011 Raj Rajaratnam the chief executive of one of the world's largest hedge funds, The Galleon Fund, was found guilty of all the fourteen charges made against him of conspiracy to defraud and committing securities fraud. For many years apparently, the performance of Rajaratnam's fund had been sustained by information about deals which he had been fed by insiders from companies which included IBM; Advanced Micro Devices; Goldman Sachs; Intel;

---

[41] Lex Column, *Financial Times*, 16 February 2012.
[42] B. Masters, 'FSA raises hackles over Hannam', *Financial Times*, 5 April 2012.

Moody's and McKinsey. Rajaratnam received a sentence of eleven years in jail after the jury found him guilty of making $63 million in illegal trades. Numerous associates of his were then subsequently pursued through the legal process.

The Paulson Fund, Abacus and Goldman Sachs

In 2010, evidence came to light that Goldman Sachs had compiled sub-prime mortgage CDOs which it had then sold to its customers, without disclosing that John Paulson – through his hedge fund Paulson and Co – had been closely involved in the selection of the 'assets' underlying the fund and was actively betting against the success of the instruments. Paulson's fund is reported to have made $15 billion in profit in 2007 on $12.5 billion under management.

In the USA, hedge funds are specifically excluded from the provisions of the legislation that otherwise cover insider dealing.

At the time of writing, Goldman Sachs is expected to negotiate a deferred-prosecution agreement (see Chapter 6). The performance of the Paulson Fund was disappointing during 2011.

The case for prohibiting insider trading is not universally accepted, however. There are a number of grounds for these objections. In some limited respects the Rhenish model of bank shareholding is a contradiction of the insider trading principles in standing form; dealing in the shares of a company in which a bank has an interest may be seen as a signal to the rest of the market. Equally, both the UK and American codes recognise the concept of directors' trades being legitimated insider action, prohibiting transactions only in certain closed periods when the directors might be in possession of 'confidential information' (but isn't all information from a company not released to the outside world confidential?). Milton Friedman believed that the action of trading released information into the market and that more trading freed the market up and acted as a valid conduit for information which might otherwise take time to enter the market. Such delays might result in a mis-allocation of resources.[43]

Furthermore, it would appear that some of the strictures applied to shares are not offered as protections to other trades – in land for instance – where superior knowledge not known to one party may confer a legitimate advantage upon a counter-party to the transaction.

What can certainly be said is that, in the course of less than a generation, the use of information in share markets has changed radically. Information about trading conditions, contracts, likely levels of profit and competitors, was part of the common

---

[43] L. Harris, *Trading & Exchanges* (Oxford University Press, 2003), Chapter 29, pp. 591–7.

currency of conversations between analysts and finance directors of listed companies in the City of London before the advent of 'Big Bang' in 1986. This information, which was then passed on to clients, would now certainly attract a prison sentence for both parties to the conversation if any form of trading action resulted. Yet the stock market is not cleaner to any marked degree, in this respect, as the high profile cases pursued in the past few years by the FSA have demonstrated. The change in regulatory environment has driven the exchange of information into different avenues.

In February 2012 a comparatively rare event occurred in the London Stock Market, when the price of shares in a small oil exploration company surged on clear rumours of a takeover. Although the potential acquirer was mis-identified initially, the rumours proved correct. Such leaks have fallen in number on the London market – partly because of tougher regulation by the FSA and partly because of the lower level of takeover activity in recent years. Since 2000 the FSA has collected, in conjunction with the research division of the LSE, details of abnormal movements in prices of shares and these have shown a trend downward coincident with the stronger enforcement practised by the regulator: in 2009 rumours of takeovers seem to have affected 44 of the 144 takeovers announced while in 2010, only 25 of 118 deals seem to have been compromised.[44]

But the FSA itself is not entirely sure that its statistics are reliable: share prices move for all sorts of reasons and there may be no correlation between every transaction and an exterior event. While the stock market is possibly cleaner, in the sense that there have been fewer superficial leaks in the past couple of years, it is not necessarily fairer in respect of the position of all shareholders. The regulators have not yet managed to devise a mechanism for smoothing the impact of company announcements on share prices, so that sudden bursts of information, emanating from companies (the Exchange offers no advice on what companies should release to the market, leaving it entirely to the discretion of each company's interpretation of what is 'significant'), can result in share prices being more volatile than they would otherwise be. This enables the unscrupulous and knowledgeable to adopt different tactics to capitalise on their asymmetry of information.

The private shareholder

The fundamental problem of fairness (as defined by the Exchange's mechanisms) still by-passes the interests of the private shareholder, who is always at a disadvantage in share trading and shareholding because there will be a circulation of information

---

[44] B. Masters, 'Suspicious trades mar 30% of UK takeovers', *Financial Times*, 10 June 2010; FSA Market Watch, Issue 37 (September 2010); see also B. Dubow and N. Monteiro, 'Measuring Market Cleanliness', FSA Occasional Paper 23 (September 2006); and N. Monteiro, Q. Zaman and S. Leitterstorff, 'Updated Measures of Market Cleanliness', FSA Occasional Paper 25 (March 2007).

among professional shareholders to which he or she will not be privy. The private or small shareholder is a bit like the small boy in the crowd at a football match, continually trying to see the game from between the legs of his older and bigger brothers; theoretically, if he has bought a ticket, he has the same access to view the pitch as every one else but in reality he might only hear the roars of the rest of the crowd when something significant happens.

Market controls could be devised, theoretically, to solve this problem by controlling the release of information to such a degree as to reduce all movements to ones based simply on differences in the perceived appetite for risk; or by allowing trading only at set times after information has been released, but by doing that – apart from the very obvious problems of market mechanics – the problems of misallocation of resources which Friedman pointed to, would still not be avoided.

Regulation of takeovers

In February 2012, not-long-listed Glencore (May 2011 on the London Stock Exchange and an immediate constituent of the FTSE 100) and Xstrata announced that they intended to merge.[45] It was to be, according to the Press releases issued by the two companies, a merger of equals (a slightly redundant explanation, since one of the definitions of a merger is in fact that it is exactly that – two companies that are roughly comparable pooling their resources rather than one company taking over the other). The reasons advanced for the merger were principally the enhancement of earnings of the two companies and the strategic possibilities opened up by combining the world's largest trading house with one of the biggest mining groups. The names of both companies had been linked before the flotation of Glencore in May 2011, when a link was seen as a natural route to release some of the wealth accumulated by the (unlisted) Glencore shareholders.

The academic literature based on studies suggests that over the long term shareholders do not benefit substantially from merger and acquisition activity[46] (or 'murders and executions' as the alternative City slang has it), the disposition of the property represented by a share is not the concern of the market regulator. (In the case of the merger announced in February 2012 there was immediate hostile reaction from some London fund managers, one of whom described it as 'fabulous for Glencore; a great deal for the Xstrata management but a poor deal for Xstrata's

---

[45] J. Blas, 'Time nears for a Glencore and Xstrata deal', *Financial Times*, 11 October 2011.
[46] B. Holmstrom and S. N. Kaplan, 'Corporate governance and merger activity in the U.S.: making sense of the 1980s and 1990s', NBER Working Paper No. 8220, issued in April 2001.

majority shareholders'.[47]) The market as a market and regulators as regulators are not (usually) interested in the specific and purely financial terms of a deal – in terms of valuations – or with what shareholders wish to do with their shares once they have been offered a price for them. The economic outcomes of a particular bid are of no concern to the market regulators. What they are concerned about is that all shareholders are treated equally – both within the same class and between classes, if appropriate – and that nothing is done by a bidder to distort a market to its own advantage or to one set of shareholders.

Regulation of market activity of this type in the UK is the responsibility of one particular body – the Takeover Panel, which was originally established in 1968 to oversee the City Code on Takeovers and Mergers. The provisions of the Code are now largely mirrored in the provisions of the EU Takeover Directive of 2004.

The 2006 Companies Act, Pt 28 (Chapter 1) gave the Takeover Panel statutory power to regulate the conduct of participants to a bid and to sanction behaviour if it deemed it to be in breach of the City Code. Until the passage of the 2006 Act, the Panel existed with significant moral power but no legal teeth. In 2010, the Panel commenced a review of its powers[48] and announced from 2011 a number of technical changes would also be implemented – including the so-called 'put up or shut up powers' (PUSU) which required a bidder to make a definite bid after a specified period; moves to prohibit restrictive undertakings about soliciting alternative bids and the elimination of so-called break fees (which were designed to defray a bidder's outlays in the event of an unconsummated deal).

The effect of the changes is supposed to provide greater protection for the shareholders of targeted businesses. However, one of the consequences of the changes may be to make bids more difficult to accomplish: the cumulative effect of the changes is to make the collection of information about a potential acquisition much more costly or force it to run to much tighter timetables (which often reduces to the same point about cost). This may not be in the long-term interest of any set of shareholders.

Very large bids are occasionally made on the flimsiest of information – the disastrous RBS bid for ABN Amro was apparently based on the contents of three lever arch files and some CDs.[49] This was on the basis that Barclays were also bidding and they would have done their own 'due diligence' and if they weren't frightened off everything must have been all right. Nor are smaller bids exempt from such failings: the circumstances of the bids that brought Mouchel low (which were not conducted

---

[47] K. Burgess, J. Blas and T. Burgis, 'Glencore and Xstrata face blocking threat', *Financial Times*, 7 February 2012.

[48] A. Smith and L. Saigol, 'Panel gets mixed response to change', *Financial Times*, 21 October 2010.

[49] S. Blowers and J. Treanor, 'RBS "gamble" on ABN Amro deal: FSA', *The Guardian*, 12 December 2011.

under such tight time constraints) have already been dealt with. Under the new proposals the analysis of more and better information from a target company's own data will be subject to a very tight time limit. This might of course bring about fewer and more considered bids. But since, as has been alluded to above, few bids appear to bring benefits to shareholders in the long run but mostly appear to benefit the incumbent management of the acquiring business for a brief period (partly due to the scope allowed for technical and quite legal 'improvements' in the combined accounts) the auguries are not good.

Regardless of the effect of proposed new powers, the Takeover Panel does not seem to have exercised those it already possessed consistently or uniformly. Mitchells and Butlers appears to have become the plaything of a group of wealthy investors who might be said to have controlled the company's fortunes to the detriment of other shareholders without being forced to make a bid; or have been able to use information they are in possession of to make bids which distort the market for the company's shares. In the case of Kraft's takeover of Cadbury, the acquiring company made specific undertakings during the bid which it then decided to renege upon after the acquisition was completed.[50] The Panel found itself unable to do anything practical to censure Kraft. Under its new head (who had also been Kraft's chief external legal adviser before being seconded to the Panel) the Panel decided not to press any for any action against statements made by or on behalf of the company during the bid, the failure to follow through on which later cast doubt on Kraft's good faith during the bidding.

Conclusion

The idea behind the regulation of stock markets is to protect all market participants by ensuring that powerful or sectional interests do not distort patterns of trading by using asymmetries in knowledge or resources of money to their own particular advantage. In the corporate governance framework in the UK and elsewhere, many procedural aspects of good governance are reinforced by market obligations. In many respects the contracts which companies agree with stock markets to provide large amounts of information on entry and then to abide by the rules on the release of information and their behaviour towards their shareholders afterwards have pre-dated statutory obligations. The supervisory policing role of the stock market thus has an integral contribution to the maintenance of good governance.

However, the regulation of the market is not infallible and to rely on it too strongly as a prime source of governance is to fall into the reductivist trap of believing that the powers of the market – alone and unfettered – will elicit behaviour among

---

[50] Concerning factory closures.

companies and information from them that will bring about all that investing shareholders require. Such mistaken reliance will further reduce the effectiveness of fragile governance structures that are derived from a traditionalist theory of governance entrenched in a belief in the moral, legal and operational supremacy of the shareholder. The force of the market is generally more powerful than actions that can be undertaken by individual shareholders – which may sometimes work to the collective of advantage of all shareholders but may also work to the disadvantage of minorities.

In some cases the stakeholder appears to have supplanted the shareholder as the locus of power in respect of company behaviour – particularly where externally-orientated behaviour, involving activity that can affect a publicly-listed company in a forward-looking sense, is involved.

This subject will be pursued further in the next chapter which will deal with the ramifications of the financial regulatory regime in the UK following the break-up of the FSA into two constituent parts.

CHAPTER 11

Changes in regulatory structures – the PRA, the FCA and the ICB recommendations

This chapter will review the following issues:

- changes in regulatory organisation brought about by the splitting of the FSA into two components;
- the argument for treating the regulatory control of the financial sector as a special case embedded in the changes;
- the continuation of the development of the role of the FSA as a shareholder proxy;
- the changes brought about by the ICB recommendations;
- shortcomings of the proposed changes;
- transparency charges.

Regulatory activity over companies may include aspects of both procedural and behavioural activity as well as systemic regulation. Thus it concerns itself with the detail of individual transactions; with the culture against which those transactions are effected (structural governance) and the inter-relationships between those two at the level of the whole system. In the UK the landscape of regulatory activity for the financial services sector will be changed substantially in early 2013 when the FSA splits into two parts to become the Prudential Regulation Authority (PCA) and the Financial Conduct Authority (FCA). While this change is essentially a matter of sectoral regulation its impact goes much further. The change emphasises the significance of the financial sector to the UK economy – not only in terms of companies that are involved in operations in finance but also through their activities as investors and financiers of other companies.

What the financial crisis of 2007–8 threw into sharp relief were the gaps between the co-ordinating functions of the triumvirate of the Bank of England, the Treasury and the FSA. While the crisis was essentially confined to the finance sector initially, it rapidly spread throughout the whole economy. Within hours, once it broke out, it began to affect stock market behaviour; domestic borrowers and deposit makers; insurance companies and pension funds; industrial companies and retail concerns. The crisis therefore spilled over extremely rapidly from a localised, sectoral problem to one which affected all of the economy. It affected all of the functions of the State that supervised in some way the machinery of the economy: the Bank of England, charged with the control of borrowing and lending and interest rates; the Treasury, charged with the overall wellbeing of the economy; and the FSA, charged with the supervision of the financial sector, which underpins all other economic activity.

At the sharpest point of the crisis, it appeared that none of these bodies had had a clear idea of what should be done, or even what the basic cause of the problems were. The FSA had been watching individual companies in the financial sector – with greater or lesser diligence; Lord Turner, in an interview on UK television in February 2009, accepted that the FSA had been focusing too much on processes and procedures rather than looking at the bigger economic picture. During the boom years, the Treasury had been congratulating itself on the progress of the economy, even though it was fuelled by swilling debt; and the Bank of England had apparently missed much of the significance of the information it routinely collected (see Figure 11.1). Everyone was looking at their part of the picture – often in some detail – but not relating it to the overall landscape – and to continue the allusion drawn at the start of the book, they were often looking at the landscape without any appreciation of the geology that underlay the topography. The figure below, taken from a much later edition of the Bank of England's *Financial Stability Report*, illustrates the point.

The information in Figure 11.1 clearly indicates the rapid rise of gearing in banks' balance sheets just before the crisis hit. The use of other data about banks' deposits and inflows, regularly collected by the Bank, would have helped point to the conclusion

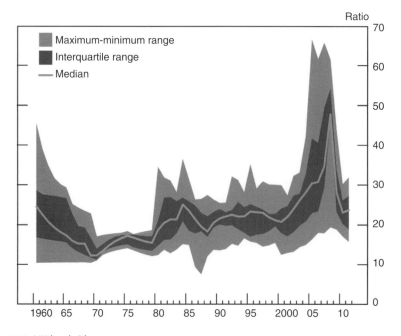

Figure 11.1 UK banks' leverage
Source: Published accounts and Bank calculations.

that the steep rise was nothing more than inter-bank indebtedness. In short, banks' balance sheets were becoming swollen with the 'assets' that they traded between themselves and from which they were deriving 'profits'. The Treasury the Bank and the FSA all had access to this information – it is regularly collected and published publicly – but for whatever reason no-one appears to have recognised the significance of the over-heating of activity and the increased amount of inter-bank activity that diminished capital ratios and reduced effective liquidity.

The supposed points of contact between the three institutions were where systemic control of governance was weakest. Just as weeds flourish in the gaps between paving stones, so the seeds of systemic failure (and counter-governance, see Chapters 15 and 16) are most able to develop where the regulatory reach does not extend – either by accident, or by design, or by neglect. By the time that the high point of the financial crisis had passed it had become obvious that the FSA was not operating as it should. The Turner Review had stated quite bluntly that the Authority had not acquitted its obligations (see Chapter 8) in respect of the governance of the market – the systemic issue of governance.

Whether the failure was a consequence of 'light touch' regulation; a failure of strategy within that overall policy; failure on the part of senior individuals to exercise the authority that they were equipped with; or a blend of all those factors, is uncertain. Certainly just before the financial crisis the FSA was becoming more determined in its prosecution of the failings of market operators – corporate or individual – a change which was probably due to major changes of staffing responsibilities inside the Authority, and an indication that some of the policing powers had been previously under-used.

The FSA Charter

From its creation in 2001 under the Financial Services and Markets Act the FSA had four chartered aims:

1. *Maintaining confidence in the UK financial system* by, among other things, supervising exchanges, settlement houses and other market infrastructure providers; conducting market surveillance; and transaction monitoring.

A systemic function

2. *Promoting public understanding of the financial system.* FSA are supposed to help people gain the knowledge, aptitude and skills they need to become informed consumers, so that they can manage their financial affairs more effectively.

A sort of 'reverse-behavioural' function, bearing on the customers' interests to promote adequate behavioural governance on the part of firms in the financial sector through demand-pull.

3. *Securing the right degree of protection for consumers.* Vetting at entry aims to allow only those firms and individuals satisfying the necessary criteria (including honesty, competence and financial soundness) to engage in regulated activity. Once authorised, firms and individuals are expected to maintain particular standards set by the FSA. They monitor how far firms and individuals are meeting these standards and investigate and, if appropriate, discipline or prosecute those responsible for conducting financial business outside the rules.

Both procedural and behavioural functions

4. *Helping to reduce financial crime.* FSA focuses on three main types of financial crime: money laundering; fraud and dishonesty; and criminal market misconduct such as insider dealing.

A function which should support good structural governance

These aims will now be redistributed between the PRA and the FCA – although probably with a lesser emphasis on the educative obligation.

In the first few weeks of the new coalition Government the Chancellor of the Exchequer announced the much-trailed policy of abolishing the FSA[1] as it stood and splitting it into two component parts: the FCA and the PRA.

As far as regulated firms are concerned, the original conclusion drawn was there was unlikely to be much change in the impact of day-to-day contact with the regulator, either in style or in substance. The government was initially keen to stress that the intention was not to double the amount of regulation by splitting the old body into two, although the line now is that there will have to be some duplication and that the large financial groups which were due an inspection in the FSA's final year will now probably receive two inspections, one of which will be by the new regulators.[2] Before his resignation of the post[3] Hector Sants, the chief-in-waiting of the Prudential Regulation Authority had called upon his supervisees to adopt a different approach to the two 'pro-active and judgment-led' regulators – not adopting a narrow rule-bound attitude of what they could get away with but instead taking a broad view. He stressed that the new approach means two distinct sets of regulators – perhaps taking two different approaches to the task.

---

[1] P. Jenkins, 'Bankers resigned to change', *Financial Times*, 19 June 2010.
[2] L. M. Cannon and P. Adams, 'Twin peaks regulation', *New Law Journal*, 162(7507) (2012).
[3] K. Burgess, 'Sants gets wish and heads for FSA's door', *Financial Times*, 16 March 2012.

The Bank of England

Under the new format of regulation the Bank will have the responsibility of protecting and enhancing the stability of the financial system of the UK, by working with other relevant bodies, including the Treasury, the PRA and the FCA. As a direct legacy of the events of 2007–8 (and with echoes back to the 1972–75 secondary banking crisis 'lifeboat'), the Bank will have a Special Resolutions Unit which will be responsible for the supervision of failing banks under the special resolutions regime. The other major change is that the Bank will also constitute a Financial Policy Committee which will identify and take action to remove systemic risks.

The Financial Policy Committee

The Financial Policy Committee was proposed in the policy document 'A New Approach to Financial Regulation: building a stronger system' published by the Treasury in February 2011. The FPC is supposed to work in the following way:

> The Government envisages that the FPC will contribute to the Bank's financial stability objective by identifying, monitoring, and taking action to remove or reduce, systemic risks with a view to protecting and enhancing the resilience of the UK financial system. The interim FPC will undertake, as far as possible, the forthcoming statutory FPC's macro-prudential role. An important initial task will be to carry out preparatory work and analysis into potential macro-prudential tools. The Government's consultation document states that the interim FPC …will play a key role in the development of the permanent body's toolkit by sharing its analysis and advice on macro-prudential instruments with the Treasury, to help inform the Government's proposals for the FPC's final macro-prudential toolkit.[4]

This is the component of the changes that is probably of the greatest value to the improvement of the sturdiness of the regulatory regime, since it will be pointed towards the issue that seems most commonly agreed on – that one of the major failings of the previous arrangement was that despite whatever tasks they thought that they were doing, no-one was paying concentrated attention to the overall picture.

It will be the purpose of the FPC to scrutinise such information and to alert both the other arms of the regulatory structure – the Treasury (and therefore Government), the FCA and the PRA – to changes in market conditions which might jeopardise systemic stability. This power extends beyond recommendation to a directive power to effect change.

---

[4] Bank of England website, www.bankofengland.co.uk/financialstability/Pages/fpc/default.aspx.

The Prudential Regulation Authority

The PRA will report to the Bank of England and is tasked with the obligation to enhance financial stability by promoting the safety and soundness of authorised persons, including the minimisation of any impact of their individual failure. It will be looking after 'prudentially significant firms' – deposit takers (the banks), insurance companies and some investment firms.

The Financial Conduct Authority

It will be the responsibility of the FCA to enhance confidence in the UK financial system by facilitating efficiency and choice in services; securing an appropriate degree of consumer protection; and protecting and enhancing the integrity of the UK financial system. It will thus regulate the conduct of firms under its supervision and also give some support to consumers of financial products.

Comments by the Chair of the Treasury Committee, Andrew Tyrie MP, on publication of the Committee's report into the FCA proposals

'We need a fresh approach to regulation. The plain fact is that the FSA did not succeed in protecting consumers from spectacular regulatory failures. The mis-selling of PPI and endowment mortgages are just two examples. The FSA is not only expensive, for which the consumer always pays, but many have told us that it has also become bureaucratic and dominated by a box-ticking culture.

The creation of the FCA is an opportunity to create something much better. Too often we've heard that the FSA is aloof and unapproachable and that, in any case, firms are nervous about approaching them – we must break with that culture. Encouraging a greater level of engagement between firms and the regulator is in the consumer interest.

If we are not careful, the FCA will become the poor relation among the new institutions. But it is the one that will matter most to millions of consumers.'

Treasury Committee policy recommendations

Among the Treasury Committee's recommendations are:

That the Government should legislate to give the FCA a primary objective to promote effective competition for the benefit of the consumer. This is closely in line with the thinking of the Independent Commission on Banking and the Office of Fair Trading.

That the FCA develops far more reliable estimates, in collaboration with the industry, of its own cost effectiveness.

That the Government differentiates between retail and wholesale consumers.

That both the FCA and the financial services industry make better efforts to communicate with each other.

That the current legislative proposals be revised to ensure that the FCA is properly accountable to Parliament and that tools are available to enable the required level of explanation from the regulator.

The regulatory stance is therefore what has been described as 'twin peak'. There are inevitably, however, valleys between peaks.

Shortcomings of the new structure

First, one of the most obvious – although not the most significant – issues will be the additional cost of regulation. Staff numbers at the FSA increased by a third after the crisis up to the point where the organisation split and the first year will see an increase in staffing costs of 15 per cent with a further 10 per cent in each of the next two years.[5]

Second, in some ways the splitting and division of responsibilities is a reversion to the multi-regulator structure that characterised regulation after the Big Bang – and which was found to be wanting. Other countries generally have not adopted such a radical approach after reviewing their regulatory stances (and most commentators agree that few regulatory systems came out of the crisis untarnished).

Third, it is to be hoped that the regulatory agencies get time to 'bed down' before the next crisis occurs – and the lengthy timeline for changes required by the report of the Independent Commission on Banking, together with continuing incipient problems in some financial products allows plenty of scope for another crisis. The FCA will be particularly in need of recruits since many of the FSA's existing staff are moving to the PRA.[6]

Fourth, as a consequence of this nothing is being done – apart from exhortations to the supervisees to be better behaved – to avoid the chronic problem of regulatory lag. The market moves faster than the regulator can hope to keep up in most areas – that was largely the problem of the last crisis. Although the introduction of the FPC may go some way to ameliorating this, the phenomenon is unlikely to go away and many new staff are going to have to learn their jobs and the implications of the new regulatory structure at the same time as they learn about their supervisees.

[5] B. Masters, 'Financial regulator seeks 15% rise in budget', *Financial Times*, 2 February 2012.
[6] J. Kollewe, 'Hector Sants quits FSA', *The Guardian*, 16 March 2012.

Fifth, some of the narrow reactions to the control and management of the large financial institutions that were introduced in the immediate aftermath of the crisis may have to be reviewed. Between 2008 and 2011 the FSA vetted the appointments of more than 550 prospective directors to the boards of banks[7] to try to assess the extent of their market knowledge and understanding of risk and corporate governance. In the exercise it conducted to review the appointment of potential directors of financial institutions the FSA effectively displaced the shareholders of those organisations as the selectors of directors.

A narrow focus on non-executive directors of banks having appropriate experience, such as that required by the FSA after the Walker Review, may worsen the problem of group think rather than reduce it. The example of the board of Lehman served as an example of the need for reform but the author of the Davies Report on Women on Boards said in 2011 that he was 'appalled that the FSA is forcing a thinking that boards of a financial institution can only be made up of people who have an extraordinary amount of experience in that industry … We will look back in decades to come and say that was a mistake. The whole idea, even on bank boards, is to have different sorts of thinking'.[8]

Significantly, the principle that shareholders should have a slate of directors approved by the State runs counter to the concepts of the independence of the incorporated business and of the primacy of the shareholder, which are supposedly fundamental to the conventional view of the operation of corporate governance.

Lehman's Board, pre-crash

The board members included:
- John Macomber, 80 years old, a former McKinsey & Co. consultant and chief executive of chemical-maker Celanese Corp;
- John Akers, 74, former IBM chief;
- Thomas A. Cruikshank, 77, chief executive of Halliburton Co. prior to Vice President Dick Cheney;
- Henry Kaufman, 81;
- Sir Christopher Gent, 60, the one-time chief of mobile-phone company Vodafone PLC (second youngest member);
- Theatre producer, Roger S. Berlind, 75;
- Former Telemundo Chief Executive, Roland Hernandez, 50;
- Michael Ainslie, 64, former chief executive of Sotheby's Holdings;

---

[7] E. Moore, 'Davies raps bank boards' "fatal mistake"', *Financial Times*, 22 February 2012.
[8] *Ibid.*

- Marsha Johnson Evans, 61, one-time head of the US Red Cross and a former Navy rear admiral;
- and, until 2006, Dina Merrill, an 83-year-old actress who once featured in the film *Desk Set* (1957) as well as *Caddyshack II* (1988).

Last, nothing has been done specifically about two major problems – the first being the scope and coverage of the regulatory regime; the second being the problem of international systemic coverage.

The shadow banking sector, hedge funds and Exchange Traded Funds (ETFs) all remain outside the scope of the new regulatory structure. The last crisis showed that the problems arise as much as anything else from areas where regulation does not extend. Shadow banking, hedge funds, ETFs and other structured funds all have the potential to distort dramatically the level of financial activity and throw the system out of kilter.[9]

Structured products – which superficially resemble unit trusts but are effectively less transparent because of the discretion allowed to providers in terms of the assets that they load into the composition – have great potential to go badly wrong for their investors and are effectively unregulated. Sales of these instruments (mostly but not exclusively to the private saver) exceeded £9 billion in the UK in 2011.[10] This was down from the previous year's total of £12 billion but with the number of individual products launched at the same level, at 900. One-third of these were inflation linked. So-called collateralised products accounted for many of these new launches, attracting investors away from low-yielding deposit accounts and into higher yielding funds where the exact composition of the product is at the discretion of the provider. Some of these products track one index with complicated synthetic compositions that may in fact be nothing like the apparent make-up; others are yet more complicated and are called hybrid funds since they track a composite index. Such funds can be loaded with very obscure baskets of assets, not all of which may be fully described and all of which are at the discretion of the provider in pledging against the fund.[11] Even supposedly collateralised (security-backed) funds are not immune from problems: Lehman Brothers defaulted on its structured product pay-outs when it collapsed in 2008.[12]

---

[9] C. Flood, 'ETF providers attack systemic risk warnings', *Financial Times*, 17 April 2011.

[10] E. Moore, 'Sales of structured products soar', *Financial Times*, 13 March 2012.

[11] J. Grant and N. Tait, 'Europe set for overhaul of rules on share dealing', *Financial Times*, 29 July 2010.

[12] S. Grene, 'ETF Q&A: the good, the bad and the synthetic', *Financial Times*, 31 January 2010.

UK banks still continue to use US and Euro denominated Residential Mortgage-Backed Securities (RMBSs), collateral swaps and secured debt private placements to trade between themselves on their 'prop desks'. More competition among banks – something actively cultivated by the ICB report, coupled with regulatory uncertainty may lead to more – not less – usage of shadow banking instruments, thereby furthering instability but 'under the radar'. Some banks are considering the bundling of international trade debts into CDO format; shadow banking and the regulated sector thus merge together.[13]

The new 'twin-peak' structure in the UK will have to absorb – in due course, by 2019 – the Independent Banking Commission's (the Vicker's Report) proposals for ringfencing domestic banks, which have been accepted by the UK Government. Yet there are problems inherent in the existing structure of the sector which have not been dealt with in reasoning behind the ICB's proposed structure. These pivot on the widely-used concept of 'moral hazard'.

The term was current in economic debates in the 1960s.[14] Its provenance as a philosophical term goes back to the seventeenth century and as an operational concept it was widely used by English insurance companies in the late nineteenth century.[15] But in the specific context of the banking crisis – and as attributing a rationale for the behaviour of directors of banks – its use is much more recent. Appearing before the House of Commons Treasury Select Committee in September 2007, the Governor of the Bank of England used the term to explain why the Bank had held back from supplying funding to Northern Rock prior to the run on that bank two months earlier, even when it became obvious that it was struggling given that its funding sources – the wholesale money market – were drying up. He said it would have been 'irresponsible' for the Bank of England to have intervened earlier, citing the concept of moral hazard.[16] The idea he wanted to convey was that by signalling too early that it would bail out banks that got into trouble, bankers would be encouraged to take even larger risks, certain in the knowledge that they would not suffer insupportable consequences.

This interpretation of a central bank's role flies in the face of the long-recognised obligation of central banks to be lenders of last resort – although admittedly that term was never intended to imply *funders* of last resort and was supposed to apply to strictly temporary imbalances in commercial banks' financing. However, as the UK secondary banking crisis of 1972–75 showed, there was no reason – of policy, practical, political

---

[13] Leader Column, *Financial Times*, 10 April 2012.

[14] K. Arrow, 'Uncertainty and the welfare economics of medical care', *Am. Econ. Review* (December 1963).

[15] A. E. Dembe and L. I. Boden, 'Moral hazard: A question of morality?', *New Solutions*, 10(3) (2000), 257–9.

[16] P. Stevens, 'It is time to abandon imprudent caution', *Financial Times*, 6 October 2008.

or operational – why the Bank of England should not assume a longer-term view and there were many reasons why it should. The Bank has itself now recognised this through the introduction of the supervisory powers of the Special Resolution Unit, embodied in its new structure after the Banking Act 2009.

The Bank of England's Special Resolution Regime

The Banking Act 2009 created a Special Resolution Regime (SRR) which gives the Tripartite authorities a permanent framework providing tools for dealing with distressed banks and building societies. And it gives the Bank of England a new role in selecting from the statutory resolution tools. The SRR powers came into force on 21 February 2010 following the expiry of the emergency legislation in the Banking (Special Provisions) Act 2008. That Act had made provision to enable the Treasury in certain circumstances to make an order relating to the transfer of securities issued by, or of property, rights or liabilities belonging to, an authorised deposit-taker; it was used to nationalise Northern Rock.

The SRR powers allow the authorities to:
- transfer all or part of a bank to a private sector purchaser;
- transfer all or part of a bank to a bridge bank – a subsidiary of the Bank of England – pending a future sale;
- place a bank into temporary public ownership (the Treasury's decision);
- apply to put a bank into the Bank Insolvency Procedure (BIP) which is designed to allow for rapid payments to Financial Services Compensation Scheme (FSCS) insured depositors;
- apply for the use of the Bank Administration Procedure (BAP) to deal with a part of a bank that is not transferred and is instead put into administration.

The Banking Act creates clearly-defined roles for operation of the SRR. The Financial Services Authority, in consultation with the Bank and the Treasury, makes the decision to put a bank into the SRR. HM Treasury would decide whether to put a bank into temporary public ownership, and otherwise, the Bank of England, in consultation with the other authorities decides which of the tools to use. The FSCS has a role in relation to depositors covered by its depositor compensation scheme.

The Act sets out five key objectives in choosing which resolution tools to use:
- to protect and enhance the stability of the financial systems of the UK;
- to protect and enhance public confidence in the stability of the banking systems of the UK;
- to protect depositors;

- to protect public funds;
- to avoid interfering with property rights in contravention with the Human Rights Act 1998.

To carry out its new responsibilities the Bank has set up a Special Resolution Unit which will lead in the work required to select and implement a resolution tool.

Since its use by the Governor, the term has now become more widely accepted among some academic economists and policy-makers as a factor to be considered in the structure and processes of banking regulation. It formed part of the basis of the ICB's remit (see Chapter 8). The Treasury instructed the Commission to assess how to:

- reduce financial stability risk in the banking sector, by exploring the risk posed by banks of different size, scale and function;
- mitigate 'moral hazard' in the banking system – this is where institutions are insulated from the natural consequences of taking risks due to their size and importance;
- deal with the issue of banks being seen as 'too big to fail';
- reduce the likelihood and impact of firm failure; and
- promote competition in both retail and investment banking.

The concept in the remit is different from the interpretation placed on the term subsequently. The National Institute of Economic and Social Research (NIESR), while agreeing that moral hazard 'is central to the crisis' still questioned the application of the concept: papers produced by NIESR staff[17] have suggested that bankers' appreciation of risk was poor both collectively/corporately and personally and that while the bankers were supposedly so certain about the likely response of regulators, the regulators exhibited no such certainty about their own likely responses. The use of the moral hazard argument appears therefore to be a retro-fitted theory, consistent only with the outcome and not with the causes.

A far more likely explanation is that given by Chuck Prince, the then chief executive of Citicorp in an interview with the *Financial Times* in July 2007:[18] 'When the music stops, in terms of liquidity, things will be complicated. But as long as the music is playing, you've got to get up and dance. We're still dancing.'

---

[17] A. Armstrong, 'Never Again – an evaluation of the ICB's proposals for structural reform', ESRC/ NIESR Financial Stability conference, London, February 2012.

[18] M. Nakamoto and D. Wighton, 'Citigroup chief stays bullish on buy-outs', *Financial Times*, 9 July 2007.

In other words banks' behaviour is driven by what their competitors are doing. This is a far more plausible explanation than that of discounting disaster because the State will intervene. It would have been a very strange board meeting if Sir Fred Goodwin (as he then was) had told his fellow directors as justification for RBS buying ABN Amro, that the risks of things going wrong could be discounted because the Bank of England would step in to help out. Bankers wanted to see their share price rising – that is what drove their conduct – and looked for ways of doing that, not least to benefit themselves too. It seems unlikely that they were blinded to the possibilities of a zombie life for their bank's share price – and their reputations and legacies, their livelihoods and their own wealth – by the potential of a State safety net.

The ICB report, in seeking to break up the large 'universal' banks into smaller models, does not reduce the issues of competition which promoted the environment of risk-taking which Chuck Prince described as being the most important. The ICB's report largely ignores the issue of how banks will still compete with one another under the revised structure it advocates. The so-called 'challenger banks' which raised funds by methods which were seen at the time as innovative and highly competitive[19] were largely where the problems were greatest – Anglo Irish, Northern Rock and IceSave would all fit into this category. Further, Figure 11.1 showed the systemic effect on bank gearing of deep changes in the asset holding behaviour of competitive banks. If banks are still to be encouraged to be innovative and competitive under the ICB recommendations, more regulatory attention will have to be paid to the bellows effect of expanding and contracting balance sheets. With banks trading assets extensively with each other, as support for their lending policies, there are positive and negative effects for individual banks of each change in asset value and gearing of their counter-parties. Reducing the supposed likelihood of 'moral hazard' by virtue of not guaranteeing support for a failed bank might still not prevent the gradual accretion of systemic risk.

As later chapters will show (Chapters 12 and 13), the problems with the banks were manifold – not so much that they were too big to fail but that they were inherently too big to audit. This is a general problem of large organisations which impacts upon the systemic nature of governance and affects the individual, behavioural governance culture.

Dealing in monetary assets and very large numbers of transactions, using novel and dynamic products, banks are more opaque as commercial entities than most other types of business, for an outsider. As has already been noted they resemble federated structures rather than unified business entities. Within this opacity managers will constantly be trying – legitimately – to shift risk to different levels and to different vehicles within the organisational structure. This produces vulnerability to

---

[19] T. Braithwaite, 'Banking costs more for small businesses', *Financial Times*, 14 October 2005.

systemic problems – and structural governance – unless managers are always able to correctly predict systemic changes. Because of the opacity, regulators will be unaware of the changes and the varying levels of vulnerability at any given time. Although academic studies are far from unanimous on the way that competition and risk are traded off,[20] there seems to be a convergence around the idea that franchise value – simply put, the firm's standing and reputation – and risk-taking are trade-offs: more respected firms are less likely to indulge in risky behaviour. However, there appear to be no safeguards in the anticipated regimes of either the proposed ringfenced banks or the regulatory structures that are being developed, to prevent the use of inter-bank products which might be regarded as systemically risky once a certain volume arises. In short certain activities which are going to be outside the anticipated regulatory perimeter might produce the feed-stock for competitive banks inside the perimeter, thereby allowing osmosis of systemic risk into the regulated sector unless the regulator is particularly alert.

The division of the FSA into the two new bodies does seem to address most of these problems, since it will specifically target *prudential* regulation and financial *conduct*. It is not certain however that it will have the conceptual tools to enable it to do this in the light of the discussion above.

The problems of the integration of regulatory techniques and opacity of the regulated sector are multiplied by the international dimension. The contagion that affected financial markets swept across the whole globe because of the international mobility of capital and the global reach of the large banks. Global regulatory standards are loose or informal; if standards are to be pursued they must be enforced so that the development of appropriate – and enforceable – standards for the regime of banking regulation through the Basel III agreements must be a priority, as the PRA itself has pointed out.

In this international aspect there is a fundamental disjuncture between the characteristics of the financial sector and the regulatory machinery set up to supervise it. The products of the financial sector are international and mobile; constantly morphing into new forms; highly dynamic and evolutionary. National regulations are devised locally and enforced territorially; fixed in a point in time by virtue of being structured and without any innovative component – for them to have an innovative characteristic would largely be a contradiction of the cardinal qualities of regulation as being fair, predictable, certain and enforceable.[21]

---

[20] F. Allen and D. M. Gale, 'Competition and financial stability', NYU Working Paper No. S-FI-03–06 (September 2003), available at http://ssrn.com/abstract=1297769.
[21] Cf. Adam Smith's Four Canons of Taxation: Smith, *Wealth of Nations*.

CHAPTER 12

Failure – the abiding characteristic of regulation

This chapter will consider the issues of:
- audit and its failings;
  - audit failure;
  - 'good audits';
- accountants' and auditors' judgement;
- the application of accounting standards;
- auditor defensiveness;
- international developments;
- limitation of liability – shareholder issues;
- audit firm governance and related issues;
  - UK;
  - European dimension;
- regulatory lag.

Introduction

Previous chapters have built up a case, by taking a variety of perspectives on the components of the mechanism of corporate governance, that the traditionalist, conventional view of how governance operates does not describe what actually happens in companies or in the marketplace. As a consequence of this, the individual components of the governance system, put together under the principles of the conventional view, are not well linked and do not operate together effectively because the traditionalist view over-emphasises the importance of some aspects and reduces the significance of others.

There is a further problem which now needs to be considered concerning the standing of one of the individual components of the governance mechanism, that of the audit of companies' financial information.

Audit is central to much of the architecture of corporate governance since it is the check mechanism on which the traditionalist view of the governance system largely depends. Audit has a central regulatory role at every level of governance – from the self-checking by the organisation of procedural aspects; through the process of reporting to shareholders on the behavioural aspects of company processes; to the systemic aspects of providing information on which other parts of the market/ governance system rely.

Yet audit typifies much of the fundamental problem of all regulation – it is an activity which is almost fated not to produce the outcome anticipated of it – and this is more than in the sense of failing to produce either evidence of the failing of a system or failing to produce a clean bill of health. On anything more than superficial examination the practice of audit appears to be an activity that adds little of real weight to the purposes of governance in terms of purposive effect for listed companies. Other regulatory activities do not always achieve their expected or desired objectives on a consistent basis but the problem with auditing, as will be demonstrated, is that it *almost always* fails to do what is required or expected of it. Michael Power describes this as the 'expectations gap'.[1] The gap is not simply about what audits can actually deliver in terms of the reality against the ideal but also what the public expects of audits – and public perceptions of audits are relatively unsophisticated in comparison with those of practitioners.

Audit and its failings

The act of checking stands as a substitute for complete trust. As Julian LeGrand has pointed out,[2] regulation and trust are difficult to reconcile. The need to check implies that there is some potential for a breakdown in the relationship of trust between the entity or person being checked and the person to whom the report of the check will be made; the first problem that audit faces is that if this breakdown is the result of intentional mischief or the suspicion of such, then the evidence of the failure will probably be concealed, making the uncovering of it difficult.

Concealment is also aided by volume just as verification is hindered by it: in a simple organisation it is perhaps possible to check physically every transaction. Where transactions annually run into many multiples of millions as they may do with very large financial institutions, it becomes impossible for every transaction to be checked individually and sampling procedures have to be developed to provide some degree of confidence that problems will be revealed by looking at only a small fraction of the total number of transactions.

Thus any audit starts off on the back foot in any but the simplest of organisations: it is trying to discover something that has already been done recorded by systems that are prone to (at least) normal error; something that will probably not be readily

---

[1] M. Power, *The Audit Society* (Oxford University Press, 1997).
[2] J. Le Grand, *Motivation, Agency and Public Policy* (Oxford University Press, 2003).

evident if it is damaging to the organisation; something that may be concealed by deliberate action or simply by volume; and all that from a position of externality to the main organisation. (Even internal audit functions have to be distanced, by their very nature, from the activities of the main organisation by which they are hosted.) Audit teams are used as training grounds for entrants to the profession, although they are supervised, of course, by qualified professionals;[3] nonetheless as a consequence of this a good proportion of the members of an audit team will start out without detailed expert knowledge of an organisation's specific processes or idiosyncracies. Added to this is the constraint of time and agreed cost bulking large in the timetable for the audit: auditing is a fiercely competitive business despite the relative oligopoly of the major accounting firms, who always have eager competitors snapping at their heels. In an attempt to overcome some of these problems the auditor is forced to adopt a partial approach and to use a series of tests that – while they may be scientifically based using mathematical techniques – are essentially applicable only to the purely numerical aspects of transactions.

It might be contested that audit is more than mere numerical checking in the hope of finding a discrepancy; it does not have to be a hostile activity seeking to trip up those it is checking up on, but can produce organisational benefits (although some authorities contend that fraud discovery appears to have been the primary purpose of auditing until well into the twentieth century, others point to the neutral issue of verification being documented as the main purpose a century earlier).[4] While this might reduce the incidence of foredoomed failure it still leaves unsatisfied the issue of the exact value of audit as an action. It is more a ritual than a purposeful activity, sanctifying the books of companies that are probably only marginally out of accounting kilter and failing to root out the problems that have something more seriously wrong. For whatever the description of the primary purpose that is chosen, some simple facts remain.

First, some form of account is being given by one party (an agent) to another (a second agent) to enable a third party (a principal) to assess how well the first party is acquitting his agency obligations and that therefore there is an element of distrust or, at the very least, a gap of credulity which needs to be filled by the auditor's report (despite its limitations). Second, there will be limits to what can be tested for verification – these will be limits imposed by practicality or limits imposed by time or limits imposed by cost. In the commercial world it becomes pointless to pursue the audit process (for most routine purposes) beyond the point at which its marginal cost exceeds its marginal benefit to the organisation (or its stakeholders); the public sector may have different priorities. Third, the situation of any business or organisation is dynamic in respect to the passage of time and consequently the validity of the auditors'

[3] Power, *The Audit Society.*   [4] *Ibid.*

opinion is highly temporary; what is true now for this moment will not necessarily be true after the passage of a brief period of time or after more transactions have been completed. (This particular issue has formed the basis of several significant legal cases about the ways in which an auditor's opinion has value and to whom – see below.)

In addition, there will be areas – which may occasionally be crucially important to an individual organisation's financial position – where the auditor relies on the opinion of others in order to form an opinion of his own.[5] This occurs not only where the auditor has no specific expertise that he can bring to bear – for instance in cases where special assets or special transactions have to be evaluated – but also where audits are conducted by teams of auditors working on different parts of the audited organisation – who may or may not belong to the same auditing organisation, perhaps interpret standards differently or have different approaches to the interpretation of specific judgemental problems. Power characterises this as 'the hierarchy of opinion'[6] – a condition which gives rise to potential problems of consistency and replication.

The Parmalat Affair

In 1999, the firm of Grant Thornton who were the auditors of Parmalat, an Italian dairy products company that had expanded rapidly into a major producer of processed foodstuffs worldwide, was replaced by the multi-national firm of Deloitte – one of the then 'Big Six' accounting firms. Because of the smaller firm's specialist local knowledge (and partly due to the specifics of Italian company law) Grant Thornton was retained as sub-contractor to Deloitte for some of the subsidiary audits.

In 2003, the company collapsed in what turned out to be Europe's biggest fraud to date, with €14 billion of funds improperly accounted for.

In 2005, Deloitte accused Grant Thornton of having withheld information from Deloitte which contributed to making the audits inadequate. Deloitte's chief executive was reported as saying:[7]

'It … appears that possibly other professionals were lying to our people … Based upon the way the prosecutors have dealt with Grant Thornton, it would be reasonable to expect, in the final analysis, that they had information we did not have, and we wished we had.'

In 2004, Grant Thornton (which has the corporate form of an international association of companies) expelled its Italian businesses. In 2008, a court dismissed a legal action against Bank of America and Grant Thornton in respect of the bankruptcy.

[5] *Ibid.*   [6] *Ibid.*
[7] A. Parker, 'Deloitte blames Grant Thornton', *Financial Times*, 3 January 2005.

Audit failure

Even at its most innocent level, as nothing more than a summarised record of trading, the consolidation of a year's transactions in isolation, into a few lines of numbers does violence to the true narrative record of experience of the company (and those who work for it). Skilled analysts can derive much information from the accounting records of companies and can re-construct events with a reasonable degree of accuracy if the information is basically 'wholesome' – in the sense of having been prepared by honest and reasonably diligent individuals tasked with the maintenance of the company's books.

However, if the information has been prepared – falsified – with the intention of deceiving outsiders, then it becomes very difficult within the constraints of time and cost that are the boundaries of a 'normal' audit to unearth evidence of mischief and track it back to a source.[8] As part of the process of developing audit routines that are supposed to be reliable, the external auditor has therefore handed off much of such 'monitoring activity' to the internal audit function, which is tasked (among other things) with routine policing of accounts on a continual basis. The corollary of this is that to succeed as a company fraudster, the perpetrator has either to have the active collusion of some appropriate level of management or the collusion of the internal auditor. In either of these cases, the likelihood of immediate discovery is slim as the numerous examples of account falsification indicate. In the five years from the start of 2006 to the end of 2011, for instance, the accounts of Bernard Madoff's ponzi scheme in America;[9] the hidden loans of Anglo Irish Bank;[10] the falsified accounts of Satyam Computer Services in India;[11] the Lehman Brothers Repo 105 transactions[12] and the Olympus 'tobashi' schemes,[13] all came to light. All these schemes had involved some form of collaboration between managers internally or with outsiders; all the schemes had all been running for many years before discovery. All involved – with the exception of the Madoff scandal – audits being conducted by branches of the very largest firms of accountants. (The use of a one-office firm of accountants by such a large and, purportedly, successful firm as that run by Madoff should have alerted regulators and was therefore an issue of culpable regulatory stupidity – against which no system can be proofed.) The list could be extended backwards indefinitely,

[8] Jones, *Creative Accounting*.
[9] E. Arvedlund, *Madoff: The Man Who Stole $65 Billion* (London: Penguin 2009).
[10] V. Boland, 'Anglo Republic', *Financial Times*, 9 October 2011. Review of S. Carswell, *Anglo Republic: Inside the bank that broke Ireland* (Dublin: Penguin Ireland, 2011).
[11] J. Fontanella-Khan, 'Timeline: the Satyam scandal', *Financial Times*, 7 January 2009.
[12] J. McDermott, 'Dick Fuld and E&Y fail to dismiss Repo 105 case', *Financial Times*, 27 July 2011.
[13] J. Soble, 'Olympus Q&A', *Financial Times*, 10 November 2011.

suggesting that many similar such schemes are being run now and are merely waiting their moment to be revealed, when adverse circumstances push them into the light.

It is generally problems with prevailing economic circumstances which produce evidence of some form of regulatory problem. Regulatory systems are usually strongly pro-cyclical in their impact – light touch during good times (so as 'not to kill the goose that lays the golden egg') and thereby allowing sharp practice to develop which is concealed in the general increase in well-being and the feeling of well-being. Rules are then introduced after the event to try to prevent the same things happening again which, mixing metaphors, is firmly bolting the stable door after the horse has scarpered. Such problems, when they come to light, are often revealed by economic activity receding, leaving firms beached as sources of funds become restricted when they could otherwise survive on the forward momentum produced by advancing economic activity.

Auditors urged to be more medieval

Auditors should imagine themselves as loyal medieval servants to ensure they vet company accounts with sufficient scepticism.

This was the advice given to the profession on Friday by the Financial Reporting Council, the accountancy and corporate governance regulator.

Frustrated by the failure of some auditors to challenge figures produced by company executives, the FRC has tried to define the scepticism it wants them to demonstrate in a wide-ranging paper.

As well as exploring analogies from Greek philosophy and Victorian capitalism, the FRC guidelines suggest that auditors consider the origins of the modern audit, which they trace back to English manor houses in the 14th century.

Then, the most trusted servant was asked to vet the way other servants had looked after their master's assets. Modern auditors could understand their role by putting themselves in the shoes of these loyal retainers, the FRC said.

The regulator said such servants were sure to ask the questions their aristocratic masters would have asked, and demand the same amount of supporting evidence. Modern auditors ought to represent the needs of investors and other stakeholders in the same way, it said.

'If you go into that mindset, you should be able to make the right judgments,' said Marek Grabowski, FRC director of audit policy. Scepticism is 'the absolute cornerstone of an effective audit', he added.

The performance of auditors in the run-up to the financial crisis has come under intense regulatory scrutiny in various countries, particularly with regard to the profession's failure to give advance warning of bank collapses.

The FRC said properly sceptical audits needed to consider whether there was any evidence that would contradict management assertions, rather than just vetting evidence supplied by the audited company.

It also questioned whether some audits might be done more effectively if auditors employed more people with business experience outside the audit profession to do the work.

The traditional 'pyramid' structure, in which recent graduates do much of the work under the supervision of a relatively small number of senior staff, 'may not always be appropriate', the FRC said.

Audit committees – the non-executive directors who manage a company's relationship with its auditor – also needed to encourage others in the business to respond constructively to any challenges made by auditors, the regulator added.

The fact that auditors were paid by the audited company, 'in a way that is relatively detached from shareholders', could be a threat to scepticism, the FRC said.

It said the strong relationships that audit firms built with audited companies and their managers could also compromise auditor independence.

Source: A. Jones, *Financial Times*, 30 March 2012

'Good audits'

The problem of companies failing after they have been cleared, in investors' eyes, by a prolonged series of satisfactory audit opinions usually brings with it some degree of professional self-examination and then possibly some censure. This is then followed by some academic discussion about the need to effect changes in the rules and regulations – or their application – and then a period of quietude until the next problem arises. In some jurisdictions the period between the occurrence of the event and the occurrence of the rule change can be substantial: in the UK the changes that were identified as being necessary to make insolvency law work properly after the secondary banking crisis between 1972 and 1975 were not enacted until over a decade later in 1985;[14] in the USA, by contrast, a piece of legislation passing through Congress at the time of the Enron collapse[15] was dramatically strengthened (perhaps too much so) and became the Sarbanes–Oxley Act of 2002.

---

[14] Insolvency Act 1985.
[15] The legislation had been prompted by problems at World.com and Tyco which occurred before Enron fell.

In the light of such regulatory or legal changes, the public view might be held to be that the audits had failed – in that they did not indicate a problem with the companies which collapsed soon afterwards; that view would certainly be valid in the case of Parmalat, for instance.

Practitioners would maintain though that not every collapse of a company is an indication of a poorly performed audit. The practitioners' view might be that the audit achieved its objectives, in that it was performed properly according to the objectives established and the procedures set and reviews all the information that should have been reviewed against the standards in operation at the time. It is thus possible to have a 'good' audit by (the limited) professional measure which produces information which is essentially worthless in the eyes of the public and the people for whom it should have been most useful – the shareholders.

This issue became a matter of public scrutiny in the wake of the financial crisis of 2008 when the 'culpability' of auditors and the application of auditing standards in contributing to the collapses, was aired. Conventional wisdom has it that banks were too big in terms of their systemic importance to be allowed to fail. Instead, it might be said that one of the reasons for the lack of any signals about the problems that were heeded was that they were *too big to audit*. The size of the banks and the disparity of their range of activities made the product of the audit investigations almost worthless simply because the audits were trying to produce a consolidated opinion on a range of products with vastly different operational characteristics. The audits were probably technically unimpeachable but produced no information of usable value because of the scope of the task. The consolidation of vast amounts of information produced lots of numbers but little insight, largely because of what has come to be called the 'granularity' of the picture they produced.

Accountancy rules aim to cut probes backlog

In 2011 the backlog of disciplinary cases being brought against auditors stretched back over a decade, leading to a proposal that the Financial Reporting Council should allow negotiated settlements to clear the queue of old cases. The FRC oversees the accounting profession in the UK and establishes the rules of governance for the profession.

In October 2011 the FRC was investigating over a dozen claims against firms including Ernst & Young's auditing of Lehman Brothers and Deloitte's auditing of MG Rover, the car-maker which collapsed under the weight of its debts in 2005 after four major shareholders had extracted large amounts of cash for their own pension schemes (they voluntarily agreed to refrain from acting as company directors in 2011). It had lost a major case against PWC in 2007 over the auditing of a bus-maker that then went bust.

One of the problems faced by the FRC was that it has no powers to compel companies to supply information – only accountancy firms – and that its scope to pursue firms was limited in the face of regulation by the profession itself.

The FRC would like to transfer some more peripheral audit oversight to the professional bodies so that it could focus more on larger listed companies.

The FRC had been criticised for moving towards 'light touch' regulation and accused of taking a much less aggressive approach to regulating auditors than the European Commission which had contemplated banning auditors from providing some consulting services to their audit clients.

Accountants' and auditors' judgement

The preparation of accounts is far from being a completely mechanistic exercise and both accountants and auditors are keen to stress the judgemental aspect of their professions. Not all transactions are straightforward and individual circumstances have to be taken into account in determining the necessary balance between the complete accuracy of information – and its consequent probable redundancy – and usefulness. However, while the unfettered judgement of individual accountants in compiling books of account is constrained by established conventions the degree of discretion allowed between individual unique transactions may be significant. The accounting conventions internal to companies' own standards may only be changed so often before shareholders and auditors become suspicious but within the level of operational discretion, considerable latitude may be exercised. This then becomes subjected to a further degree of judgemental discretion when auditors review the books compiled by the company – leading to a potential compounding of effect.

The application of accounting standards

There is a further issue which revolves around judgement and standards in respect of the audits conducted immediately prior to the financial crisis – that of the appropriateness and the application of established accounting standards, irrespective of any issue of individually exercised discretion.

Following the collapse of Lehman Brothers in particular, the effects of two accounting devices have been called into question in precipitating problems: the standards which control the valuation of assets – so-called 'mark-to-market' or 'fair value' accounting (FAS 157/IAS 39) – and the use of what are called 'repo instruments' in the USA and 'repurchase agreements' in the UK.

Fair value accounting was a development of the 1990s. Companies have always been supposed to value their assets at the lower of purchase price and realisable cost but this poses some substantial conceptual and accuracy problems for the 'true and fair view'. In an attempt to provide some sort of benchmark for these valuations, in the period when financial products were rapidly increasing as a component of economic growth, accounting regulations were developed and extended to enable the market value for a financial instrument (for which there might be no other easily identifiable proxy value) to be adopted. This could – and did – lead to obvious abuse but equally could often be justified as a legitimate usage by a suitably robust case advanced by expert managers. Assets could therefore be held in a balance sheet at a particular value when there was no other alternative method of ascertaining value (or equally, no other effective market). Whether this value could be realised in a falling market then became a serious issue for auditors to have to deal with and for shareholders to interpret.

Repurchase agreements are a method of classifying what is a conditional agreement to sell and buy-back an asset (or obligation), as an outright sale with no recourse. This is obviously a method of effectively reclassifying debts temporarily to the benefit of the seller. Companies may thus appear to lighten their balance sheets of debt temporarily by choosing to undertake such transactions at an appropriate time – that is, at the year end. One day after the year end (or perhaps two, to maintain some appearance of probity) the debt is bought back at a fee to recompense the counter-party for his trouble. These devices are then known in shorthand by the rate of fee or interest they bear – so Repo 105s or Repo 106s, meaning that they would be repurchased at a previously established increment of their original transfer value.

Both these devices were – and are, at the time of writing – entirely legal but their effects on company balance sheets can be extremely damaging, as the financial crisis demonstrated. However, under the rules prevailing at the time their use could not be contested by the auditors. The audit would be performed completely in accordance with the rules and conventions but would produce a perverse result because the rules had not caught up with the effects of reality – 'regulatory lag', indicating the basic reactive and reflexive nature of most regulation.

Auditor defensiveness

To be valid the statements prepared by auditors must contain a number of set clauses and features: they have to specify the period to which they relate; the company to which they relate; they have to be dated; they have to have a form of words which indicates that the auditors have formed an opinion which is based on a 'true and fair view' that the company is a 'going concern' and they have no reason to offer any qualification to that view. They also have to be signed by the audit firm taking responsibility for the audit overall – and since the passage of the 2006 Companies Act, in the UK, the senior auditor has to be identified by name and to sign in his own capacity.[16]

Chapter 2 dealt with the comparatively recent introduction (in the UK at least) of the legal requirement for accounts to show a true and fair view. To be fair, previous legislation had included such an obligation but the pressure from companies for commercial secrecy had allowed latitude in the definition of what was true, fair and complete. Best practice and Stock Exchange rules had often exceeded the statutory requirement but as the Royal Mail case showed it was common practice for companies to use secret funding to pad their dividend capacity.

However, under the rules as they exist now the auditors can seek to protect themselves in a number of ways against the sort of situation which they faced as a consequence of interpretation of the rules at the time of the Royal Mail case. They are able to do this to some extent by stating that the information which they have relied upon to conduct their audit has been prepared by the company under the authority of the directors and that it effectively is only good for the period which is reviewed. As the result of several legal actions (the most significant of which in the UK is *Caparo Industries plc* v. *Dickman* [1990] UKHL 2) the auditors' liability is also circumscribed in respect of the liability he has to other users of the accounts. Auditors have thus sought to restrict the extent to which the product of the efforts can be held against them by limiting the usefulness of their audits, hedging the terms about with restrictions on liability and indicating the involvement of others in the production of the reports.

International developments

The collapse of Enron in the USA as a result of accounting frauds led to the consequent collapse of that firm's auditors too. Arthur Andersen's Houston office had been based in Enron's premises and the firm had effectively been internal auditor, external auditor, corporate finance adviser, company archivist and tax adviser to its client.[17] The demise of the company meant that Andersen effectively collapsed too, some might say under the weight of its own ethical contradictions, surrendering its US practice licence in 2002, thereby bringing the number of large auditors down from five to four. In the space of little more than a decade, through national and international amalgamations and financial problems, the Big Eight had reduced to the Big Four.

This reduction severely disturbed financial markets through a secondary effect: investors supposedly became concerned about the effect of not having auditors with sufficient international reach, experience and competence to audit the large numbers of international companies into which international investment funds had

---

[16] Companies Act 2006, s. 447.   [17] See Cruver, *Enron*.

migrated.[18] The European Union regulators were allegedly particularly concerned following the Parmalat affair and the forthcoming implementation of the UK's Companies Act provided an ideal way of ameliorating the burden of liability on auditors to shrink the pressures that were encouraging amalgamations and potential actions by aggrieved shareholders (some actions had been initiated already or intimated in respect of alleged negligence).

Limitation of auditor liability – shareholder issues

Sections 532 to 538 of the UK Companies Act 2006 allowed companies to negotiate with auditors to limit the liability of the auditors in performance of their duties (provided this is agreed by the shareholders) in return for a reduction of the audit fee. The agreements are known as LLAs (Liability Limitation Agreements). (The auditors would of course benefit since their own insurers would be off the hook for professional negligence claims and the auditors' professional indemnity premia would reduce.) Such agreements have to be renewed annually and must have the explicit approval of the shareholders: in public companies this must be secured at an AGM; in private companies the shareholders can pass a waiver by means of a written ordinary resolution. The enabling clause in the Act uses the word 'purport' in describing what such arrangements do:

> an agreement that *purports* to limit the amount of liability owed to a company by its auditor.

The Act does not specify how the limitation should be agreed and states only that it should be 'fair and reasonable', so any court adjudicating on the matter has to take into account the liability of any other party which occasioned a problem.

A number of obvious problems arise in consequence of this. First, given that directors have express statutory duties to the company, for them to recommend a liability agreement be put in place might be thought to be an abrogation of those duties. The 1929 Companies Act included a provision to prevent such agreements because of the conflict with directorial liability. Legal opinion[19] in respect of the introduction of LLAs – yet to be tested in a case – suggests that, under the enhanced obligations of the 2006 Act directors would not be in breach in recommending such agreements.

Second, given the international nature of large company shareholdings, it is not clear that such an agreement would limit an action being taken by any overseas

---

[18] I. P. Dewing and P. O. Russell, 'Accounting, auditing and corporate governance of European listed companies: EU policy developments before and after Enron', *Journal of Common Market Studies*, 42 (2004), 289–319.

[19] Mark Hapgood QC to ICAEW, www.icaew.com/en/technical/audit-and-assurance/working-in-the-regulated-area-of-audit/audit-liability/guidance-on-limited-liability-agreements.

shareholder and the SEC in particular has given no assurance that a limitation agreement would be respected in the American courts.

Third, the use of an agreement opens up the possibility that the engagement letter and the limitation agreement may not mesh properly. This will involve additional operational costs in the form of lawyers' fees in reviewing and drafting revised engagement letters and – if things go wrong – the additional costs of trying to prove the case for recovery.

Fourth, in private companies, the resolution affirming the use of an agreement is an *ordinary* resolution requiring a simple majority of votes to be passed. This may mean that in private companies otherwise substantial enough to command a listing if they wished, director-shareholders in possession of a majority of votes get their own way in respect of such agreements being implemented while other shareholders – whose access to information will be limited only to that which is formally published – may strongly object to the principle of such arrangements. In listed companies, the small shareholder, whose proportion-at-stake may well be substantially larger than that of an individual fund, is inevitably disadvantaged.

Fifth, aside from benefiting the auditors and their insurers it is difficult to see what use these arrangements have. Why should shareholders wish to compromise the prospect of recovery of compensation which might be available to them if the auditors have not done their jobs properly? If the auditors perform their tasks properly – that is within the terms of their professional obligations and the engagement letter – there is no prospect of litigation (as the case involving Barings and Price Waterhouse Coopers showed), so the ordinary prospect of a court action, an adverse decision and damages is negligible. The issue reduces to the equivalence of the 'guaranteed bonus' that bedevils the issue of directorial remuneration (see Chapter 14) – being paid extra (through having costs reduced) for the job which the auditors are contracted to do.

The prosecution of the argument for introducing LLAs was undertaken by the major accounting firms who lobbied hard for its introduction. As late as 2004, just two years before the Companies Act was passed, the then Secretary of State at the Department of Trade and Industry, Patricia Hewitt, appeared to reject pleas for the introduction of limitations on liability when lobbied by the international chairman of KPMG.[20] During the 1900s, auditors had exerted considerable pressure to dispense with unlimited liability; the professional obligation to accept complete responsibility in return for professional standing was also seen as a barrier to the commercial development of auditing.[21] However, the UK Government appeared to be swayed by the auditors' arguments that national rules on auditor independence inhibited the development of higher auditing

[20] M. Dickson, 'Fair destination, shame about the driving', *Financial Times*, 9 September 2004.
[21] C. Napier, 'Intersections of law and accountancy: unlimited auditor liability in the United Kingdom', *Accounting, Organizations and Society*, 23(1) (1998), 105–28.

standards internationally since the global leaders were unable to issue direct instructions to other member partnerships in territories which guarded their independence. The argument was thus turned on its head by the auditor firms who suggested that regulators' complaints about variations in the quality of audit work would produce pressure for closer associations which would require relaxations in liability for everyone of the partnerships to be able to agree, since the construction of global partnerships would require global pools of profits which partners would share in. This arrangement, so the audit firms' argument ran, would be a non-starter if the partners of better regulated profit-pools were subjected to the risk of having their profits compromised by liability claims.

The benefit seems to work one way, in consequence, with any reduction in audit fees likely to be minimal in terms of the totality of fees borne by shareholders for the comfort of audited books. Not surprisingly, the attitude of the bodies representing shareholders – the ABI and NAPF in particular – to the introduction of such agreements, while it could not be described as hostile, has been generally unsympathetic.[22]

Audit firm governance

In October 2007 the Market Participants Group – a review body established by the Financial Reporting Council – produced a report on their deliberations to align the governance obligations of audit companies with those of the companies that they audit. After a series of review and consultation processes, a report was finally produced in January 2010. The Audit Firm Governance Code applies to eight audit firms that together audit about 95 per cent of the companies listed on the Main Market of the London Stock Exchange and stems from recommendation 14 of the original report.

Introducing the report on its website the Institute of Chartered Accountants in England and Wales (ICAEW) said:

> The reputations that the audit firms have built upon their licence to audit are of vital public interest. One way in which they can maintain public trust in their brands is by being seen as exemplars of best practice governance. In this context, it is however important to recognise that the governance challenges faced by audit firms are different from those faced by listed companies.

The report included a statement of objectives which elaborates the intention of its authors. The Code was intended to 'support firms in their objectives of performing high quality work that gives confidence to shareholders' but also to play four additional roles:

---

[22] J. Eaglesham, B. Jopson and S. Tucker, 'Investors disappointed by audit reform', *Financial Times*, 20 July 2005.

1. enhance the stature of firms as highly visible exemplars of best practice governance;
2. enrich firms' transparency reports;
3. encourage changes in governance which improve the way that firms are run; and
4. strengthen the regulatory regime by achieving transparent and effective govern-ance without disproportionate regulation.

In the same paragraph, a further clue to the intentions of the Code's authors was given which seems to attempt to square the code with the availability of LLAs:

> [The Code] should also benefit capital markets by enhancing choice and helping to reduce the risk of a firm exiting the market for large audits because it has lost public trust. Exit from the market would not only signal the loss of a firm's substantial investment in its reputation, but would also have adverse effects on the functioning of markets and on the availability of choice for users of audit services.

The Code is formed of twenty principles and thirty-one provisions. Its main recom-mendations (it is of the 'comply or explain' variant like the main UK Corporate Governance Code it seeks to emulate) are mostly recitations of what would be expected of any competently run accounting firm based on systems principles. The main departure from what might otherwise have been expected is the proposal that independent non-executives be brought in to assist the directors of the businesses to evaluate policy – especially where as the report notes:

> Audit firms often share operations, brands and reputations with businesses that are subject to little or no regulation and this can pose significant risks to the reputation and continued existence of the firm including its audit practice. The Code envisages independent non-executives playing a role in helping to address those risks, as well as enhancing confidence in firms' decision making and ensuring that stakeholder concerns are properly communicated at the highest level.

The Audit Firm Governance Code

A Leadership

A.1 Owner accountability principle

The management of a firm should be accountable to the firm's owners and no individual should have unfettered powers of decision.

Provisions

A.1.1 The firm should establish board or other governance structures, with matters specifically reserved for their decision, to oversee the activities of the management team.

A.1.2 The firm should state in its transparency report how its governance structures and management team operate, their duties and the types of decisions they take.

A.1.3 The firm should state in its transparency report the names and job titles of all members of the firm's governance structures and its management team, how they are elected or appointed and their terms, length of service, meeting attendance in the year, and relevant biographical details.

A.1.4 The firm's governance structures and management team and their members should be subject to formal, rigorous and on-going performance evaluation and, at regular intervals, members should be subject to re-election or re-selection.

A.2 Management principle

A firm should have effective management which has responsibility and clear authority for running the firm.

Provision

A.2.1 The management team should have terms of reference that include clear authority over the whole firm including its non-audit businesses and these should be disclosed on the firm's website.

B Values

B.1 Professionalism principle

A firm should perform quality work by exercising judgement and upholding values of integrity, objectivity, professional competence and due care, confidentiality and professional behaviour in a way that properly takes the public interest into consideration.

Provisions

B.1.1 The firm's governance structures and management team should set an appropriate tone at the top through its policies and practices and by publicly committing themselves and the whole firm to quality work, the public interest and professional judgement and values.

B.1.2 The firm should have a code of conduct which it discloses on its website and requires everyone in the firm to apply.

B.2 Governance principle

A firm should publicly commit itself to this Audit Firm Governance Code.

Provision

B.2.1 The firm should incorporate the principles of this Audit Firm Governance Code into an internal code of conduct.

B.3 Openness principle

A firm should maintain a culture of openness which encourages people to consult and share problems, knowledge and experience in order to achieve quality work in a way that properly takes the public interest into consideration.

C Independent non-executives

C.1 Involvement of independent non-executives principle

A firm should appoint independent non-executives who through their involvement collectively enhance shareholder confidence in the public interest aspects of the firm's decision making, stakeholder dialogue and management of reputational risks including those in the firm's businesses that are not otherwise effectively addressed by regulation.

Provisions

C.1.1 Independent non-executives should: have the majority on a body that oversees public interest matters; and/or be members of other relevant governance structures within the firm. They should also meet as a separate group to discuss matters relating to their remit.

C.1.2 The firm should disclose on its website information about the appointment, retirement and resignation of independent non-executives, their duties and the arrangements by which they discharge those duties and the obligations of the firm to support them. The firm should also disclose on its website the terms of reference and composition of any governance structures whose membership includes independent non-executives.

C.2 Characteristics of independent non-executives principle

The independent non-executives' duty of care is to the firm. They should command the respect of the firm's owners and collectively enhance shareholder confidence by virtue of their independence, number, stature, experience and expertise.

Provision

C.2.1 The firm should state in its transparency report its criteria for assessing the impact of independent non-executives on the firm's independence as auditors and their independence from the firm and its owners.

C.3 Rights of independent non-executives principle

Independent non-executives of a firm should have rights consistent with their role including a right of access to relevant information and people to the extent permitted by law or regulation, and a right to report a fundamental disagreement regarding the firm to its owners and, where ultimately this cannot be resolved and the independent non-executive resigns, to report this resignation publicly.

Provisions

C.3.1 Each independent non-executive should have a contract for services setting out their rights and duties.

C.3.2 The firm should ensure that appropriate indemnity insurance is in place in respect of legal action against any independent non-executive.

C.3.3 The firm should provide each independent non-executive with sufficient resources to undertake their duties including having access to independent professional advice at the firm's expense where an independent non-executive judges such advice necessary to discharge their duties.

C.3.4 The firm should establish, and disclose on its website, procedures for dealing with any fundamental disagreement that cannot otherwise be resolved between the independent non-executives and members of the firm's management team and/or governance structures.

D Operations

D.1 Compliance principle

A firm should comply with professional standards and applicable legal and regulatory requirements.

Provisions

D.1.1 The firm should establish policies and procedures for complying with applicable legal and regulatory requirements and international and national standards on auditing, quality control and ethics, including auditor independence.

D.1.2 The firm should establish policies and procedures for individuals signing group audit reports to comply with applicable standards on auditing dealing with group audits including reliance on other auditors whether from the same network or otherwise.

D.1.3 The firm should state in its transparency report how it applies policies and procedures for managing potential and actual conflicts of interest.

D.1.4 The firm should take action to address areas of concern identified by audit regulators in relation to the firm's audit work.

D.2 Risk management principle

A firm should maintain a sound system of internal control and risk management over the operations of the firm as a whole to safeguard the owners' investment and the firm's assets.

Provisions

D.2.1 The firm should, at least annually, conduct a review of the effectiveness of the firm's system of internal control. The review should cover all material controls, including financial, operational and compliance controls and risk management systems.

D.2.2 The firm should state in its transparency report that it has performed a review of the effectiveness of the system of internal control, summarise the process it has applied and confirm that necessary actions have been or are being taken to remedy any significant failings or weaknesses identified from that review.

It should also disclose the process it has applied to deal with material internal control aspects of any significant problems disclosed in its financial statements or management commentary.

D.2.3 In maintaining a sound system of internal control and risk management and in reviewing its effectiveness, the firm should use a recognised framework such as the Turnbull Guidance and disclose in its transparency report the framework it has used.

D.3 People management principle

A firm should apply policies and procedures for managing people across the whole firm that support its commitment to the professionalism, openness and risk management principles of this Audit Firm Governance Code.

Provisions

D.3.1 The firm should disclose on its website how it supports its commitment to the professionalism, openness and risk management principles of this Audit Firm Governance Code through recruitment, development activities, objective setting, performance evaluation, remuneration, progression, other forms of recognition, representation and involvement.

D.3.2 Independent non-executives should be involved in reviewing people management policies and procedures.

D.4 Whistleblowing principle

A firm should establish and apply confidential whistleblowing policies and procedures across the firm which enable people to report, without fear, concerns about the firm's commitment to quality work and professional judgement and values in a way that properly takes the public interest into consideration.

Provision

D.4.1 The firm should report to independent non-executives on issues raised under its whistleblowing policies and procedures and disclose those policies and procedures on its website.

E Reporting

E.1 Internal reporting principle

The management team of a firm should ensure that members of its governance structures, including owners and independent non-executives, are supplied with information in a timely manner and in a form and of a quality appropriate to enable them to discharge their duties.

E.2 Financial statements principle

A firm should publish audited financial statements prepared in accordance with a recognised financial reporting framework such as International Financial Reporting Standards or UK GAAP.

Provisions

E.2.1 The firm should explain who is responsible for preparing the financial statements and the firm's auditors should make a statement about their reporting responsibilities.

E.2.2 The firm should report that it is a going concern, with supporting assumptions or qualifications as necessary.

E.3 Management commentary principle

The management of a firm should publish on an annual basis a balanced and understandable commentary on the firm's financial performance, position and prospects.

Provision

E.3.1 The firm should include in its management commentary its principal risks and uncertainties, identifying those related to litigation, and report how they are managed in a manner consistent with the requirements of the applicable financial reporting framework.

E.4 Governance reporting principle

A firm should publicly report how it has applied in practice each of the principles of the Audit Firm Governance Code excluding F.2 on shareholder dialogue and F.3 on informed voting and make a statement on its compliance with the Code's provisions or give a considered explanation for any non-compliance.

Provision

E.4.1 The firm should publish on its website an annual transparency report containing the disclosures required by Code Provisions A.1.2, A.1.3, C.2.1, D.1.3, D.2.2 and D.2.3.

E.5 Reporting quality principle

A firm should establish formal and transparent arrangements for monitoring the quality of external reporting and for maintaining an appropriate relationship with the firm's auditors.

Provision

E.5.1 The firm should establish an audit committee and disclose on its website information on the committee's membership and terms of reference which should deal clearly with its authority and duties, including its duties in relation to the appointment and independence of the firm's auditors. On an annual basis, the firm should publish a description of the work of the committee in discharging its duties.

F Dialogue

F.1 Firm dialogue principle

A firm should have dialogue with listed company shareholders, as well as listed companies and their audit committees, about matters covered by this Audit Firm Governance Code to enhance mutual communication and understanding and ensure that it keeps in touch with shareholder opinion, issues and concerns.

Provision

F.1.1 The firm should disclose on its website its policies and procedures, including contact details, for dialogue about matters covered by this Audit Firm Governance Code with listed company shareholders and listed companies. These disclosures should cover the nature and extent of the involvement of independent non-executives in such dialogue.

F.2 Shareholder dialogue principle

Shareholders should have dialogue with audit firms to enhance mutual communication and understanding.

F.3 Informed voting principle

Shareholders should have dialogue with listed companies on the process of recommending the appointment and re-appointment of auditors and should make considered use of votes in relation to such recommendations.

Source: www.icaew.com/en/technical/corporate-governance/audit-firm-governance-code

However, the application of the rules is already beginning to give some problems as can be seen from recent cases involving the disciplining of some senior members of audit and accounting firms for alleged shortfalls in their behaviour in high-profile cases.

MG Rover auditor given clean bill of health

Deloitte, the auditor and tax adviser to MG Rover, has received a largely clean bill of health from the independent report on the collapse of the carmaker.

Speculation has circulated for years in Birmingham that Deloitte could be censured by the study produced by barrister Guy Newey and forensic accountant Gervase MacGregor. Their 850-page report, published on Friday, revealed that Deloitte charged fees to the struggling automotive business of £30.7m over five years. Some of the advice concerned ways in which the so-called 'Phoenix Four' directors led by John Towers could extract 'excessive' rewards from the business, which they bought for just £10 from BMW in 2000.

However, the inspectors found 'no evidence' that the high level of non-audit fees compromised the independence and objectivity of Deloitte as auditor. They concluded that Deloitte acted properly in qualifying MG Rover as a going concern at the end of 2004, just a few months before the collapse of the company with 6,000 job losses.

One suggested angle of attack for opponents seeking to bring legal actions against the Phoenix Four directors would be that they went on trading the car company after it was no longer viable, a breach of their duties. But the inspectors found that a partnership deal with Shanghai Automotive Industry Corporation could have proceeded, underwriting the future of the group.

Creditors may therefore look elsewhere in the report for ammunition to support potential legal actions to claw back money from the Phoenix Four. The inspectors calculated that the men stand to gain £14m in extra payments from MGR Capital, the Rover car loans arm, which they owned separately from MG Rover. The Four have said they will defend vigorously any lawsuits brought in the wake of the report's publication.

Deloitte does not escape criticism when the report addresses the talks with Ian Whyte, a risk controller at BMW responsible for the disposal of car loans books for Rover. The report says Deloitte 'sought to use the prospect of involvement in an MBO to persuade Mr Whyte to supply to them potentially confidential information, or information BMW would or might have preferred Mr Whyte not to disclose.' Meanwhile, Ian Barton, Deloitte assistant director, is criticised for leading a briefing on the purchase of the Rover car loans book for directors of MG Rover outside the circle of the Phoenix Four.

In a statement, Deloitte said: 'All the engagements we carried out for the group provided manifest benefit to the business of the group.' Fees were 'fair and reasonable', it said.

Source: J. Guthrie, *Financial Times*, 13 September 2009

Concluding remarks

The comfort that an audit is supposed to offer shareholders is less solid than a casual observer might suppose. The audit is supposed to confirm to the shareholders that the company which carries their investment is operating properly in the three dimensions of procedural, behavioural and structural governance. Yet practitioners have serious concerns about the validity of such assurances – which have for many years been wrapped around with verbal protection to deflect attacks on the liability of the auditors – and their ability to show a 'true and fair view'.

While the new practice of requiring the auditor to sign in a personal capacity may appear to be a strengthening of personal responsibility, the ability of directors to negotiate liability caps with auditors allows both directors and auditors off the hook to some extent – solely at the betterment of the auditor through relaxation of professional indemnity premiums.

Such behaviour does not square easily with the extensive code of governance for audit firms introduced in 2010 reproduced in full extent in the text box. While this appears to align the running of audit firms with the running of those organisations they review, this is merely cosmetic. Audit is a statutory obligation: companies cannot choose whether or not to take it on and the limitation of liability is consequently a retrograde step, propelled by a motivation based on profit maximisation and back from the standards of professionalism.

In April 2012 PIRC advised investors to vote against the annual accounts, and the directors and the re-appointment of the auditors of several large UK banks for their failure to reflect the true position of the banks because of the reliance on historical information about assets,[23] which may not reflect the banks' actual position. This spills over from concern about the problems over bank audits immediately before the financial crisis, when audits provided little comfort for shareholders because the audited companies were too big to audit and too complex to understand.

---

[23] J. Treanor, 'Pirc takes on banks over "true and fair" reporting', *The Guardian*, 11 April 2012.

CHAPTER 13

Accounting for profits: the root of information asymmetry

This chapter will consider:

- how accounting and governance interact;
- the nature of the information in accounts;
- specific and general governance problems in the treatment of the components of accounts;
- accounts and the shareholder;
- accounts and the stakeholder;
- accounts and the marketplace;
- narrative reporting;
- intangibles and CR.

Introduction

It may seem back-to-front to deal with the preparation of company accounts after dealing with audit issues, but the linking theme between chapters has been issues of governance – and audit is a part of the structure of corporate governance and corporate regulation. Whereas, on one level at least, the preparation of accounts is essentially a managerial matter in terms of controlling the organisation on a day-to-day basis.

Another reason for considering the issues concerned with accounting in governance at this point rather than earlier is that this chapter will also provide a platform for subsequent chapters in considering issues of the abuse of the management of companies and company governance that lead to further difficulties for shareholders and stakeholders.

This chapter will consider some basic problems with the accounts that are provided to shareholders in terms of governance; some consideration of the provision of accounts information to stakeholders in the light of their collectively increasing power over company regulation and some consequential aspects of company governance; and it will also touch upon some issues concerning the release of accounting information to the market for capital, in governance terms. None of the treatment requires a technical appreciation of accounting detail.

Accounting and governance

The obligations of good managerial practice require that a good governance system will possess the following characteristics:

● *Fairness*

Individuals – or perhaps classes of individuals – are treated in the same way.

● *Openness/transparency*

The system works by revealing information – or as much information as is consistent with simple commercial confidentiality; or at least with the requirements of the law.

● *Independence*

Decisions are not influenced by persons or other actors outside the disclosed circle of participants – an example of the infringement of this characteristic would be the 'shadow directors' issue in English company law.

● *Probity/accuracy*

Information, when it is disclosed, is accurate and truthful; actions are morally correct.

● *Responsibility*

Individuals take responsibility for their own actions in determining matters of governance.

● *Accountability*

Individuals are held accountable for their actions.

● *Reputation*

Issues of good reputation are considered to be paramount in acquitting tasks of governance.

● *Judgement*

Where issues of judgement are required they are taken using the other characteristics as lode-stars.

● *Integrity*

Issues of governance are at all times subjected to scrutiny for their integrity in respect of all the other characteristics.

It is easy to see that information is at the heart of all this. So, to support a good governance system and ensure that the system is internally consistent, the characteristics of the information in the system should presumably mirror the overall characteristics of the system.

Accounts are a form – perhaps the principal form – of information by which shareholders are informed of the progress of a business. The form and content of accounts statements are governed by rules developed by professionals and regulators to ensure consistency, completeness and accuracy. As a consequence these regulations, as applied inside the company, then become part of the procedural governance of the company. To decide whether the accounting regulations serve governance well, the accounting regulations and their consequences have to be evaluated in respect of the requirements of good governance detailed above to ensure that shareholders and managers are both properly served by the provision of information between them.

The information made available

For governance purposes accounts perform at least three functions: first, to enable managers, shareholders and stakeholders to run their businesses properly and legally; second, to help allocate resources efficiently; and third, to parcel out rewards to the various parties to the enterprise in some way proportionate to their economic interests.

Information collected for these purposes is then subject, by both the accounting regulations and also by the terms of the contract which exists between shareholders, managers and the company itself, to a number of tests or constraints to filter out and organise what is necessary to fulfil the function. In strictly accounting terms, these tests and constraints revolve principally around four technical matters:

1. *Issues of recognition*
Whether an item ought to be included in the accounts of a company.

2. *Issues of measurement*
If it is to be included how the item is to be measured – which goes beyond consideration of whether it is 'value-able' to include considerations over the timing and duration of the measurement.

3. *Matching*
A consequence partly of the double-entry book-keeping system which requires every entry to be effectively self-checking, and also of the issue of timing noted above.

4. *Prudence*
Which might be thought of as a consideration of the quality of the item being recorded – what is the reliability of the valuation being placed on it and how this might be further affected by timing and duration issues.

As a consequence of these four technical aspects and the intervention of timing, accounts are then perpetually in tension with respect to a fifth concern, from a governance point of view, the tussle between reliability and relevance – between accuracy and usefulness.

This would be bad enough were the problems limited to those five concerns, but at the same time accounts are used to do a number of different things, not all of which are compatible or consistent.

Among the functions which accounts are used to perform are the following:
- to record changes in the value of assets, calculated by reference to money;
- to record changes in the company's value over the passage of time;

- to attempt to apportion the values of variable components of input to the production of outputs;
- to provide a measure of efficiency;
- to act as a control mechanism;
- to attempt to compute the value of obligations to different parties involved with an organisation;
- to provide a measure of commercial viability.

Yet another level of complication is added by the fact that there are many users of accounts – management, shareholders, potential shareholders, stakeholders and the State, a particular type of stakeholder – who will come at them from different starting points and put them to different uses.

And as with all information that is shared, accounts have a fundamental characteristic that they have to be both conceptually and formally agreed by parties to a transaction to be of any value. This then produces an additional complication.

At a domestic level, these issues obviously provide a very complicated framework in which accounts are utilised. However, listed companies are increasingly owned by shareholders worldwide. International comparability of information further increases the complications since it is aggravated by matters of:

- local culture and tradition, which has particular significance when companies own subsidiaries in different parts of the world, where rules about accounting and governance differ from that of the country in which the parent is located;
- jurisdictional legal constraints which may impose specific conditions on the compilation of accounts;
- occasional political interference in the activities of companies for local or economic planning reasons;
- questions of partiality in respect of the balance between all stakeholders, perhaps motivated by political change or economic circumstance;
- issues of expediency;
- the tension between rule-based systems and principle-based systems; issues of legalism versus the judgemental approach to governance, for instance.

A full evaluation of the detail of the ways in which technical accounting conventions affect the preparation of financial statements, for instance through both the differences *between* GAAP and IFRS and the problems of application *within* the separate conventions, is beyond the scope of this book (readers interested in the subject should consult the list of Further Reading at the end of the book). However, the control of accounting information largely determines the size of the imbalance occasioned by the asymmetry of information between managers and shareholders. So the degree to which different accounting formulations can legitimately impact upon governance needs to be considered in evaluating how well the current theories of governance describe the relationship between the parties to the arrangements of governance, for public companies. An indication of how accounting information may produce a partial picture (in the sense that it favours one party in the governance arrangement) is necessary since it will also form the basis for consideration of some of the issues of 'counter-governance' dealt with in Chapter 15.

There are, for instance, significant governance implications in the latitude allowed companies in the valuation of assets. These may impact upon issues of fairness, transparency, accuracy and judgement in the most correctly run of companies – and this is to say nothing of those companies where probity and integrity are not consistently highly valued as obligations to shareholders and stakeholders. Certain processes may require assets of a unique or very unusual character to complete them. The market for these assets is then very narrow; how are managers to value them on this basis and how are shareholders to interpret the information?

As a general example to illustrate the problems of imparting information, the central issue of ascribing fair value to an asset can be taken. While certain jurisdictions do not require that assets be revalued – on the basis of prudence, since they always ascribe a low value to the asset – the Anglo-American view is that not to do so may result in an inaccurate view being taken by shareholders of the value of the business. Some assets may occasionally appreciate in value – and not to reflect this increase will therefore understate the realisable value of the asset to shareholders. Consequently, the valuation of an asset and reflecting that value in the accounts of the company can be of central importance since it can affect, at the very least, matters of solvency; issues surrounding the further raising of funds and considerations of the distribution of dividends – or the value of a company being acquired. (It is interesting to reflect that hostile acquisitions were unknown in both Germany and Japan until quite late in the twentieth century,[1] so issues of being able to value companies being taken over were largely unnecessary. By contrast the USA and UK have had active takeover markets for much longer.) This wraps up issues of recognition, measurement, matching and prudence. The situation about determining fair value was considerably complicated by the intricacies of financial assets.

The example could be repeated numerous times for different categories of accounting items involving all the major statements of information received by shareholders: the balance sheet, the profit and loss account and the cashflow statement (some of these will be indicated in this chapter – but not exhaustively). As a consequence of these problems – in the valuation of assets; in the identification of profit and in the classification of funding – the characteristics of the information produced often run

---

[1] The UK takeover of Mannesmann by Vodafone in 2000; the takeover of the Long Term Credit bank in Japan by Ripplewood Holdings in 2000.

against the characteristics of good governance systems, either through flawed conception, flawed implementation or the possibility of managerial manipulation.

In public companies shareholders have no right to see managerial accounts and are only legally obliged to be given an annual statement of accounting information; listed companies are also obliged to provide very limited amounts of information at the half-yearly stage. As other earlier chapters have shown, even this has been subject to differing interpretations over the years, with the concept of 'true and fair' being a relatively recent introduction in legally prescribed formats of accounts, in the UK at least. For the most part, the precise form of accounts has been left to experts to adjudicate, with informal obligations developed by the Stock Exchange preceding the legal obligation. (In private companies, of course, the arrangements for governance are at the discretion of the shareholders, in accordance with the articles of association of the company, which may give private company shareholders greater or lesser rights than those enjoyed by shareholders in public companies, subject always to the minimum requirements of the law.)

Specific problems in the account process

Any attempt to capture information about a company is subject to the difficulty of pinning flows of information down to precise portions of time and activity, and dividing costs between different activities. (The problems this poses for audit have already been aired in the previous chapter.) Because of these problems more fundamental difficulties with direct impact on governance occur in three specific areas: the discretion allowed managers to formulate costs and allocate them according to arbitrary judgement (an inevitable but nonetheless important issue from the point of view of the valuation of parts of the company or the way in which managers may be rewarded); the basic interpretation of information by shareholders and others; and the purpose to which accounts are directed.

Managerial discretion: issues of timing and valuation

Managers might choose to take a subjective view of revaluations and changes in the value of assets over time in order to help smooth profits; this is because changes to the value of items on the balance sheet can be taken through the profit and loss account. Consequently, in bad years managers tend to pile as much bad news as possible into the profit and loss account to disguise the true picture and to enable a very effective bounce-back in subsequent years. It is possible under accounting conventions to have three potential, different bases for valuation (because of the application of the impairment rules) in one balance sheet. Some assets may be valued at historical cost; some might be valued at net selling price and some might be ascribed a value to the business because of uniqueness or rarity. Provided each class is valued consistently, and the accounts state the basis of valuation, the rules allow this. There is consequently considerable allowance for managerial discretion about how to value individual items.

For instance, in the event that a company finds that the value of a current asset is materially different from the value at which it was purchased – which it held in order to sell on perhaps – then the accounts are constructed to reflect an 'impairment' in the value of that asset. The term has come to popular currency with the problems over loans that banks bought from other banks and then found to be worth substantially less than they had paid for them. In the case of the banks' loans, over time some of the value may be recovered but in the meantime the loans are 'impaired' and their value is recorded as such in the balance sheet. From a governance point of view this has particular problems, mostly connected to issues of the timing of impairments and the quantity of such impairments affecting the apparent value of the company. The essential characteristic of such a provision is its *uncertainty*; therefore, the inclusion on the balance sheet of such values generates problems of judgement over implementation and measurement which may affect company value in the short term.

In businesses where sales are effected by contracts which take some time to complete there is judgement to be exercised to determine at what stage *revenue recognition* occurs – how much profit can be taken on completion or physical delivery or sign off by customer, for instance. While there are necessary conventions which must be adhered to (both in terms of comparability with other organisations and consistent application year-on-year), the answer to this problem is that revenue recognition effectively depends upon the particularities of each sale – and consequently international accounting conventions can only compromise in their formulations between blandness and precision, between usefulness and relevance. If profit is recognised too early, the information is highly suspect for shareholders; if a decision of extreme prudence is taken to recognise profit only at the conclusion of the selling cycle, then the information is highly reliable but virtually useless – especially for managers. So, in the short term at least, the interests of managers and shareholders are in conflict on this issue.

The effects of profit recognition: an (exaggerated) illustration

Consider two investment trusts run by the same set of managers, Trust A and Trust B.

Both start with capital for investment of £10 million. Both invest in shares and reap returns of 20 per cent in the first year raising the value of their Trusts to (notionally) £12 million plus a small amount of interest on the uninvested balance.

However the managers of Trust A decide to cash the shares that have increased in value realising the profit made. They are thus able to report the value of the Trust has increased. They then reinvest the profits into more shares.

Trust B cannot report an equivalent increase in profits since they have not been realised; they can merely report that the Trust has received income from interest.

The share price of Trust B drops. The managers sell some of their own holdings in Trust A and buy shares in the depressed Trust B.

The following year Trust B has another good year and realises and reinvests just like Trust A did. Its share price soars. The managers are very pleased – on two counts, of course since they bought the shares cheaply.

Trust A decides not to realise and cannot report realised profits, so its share price dips, since it reports only interest this time. The managers sell some of their own holdings in the now highly-valued Trust B and buy shares in Trust A at the depressed price.

They then repeat the same trick year after year, enriching themselves at the expense of the other shareholders.

Source: adapted from K. McNeal, *Truth in Accounting* (Houston, TX: Scholars Book Co., 1939)

Classification of expenses

Managers are also able to manipulate the apparent profitability of certain parts of a company by the way that they allocate costs. There are basically two ways of allocating costs: by nature such as heat, light, power; advertising, legal and so on; and by function or department – advertising department, company secretarial department, other operating departments and so on. Where allocation is by nature, the information provided is more reliable from an outsider's point of view since allocation to function often tends to be arbitrary. On the other hand, allocation by function is claimed to give more relevant information managerially (although this is contestable) and is consistent with accounting to help determine levels of break-even – but it has the disadvantage that it allows 'managerial' manipulation and interference.

Managers control the information released to shareholders in form and in content. There is a profound asymmetry in the relative possession of information between the manager and the shareholder in a number of different respects – at the very least in terms of timeliness, content, comprehensibility, comprehensiveness – possibly even accuracy. But in summary, issues of asymmetry of financial information centre around three major aspects: the recognition or timing of transactions (which are not necessarily the same thing); issues of valuation or measurability of individual transactions;

and issues of prudence. Aside from any other consideration, all three are affected by the continual tension between the usefulness of information and the accuracy of information touched on above – a tension which is normally resolved in favour of usefulness (and therefore might be against the short-term interests of the shareholder; in the longer run the interests of shareholders and managers are likely to be coincident on accuracy).

The issues have three major consequences, which impact principally on the balance sheet and the income statement rather than on the cashflow statement: they can affect the value of assets as they are placed on the balance sheet or as they are re-valued; they may alter the way in which profit is recorded in any given accounting period; as a consequence of the interaction of the first two factors, they may affect the way that companies are valued by outsiders. They may also affect the distribution of rewards between shareholders and managers. A good example of this issue in practice is the clawback of bonuses from senior bank staff during early 2012[2] – all the relevant tests had been 'properly' completed by the standards of the contemporaneous accounts yet bonuses were obviously overpaid because of the subsequent huge losses that the banks incurred, prompted by the use of devices that the directors at least did not understand. Yet the banks' accounts had been audited and the shareholders had passed them.

While not immune from manipulation, cash is less easy to distort as an accounting item, because, in the simplest form, it is either there or it is not. However, companies with foreign subsidiaries may produce accounting information (as a consequence of the translation of foreign currency) which is not immediately straightforward. Beyond this though, instances of the manipulation of cash values usually imply some form of outright fraud, where the actions of managers have moved beyond the grey areas of information asymmetry and into the dark ground of outright fraud.

Problems arising for the shareholder

The first and most obvious example of problems that arise for the shareholder in terms of interpreting the information from accounts is that of asymmetry.

The shareholder, in listed companies at least, only receives information at the end of an accounting period – a half-year or a full year in normal circumstances. The managers of the company, by contrast, receive financial information on a continual basis and in much greater detail than the limited number of headings under which statutory accounting information is aggregated and then passed to the shareholder. So, when the shareholder does receive the financial information (in the prescribed statutory form), it is first, months out-of-date; second, refers to a period of trading that may be significantly different from

---

[2] S. Goff and M. Murphy, 'Lloyds 13 to lose total of £1.5m', *Financial Times*, 20 February 2012.

that which the company is currently experiencing; and last, is produced in a form which while accurate, provides little information about the shape of trading during the year and the way in which the company's trading developed during that time. The missing information has to be filled in by a narrative statement about trading prepared by the directors, in order to make more sense (of which more below).

This might be dismissed as an inevitable by-product of the arrangements by shareholders to manage the affairs of the company on their behalf. Supporters of the traditionalist view might hold that first, the shareholders should only appoint managers they believe to be competent; and second if every one of the shareholders is in the same position then it doesn't really matter. There may be some truth to this last point – except that not all shareholders are usually in the same position for the purposes of gaining access to the market for trading. The accuracy and fullness of information does have significance in respect of the stewardship of their own wealth for shareholders (if not the stewardship of the company) and it has even more significance when directors and managers own shares – as will become plainer when issues of managerial reward are concerned in Chapter 14.

Occasionally, as a result of some specific event – such as a takeover bid or a rights issue (see below) – companies may release more up-to-date information about profitability or specific balance sheet items which may help outsiders to probe more deeply than normal into the pattern of trading. Those skilled in interpreting accounting information may also be able to extract some additional information by comparing the pattern of half year result with those of the full year, tracing the relationships between balance sheet items between years and comparing those with cash flow information and the company's public statements. Large fund managers employ many such staff.

The information which the manager of the company receives is therefore, more complete in itself, fuller in extent and produced more promptly. In short it is biased towards the useful end of the range, while the information that the shareholder receives is biased towards the complete or accurate end – and is probably less useful for being so.

Accounts and the stakeholder

While all parties who are users of accounts have an interest in their technical accuracy and consistency, the detailed issues of the recognition or timing of transactions – individual valuations of accounting events, issues of measurability and prudence – do not impact on stakeholders to such an extent, with the exception perhaps of the State.

The State requires that accounts be prepared specifically for the purpose of tax collection – with the result that such accounts bear only passing similarity in many cases to the accounts prepared for shareholders (on the so-called statutory basis) and still less with the managerial accounts prepared for operational purposes. Every company therefore usually has three books of accounts: the managerial accounts used for operational control prepared and up-dated on a rolling basis; the accounts prepared for shareholders on a statutory basis which summarise the events of the year; and the accounts prepared for the tax authorities, which take advantage of specific permissions and conventions regarding the collection of tax.

The laxity or precision of the tax system will itself contrive to produce different types of accounting systems. Where taxation is a significant and inescapable obligation then accounting systems will probably have a theoretical and practical character designed to minimise the impact on businesses' accounting structures, both in terms of presentation and operationally. However, the need to provide for the information needs of taxation may also result in enterprises being run to minimise taxation consequences in the short term – impeding investment, perhaps promoting wasteful investment, altering retirement and investment considerations, impeding innovation – all as a result of the accounting response.

This may have follow-on consequences for other stakeholders, since the present accounting regime is based on the needs of what is essentially a shareholder-centred, profit-maximising environment.

The central problems for stakeholders in trying to assess the information contained in company accounts are that first, the accounts are not designed for their use and so merely re-hash existing information under different headings without adding much (if any) value to the mix, and second, while they are as a group probably more numerous *in total* than the shareholders or the managers for whom the accounts have been constructed they are *an aggregate of interests* with only tenuous common links between them as to the type of information they need.

The triple bottom line

Developed from the ideas in a 1999 book – J. Elkington, *Cannibals with Forks* – the 'triple bottom line' approach has three intentions rather than the single purpose of normal accounts. There is a 'bottom line' for each of the shareholders, the environment and the stakeholders intending to demonstrate to each party what the company has done during the year for which the accounts are prepared.

The process of compiling the accounts uses existing information but re-orders it in a different way.

Traditionally formulated accounts start with

Step 1

Turnover – the amount generated in sales.

Step 2

Take off costs (of several and various types) to give a 'gross margin'.

Step 3

Add back any investment profit or interest earned on cash balances.

Step 4

Take off any interest paid on borrowings.

Thereby arriving at a pre-tax profit figure.

After the application of a tax charge this shows what shareholders get.

Triple Bottom Line Accounts identify a different set of beneficiaries of the company's activities

Customers

Suppliers

Company Value Added

Employees

Community

Public sector

Investors

Step 1

Start with cash received from customers – the equivalent of turnover under most accounting conventions.

Step 2

Add to this Investment income received from investments the company has made in a variety of assets and any income received from cash holdings.

Step 3

Subtract any Payments to suppliers for goods and services received (but not for labour only – the company's payroll charges).

Step 4

This gives an amount known as the Company Value Added.

Step 5

Then allocates payments incurred during the period under review to the beneficiaries:

Employees (who are paid wages)

The Community (which arrives in the form of corporate social and environmental investment)

The Public Sector (taxes)

Investors (dividends and interest)

Money retained (profit for the use of the company in increasing its assets base or improving liquidity).

These amounts in total have to balance the Company Value Added.

Because of this the largest aggregated group of interests is left out of this structure of information presentation. Accounts are not prepared for the use of stakeholders. Even where information is provided for stakeholders in a format which involves a different structure from the standard – for instance, the triple bottom line format (see text box) – the components used are merely re-manipulations of the information already collected. This has led to the criticism 'that what is sound about the idea of a Triple Bottom Line is not novel, and that what is novel about the idea is not sound'.[3]

Furthermore, 'the Triple Bottom Line paradigm cannot be rescued simply by attenuating its claims: the rhetoric is badly misleading, and may in fact provide a smokescreen behind which firms can avoid truly effective social and environmental reporting and performance'.[4]

But the stakeholders are not alone in finding their information needs unsatisfied. Professor Charlotte Villiers suggests that the reporting regime may not promote the integrity of capital markets or even assist the internal house-cleaning function of companies.[5]

Accounts and the marketplace

The Companies Act 2006, like all previous Companies Acts, does not specify the detail of accounts. It places the burden on the company by requiring that companies must keep books of account which are proper and comply with recognised accounting standards; beyond those stipulations it is silent as to the exact natures of form and content. The structure of accounts prepared for shareholders largely rests on the professional competence of those constructing the accounts and the professional codes and obligations they work under.

Aside from the issues of professional competence and sanction, obligations to prepare accounts in specific ways are also enforced by the Stock Exchange, through the Listing Agreements – with slightly different requirements for AIM and the main market. In many ways stock markets have led the development of enhanced standards of reporting, often requiring more information of the companies on the Exchange than they are legally required to disclose.

It is not surprising that the explosive growth in accounting sophistication – beyond the mere recording of numerical information – developed in tandem with the growth of major stock markets and especially their shift away from trades in government

---

[3] W. Norman and C. MacDonald, 'Getting to the bottom of the Triple Bottom Line', *Business Ethics Quarterly*, 14(2) (2004), 243–62.
[4] *Ibid.*
[5] C. Villiers, *Corporate Reporting and Company Law* (Cambridge University Press, 2006).

stocks to acting as primary and secondary markets for shares in industrial companies. The direct provision of finance by investors requires appropriate information to be conveyed to enable potential financiers to calculate the likelihood of risk and reward. Increasing stringency of regulation of market intermediaries has also led to them pressing for more information to protect themselves – witness the complexities of the verification of information produced for the listing process and the preparation of prospectuses for offerings of shares to the public.

Primary and secondary economic activity (extractive and manufacturing) does not normally require the development of intangible assets as a class, until the development of sophisticated trading activity. But with the growth in tertiary economic activity – service activities, financial activities not related to the support of the primary and secondary sectors and the growth of 'thinking' activity – the need arises for the creation of classes of asset that identify value in non-physical assets. The effect of these changes can be very substantial: between 1973 and 1993 the median ratio of market value to book value of American companies doubled as they began to develop accounting techniques to represent their intangible assets – inventions and IP, brands and up-valued assets.[6]

In addition, the different information requirements of debt and equity – and more sophisticated usage of both – have further accelerated the pressures for information so that as financial markets have become bigger and more sophisticated, more information is required. But the complexity of the financial information has not always resulted in better information being provided: attempts to produce more comprehensive information have often resulted in providing opportunities for confusion and obscurity, sometimes deliberately as a device to conceal information that might be thought commercially harmful. The use of off-balance sheet vehicles inside Enron and the problems encountered in the abuse of definitions of ownership of associated and subsidiary companies in the UK in the 1960s and 1970s would be cases in point.[7] One of the most tangled areas of this effect is in the valuation of intangible assets.

The problem of intangible assets

Intangible assets are best described by what they are not: they are not physical and they are not, in the strictest sense, monetary. They may represent the price paid for control of an asset above its strict monetary worth (in which case they are accounted for as 'goodwill') or they may be an estimate of value for an item such as intellectual property or some form of brand reputation.

---

[6] 'A price on the priceless', *The Economist*, 10 June 1999.
[7] J. Flower and G. Ebbers, *Global Financial Reporting* (Basingstoke: Palgrave, 2002), Chapter 19.

Without adequate means to represent these values some companies' valuations – that is valuations made by the market-place – appear to be seriously adrift of their asset valuations. If, for instance, a comparison is made of the market valuations of companies such as Microsoft or Apple with their balance sheet totals, there is a serious disparity between the market's valuation of the companies and what the balance sheets 'appear' to show. Only part of this can be explained by market sentiment and other non-financial factors, since the disparity is so large. As has already been noted IBM's primary assets, which are software and software development skills, do not show up on the balance sheet at all.[8]

Since intangible assets are, by their nature, difficult to value and may not be 'properly' valued initially, some companies may have reassessments of their value occur in lurches after the market becomes aware of some factor which was previously unrecognised. The share market may also discount the accountancy and prefer its own assessment, positive or negative. Such movements obviously affect the value of share-holdings and may have adverse governance effects, in that shareholders are affected by perceived value and the control that managers have over this.

Goodwill and its forms

The accountant's view of goodwill is not limited to the standard dictionary defin-ition – which has connotations of some form of friendly disposition or sympathetic feeling – although there are elements of this in the concept.

Technically, goodwill is the difference between the value of the assets as a whole and the sum of the assets of the individual parts. It is thus a strategic concept which can be used to justify the value of an asset which has been purchased from another entity at a price above its previous valuation – as in the case of takeovers, where some form of premium usually has to be paid to existing owners for them to cede ownership of an asset that yields economic benefits. The German term for this is 'Firmenwert'; the French call it 'fonds de commerce' – both of which avoid the 'friendly' connotation of the definition that attaches to the English term, because of its common usage in a non-technical sense.

As well as the concept of a 'premium for control' in ownership terms, goodwill also represents the value of organic skills, abilities, culture or brand recognition (or perhaps 'going concern' value). This explains why established businesses are more valuable – usually – than those just formed, since they possess all or some of these characteristics whereas start-ups perhaps few or none of them. It also goes some way to explaining why some companies may achieve a huge valuation even without recording any

---

[8] See interview quoted in Chapter 2.

profit – the examples of Facebook and Amazon being appropriate. It is also possible – on the basis that goodwill is the difference between the value of the assets collectively and the sum of the individual parts – for consolidated goodwill to be higher than that of individual operating units in a group structure. This can then affect managers beneficially in terms of the apportioning of rewards between shareholders and managers.

However, in terms of its accounting treatment, goodwill is crucially dependent on its origin. Internally generated goodwill – the cost result of policies designed to hold the enterprise in customers' regard – is always charged to the P&L account, since it is impossible to calculate, at least in an asset-based sense. Acquired goodwill on the other hand can be readily calculated since it is the excess paid for a business unit over the value of the assets acquired. This may, for instance, involve securing a line of supply or a line of distribution, for which some premium is paid. The governance consequences of these differing treatments mean that managers are potentially able to manipulate the value of an asset by judicious definition of what it is that has been acquired – although to a lesser extent than was once the case. In 1971, for example, the British engineering company Rolls Royce was forced into bankruptcy because its accounting policies allowed it to capitalise expenditure on developing jet engines and treat research and development spending as an addition to the company's asset base, rather than take it through the profit and loss account and reduce the company's earnings.[9]

One of the purposes of keeping the earnings of a listed company high, of course, is to make it more difficult for other companies to persuade the existing shareholders to part with their shares; a change in ownership may well result in significant reduction in the ranks of senior managers. A consistent and increasing level of earnings will encourage shareholders to buy shares and hold them, thus safeguarding managerial jobs and perhaps allowing them to participate in the increasing value of the shares too. But the preyed-upon may also be predators themselves: one method of maintaining growth after organic potential becomes thinner is to buy into the growth potential of younger companies or those in different sectors.

Consequently the market for control of companies also requires increasing amounts of accurate information. Since the amalgamation of companies is a complex exercise and may involve the blending together of different accounts conventions as well as the combination of physical and cultural regimes, aspects of both procedural and behavioural governance may be affected. Alert managers are able to take advantage of this to their own benefit.

In particular, it is possible to some extent for managers to choose between two types of amalgamation – merger and takeover – if the two entities which are combining are

---

[9] E. Lowe and A. Tinker, 'Siting the accounting problematic: towards an intellectual emancipation of accounting', *Journal of Business Finance & Accounting*, 4 (1977), 263–76.

not of substantially different sizes. If they are of very different sizes then the scope allowed to managers to juggle the numbers and concepts is much more limited, since the option of calling the combination a merger becomes implausible. This produces a number of accounting considerations which may sway managers to choose the option of merger. Although the accounting considerations are essentially cosmetic in nature, and are short-lived, they may have significant governance effects.

The first and most significant consequence is that since both sets of shareholders (mostly) stay the same in terms of their continued existence in the merged business, they are both entitled to see the combined profits for the merged entities for the entire year. Shareholders who are bought out in a takeover, yield their ownership of the previous company for cash or shares in the acquiror and have no residual interest in the company that was. The acquiror takes on the turnover and resultant profit from the date of acquisition only and so only consolidates profits from the date at which the acquisition formally took place. So profits for the merged entity appear to get an instant boost, since there is no goodwill problem; there is no goodwill amortisation and as a result of this the return on assets, both now and in the future, becomes instantly higher (there is no premium for control – goodwill – to artificially inflate the value of the assets which has to be written down over time).

The effects of this can be significant in terms of (supposedly) sustained earnings and managerial justification of the deal, occasionally leading to anomalous effects from an outsider's point of view.

The consolidating arrangements may obscure certain critical information. The merger method is held to be conceptually unsound, because the principles of historical cost accounting may be flouted (in terms of asset valuation). Since mergers almost without exception involve an exchange of shares, this may then dictate the way in which amalgamated assets are valued. The merger method produces less clarity in the provision of financial information, after the event, than does the takeover method; and as a consequence of all this resources may be misallocated under the effect of different methods.

Very large companies which have chosen to use merger accounting include DaimlerChrysler, Exxon Mobile, Aventis (formed in 1999 when the French pharmaceuticals company Rhône-Poulenc S.A. merged with the German chemicals concern Hoechst Marion Roussel) and BP Amoco.

BP and Amoco – a merger of unequals

In the case of the merger of BP and Amoco in 1998, BP – a British company and subject to the FRS rules on accounting promulgated by the FRC – was roughly one and half times the size of Amoco – or in asset terms broadly 60 per cent of the combined entity as opposed to Amoco's 40 per cent. But on completion of the deal the final shareholding proportions of the new entity were allocated at 59.98 per cent to BP's shareholders and 40.02 per cent to Amoco's shareholders. This allocation was such as to make the deal fall under the FRS 6 rules which stated that if one entity were more than 50 per cent larger than the other then acquisition accounting (takeover accounting as opposed to merger accounting) would have to be applied.

Because of the consequences on the companies' accounts and the potential for managerial benefit, in practice most local accounting regulations prohibit the use of merger accounting except where it is very obviously a share exchange of two nearly equal entities. This is the case in all European countries, Australia prohibits merger accounting under any circumstances, while American rules may allow merger accounting even for the amalgamation of entities that would also fall under the acquisition rules in other jurisdictions.

Fuzzy oversight will not solve standards issue

The setters of international financial reporting standards have new bosses. Last Friday, the IASC Foundation announced that its trustees would from now on, in effect, be appointed by a 'monitoring board', which thus gains ultimate if indirect power over the International Accounting Standards Board.

The new group includes representatives of the US Securities and Exchange Commission, the European Commission, Japan's Financial Services Agency and two other members of the International Organization of Securities Commissions, with the Bank for International Settlements as observer.

But this move will hardly end the controversies about IFRS.

The IASB has not had a good crisis so far. It failed to lead when bankers in the EU and US unfairly scapegoated 'mark-to-market' accounting, which forced them to disclose losses they did not want to believe in. Only last month did an IASB group start a serious review of this still burning issue.

In October, the IASB agreed to amend a standard on financial instruments to placate angry governments, in violation of its own due process and to the despair of investors. David Tweedie, its chairman, nearly resigned but eventually knuckled under.

Republican Christopher Cox, the former SEC chairman and champion of IFRS, left without a firm road map for their adoption in the US. His successor Mary Schapiro has declared herself in confirmation hearings 'not prepared to delegate standard-setting or oversight responsibility to the IASB'.

The monitoring board serves defensive purposes. The trustees can no longer be lambasted as a self-appointed group.

But the substantial legitimacy problems remain. A growing part of global markets, including China, is not represented in the new group. No link is established between the standard-setter's accountability and its funding, which for the moment remains a case of taxation without representation.

The identity of the monitoring board itself is fuzzy. It is not known whether it will have any formal decision-making processes, such as a chair or voting rules. The risk is of opaque proceedings which do little to bolster public acceptance.

The trustees seem hesitant about the very nature of their organisation. They try to replicate the relationship that exists between national standard-setters and governments.

But the success of IFRS has come from its orientation towards investors and other global market participants.

By missing the opportunity of clear empowerment of users in IFRS governance, the trustees risk finding themselves torn between conflicting objectives.

A case in point: some have proposed that financial stability become a formal aim of the IASB, but no consensus exists on what that means exactly. If buffers or 'dynamic provisions' are introduced to correct procyclical effects of capital regulations, it is not the same to embed them in IFRS or in separate calculations. Financial transparency and stability are not mutually incompatible but are best served by different institutions with clearly defined objectives. Otherwise, the scope for cooking banks' books is just too large. Think of France's Crédit Lyonnais in the early 1990s.

The IASC Foundation's trustees need to do more to ensure the sustained success of IFRS. This might include finding a firmer voice in the public debate; recognising that IFRS will not be adopted immediately in the US and that a rushed approach serves nobody; and preparing for more direct representation of users, not only in the standard-setting process but also in formal governance arrangements.

Source: N. Véron, *Financial Times*, 5 February 2009

Narrative reporting

In an attempt to overcome some of the communication problems of relying on numbers to convey a company's position and health financially, several attempts have been made to bolster the information available to shareholders with supplementary reports prepared by the directors.

The most significant of these proposals was that made to include an 'Operating and Financial Report' which might – had it been implemented – have gone a long way to providing more meaningful information to stakeholders and begin to alter the balance of company reporting away from the short-term, the historical and the formulaic. This would have given shareholders and stakeholders much better insight into the position of companies, improving governance behaviourally and, to some extent, systemically.

OFR: extracts from a statement by the Accounting Standards Board 2005

On 28 November 2005, the Chancellor of the Exchequer announced the Government's intention to remove the statutory requirement for quoted companies to publish an OFR for financial years beginning on or after 1 April 2005. This had implications for the ASB's Reporting Standard (RS) 1 'The Operating and Financial Review', which has now been formally withdrawn. As a result, the Board has converted RS 1 into a Reporting Statement of best practice on the OFR, which will have persuasive rather than mandatory force. The statement was published on 26 January.

The principles in particular make clear that the OFR should reflect the directors' view of the business. The objective is to assist members of the company (the current shareholders) to assess the strategies adopted by the entity and the potential for those strategies to succeed. While the OFR should focus on matters that are relevant to members, the information in the review will also be useful to other users.

The Reporting Statement sets out a framework of the main elements that should be disclosed in an OFR, leaving it to directors to consider how best to structure their review, in the light of the particular circumstances of the entity. It contains recommendations on the disclosures that should be made in respect of any Key Performance Indicators (KPIs) included in an OFR, but it does not specify any particular KPIs that entities should disclose, nor how many, on the grounds that this is a matter for directors to decide.

The process of developing the standard was started in May 2004, when the Government announced its proposals for a statutory OFR and indicated that it intended to specify the ASB as the body to make reporting standards for the OFR. An Exposure Draft of the Standard (RED 1) was issued on 30 November 2004 and attracted some 60 responses.

RS 1 built on the requirements of the OFR Regulations and the ASB's 2003 statement of best practice on the OFR, which RS 1 superseded. The standard applied to quoted companies in Great Britain and to any other entities that purported to prepare 'Operating and Financial Reviews'. It was a principles-based standard, which in particular made clear that the OFR had to reflect the directors' view of the business.

Source: ASB website, www.frc.org.uk/FRC-Documents/ASB/Reporting-Statement-The-Operating-and-Financial-Re.aspx

Much work had gone into the preparations for the OFR and its withdrawal at a comparatively late stage aroused considerable anger – not least from the auditors who had seen another lucrative field of work opening up (because the OFR would have been a formal statement by the directors it would have required formal auditing) which was then snatched away.

Six years later, under a new Government, the issue was revisited with watered-down proposals simplifying companies' annual reporting requirements into two separate documents. In September 2011 the Government announced[10] that the proposals would take effect from April 2013 to allow companies time to make preparations. A Strategic Report will provide information on financial results, the company's business model and strategy, risks, remuneration and environmental and social issues. The Annual Directors' Statement will provide more detailed information, and will be published online. The Government claimed that these simpler reports would 'increase transparency and accountability in the investment chain and enable shareholders to get a real picture of what is happening to their investments'. The Government also expected the report to enable shareholders to link performance criteria published by the company with the remuneration of directors – even though a specific report has to be prepared in respect of pay already – which, although it must be voted upon at the AGM, has no binding force on the company.

Intangibles and CR

Accounting techniques became more sophisticated as the entities which they dealt with became larger, more complicated and more diffuse. As the significance of the tertiary parts of the Western economies became greater at the end of the twentieth century so the conceptual complexity of accounting became greater – but all the while devoted to the needs of the shareholder, even though the stakeholder became an increasingly powerful factor in the governance of companies.

But the development of techniques for dealing with intangible assets began to erode the conceptual dominance of the shareholder. Even though the International Accounting Standards Board's rules on intangibles still work against the identification of stakeholder interests, the concepts of internally generated goodwill – actions designed to enhance the standing of the company in the eyes of customers, through investing in employee training, securing 'brand values', reducing externalities – all open the way, potentially, for more sympathetic treatment of the interests of stakeholders. Thus, however flawed the concept of CR may be – and it has many difficulties, as shown in Chapter 3 – developments in recognising the wider value of company investment to

---

[10] 'Greater transparency in company pay and reporting', available at www.bis.gov.uk.

secure corporate value, may well contribute to increased appreciation of the part played by stakeholders in the development of the company.

Summary

The accounts are the primary method by which information about a company is conveyed to shareholders. In the case of a listed company, because of the strictures on insidership and the limited contact between (most) shareholders and the company this is a very important channel for communicating vital information about procedural and behavioural governance.

However, the regulations which control what goes into the accounts are open to different interpretations by those who compile them just as the information imparted by the accounts is open to different interpretations by outsiders. While much of the interpretation is value-neutral, occasionally the asymmetric nature of the information-giving and accounting process leads to significant distortions in favour of managers and to the disadvantage of the shareholder, the potential shareholder and the marketplace.

Because of the focus on the information needs of the shareholder, and because the collection of information is embedded in a profit-driven and return-orientated mechanism, the needs of stakeholders – apart from the State which has the power to enforce provision of its requirements, through the collection of tax information – are incidental to the process by which information is collected and then relayed through the accounts. Yet this is at odds with the increasing power of stakeholders to influence companies. The State is always an exception since it has the power to compel compliance with its requests.

The precepts of shareholder dominance which underpin the conventional theories of governance are weakened further by a more specific view of how accounting works in the various interests of shareholders, stakeholders and managers.

CHAPTER 14

Reward and performance

This chapter will consider:

- the problem of managerial performance and the balance of reward between the parties to the governance arrangement;
- the policy origins of recent problems;
- trends in bonus and option implementation;
- the fundamental flaws in the bases of remuneration structures;
- the pernicious effects of management share options and the operation of 'moral hazard' in respect of options;
- different approaches to the problem.

Introduction

More than any other issue, the problem of apportioning reward to managers and shareholders has typified the breakdown of effectiveness of the traditionalist view of corporate governance. It is the issue which generates most heat and least light over how corporate governance should work – but it also indicates how the policy levers that are pulled are, in reality, disconnected to the governance structure. The problems brought about by the use of inadequate and improper bonus systems therefore affect the behavioural and structural aspects of governance and, through failings in the individual exercise of these they go on to affect, the systemic aspects of governance. The prevalence and inflammatory significance of the popular shorthand phrase – 'the bonus culture' – signifies the way in which the issue has achieved notoriety in the minds of those who would not ordinarily be interested in such matters.

The debate is not limited to the UK: American shareholders have complained about levels of pay and rewards for many years.[1] The issue of executive pay entered politics in France in February 2012 when the presidential candidate of the French Socialist party, François Hollande, said he would impose a 75 per cent marginal tax on annual incomes above €1 million, if elected.

---

[1] R. Monks, *Corpocracy* (New Jersey: Wiley, 2008).

The problem of managerial performance – balancing managerial reward and shareholder interests

A tale of remuneration at four companies

Reckitts

The corporate governance consultancy, PIRC, has consistently recommended that shareholders vote against Reckitt Benckiser's remuneration report since 2003, saying that the share-based scheme is not sufficiently challenging to directors: no absolute limits apply to the awards that can be made under the scheme.

In 2010 the chief executive of the company Bart Becht, who – before he left Reckitts – also sat on the boards of Coty in New York and a small Los Angeles-based aircraft manufacturer called Icon Aircraft, retired from the company after ten years as chief executive. His pay in the last year was £18.2 million (including shares cashed) and the previous year he had been paid £92 million (including shares cashed). Becht became chief executive as a result of the merger of Britain's Reckitt & Colman with Benckiser of the Netherlands in 1999. At the time of the merger the combined group had a turnover of £3 billion. By the time of his departure the company had increased annual turnover to £23.5 billion, helped by the £1.9 billion acquisition of Boots's over-the-counter medicines wing in 2006 and the £2.5 billion purchase of SSL International.

On the news of Mr Becht's departure the share price fell nearly 7 per cent.

Cable and Wireless Worldwide

In March 2010 Cable and Wireless Worldwide split from its parent company with John Pluthero as its then chairman. He had been the company's chief executive before the split and later reverted to that after relinquishing the chair after the incumbent MD resigned following profit warnings. The newly floated company had carried with an incentive plan that it had put in place in 2006, where senior executives were to receive large cash payments – a so-called 'private equity based' plan. Mr Pluthero, a chartered accountant who had previously been chairman of Energis when it went into administration, received a £10.2 million payment under a previous incentive plan running prior to the demerger. In the last year of his tenure at CWW he received remuneration of £740,000. CWW was capitalised at £1.2 billion; the chairman of Vodafone (market capitalisation £84 billion) received £600,000 on the same basis.

Within the space of sixteen months the company issued three profit warnings, retreating from the forecasts made at the time of the split. By the time of the third warning the shares had lost half their value; total shareholder return had fallen by 42 per cent; and the dividend – which was uncovered by cash flow – was to be halved.

The *Financial Times*, in July 2011, commenting on the third profit warning, said that Mr Pluthero's tenure had been characterised by showy announcements and over-optimistic forecasts coupled with a focus on short-term performance at the expense of long-term goals – all of which the newspaper believed were characteristic of managerial behaviour coupled to share price targets.

In November 2011, Mr Pluthero left the company, waiving his severance payment, after he apparently indicated that he was not prepared to see through the three to five year plan that restructuring and restoring it to profitability would require after it announced half-year losses of £590 million. CWW revealed in its results statement that it taken exceptional items totalling £624 million against profits – including a £436 million goodwill impairment against previous acquisitions and a £146 million write-down on deferred tax assets.

VW

In March 2012 the German car-maker VW announced that its chief executive Martin Winterkorn would receive €17.5 million in salary, bonuses and long-term incentives – making him the highest paid executive of a publicly-listed German company. The car-maker had recorded record revenues and earnings in 2011, selling more than 8 million vehicles and making €11.3 billion in operating profit.

Much of the payout was geared towards rewarding profitability over a number of years but the size of the payout raised questions about whether it met the criterion of 'appropriateness' under German corporate governance standards. Mr Winterkorn's pay consisted of a €1.9 million fixed salary and €11 million bonus, as well as contributions from a long-term incentive plan. His pay almost doubled from €9.3 million in 2010 to a total far in excess of Daimler chief executive Dieter Zetsche, who earned €8.7 million and Peter Loescher, chief executive of Siemens, who received a similar amount. The chief executive of Ford, Alan Mulally, received company shares that vested in 2011 worth $58.3 million.

In total, VW paid out €70.6 million to its eight board members compared with €36.7 million in the previous year. Hans Dieter Poetsch, chief financial officer, received €8.1 million in total pay. VW's executive bonus payment is primarily based on the financial results achieved in the past two years, while the long-term incentives are tied to four-year performance measured according to customer and employee satisfaction, unit sales growth and return on sales.

VW proposed to pay a dividend of €3 per ordinary share compared with €2.20 the year before and its workers last year received a bonus of €7,500 each.

Premier Foods

Mike Clarke was appointed by the board of Premier Foods as its new chief executive in September 2011 on a package potentially worth approximately £10 million ($16 million) over five years.

The company had a market capitalisation at that time of just over £300 million and had shed more than 80 per cent of its value since its flotation in 2004. A fundraising in 2009 that saw Warburg Pincus, the private equity firm, become the largest shareholder, was a rescue rights issue in all but name.

The pay package is modelled so as to contribute to reversing the destruction of value suffered by Premier's shareholders following its takeover of rival RHM in 2007, with the maximum payout applying only if shareholders also benefit.

The divisive issue of directors' pay

Critics in the UK of the apparently excessive rewards being appropriated by management, in financial institutions in particular, have been attacked by the CBI, by politicians and by the IoD for being 'anti-business'. This is itself odd, since the two organisations in the UK whose stances are often taken as proxies for the views of senior managers and directors are far from being co-incident over the issue.

The Confederation of British Industry's view is supportive of the bonus as a means of 'incentivising' senior managers, but the Institute of Directors believes that the rate of increase in the level of remuneration is unsustainable[2] and has made recommendations to address the problem by altering board composition and making shareholder voting binding on companies, since it believes that directors from different backgrounds are more likely to exhibit 'objective scepticism' on matters of remuneration. Binding votes are hotly contested by the CBI as being 'micro-management' by 'Machiavellian shareholders'.

---

[2] Written evidence to the BIS, November 2011.

The CBI's position on bonuses

In an interview published in the London *Evening Standard*, John Cridland, director-general of the CBI, reinforced his message that rewards should be given only where they are justified – comparing high-performing directors to top footballers:

'The whole football team knows that their performance requires one or two star players, and I think it's the same with a board of directors,' he said. 'That is why some payments will be high but they should only be high if they are for the equivalent of a goalscorer in the Premier League.'

'The anti-business rhetoric that we saw in the autumn at the three party conferences has increased since. I don't think it's an accident that it has increased as public nervousness at the state of the economy has increased.'

The President of the CBI's view

'We have all seen the social symptoms of a depressed economy inflamed by anti-business political rhetoric. The initial, and in some cases justified, attack on bank bonuses is now infecting the public perception of big business – seen as the undesirable led by the untrustworthy.

The corrosive anti-business sentiment feeds the view that all banks are despicable; all energy companies rip you off; all defence firms profiteer; all boardrooms are full of cronies and all in private equity are asset-strippers. In such a world, anyone who earns more than the Prime Minister is overpaid and bonuses go to the greedy and self-serving – never the over-performing.

Facts are ignored, prejudices easily confirmed and the position of business irrevocably weakened. For the unemployed and those struggling on low incomes, it can be an easy message to absorb.

When most people earn less than $2 a day, the fairness of those earning $2 a minute – however able – will always be questioned. But it is a function of markets, not morals.

So, just as football clubs pay millions of pounds for their top talent, and Hollywood pays millions of dollars for its stars, global business pays similar amounts to its top tier.

Increasingly, responsible boards are clear that it is their duty to be both market-aware and socially sensitive when determining performance and remuneration levels today.

Those that fail in their duties deserve neither the support of their peers nor the approval of their shareholders.

Responsible shareholders must be engaged as stewards, empowered as owners and equipped with the tools to facilitate informed, constructive involvement, but not meddling micro-management.

Business recognises the own goals scored by banks, media companies and multi-nationals. Increased self-discipline and proportionate regulation has become a necessary and appropriate outcome.

But sadly the volume of abusive rhetoric – while justified for the few – undermines the many. Damaged businesses run by demoralised managers are not a firm foundation for encouraging vital inward investment.

Mining the seam of popular anti-business feeling may be successful for short-term poll ratings, but risks weakening the industrial wealth-creating foundations on which our whole society depends.

It is time to leave the greed debate and return to the growth agenda.

Greater transparency in reporting, thoughtful judgment in rewarding and wider diversity on boards will help rebuild the reputation of business. Trust and respect – like bonuses – must be earned.'

Source: extract from Sir R. Carr, 'Let's end the executive greed debate and focus on growth', *Sunday Telegraph*, 12 February 2012

The debate about what managers should get from their efforts stems partly from a confusion about who their efforts are intended to benefit – themselves, the company or a wider constituency – since the question of the legitimacy and quantum of bonuses arises from harnessing shareholder value concerns to issues of the remuneration of the senior ranks of a company. Such concerns are not new, they stretch over 120 years from Vanderbilt's famous 'the public be damned' comment in 1882[3] through to Jack Welch's conversion to a wider purpose, after preaching the gospel of shareholder primacy for twenty-five years while at General Electric: 'Shareholder value is a result not a strategy. Your main constituencies are your employees, your products and your customers'.[4]

The last comment from Welch also highlights one of the problems with the principal-agent formulation of corporate governance and its association of directorial effort with shareholder value – why should the moral problem (if not the strictly financial one) of distribution of rewards between the parties to the governance arrangements terminate at the level of directors? True, they control the deployment of the company's assets on behalf of shareholders in a formal and legalistic sense – but their physical contribution to the success of a company is no more than one

---

[3] Vanderbilt to reporter Clarence Dresser, Chicago 1882.
[4] F. Guerrera, 'Welch condemns share price focus', *Financial Times*, 12 March 2009.

contribution among many other functions. Some of these functions make far greater additions to shareholder value than the directors' activities.

The policy origins of the bonus culture

Chapter 6 has already dealt with the Greenbury Committee Review of 1995 which effectively formally propelled the use of bonuses into the structure of directorial pay in the UK, by suggesting that pay should be linked explicitly to shareholder returns to try to reduce the effects of the principal-agent problem.

The Greenbury Committee, set up in the turmoil of public feeling about 'fat cat' salaries, effectively sanctified the structure of pay then coming into in vogue – where companies were encouraged to use self-referential 'benchmarking' (in the sense of selecting a group of supposedly 'peer' companies to indicate the need to increase salaries, either to attract the best to help the company catch up, or to allow it to retain its existing executive complement against poachers wanting to promote *their* company) to justify increasingly high salaries, which were then approved by remuneration committees advised by 'reward consultants' – who had collected, collated and reviewed the information on which the remuneration committees based their judgements. These consultants were also usually engaged in the business of 'headhunting' senior managers from one organisation to another and their fees for doing this were based on a proportion of the salary of the individuals they secured for their clients. As a result, it is not surprising that they had an interest in seeing levels of pay in boardrooms rise continually and rapidly.

By formally adding the use of bonuses, options and other incentives to the platform of basic pay, and encouraging the use of expert support in the form of the reward consultants, the Greenbury Committee laid the structure for executive pay to both outstrip and out-distance shareholder returns and to break the link with un-restructured basic pay received by the majority of workers, who are not able usually to incorporate such elements in their pay.

By going through such a process of scrutiny, advice and review, the remuneration committee has been held (quite correctly) to have legitimated decisions over pay. The trouble has been that the legitimising has been based on flawed foundations, because of fundamental errors in the theorising behind the installed changes. It is not possible to hold that the level of pay increase seen in recent years merely 'reflects the result of bargaining processes between shareholders' elected representatives and managers';[5] too many shareholders representatives are themselves managers elsewhere with interests in overall levels of remuneration that will benefit their own.[6] Regardless of any

---

[5] J. Macey, *Corporate Governance* (Princeton University Press, 2008).
[6] A. Smith and K. Burgess, 'Peer pressure matters with executive pay', *Financial Times*, 18 January 2012.

judgement on consequential social issues (value-laden or otherwise), the bonus system has had the effect of building structural rigidity into the system and reducing flexibility, all compounded by issues of deliberative groups which are essentially closed and largely insulated from a critical objective voice: shareholders' votes on remuneration are only advisory in the UK and have only recently been made more powerful in the USA.[7] The 1995 Greenbury proposals were the pay-and-rewards equivalent of bolting an after-burner on to a jet engine, without fully appreciating that an after-burner only works to boost thrust.

Bonus and option implementation

Although studies of executive pay have been conducted for many years, apart from those conducted for commercial purpose, reports had mostly been based on empirical evidence derived from company reports.[8] Initially, because of reporting obligations, these reports were only available for American, Canadian and British companies but the increasing obligations on companies across Europe to increase levels of disclosure have now indicated more widespread trends.

In the early part of the present century the trend of growth of executive pay was very rapid and largely undisturbed by the stumbles of the world economy in 2002 (the dot.com bust). This is largely because of gains made in the first two or three years of the new millennium when salaries of senior European executives saw substantial increases: in Switzerland the average pay of a chief executive almost tripled between 2001 and 2003; in Germany it more than doubled over the same period.[9] Much of the increase was not due to changes in basic cash payment but because of the introduction of incentive payments linking overall remuneration to changes in share prices. The use of such devices increased dramatically; by 2003 95 per cent of German listed companies and 80 per cent of Swiss listed companies had incentive schemes linked to share price change against a lowly 20 per cent for both only six years earlier.[10] Once share price plans are installed they tend to have the effect of acting like ratchets. They are best employed where there is a reasonable degree of disclosure and this results in directors making sure – via various types of pressure on remuneration committees – that they are paid amounts consistent with 'comparable' individuals in 'comparable' organisations.

In the late part of the twentieth century it became increasingly common to engage senior managers from outside an organisation, rather than grow talent internally: the

[7] Groom, 'Executive pay: The trickle-up effect'.
[8] K. J. Murphy, 'Executive compensation: Is Europe catching up with the US and should it do so?' in Owen, G. et al., *Corporate Governance in the US and Europe* (Basingstoke: Palgrave, 2006).
[9] *Ibid.*   [10] *Ibid.*

increasing scope of operations of large companies geographically and corporate amalgamations encouraged this trend. External engagement usually requires a premium to be paid to tempt those who are employed elsewhere and, in the USA, at least, at the higher reaches of organisational structures, the negotiation for pay is often done through agents,[11] usually lawyers, acting on behalf of their clients (who are of course, their principals) and who benefit from some proportion of the overall package they are able to achieve.

The trend for increased share options, as a component of overall salary, followed the pattern established in the USA but lagged substantially behind it. For instance, in 1997, one chief executive – Michael Eisner of the Disney Corporation – was paid as much as the entire cohort of managing directors of the FTSE 500 in the UK.[12] A mere $6 million of his $576 million was down to cash, the rest was due to the exercise of share options.

In 1992 American firms granted their employees options worth $11 billion at the time of grant, by 2000 that had increased to $119 billion on the same basis, although it fell back in later years.[13] Since 1995, share options have also been the preferred method in the UK of supposedly aligning directorial interest with that of shareholders.

What the studies on the market have also produced is clear evidence that while the market for senior managers is extensive it is also subject to serious imperfections in the alignment of pay structures with company performance: the size of company explains 40 per cent of the variation in the pay of senior executives, according to one study, with performance affecting only 5 per cent.[14]

There appear to be three major areas which are the causes of problems. These are first, institutional influences, second, prevailing theories of motivation, and third, fundamental problems with the construction of share option schemes.

Institutional influences

There are two distinct schools of thought about the use of options, one academic group maintaining that they bring about adverse outcomes because of the risk-averse behaviour which they prompt;[15] the other maintaining the exact opposite, suggesting that they encourage reckless behaviour. There is academic evidence to support both positions.[16]

---

[11] *Ibid.*   [12] *Ibid.*

[13] B. Hall and K. J. Murphy, 'The trouble with stock options', NBER working Paper 9784 (2003); M. J. Conyon and K. J. Murphy, 'The Prince and the Pauper? CEO Pay in the United States and United Kingdom', *The Economic Journal*, 110(467) (2000), 640–71.

[14] H. Tosi et al., 'Managerial Control, Performance, and Executive Compensation', *The Academy of Management Journal*, 30(1) (1987) and *Journal of Management*, 26(2) (2000), 301–39.

[15] B. S. Frey and M. Osterloh, 'Stop tying pay to performance', *Harvard Business Review*, Jan–Feb 2012.

[16] B. G. M. Main, 'The question of executive pay' in Owen et al., *Corporate Governance*.

The first group maintains that most executives do not hold widely diversified investment portfolio positions, like the fund managers who would be familiar with the intrinsic future value of shares, but are instead heavily invested in one asset – their careers – in terms of both personal and financial capital. This leads them to be risk averse and provides them with strong incentives to attempt to 'smooth' the price of the shares which they are given options over.[17] It also requires them to have tangible additional 'hard' (cash) returns to offset the volatility of the 'soft' returns represented by the options, pushing up remuneration packages overall.

The second group maintains that the reverse happens and that executives become reckless in attempting to push the share price up to meet or exceed levels where they will be able to exercise option rights. A further consequence of this is that such actions often lead directors to focus exclusively on areas covered by the criteria and neglect other important tasks, bringing a double dose of damage – doing more than they should in one direction and less than they should in another. The problems are compounded by the demands of a modern economy, where new challenges emerge constantly, and it is impossible to determine the tasks that will need to be done in the future precisely enough for variable pay for performance to work well.

Psychological influences

Evidence has emerged from psychological studies[18] which suggest that managers behave differently from that suggested by the simplistic strictures of principal and agent theory. Most people react to a combination of monetary reward (extrinsic motivation) and personal factors such as a sense of accomplishment, self-esteem and personal satisfaction (intrinsic motivational factors). Unfortunately since all of the last can be confused with, or supplanted by, external motivation factors, remuneration committees have concentrated on the former, perhaps spurred by some individuals whose extrinsic responsiveness outweighs their ability to discriminate between extrinsic and intrinsic motivation. This then leads to the eventual collapse of corporate relationships – and to attempts at increasing shareholder value – as individuals are forced to concentrate on short-term measures to maximise the levels of return that their poorly-constructed pay structures demand.

---

[17] R. Skovoroda et al., 'The Minimum assumed incentive effect of executive share options', ESRC Paper 2003; and A. Bruce et al., 'Executive bonus and firm performance in the UK', *Long Range Planning*, 40(3) (2007).

[18] B. S. Frey and R. Jegen, 'Motivation crowding theory', *Journal of Economic Surveys*, 15 (2001), 589–611.

The fundamental flaws in the bases of remuneration structures

In addition to these underlying problems there are also governance problems stemming from the individual nature of remuneration plans which incorporate some form of link to share prices.

From the shareholders' point of view many schemes are badly constructed or do not hold to the original purpose by being overly weighted towards the benefit of managers and directors. There are more than a dozen ways indicated below in which this happens and more could possibly be distinguished.

No limits schemes

Mention was made of the Reckitt Benckiser bonuses at the outset of this chapter. The scheme has been castigated by PIRC for over a decade for effectively setting no limit upon the rewards achieved by directors – but nothing has been changed in terms of the balance of rewards. This may appear to be of marginal significance if the share price rises and keeps on rising – but eventually share prices plateau, especially if the increase in the share price has been fuelled by acquisition. Such 'no limits' schemes then begin to bite the shareholders hard as earnings stall and the positive link between earnings and share prices begins to reverse with higher numbers of shares in issue acting in a way to reduce shareholder value.

The aspic schemes

Because of the natural tendency of remuneration committees to take what is available as a starting point for basing future returns, the balance is always loaded in favour of the executives; no schemes effectively start from the position of a blank slate. Such arrangements effectively place in aspic the gains already achieved by directors and then add to them.

Improper base selection

By not selecting the proper base against which to measure achievements, on the basis of the asymmetry problem – that the executives are always in possession of more and better knowledge than the non-executive directors, acting as proxies for the shareholders – results tend to be skewed in favour of executives, this is especially the case where the option then displaces the shareholder as the principal in the supposed principal-agent relationship (see below). Where the base then works against the executives they are able to claim that they will consider exercising their right to depart and remuneration committees then adjust the schemes in their favour – the Thomas Cook example being a case in point.

Lack of shareholder redress

Because votes cast on remuneration reports are non-binding, there is little share-holders can then do apart from grumble. Any revisions to directorial pay policy and structures made 'voluntarily' may well be inadequate – as the response by Tesco showed in 2011, after a near 50 per cent rebellion by shareholders the previous year.[19]

Herd movement

Stockbrokers have long been aware of the fact that good results from one company in a sector will produce a sympathetic response in other companies' share prices. Similarly, when markets are confident share prices overall become buoyant. Research[20] has verified what stockbrokers have long known – that many share price movements are due to herd effects as shares are bought – or sold – in response to market movements. Obviously, if share prices go down because of these effects, those in possession of options become disadvantaged, but they have not risked or lost their capital as shareholders do – and as has been suggested they may well have compensated for this in their other demands over pay structures.

Luck

The Nobel prize winner Daniel Kahneman has estimated the correlation between firm success and managerial input as determined by the perceived quality of the chief executive.[21] His analysis is stark: 'Even if you had perfect foreknowledge that a CEO has brilliant vision and extraordinary competence, you still would be unable to predict how the company will perform with much better accuracy than the flip of a coin'. Luck is, of course, by its nature unsustainable.

Valuation problems (1)

Issues of proper valuation are legion and have been exploited dramatically in some of the most egregious examples of misbehaviour: the case of Enron serves as an example for the rest. By the end of his first year in office (1997), Enron's CEO, Jeffrey Skilling, had increased the number of share options held by senior managers by over 56 per cent over the previous year. By the end of 2000, the equivalent of 13 per cent of Enron's issued shares was held in the form of options owned by management[22] – thereby

[19] A. Felsted, H. Kuchler and K. Burgess, 'Investors censure Tesco on pay plans', *Financial Times*, 2 July 2010.
[20] A. Puckett and X. S. Yan, 'Short term institutional herding and its impact on stock prices', University of Missouri Working Paper 2005.
[21] D. Kahneman, *Thinking Fast and Slow* (London: Allen Lane, 2011).
[22] R. Bryce, *Pipedreams* (New York, NY: Public Affairs, 2002).

representing 93.5 million reasons why senior executives wanted to propel the company's 'earnings' forward regardless of proper accounting conventions. Rules become flexed to their maximum by the unscrupulous in the desire to achieve the exercise of options – which involved no real wealth being risked, as in the case of the shareholder, only the prospect of wealth – thereby continually eating away at the structural foundations of good corporate governance.

Valuation problems (2)

There is also evidence to suggest that options are, somewhat perversely, a badly under-valued method of remuneration at the time of issue, which become more costly to the issuer over the passage of time; it is difficult to value an option on grant because of the uncertainty attached to the exercise. Boards of directors issuing the shares perceive them as low-cost because they have favourable tax treatment attached to them (provided they are properly set up) which results in an over-generous allocation, which then becomes the norm, but affects shareholders' wealth in due course by both the dilution of earnings effect and the overhang of shares in the marketplace.

Valuation problems (3)

The point about the indeterminate value of the option, on issue, has already been made. Because of uncertainty about the point at which the option will be exercised its monetary value is imprecise. However, it is possible to assign a putative value using a technique known as the Black-Scholes equation. The outcomes of such calculations often reveal much greater impact on other shareholders than might be anticipated. In June 1998, a firm of fund managers in the USA calculated that the 16 million options granted annually by the drug company Merck had a Black-Scholes valuation of about $750 million which would require off-setting share repurchases from other share-holders of more than $2 billion each year (at the then-prevailing share price) to balance the dilution effects.[23] The effect of options granted in this fashion then turns an incentive into a very attractive share-ownership plan on instalments at considerable cost to the company and other shareholders.

Dilution

In June 2011, UKFI, the body that manages the taxpayer's stake in the country's bailed-out banks, informed investors that its stake in the bank's shares had fallen below two-thirds. Under FSA regulations, a shareholder is obliged to issue a statement to the stock market if its stake changes by more than 1 per cent.

---

[23] E. Chancellor, *Capital Account* (New York, NY: Texere, 2004), p. 188.

According to a statement to the stock market, released by RBS on behalf of the government, the UKFI stake in the bank now stands at 66.46 per cent. At its height, the government owned 70.3 per cent of voting shares in RBS.

In total, the UK Government's overall economic interest in RBS – after it injected £45 billion to bail it out during the crisis – is now 82 per cent, after including other non-voting interests, such as a large tranche of B-shares. This is a decline from its peak of 84 per cent.

The dilution is due to remuneration of bank staff – with employees exercising options to take new shares on the market as part of deferred bonus packages. Six hundred and fifty million shares were given to RBS employees, mostly in its investment banking unit, in the 2009 bonus round – when RBS was not allowed to make cash payments.

When these were placed in the market, more than half were sold immediately – bringing about a 4 per cent fall in the bank's share price.

Inappropriate measures and Goodhart's Law

The exercise of options encourages directors to think exclusively in terms of earnings-based measures of performance – the return on equity. This then leads to the problem of distortion in what the return on equity represents. Charles Goodhart has already been mentioned. He was an economist at the Bank of England who, in the 1970s, propounded a theory – now known as Goodhart's Law – suggesting attempts to tax or regulate one area of economic activity rapidly led to the same activity being conducted under a different name through another (untaxed) channel. He noticed that attempts by the Government to control inflation by relying on particular statistical relationships were thwarted when the market became alert to the problem and the relationship broke down. In short, Goodhart's Law suggests that when one measure became a target it ceased to be a good measure.

Barclays' plan to boost revenue

In mid-2011 the *Financial Times* reported that Barclays' chief executive, Bob Diamond, planned to boost the revenues of the bank by 20 per cent in order to achieve a return on equity of 13 per cent by 2013.[24] The largest boost is anticipated to come from BarCap where merger and acquisition activity and equity business are required to expand; the corporate and 'wealth' divisions are also expected to make substantial contributions.

---

[24] S. Goff, 'Diamond vows to try harder as Barclays disappoints', *Financial Times*, 10 February 2012.

Retail banking traditionally makes a return of 4 to 5 per cent *at most* in what is a mature business with little scope for change. Corporate banking makes perhaps 10–11 per cent. These two functions account for nearly half of the turnover of the bank, worldwide, implying that the remaining functions will have to make proportionately higher contributions to the banks profitability than their turnover contributions, as measured by return on equity (ROE), if the overall planned return is to be achieved. In banking, return and risk are directly correlated.

Different perceptions of shareholder value

Different shareholders may have different perceptions of value and these may not necessarily be commensurate with the views on which the reward system involving the exercise of options or the use of bonuses is based.

The obvious rejoinder to this objection from a conventional viewpoint is that the shareholders have appointed directors – and through the directors the remuneration committee – to act for them and so they have no particular position to interfere from, either in law or from a moral standpoint: shareholders not in agreement should sell their holdings and move on to a different investment which better suits their risk appetite or their preference for a certain type of reward. Yet in an arrangement where votes on the remuneration report are non-binding, shareholders are denied any attempt to influence – let alone change – the structure and so are forced to exercise the 'exit' option, since 'voice' is effectively denied them and 'loyalty' is discounted. The traditionalist view of how the operation of the governance process works therefore has a broken lever – the agents are not required to take note of what the principals require; such votes have a signalling effect but this is not always heeded as numerous reports of interaction between remuneration committees and shareholders attest.[25] If the shareholders then have no option but to sell their shares, in order to preserve their investment according to their own risk preferences, the whole edifice on which the promotion of the idea of stewardship is founded is once again found to be wanting.

The problem of 'clawback'

During 2011 and 2012 the major banks in the UK were forced to repay many billions of pounds to previous customers who had been obliged to take out unnecessary insurance when they took out loans with them.[26] The provision that Lloyd's alone made for the repayment of these loans amounted to over £3 billion, and collectively

---

[25] For example: HSBC, Barclays, Tesco, Thomas Cook.
[26] Moore, 'Banks face £3bn bill in PPI scandal'.

the banks had made provisions of £6 billion by the end of 2011.[27] These loans had contributed strongly to the banks' profits over the previous decade, since in many cases they could be regarded as an additional fee charged to borrowers as they had no prospect of ever being exercised as insurance contracts.

In February 2012, Lloyd's announced that it would be 'clawing back' £580,000 of the bonus of £1.45 million awarded to the previous chief executive, Eric Daniels for the year 2010. This announcement was received with acclaim (apart, presumably, from Mr Daniels) as evidence that the bonus system was responding properly and that failure would not be rewarded.

What the clawback implied though was that, despite the bank having taken a charge of £3.2 billion to compensate customers who were effectively treated fraudu-lently (fraud is defined by the OED as 'a dishonest artifice or trick'), the remuner-ation committee would still have awarded the chief executive £870,000 for his performance that year. This is far from being evidence that the bonus system operates properly – especially since at the time of writing no other bank has operated such a mechanism – more an indication that expensive lawyers were brought in to negotiate a settlement, since the basis on which the clawback and the retention were calculated was not disclosed. (It also has serious implications for the health of structural governance in Lloyd's.) If the £3.2 billion provision had been taken in the 2010 accounts, Lloyd's would have recorded three consecutive yearly losses on its preferred 'combined business' measure, thereby eliminating any bonus awards to the directors.

Boundaries – time and obscurity

The Lloyd's clawback indicates another feature of imbalanced rewards structures that was prevalent during the financial crisis of 2007–8 – that of the timing boundaries within which bonuses operate. Bonus structures are now complicated arrangements for outsiders to disentangle, since they operate on a rolling basis and may apply to the performance of the company achieved over years previous to when they 'vest' or are exercisable.

This has been an element introduced to try to reduce the effects of short-termism and behaviour designed to manipulate profits. The FSA remuneration code is intended to end the practice that was common before the banking crisis that bankers received 100 per cent of their annual bonus in cash. The basic elements of the code are that 40 per cent of a bonus must be deferred for at least three years, although this rises to 60 per cent in some cases. Also, at least 50 per cent of any bonuses must be paid in shares or other non-cash instruments. No guaranteed

---

[27] S. Goff, 'Barclays' PPI complaints soar', *Financial Times*, 22 February 2012.

bonuses of more than one year can be paid and only then 'in exceptional circumstances to new hires for the first year of services'.[28]

While the intention was admirable one of the consequences, from the shareholders'
point of view, has been over-complication and a loss of clarity. While at the senior
reaches of a company the operation of bonus structures and share option schemes
can be disentangled because the information is disclosed, it is not so easy to do this
for levels below the obligatory disclosure levels. This then leads on to other issues,
principally the absolute balance of returns to shareholders and managers – not the
division of the spoils after targets have been achieved, and the issue of the cultural,
structural governance of the company.

Quantum – cash bonuses

After the collapse of inter-bank lending in the wake of the problems of 2007–8, investment banking activity diminished rapidly – and so did profits from those activities. The
shift away from bonuses that had been required by regulatory authorities across the
world as an immediate response to the perceived 'bonus culture' problem, mean that
financial institutions began to pay their staff in terms of higher fixed salaries with
bonuses being reduced as a proportion of overall pay – an unforeseen outcome of the
policies. However the reduced emphasis on bonuses had the effect of driving fixed costs
higher, with some salaries increasing by 50 or 100 per cent at the major banks.[29] For
some of the large 'universal' banks this meant that they were setting aside more than
60 per cent of anticipated revenues from trading to pay staff – some much more; this
sum included salaries and anticipated 'bonus pools'. Shareholders would then, obviously,
only receive any benefit – if at all – after all other costs had been absorbed. In some cases,
as in the example of RBS in the UK, this meant that shareholders who would have
benefited from strong performance at retail banking divisions – in 2011 RBS' retail
banking division profits jumped 45 per cent to £2 billion[30] – were saddled with losses at
investment banks (where bonuses were paid) which totally eliminated the gains.
The balance of reward between shareholder and management – between principal and
agent – that the traditionalist view held to be at the root of the governance arrangement
as a necessity in aligning shareholders' interests with those of directors and managers,
has become completely skewed in favour of the agent.

[28] FSA Press release, 'New deposit guarantee limit to be £85,000', 17 December 2010 (FSA/PN/181/
2010), available at http://www.fsa.gov.uk/library/communication/pr/2010/181.shtml.
[29] S. Goff, M. Murphy and G. Parker, 'RBS bonus cuts offset by big salary increases', *Financial
Times*, 22 February 2012.
[30] P. Jenkins, S. Goff and A. Sakoui, 'Hester has task of selling off "risky" divisions', *Financial Times*,
4 January 2012.

The pernicious effects of management share options and the operation of 'moral hazard'

Regardless of which school is correct about the way that options work – either to promote aggressive pursuit of risk or to avoid risk – what appears to happen is that the *exercise of the option or the achievement of the bonus* becomes the goal of the executives who possess options or who are rewarded through bonus payments. In terms of the traditionalist view then these devices effectively become the principal for whom the agent works, displacing the human principal from the relationship that is supposed to exist. Whether the outcome is risk aversion or over-emphatic risk endorsement, the effect is the same: actions are taken which are short-termist in nature to bring about the exercise of the option or achieve the bonus being paid out and are not conducive to promoting shareholder value in the long term.

Moral hazard

The development of the concept of 'moral hazard' has been outlined before. It has been mostly applied to the supposed effects of providing psychological safety nets for managers of systemically-significant companies by suggesting that they will not be allowed to go bust to avoid the resulting systemic damage. It is more generally applied to the instance of allowing someone to do something risky in the foreknowledge that they will not suffer adverse consequences.

In this respect the linking of managerial pay to options over shares is a prime example of moral hazard: if the option fails then the manager concerned has not lost any real outlay, merely a notional return. He has suffered no materially adverse consequences, since unlike the shareholder his material wealth was never in jeopardy. There is in consequence of this, a moral 'pressure' on the option holder to undertake risky activity just as there is a displacement of the shareholder as the true principal – that is, of course, if the principal-agent argument is accepted as conventionally-formulated in the first place.

Irrational allocation

There is a final issue which needs to be aired in respect of managerial rewards – the irrational allocation of resources. This is a problem which has been touched upon incidentally in considering several of the flaws mentioned above but it needs to be identified separately and independently since, for society as a whole rather than for individual sets of shareholders, this is the single most significant problem with the linking of managerial reward and share prices. This activity therefore stretches beyond the procedural, beyond the behavioural and into the systemic realm.

At the end of 2011 commentators were becoming aware of the substantial balances of cash which were being built up by large companies – partly due to the problems that these companies were experiencing with the banks – and the distortion which this was imposing on economic activity.

In a regular column in the *Financial Times* of 16 February 2012, Martin Wolf quoted a report written by Andrew Smithers, a financial adviser to over 100 pension funds worldwide and previously a manager of high-performing investment funds. In a document published a few days earlier, and sent out only to his clients and Press contacts, which was provocatively entitled 'UK: Narrower Profit Margins and Weaker Sterling Needed'. Mr Smithers had suggested that 'perhaps the single greatest challenge to economic policy over the next decade will consist of how to turn the corporate sector's cash surplus into a deficit without pushing the economy into recession'.

Smithers had suggested that the heavy balances of cash in company balance sheets were at least partly due to perverse incentives – particularly the linking of executive pay to share prices, since in the short run, lower investment and higher prices of output boost both share prices and remuneration of management. His analysis went beyond suggesting that the current swelling of cash resources could be attributed to precautionary behaviour after the financial crisis and identified a longer term reason: these effects occurred because management is best able to affect the short-run during which time their behaviour in respect of company policy can influence share prices and it was in *their* interest to allocate resources in a way which promoted their interests – even though this had deleterious effects on the wider economy.

What Martin Wolf went on to say, unequivocally in his commentary on the Smithers' article, is that:

> UK corporates are run not for long-term health, but for executive wealth, with bad results for the businesses themselves and, still more, for the entire economy. Policy, then, has to focus on the incentives driving today's vast corporate financial surpluses. By focusing on these, we would also relearn the most important lesson of John Maynard Keynes: the fiscal position cannot be viewed separately from what is happening in the rest of the economy. The big challenge is to bring financial surpluses down elsewhere, but by raising growth not by depressing the economy.

Summary

The well-intentioned policy to link managerial rewards to shareholders' interests and thereby avoid the consequences of the principal and agent problem has had perverse effects. By concentrating on remedies which apparently link the shareholder and the manager through the operation of governance arrangements (as traditionalist views perceive they should work) the situation has been worsened at the procedural, behavioural and structural levels, leading to perverse outcomes, procedural anomalies, behavioural warping and systemic distortion.

This is not to say that the principal and agent problem does not exist; it indicates, rather, that the remedies being used by traditionalist perceptions of governance have not identified the way in which governance works in reality. The traditionalist view by-passes the interposition of the company and conceives of a contract directly between shareholder/principal and manager-director/agent, ignoring the impact of the other stakeholders and their contribution to the creation of wealth and the way that policy decisions are derived. The consequence of that is that resources have been allocated poorly, in favour of the short term rather than the long term and to one particular group of stakeholders rather than being distributed more efficiently to a wider constituency.

PART 5

COUNTER-GOVERNANCE: FAILURES OF GOVERNANCE AND CORPORATE FAILURE

Counter-governance (1): theory

This chapter, and the next, will cover issues of 'counter-governance' – those activities knowingly undertaken, usually by managers, which work against the effective governance of a company.

Chapter 15 includes an examination of the following issues:

- instances of failure of both procedural and behavioural governance;
- structural governance failure as a cause of corporate collapse;
- the development of counter-governance cultures;
- 'innocent' failure;
- the legal view of corporate failure;
- ethics and governance;
- the two ethics view: bluff and knowing misrepresentation.

Chapter 16 looks at particular instances of counter-governance in the form of some sort of abuse of other stakeholders' interests

- market abuse: cartels;
- market abuse: concealment of information;
- other forms of abuse: environmental crime;
- other forms of abuse: pension funds.

Introduction

The term 'counter-governance' is used to denote the negative aspects of governance that bring about failure to secure the objectives for which most companies are presumably established – that is, the creation of wealth for the shareholders (and, to a lesser extent, the stakeholders). It encompasses issues such as corporate insolvency; corporate criminality; market abuse; concealment or manipulation of information by managers; corrupt practices; environmental crime; pension fund abuse; and avoidance of taxation that verges on evasion by virtue of its artificial or elaborate nature. All of these will be dealt with (some in re-capitulation) in this chapter.

Counter-governance as a condition affects all three aspects of governance related to a company – procedural, behavioural and structural – but often pervades structural governance in particular. The aspect of governance derived from, and embedded in, the culture of an organisation is particularly susceptible to distortion and is easily corrupted. It has no skeleton of rules, like procedural governance, to stiffen it and does not have the armour of codes (legal or otherwise) to protect it, as behavioural governance does. It depends on the existence of the others, in valid form, for its effects.

Little attention is usually paid to counter-governance as a discrete force or corporate characteristic since it is often viewed as an absence of good governance rather than having an existence of its own. But evidence from research into the circumstances surrounding the collapse of some large listed companies[1] indicates that corporate collapse is often rooted in deliberate and specific acts rather than accidental ones and these deliberate acts are often perversions of the structural governance core, the soft heart of the company which is represented by its ethical characteristics. By and large, companies which are admitted to listing on large exchanges do not normally suffer from deliberate acts designed purposefully to defraud – although instances are hardly unknown, as the cases of Enron or Worldcom in the USA; Satyam and Sino-Forest in Asia; or Royal Ahold, Parmalat, or Langbar in Europe all indicate. But there are very many instances of the structural/ethical guidelines being warped which produce effects which counter the impact of good governance. The newspapers are full of them every day and in many ways the existence of counter-governance gives rise to the need to discuss, design and deliver good governance. Diversions from the path of correct governance do damage to the efficiency of resource allocation, and the legitimacy of the relationship between shareholders and directors: every scandal, collapse or near-collapse, whether brought about by acts of omission or acts of commission, brings with it the elimination of some amount of shareholder wealth and entails havoc to stakeholders' interests.

Counter-governance therefore is a sub-species of governance – the dark side, the photo-negative of good and efficient governance. It ought to be recognised as such and not simply attributed to bad luck or some random aberration of standard behaviour. The concept of counter-governance includes forms of action which vary from the intentional and wilful abuse of procedure (which often is disguised by the naïve title of 'corner cutting'), through behavioural disregard of the precepts of good governance (honesty, transparency, integrity and so on) to what has been termed 'control fraud'[2] (Black), and even beyond that to occasional instances of outright banditry where the whole structure of the organisation becomes corrupted. The way in which counter-governance manifests itself can be associated, by comparison, with the concept of the regulatory spectrum introduced in Chapter 10. By looking at what

---

[1] S. Hamilton and A. Mickelthwait, *Greed and Corporate Failure* (Basingstoke: Palgrave, 2006).
[2] W. K. Black, *The Best Way to Rob a Bank is to Own One* (University of Texas Press, 2005).

causes collapse and how law and corporate governance interact to prevent it – or miss the chance to deal with it – more light is thrown on the mechanisms of governance that do work well.

The failure of structural governance and corporate failure

Corporate failures which are brought about by failures of governance can stem from any aspect of the three major dimensions of governance that are located inside companies. They may be the catastrophic consequence of sloppy observance of the procedural, but occasionally they are the product of an active disregard of proper stewardship in the sense that some form of governance behaviour has failed. More often they are the product of some long-term decline of the standards of the structural dimension of governance, which becomes accepted as the norm within a company. Failures like this are often the consequences of an elevation of the crude principles of the marketplace (which cannot properly indicate multiple tangential consequences) over the intuitive and less distinct guides offered by ethical and moral principles – issues of trust, fairness and reciprocity – which temper otherwise unimaginative applications of theoretical economics and thankfully pervade most human interaction.

Instances of deliberate and specific corporate criminality are usually infrequent, although when they do occur they may be serious and attract the attention of the legal system. Companies may not be able to flee in the same way as human perpetrators of crimes, but they can and do attempt concealment or try to put themselves beyond the reach of the law by choice of domicile and structure.

Modern developments in some aspects of the law have become extra-territorial in their scope as a consequence. Chapter 5 looked at the impact of critical governance law in terms of instances of bribery and manslaughter (where infractions of the law are at least usually visible). The law in the UK now contains provisions to destroy rogue companies which severely transgress the laws on bribery, or cause death as a result of careless behaviour which is rooted in poor structural governance. Company liquidation has achieved a new depth of meaning following the enactment of these statutes.

Occasionally, instances of structural governance breakdown are so severe that the company is unable to survive the decay: Union Carbide was unable to survive the disaster at Bhopal as an independent entity; the Arthur Andersen partnerships' reputation, collectively, was irretrievably damaged by the symbiotic relationship it had with Enron. In both instances, poor judgement at the top had gradually mutated into a full-blown decay of structural governance – the dimension of governance rooted in ethics – that resulted in acts of criminality (the destruction of evidence and breach of accounting regulations to name just two in the case of Arthur Andersen, and the flagrant disregard of safety regulations in the case of Union Carbide) which produced the demise of the business.

Corporate failure and corporate criminality might occasionally accompany each other but are not in most cases directly associated in terms of cause and effect. Despite their prominence, only very infrequently are corporate failures (in 'normal' governance systems at least) the result of deliberate actions on someone's part to defraud and to cheat their way to rewards to which they are not entitled (it is after all impermissible to start a company for an illegal purpose). Instances of structural governance failure, where the whole organisational culture becomes toxic, are very unusual but not unknown (for a possible instance see the accusations levelled at Goldman Sachs by one of its departing employees in March 2012[3]). The use of the terms 'very infrequently' and 'very unusual' are qualified by setting the large numbers of quoted companies which do conduct themselves appropriately and the vast numbers of transactions which proceed completely properly, against the minority of both instances which attract attention.

However, where such counter-governance actions do bring about failure – either complete or partial and involving monetary or reputational damage – they might be categorised as a failure involving all three aspects of (individual company) corporate governance – the procedural, the behavioural and the structural – with the emphasis usually being on the structural. In many cases it is quite conceivable that the systemic aspect (governance systems outside the company) has probably also failed, in that the checks which are supposed to exist in the system – through regulatory oversight or the discipline of audit – have not worked properly either.

By themselves, procedural failings – unless they are repeated many times before being discovered or rectified, or unless they are very large in proportion to the size of the business – do not normally precipitate sudden collapse. That does not mean that they cannot do great harm. For instance, the failings of the board of Mouchel to properly conduct investigations into acquisitions were essentially procedural and brought about serious problems for that company, and the numerous instances of lax safety standards that lie behind industrial accidents. The company may avoid collapse but shareholders lose through the damage done to share prices and stakeholders often pay much more, sometimes with their lives. They are often affected by the consequences of procedural short-cuts that are shielded from view by a box-ticking approach to governance at the behavioural level but where the structural underpinning of a moral/ethical framework is absent.

---

[3] T. Alloway, T. Braithwaite and D. Schäfer, 'Goldman battles "toxic" culture criticism', *Financial Times*, 14 March 2012.

BP and the Texas City explosion

On 23 March 2005 a blast at the Texas City oil refinery owned by BP killed 15 people and injured a further 170. Following an investigation the US Occupational Safety and Health Administration imposed a then-record fine of $21.3 million for hundreds of breaches of safety regulations, and later imposed an even larger fine of $87.4 million after claiming that BP had failed to implement safety improvements it had been obliged to make following the disaster.

An official investigation into the causes of the Texas City explosion concluded in 2007 that senior BP executives, under the company's former chief executive, Lord Browne, had failed to act on numerous warnings over safety at Texas City.

In July 2008 *The Guardian*[4] reported that:

'A newly released transcript of an hour-long deposition in April this year by Browne to a US court reveals that the corporate chief denied all knowledge of safety lapses in the run-up to an explosion at Texas City three years ago which killed 15 people and injured more than 180.

"I wasn't aware of that," he repeatedly answered when asked about maintenance failures at the plant.

Insisting that he had only ever visited Texas City twice, Browne said it looked the same as any other refinery and that he did not perceive it to be dilapidated: "I didn't see that it was unusually – I didn't come away with an impression that is lasting with me that it was unusually different."

When asked about an internal document suggesting that he was personally monitoring accident statistics at Texas City because he knew of its poor safety performance, Browne gave a qualified denial: "Well, certainly to the best of my recollection, this is an inaccurate statement. I don't recall doing this."

Browne did, however, accept that a survey of employees' worries at the site was "disturbing" and he accepted responsibility for company-wide cutbacks which were blamed by certain victims for falling safety standards. "It was necessary to reduce costs to get [BP] competitive with others and to bring a degree of discipline into the management of the firm," he told a lawyer for bereaved families and injured workers.'

Behavioural problems, by contrast, may well bring about sudden collapse without any specific procedural problems being evident – they did so in the case of Lehman Brothers (although there have been indications subsequently that the failures of

---

[4] A. Clark, 'Browne speaks of Elton, elves and etiquette – but little of Texas City', *The Guardian*, 24 July 2008.

governance there were not limited to behavioural problems and may have also gone deep into issues of structural governance and probably spread into the procedural dimension). Such problems were not unique to Lehman Brothers and may well have brought down more banks had they not been bailed out worldwide by taxpayers and public funds.

Inevitable and sudden decline of a company is usually a product of all forms of governance breaking down collectively: procedural failures compounded by behavioural shortcomings, spreading through structural/cultural failure and allowed to go wrong by systemic inadequacies of the regulatory system that should trap such problems – as in the case of RBS and the over-ambitious purchase of AMRO for instance. When a company collapses all the minor problems of procedural and behavioural governance which may not ordinarily pose a threat to its existence are revealed during investigation with no-one there to cover them up or rectify them or explain them away – it becomes no longer possible to keep all the balls in the air simultaneously.

In an extensive study of corporate failure, Hamilton and Mickelthwait concluded that the recurrent themes of corporate collapse are:

1. poor strategic decisions;
2. over-expansion, often brought about by ill-judged acquisitions;
3. the dominance of one individual on the board (usually CEOs);
4. hubris resulting in nemesis – the greed or lust for power of those CEOs (wrongly) accorded the status of 'star performers';
5. poor risk management and internal controls; and
6. ineffective boards and their audit committees (especially).

All the problems listed by Hamilton and Mickelthwait are identifiable with the internal processes of the company. In the last instance which they list, they attribute the numbers and quality of available non-executive directors as a factor in bringing about decline in companies. They consider that cronyism has often been evident when collapses have been analysed, and that non-executive directors often did not have the knowledge or experience required to make an effective contribution to decisions or had allowed themselves to be dominated by the opinions of one powerful character, usually the managing director.

Such failings do not simply arise spontaneously but often extend over generations of management thereby bringing about cultural changes – structural governance changes – that affect decision-making. When George Mathewson became RBS's chief executive in 1992 the bank had been severely weakened by bad debts arising from poor lending decisions, exacerbated by the economic slowdown of the early 1990s. Mathewson instigated and led 'Project Columbus', which involved a restructuring of RBS's UK operations by a tightening of credit controls. This earned him a reputation for ruthlessness but allowed the bank to return a profit in 1998 of £1 billion. In 1999, when Barclays (because of internal problems) began to search for a new chief executive, Mathewson was sounded out.[5] He contemplated a merger of RBS with Barclays but only if it could be run from Scotland – despite RBS being only two-fifths the size of Barclays – and with a certain Fred Goodwin, his protégé, being lined up to be in charge of Barclays (the merger never occurred, for a variety of reasons more to do with Barclays' decision processes than any other).

When Mathewson left the RBS chief executive's position in 2000 to assume the deputy chairmanship (in contravention of corporate governance code provisions) Goodwin was promoted to take his place. A year later Mathewson became chairman (again in contravention of code principles) and worked in harness with Goodwin as chairman and chief executive. It was thus the experience of Mathewson's leadership – hard-driving, ruthless and intolerant of 'rules' – which paved the way for the style of behaviour later adopted by Fred Goodwin – Fred the Shred – and the prevailing culture, the corrupted structural governance, of RBS.

'Innocent' failure

In contrast to issues of criminality or corrupted governance, some companies may be brought down by 'innocent' failure: failings mostly concentrated in volume or significance at the procedural level of governance. The case of the Royal Mail Line might be categorised as such – it will be remembered that Lord Kylsant was convicted on the charge of issuing a false prospectus. The use of accounting conventions that might be looked on as highly suspect from a later vantage point was considered acceptable by at least one eminent authority who argued in Kylsant's favour.

But like most human activities, the boundary between classifications of activity is variable and indistinct: one sometimes shades into the other, so that relatively minor failings in procedural governance might well be compounded and aggravated by inadvertent, or deliberate, failings of behavioural governance. Procedural problems – although they may appear to be of less significance than behavioural inadequacies – may well spread through an organisation like dry rot in a house. The developing extent of problems will be concealed by supposedly compliant behavioural governance – the appropriate number of committees, appropriate remits for committees, in-place succession plans, prompt reporting – but without any framework of structural governance that encourages and supports 'the right thing' being done. Problems become widespread and severe over a long period, so that problems eventually manifest themselves because the company's systems cannot cope with a marginal extra amount of pressure.

Sometimes procedural failings which are not rectified – legacy failings which survive changes of management – lead on to give false information about the health of an

[5] M. Van der Weyer, *Falling Eagle* (London: Wiedenfield, 2000).

organisation, which themselves then produce more debilitating behavioural problems. It is here that the issue of the integrity of operational and financial information come into play. Where even minor failings become persistent, the effects of both regulation and external stakeholders' interests in such actions are also significant. What may be categorised as procedural inadequacy in only small numbers of cases may become behaviourally significant in larger numbers, leading to companies and activities being heavily regulated or even outlawed and some consequently failing immediately or suffering unacceptable and unsustainable reputational damage, which leads to a longer but still inevitable decline.

The legal view of corporate failure

Aspects of law critical to corporate governance have already been reviewed in Chapter 5. Recent developments in policy have brought about changes in the legal attitude to ascribing culpability to companies as legal beings – rather than trying to find legally conclusive fault with directors as 'controlling minds' – as a consequence of their status as legal entities. The point was made in Chapter 5 that the consequences of changes in the approach to this problem, of the enforcement of the law, is one that requires cultural change – adaptations in the structural governance of companies.

However, from the point of view of solvency and insolvency, the law still maintains an un-reconstructed attitude. The operative statute in the UK is the Insolvency Act of 1986, which was partly brought into being as a result of the problems that were encountered in sorting out the Secondary Banking Crisis of 1972–5.[6] This piece of legislation firmly pins responsibility on the directors of a company for the financial failure of the organisation. The law holds that it is usually the directors who are at fault and if the failure is sufficiently clear-cut as to cause (that is not involving some catastrophic and unforeseeable event), then it is the directors who will be held liable. If the failure went beyond the bounds of normal commercial chance then they can be banned from holding directorships, fined or even jailed. It is probably the prospect of some actual consequential loss for their actions that has made directors more concerned about the issues of insolvency than – until now – about issues of bribery and corruption and corporate manslaughter.

The 1986 Act states very simply that an inability to pay debts as they fall due renders a company insolvent. However, there are a number of practical riders that have to be added to this blunt statement to make sense of the concept – all of which have some bearing on governance. The first rider is that, at some time or another, most companies – certainly most small ones – find themselves in danger of not being able

[6] M. Reid, *The Secondary Banking Crisis.*

to make payments as they fall due. This happens even to the largest companies as well as to the SME struggling along on small contracts and intermittent payments from debtors.

As an instance of this, at the time of the disaster in the Macondo oilfield in 2010, BP was within hours of not being able to make salary payments and meet debt obligations because of the extreme reluctance of banks to lend to the wounded company while they were still paralysed operationally by the effects of the financial crisis.[7] Most companies operate, to some extent, in normal circumstances, on over-draft payments to meet day-to-day obligations and if these are restricted or removed then the company – which may well be perfectly viable in the absence of such restrictions – becomes embarrassed as to the availability of ready cash.

No reasonable person could have said that BP was an unviable borrower, even suffering the sort of reputational damage that it was going through at the time. No shareholder of BP would have realistically expected the directors of BP to call in the administrators. Equally, no shareholder of any other company which can overcome the temporary problems of finding cash within a reasonable period would suggest that it be liquidated if it is otherwise healthy and with plentiful assets, even though under the strictest interpretation of the law they may be trading while unable to meet their debts as they fall due – that is, trading insolvently under a strict interpretation. The problem that this gives rise to for shareholders – and directors particularly – is to determine what is the duration of 'a reasonable period' to continue to press on trading when there is no *absolute* certainty of recovery and to identify when that reasonable period stops.

Those who have never been in this position may give answers to that problem which are very different to those who have experienced such pressures – since placing a company into some form of administration may involve very much more than a loss of mere monetary assets. It may impact on jobs, pensions, community well-being, the retention of intellectual property and future reputations. Stakeholders will be affected by such actions as well as shareholders and the stakeholders' interests – although perhaps less immediately quantifiable – may be of greater weight than those of the shareholders.

This problem is further complicated by the law recognising that there are different types of insolvency. At least three types can be identified – first, that brought about by timing differences between receipts and payments. This is another variant of the inability, on a very short-term basis, to meet debts as they fall due, as described above: a simple cash shortage may even happen to companies with large amounts of cash in their balance sheets – which just happen to be locked up in (temporarily) illiquid accounts.

The second type of insolvency is balance sheet insolvency, where the company's balance sheet liabilities exceed its balance sheet assets. This is a more serious form of

---

[7] Darling, *Brink.*

problem, and for listed companies the threat posed by its potential existence may trigger a number of actions that directors are required to take. The necessity for implementing such actions is very unusual (although the example of the electronic games retailer Game going into administration in 2012, is perhaps an example of this). The law again has a phrase which covers this situation: 'an insufficiency of assets to meet liabilities' signifying a more extended time-scale than that of a simple cash embarrassment.

As far as listed companies are concerned, as has already been touched upon, the law has special provisions. The Companies Act 2006 requires directors of listed companies which record a precipitate decline in the value of their assets (fixed assets, stock, debtors, cash balances – in other words working capital and plant) to below half the value of the issued equity of the company, to call a shareholders' meeting and apprise shareholders of the event and either propose a plan for recovery which the shareholders must agree to or allow shareholders to liquidate it voluntarily if there are sufficient assets to do so – or as a third option allowing creditors to wind it up and let them take their chances of having their debts covered by the liquidation of assets.

This is supposed to protect the interests of shareholders – and particularly the creditors of the company – who may be able to recover some value out of a company that is holed below the waterline before it sinks completely. For all types of liquidation the law provides safeguards to ensure that meetings are held with appropriate notice and at appropriate times in appropriate locations, and that the conduct of those involved in the affair is appropriately transparent – so that creditors are not cheated by crooked directors, shareholders or liquidators. These are mechanical issues which have been well provided for, in terms of governance, for many years.

The final, third, type of insolvency is one which a listed company should never get into – that of 'ultimate insolvency', where there are insufficient realisable assets to pay creditors. The checks and balances which are supposed to exist as a consequence of listing should prevent such events taking place – but have failed on at least one recent occasion.

Farepak

Farepak's origins go back to 1935 when it was started as a Christmas savings club in Fareham in Hampshire. By 2006 the company was a subsidiary of a larger group – European Home Retail plc – which went into administration after Farepak was unable to repay loans as they fell due to its bank, HBOS. The collapse of Farepak triggered the collapse of EHR plc; Farepak had 'lent' or been obliged to lend the money which it had collected from savers to its parent company, which was itself then unable to cover or repay the loans.

The liquidators appointed to oversee the distribution of the company's assets investigated the circumstances of the payment to the parent company and recommended disqualification of the directors who had formed the board of EHR plc – one of whom, Sir Clive Thompson, was the ex-chairman of Rentokil. The legal case against the directors hinged on whether the funds for savers should have been regarded as being held in trust or whether they were available for the use of the company and its parent in the discharge of normal business obligations. Savers received back only 15p for every pound they had saved with the company. The liquidators recommended that all directors be barred from holding directorships in the future.

The state of insolvency has two subordinate issues that arise for considerations of governance – one which is consequential to trading while unable to meet debts as they fall due, and one which is not consequential: both are concerned with the issue of intention.

The law recognises that the problems encountered in running businesses may be occasionally overwhelming and arise through no desire to commit mischief but through force of circumstance or occasional bad luck. Consequently there is a distinction between the legal gravity accorded to dipping into a situation of temporary cash imbalance (which most companies recover from) and the more serious issues of either trading wrongfully (continuing to trade under a *sustained* inability to meet debts as they fall due or with no hope of the situation changing), or trading fraudulently. Wrongful trading is defined as when the directors 'knew, or ought to have concluded that there was no reasonable prospect of avoiding insolvent liquidation'[8] thereby including the concept of a sustained inability to meet debts as they fall due; and when they did not take 'every step with a view to minimising the potential loss to the company's creditors'.[9] Fraudulent trading is carrying on a business with the intent to defraud creditors.

The burden of proof for wrongful trading is less – and the offence is consequently regarded as being less serious. Insolvency at the time of trading is normally a requirement to establish wrongful trading, but not for fraudulent trading.

Where the law is less able to effect some sort of result is in circumstances where the damage is not yet completely done but where there are incipient problems. The law can cope with problems stemming from contract failings – even potential ones like the rupture of the contract between the parties who make up a company, brought about by the effective demise of the company. This is because the law is concerned, in terms of aspects of corporate governance, mostly with issues of procedural governance.

---

[8] See Insolvency Act 1986, s. 214.   [9] *Ibid.*

Areas outside the procedural, when governance becomes mostly behavioural in nature, are where codes of governance are supposed to have their greatest operational impact through the sanctions afforded by hypotheses about informed shareholder choice and the cost of capital. The law is not always directly operative in these areas – comply or explain has no overt support in the Companies Act 2006 except through underpinning the contracts which listed companies strike with Stock Exchanges as part of the procedure of listing. These allow certain rules to be enforced under the threat of suspension from listing but since the 1980s, with the increasing availability of exchange platforms this threat is itself diminishing.

As long ago as 1956 the New York Stock Exchange was forced, for instance, to accept the introduction of two classes of shares from Ford when the Ford family wanted to provide themselves with the entrenching power provided by a class of shares held only by them.[10] Similarly some years later when General Motors and Dow Jones wanted to protect themselves from unwelcome bids they capitulated again and allowed an issue of non-voting shares although this was in clear violation of the Exchange's rules. In the face of the loss of prestige and income which the loss of the listing of such companies would have produced for the NYSE it backed down (both Dow and GM were able to threaten to leave since they could still have their shares traded at that time on the NASDAQ and the American Stock Exchange) and allowed the different classes of shares to be listed. The law is therefore of diminishing force at it moves away from issues of procedure and into issues of behaviour. Beyond the limits of procedural and behavioural governance lies the structural dimension of governance, where law is not directly operative.

Structural governance exists at this boundary line. It is at this point that the legal sanction of the contract between listed companies and exchanges is diminishing in effectiveness and the softer persuasive power of moral codes of behaviour and ethical frameworks is the operative restraint.

Ethics and governance

The law will probably catch wrong-doing in the form of procedural infractions and almost certainly will be enforced (if not entirely successfully) against breaches of the criminal law, provided of course that they are discovered – and, more significantly, reported. This applies in instances of revealed bribery and occasions where individuals die as the consequence of some act or omission of a company. These matters are conspicuous.

But it is issues of 'counter-governance' which may be less conspicuous than these which often provide the most damaging consequences. These are usually matters which are less obvious because they are concerned with issues of behaviour not caught by the

---

[10] Monks, *Corpocracy*.

governance codes. These are usually tacitly condoned by the theory of shareholder supremacy and its ramifications, supported by the indiscriminate application of the market theory on which it rests and concealed by a management in whose temporary interest the perversion of company culture works. They are usually concerned with issues of the pursuit of (supposed) shareholder value and the external costs of operating the company – external in the sense they are passed on to other parties not included in the immediate contract that brings the company into being or sustains it.

Economic theory – with its highly constrained conditions necessary to support its formalised predictive arguments – suggests that firms maximise their income under all conditions, irrespective of other considerations. If they do not they will fail to prosper. The doctrine of shareholder value has adopted this stance for its own – with the share price standing in as proxy for shareholder wealth. The progress of share prices is taken as a measure of increasing wealth for shareholders of growth companies – and which company does not want to be seen as a growth company? – with those that have to admit they are in mature markets, substituting what they lack in the ability to increase earnings per share (and therefore the rate of growth of their share prices) with progressive dividend policies.

No company report will ever admit to the company being limited to a mature market and with consequent limited prospects for growth in earnings into the medium and long term. The traditionalist/conventional theory appears to cleave to a view that to do so would court a rush of flighty shareholders to the exit: shareholders must be promised continually increasing wealth, under the doctrine that links wealth with rising share prices. As a consequence of this view, listed companies have to keep on moving into markets with superior prospects for growth, like sharks that must perpetually move or sink to the bottom of the sea and asphyxiate.

This is plainly not merely illogical but absurd: in any developed economy some companies, once they have exhausted the possibilities for expansion, must contemplate a mature marketplace for their products or services which will result in a reduction in the rate of growth of earnings per share. To repeat the advice given by Kenneth Boulding '[a]nyone who believes exponential growth can go on forever in a finite world is either a madman or an economist'.

But since the managements of companies are judged on their ability to maintain the super-normal rate of earnings growth expected (if they are to retain their jobs) they must do one of three things. They must either constantly seek new sources of earnings which provide such growth (but which may not result in socially-rational allocations of resources in the long term) – or if they are unable to do this then they pick strategies which appear to produce rapid returns at the expense of longer-term growth; or, in extreme cases, they resort to cheating.

Chapter 14 dealt with the issues of reward and how the attention of managers to developing company strategies that are sustainable may be diverted by a fixation on the short term, whereby stakeholders' interests may be disregarded. The intellectual and productive capital of the company may be neglected if the returns lie outside the boundary within which the market views companies' prospects (if managers' rewards are linked to rising share prices); to secure such results, financial information may be distorted.

Most cultural frameworks within which people normally operate have at their root some form of formulation of the ethical precept 'do as you would be done by'.[11] The idea of shareholder primacy, in its crudest form, appears to distort this formula to one of 'do what you can get away with'. The consequences of this re-formulation are a hollowing out of the structural elements of corporate governance. Unless it is all bound together by structural cement (which is mostly composed of an ethical content) corporate governance becomes reduced to meaningless box-ticking at one level supported by mechanistic behavioural responses at the other.

As long ago as 1968 a paper was published in the *Harvard Business Review* by Albert Z. Carr entitled 'Is Business Bluffing Ethical?'.[12] Carr likened business to a game of poker in which any stratagem short of outright cheating was a legitimate way to win the game. In his article Carr suggested that successful managers lived their lives by two sets of ethical standards – one of which operated in private life and one of which operated in the arena of business. Like poker, business had set formal rules. They could be used and interpreted in different ways to play tricks on the opposition which would never be accepted in ordinary life (where of course there are no such formalised rules). The article prompted a great deal of debate which continues to date as a trawl through the internet will indicate.

Bluff and knowing misrepresentation

Thirty-five years after the Carr article in the *Harvard Business Review*, Harvard Business School introduced a course into their prestigious MBA course entitled Leadership and Corporate Accountability (LCA). According to the account written by an English graduate of the Harvard MBA course, the journalist Philip Delves Broughton: 'the key framework for LCA divided the responsibilities for corporate leaders into three categories: economic, legal and ethical. We had to meet criteria in all three categories if we were to satisfy short- and long-term

---

[11] This formula certainly appears in Christianity, Islam, Hinduism, Buddhism, Sikhism in some way.
[12] A. Carr, 'Is business bluffing ethical?', *Harvard Business Review*, Jan–Feb 1968.

financial responsibilities without breaking the law or hating ourselves'. The Harvard course – despite all the continuing controversy – perpetuates and nurtures the concept of there being different sets of rules between 'ordinary' life and business life. Carr's debate was perpetuated in the classroom of the LCA course with students adopting different stances over the ethical appropriateness of bluffing and different ethical codes for business from standard behaviour.

This was carried over into classes dealing with negotiation where the appropriate stance as taught by a senior ex-venture capitalist, according to Broughton, was to mislead the negotiating partner while remaining within the bounds of ethical behaviour: 'Bluffing was fine. Knowingly misrepresenting facts was not.'

But the students may have been ahead of the formal teaching in their pre-course behaviour. Delves Broughton also remarked to a fellow student that he was astonished by the range of new and expensive imported cars in the student car park at Harvard. The reason, he was told, was the financing system at Harvard. Students, once accepted by Harvard, were eligible for financial aid if they had no savings or property. So the standard thing to do was to eliminate any cash balance that students might have had, in order to present empty bank accounts which then signified eligibility for aid. Hence the ranks of expensive cars lining the student car park, all paid for courtesy of the Harvard funding scheme, by clearing out whatever savings the students may have had before they filled in the application form for aid. Presumably this would be a bluff and not a knowing misrepresentation, in Harvard's terms.

For corporate governance to be effective, where the law ends and regulatory reach begins to tail off in its persuasive power, self-standing ethical and moral principles have to take over. The structural component of governance is almost entirely dependent upon the application of such moral principle and the other components of government are almost completely dependent upon healthy structural governance for their effectiveness: without the structural component to provide the glue for linking procedural and behavioural governance they become exercises in sterile, mechanical process without substance.

This then gives rise to a form of corporate hypocrisy where the company does one thing while professing to do another. The worst excesses of this type of behaviour often occur in the outward-facing aspect of governance, where companies use activities that pander to mistaken beliefs about stakeholder engagement as camouflage for activities which may be flagrantly immoral. Such activities are often mistakenly accorded the title of corporate social responsibility.

The Ford Pinto

In 1971 the Ford Motor Company introduced a new car, known as the Ford Pinto, into the North American market to defend a segment of its home market against smaller foreign imports.

The completely new design was built down to a price and weight limit – $2,000 and 2,000 pounds – stipulated by the then chief executive of Ford, Lee Iacocca. Unfortunately in achieving these limits the car also carried serious design flaws: when in a collision from the rear, the fuel tank was prone to rupture and the passenger compartment buckled, causing a lethal combination. Several grisly deaths resulted from passengers being trapped in burning cars after collisions.

Although the evidence was not completely clear-cut, a court case determined that Ford was aware of these problems but declined to modify the design – which would have involved extensive re-tooling costs, preferring instead to pay compensation to those who made claims as the cheaper option.

The controversy followed revelations in a book by Ralph Nader, *Unsafe at Any Speed*, published in 1965, that American car manufacturers routinely traded-off issues of cost against safety – at a trivial level – to save fractions of a per cent of profit.

News International

In 2010, Rupert and James Murdoch, chairman and chief executive of News International respectively, were called before a Parliamentary Committee in the British House of Commons to explain the involvement of their newspapers in the 'phone hacking scandal'. The allegations of serious invasion of the privacy of celebrities' and politicians' mobile phone calls had been rumbling around for several years but began to assume significant proportions after the revelations of the News of the World newspaper's involvement in tampering with evidence during the course of a murder investigation. The severity of the affair led to the arrest of several very senior members of the staff of News International on suspicion of the perversion of the course of justice. The activities of 'rogue' members of staff were condemned by News Corporation, the holding company through which the Murdochs' business empire was managed

In the Spring of 2012, another (former) subsidiary of News Corporation – NDS, a pay-TV business – was indicated, by the release of over 14,000 e-mail records in an Australian newspaper, as having participated in attempts to de-stabilise competitor businesses by hacking into their security encryption systems. News Corporation strongly denied the implications drawn by commentators on the content of the e-mails. The activities were not illegal under Australian law at the time (they were alleged to have taken place in 1999) but were supportive of claims made in the UK that similar activities had contributed to the difficulties which later bankrupted OnDigital, a competitor of BSkyB, the digital broadcasting company in which News Corporation owned a significant, but minority, stake and of which James Murdoch had been chief executive and then became chairman.

Ecuador – Chevron

In 2011 a court in Ecuador fined Chevron $8.6 billion for environmental damage caused during the company's operations in the Amazon delta between 1972 and 1992. Chevron did not deny that substantial pollution had occurred, nor that it had occurred while it operated in the areas[13] but claimed that agreements with the Ecuadorian Government absolved it from responsibility and called the court case and fines the products of a corrupt legal system. Chevron's spokesmen said the court's ruling formed part of a vast 'extortion scheme'[14] and claimed that the fine, imposed by a judge in the town of Lago Agrio, was 'unenforceable in any court that observes the rule of law'. Since Chevron had no assets remaining in Ecuador it refused to pay the fine, which was later increased to $18 billion for lack of an apology as required in the original ruling and therefore a contempt of court.

The duality of standards often applied in respect of business activities is an indication of a fundamental breakdown in the fabric of structural governance. Being good where you choose to be good and being bad where you think it does not matter, or where you think you can get away with it, is not an indication of a consistent approach to the objectives of good governance – more of a dual personality, which might be likened to the bi-polar condition sometimes found in humans and which is normally reckoned to be a personality disorder in its more exaggerated forms.

It indicates instead that the procedural and behavioural elements of governance are floating free of any link with each other and therefore that on any basis other than a purely time- and perspective-limited approach the company is not serving its shareholders well. This is reinforced by the evidence that in the cases cited in the text-box above such behaviour led eventually to open brigandage in the pursuit of profit and exploitation of the customer base. Bribery and theft of the property of others were routinely employed as standard tactics of business.

---

[13] *Crude*, a documentary made by J. Berlinger (Dogwoof, 2009).
[14] G. Adams, 'Chevron's dirty fight in Ecuador', *Independent*, 16 February 2011.

This is not to suggest that, despite its creaky integrity in explaining how corporate governance should work, the traditionalist theory of governance condones or supports or even suggests that such behaviour can be a legitimate instrument in the pursuit of increasing shareholder wealth. But it fails to actively prescribe such activity and therefore fails in the sense that it is silent on the issue.

Yet, except on the most limited of perspectives – and since it is impossible to tell where the 'most limited' shades into the medium and then the medium-term shades into the long-term with any consistency or objectivity – such activities are not simply ethically wrong (bad enough in itself) but also extremely short-sighted from the shareholders' point of view. In the case of the News Corporation scandal, for instance, the value of Rupert Murdoch's stake in BSkyB fell by nearly £1 billion after the extent of the hacking at the News of the World was revealed, and had fallen by nearly a fifth since the revelations in the summer of 2011 of tampering with murder enquiry evidence, wiping £2.3 billion off the company's value.[15]

Unfortunately, since the theory is creaky and limited it can be easily perverted to produce consequences that are corrupt. Non-compliance with issues of procedure (even when they are supposedly protected by law) that do not directly affect shareholder ownership rights can effectively become the norm in operating terms – as it appears to have become in the case of the News of the World. When behavioural counter-governance is established from the top of the company or allowed to flourish tacitly, it dictates a style of action in pursuit of profit in subordinate operational layers. Such actions may even be taken in the knowledge that they are in contravention of law. Corrupt activity – the ultimate expression of counter-governance and the antithesis of structural governance – is then camouflaged by the mere appearance of conformity.

The directors of the company may not be directly involved in the execution of events that are dictated by such behaviour but they will have passed down the cultural signals which suggest that the most important thing is to secure revenue and that that revenue should be at the best margin possible regardless of the outcome on others – all supposedly in pursuit of increasing shareholder wealth but often with that objective being contaminated with the furtherance of their interests.

It is this signalling behaviour which allows the development of 'toxic' financial products to be developed organisationally and then to be marketed and sold even though they are known to be against the absolute interests of the customer as was the case with Goldman Sachs and some of the CDOs it constructed; or for products to be used when they are not fit for purpose in safety-critical processes (as with the drilling mud in the BP Macondo rig disaster); or for customers to be misled that

---

[15] A. Oxlade, 'How the News Corp crisis might affect Rupert Murdoch's Wealth', *Thisismoney.co.uk*.

they need products which have no possibility of being effectively utilised (as was the case with payment protection insurance on loans offered by banks in the UK).

Summary and conclusion

In the purely legalistic sense, companies fail because they can no longer meet their obligations as they fall due. In the accounting sense this is because they run out of cash: everyone who has ever been connected with a business will be aware that it can make losses and still survive for a lot longer than it can continue to lose cash and still survive.

At the root of most large company failures – other than those innocent ones caused by some form of catastrophic change in market circumstances – is some form of breakdown of governance. Small companies fail because of the shallowness of their resources, but large companies are rarely brought low by sudden changes in market conditions since they have the resources which can be used to give them breathing space to redeploy their assets in a different way.

Large company failures are usually the consequence of some decay in the basic structural glue that holds together the more easily identifiable dimensions of procedural and behavioural governance. This glue is effectively the culture of the company which acts not only to bind the other dimensions together but also acts as the hooking-on point for the systemic governance of the environment in which the company is positioned.

As a consequence of this the interplay between the various types of governance becomes apparent. Persistent adverse changes in one will eventually lead to decay in the other two and the diffusion of values brought about by a properly-working systemic governance – a regulatory structure that works properly – reinforces the structural governance of every company it influences; this is effectively a re-statement of 'the rising tide lifting all boats' argument.

What is also apparent from this restatement is the role played by ethics in reinforcing the structural dimension. The conventional theory of governance is silent on the methods by which increases in shareholder value should be achieved, leading to an acceptance of the dual-ethics argument: business can be played by rules (which can be interpreted differently); life has no such overall set of formalised rules and requires a different ethical approach.

Where these two ethical approaches happen to coincide there is no problem for governance; where they diverge, governance is usually the loser, since the certainty of those determined to pursue the goal of shareholder value – sometimes graced by the misnomer of 'ambition' but often tainted with the rawer characteristic of greed, since their fortunes are mistakenly linked to that of increased shareholder value – is usually more powerful than those who wish to consider the claims of other stakeholders.

Counter-governance (2): abuse of stakeholders

This chapter examines particular instances of counter-governance and examines a variety of methods by which managers try to push the drag of costs that inhibit the pursuit of shareholder wealth on to other stakeholders:

- market abuse: cartels;
- market abuse: concealment of information;
- other forms of abuse: environmental crime;
- other forms of abuse: pension funds.

Introduction

The previous chapter concentrated on issues of the decay of three main types of corporate governance which brought about damage to the company because of the lack of support produced by integration of the concepts of governance. It also looked at the dual ethics argument which suggests that the culture of successful companies discards the more restrictive behaviour of transparent fair dealing in return for the advantages conferred by behaviour dictated by the pursuit of shareholder value. This chapter considers some examples of how this behaviour can lead to illegality on the part of companies and their managers and the part played by conventional governance theories in providing no barrier to this since their governance prescriptions are based on the perfect market theories of classical economics. This results in the abuse of the conceptual underpinnings of good governance – often more commonly known by the less technical title of greed. However, it would be incorrect to label all such activity in this way, as will be shown the use of the techniques employed in some instances is a response to the chaotic conditions brought about by the theoretical underpinnings of the concept of the perfect market on which the traditionalist theories of corporate governance rest. Managers are often compelled to pursue such strategies not because they are evil but because the market – shareholders – apparently require it.

Other forms of governance abuse: cartels

Adam Smith was very much aware of the tendency of merchants to consider how best to act against their customers to their own advantage. There is a famous passage from Book I, Chapter 10 of *The Wealth of Nations*:

> People of the same trade seldom meet together, even for merriment and diversion, but the conversation ends in a conspiracy against the public, or in some contrivance to raise prices.

The most egregious form of the 'contrivance to raise prices' is probably the cartel – a form of covert arrangement between firms which collude to fix prices, or output or levels of quality of what they produce. The effect of the cartel is to leave the eventual customer with little real choice and even less leverage against the producers. Cartels are largely prohibited by regulators who see them as injurious to the interest of free markets – with all the benefits that are normally accorded them. However, the cartel is a natural development of the pursuit of shareholder wealth and may be temporarily condoned by regulators under certain limited circumstances (see the 'Parliamentary view' outlined in the text box). The imaginary perfect market requires complete and perfect knowledge for all its participants in order to work properly – this is plainly an unachievable condition. In the absence of this condition holding, though, the producer faces operating conditions of great uncertainty which make it very difficult to plan: producers want to be price-setters not price takers. As far as the individual producer in a free market is concerned the free market inevitably tends to entropy unless organised in some way. External regulation of the market to ensure consistent continuation of supply is the answer of the State; internal regulation by cartel is the answer from the other side of the transaction.

Cartels

Typically, cartel members may agree on:
- prices;
- output levels;
- discounts;
- credit terms;
- which customers they will supply;
- which areas they will supply;
- who should win a contract (bid rigging).

Each of the above types of agreement is prohibited by the Competition Act and Article 101 of the EC Treaty. In addition, s. 188 of the Enterprise Act 2002 makes it a criminal offence for individuals to dishonestly take part in certain specified cartels, essentially those that involve price fixing, market sharing, limitation of production or supply or bid rigging.

Cartels can occur in almost any industry and can involve goods or services at the manufacturing, distribution or retail level.

Some sectors are more susceptible to cartels than others because of the structure or the way in which they operate. For example, where:

- there are few competitors;
- the products have similar characteristics, leaving little scope for competition on quality or service;
- communication channels between competitors are already established;
- the industry is suffering from excess capacity or there is general recession.

Only two attempts were made by the Office of Fair Trading in the eight years after the Enterprise Act 2002 provisions took effect to prosecute cartels. One of these – against four executives from British Airways – failed when it was contested; the prosecution failed to reveal documents to the defence on which the case rested thus nullifying the likelihood of a fair trial.[1] The other – an action against English executives of Dunlop Oil & Marine, a subsidiary of the listed German company Continental AG – prosecuted in 2008 was successful and resulted in prison terms for three executives who were repatriated to the UK to serve their sentences after being caught in a joint UK-American operation.

The Dunlop case

In June 2008 three English employees of Dunlop Oil and Marine Limited, based in Grimsby, were convicted for their parts in organising and running a cartel for the supply of marine hose which may have inflated prices for the product by about £15 million annually. The cartel had been running allegedly since the 1970s and required a co-ordinator to help arrange the details of the supply of marine hosing – used to transport oil from tankers to shore.

The convictions were the first successful actions brought under the Enterprise Act 2003, and were a joint operation between the Office of Fair Trading and the FBI in America, where the men were apprehended. The men had been arrested in

---

[1] M. Peel and J. Croft, 'British Airways price-fixing trial collapses', *Financial Times*, 10 May 2010.

Houston with simultaneous raids on the company's offices and the home of one of them, to seize evidence.

Two of the men were each jailed for three years and the third received a jail sentence of two and a half years.

The corporate governance principles of Continental AG (parent of Dunlop Oil and Marine)

The purpose of these Corporate Governance Principles (the Principles) of Continental AG (the Company) is to further a responsible management of the Company and the Continental Corporation (the 'Corporation') focused on value creation.

On the basis of applicable law, the German Corporate Governance Code (the 'Code') and our Basics, the Principles are intended to make the governance by the Executive Board and the Supervisory Board transparent and understandable and to promote the confidence of investors, customers, employees and the general public in the management and control of the Company as a publicly listed German stock corporation. The Supervisory Board, the Executive Board and all employees of the Corporation understand the Principles as their obligation.

Source: Continental AG website, http://report.conti-online.com/pages/for-our-shareholders/corporate-governance/cg-principles/cg-principles_en.html

The failure of the prosecution of the British Airways case of 2010, which involved fuel surcharge pricing, was not repeated when the European Union took British Airways to court – together with ten other airlines – in respect of cargo price fixing. The defending companies were fined a total of €799.4 million following a three-year probe of the cartel.[2] They then went on to face similar charges in respect of similar activities in New Zealand which were settled in 2011. The case there went back to December 2008 when the commission started proceedings against thirteen international airlines, alleging that they colluded to raise the price of freight cargo by imposing fuel surcharges on shipments into and out of New Zealand over more than seven years. The British Airways website for 2007–8 contained a copy of the corporate governance statement for the company which stated that 'the company is committed to high standards of corporate governance. The Board is accountable to the company's shareholders for good corporate governance'.

---

[2] N. Tait and P. Clark, 'Global airlines hit with $1bn cartel fines', *Financial Times*, 9 November 2010.

The Parliamentary view of cartels

'A cartel involves companies getting together to raise prices and restrict services. In addition to the highly proscribed cartels that the Government are going to act against, others are operating under their noses. I wonder whether the Government or the competition authorities have thought of looking at the Association of Train Operating Companies, which meets next week to take a collective decision to increase the price of the network card by £10, thereby devaluing it for anybody who lives within 35 miles of London. A group of business men is acting together to raise prices collectively and restrict a service – a cartel by any definition. However, it is operating under the Government's nose; indeed, I believe that the Government talk to it.

Another example – in many ways, it is more topical and important – is the banking system. As I have repeatedly pointed out in debates with the Secretary of State and the Chancellor, and as the Cruickshank* report showed, in effect, the banking system operates as a cartel. However, I doubt whether anybody expects Mr. Barrett** to go behind bars. The banking system is accepted as a legitimate structure, but the Government need to be more careful about distinguishing between small cartels – gentlemen in dirty macs in the back room of a pub who are subject to criminal sanctions – and legitimate cartels that operate in the heart of the business establishment and are totally free not only from criminal sanctions but from effective regulation. That gap in credibility needs to be bridged.'

*The Cruikshank Report was prepared by Sir Donald Cruikshank at the request of the Government and reported in March 2000. Its main conclusions were:

- Banks were benefiting from high profits by overcharging up to £3–5 billion a year for banking services to the detriment of their personal and small business customers.
- The current policy framework for banks and other financial services firms has allowed a lower level of competition scrutiny in comparison with other industries: banks are represented on the board of the industry's regulator, the Financial Services Authority.
- The banks effectively control the money transmission systems (these consist of the ATMs and credit and debit card payment networks, cheques and direct debits, standing orders and high value payments), resulting in limited competition within the marketplace and high charges for retailers and customers.
- Minimal information is provided to personal customers and small to medium sized business customers (SMEs) about banking services and banks' accountability.

- The big banks dominate the market for banking for SMEs.
** Matthew Barrett was the chairman of Barclays bank between 2004 and 2006. He famously told a Commons Treasury Select Committee 'I don't borrow on credit cards because it is too expensive' when giving evidence about the profits banks achieved on their credit card operations.

Source: V. Cable, House of Commons Debates, *Hansard*, 10 April 2002, col. 63–68

The OFT's Annual Report for 2010–11 identified three criminal investigations in the public domain which were being considered. These were investigations into suspected cartel activity in relation to input products in the automotive industry, into the supply of products for use in the agricultural sector and into commercial vehicle manufacturers. These investigations were all launched in 2010 but did not lead to any criminal charges against the executives concerned.

Cigarette and tobacco cartels

In an appeal court case in March 2012, the Office of Fair Trading suffered a significant blow to its strategy and reputation when a fine of £112 million was quashed following a seven-year investigation into alleged anticompetitive practices.

The fine was part of a record £225 million penalty levied against ten companies in April 2011 for anti-competitive promotional practices which were alleged to have taken place from 2001 to 2003 between retailers and the cigarette makers Imperial and Gallaher, which together have about 90 per cent of the UK tobacco market. The OFT claimed Imperial and Gallaher had a number of bilateral arrangements with retailers – if one manufacturer changed the price of a product, the supermarket would follow suit with a competing brand.

The fine was quashed as the Appeals tribunal found that there was 'no sworn evidence' from any witnesses that the retailers and tobacco companies entered into such an agreement.

On the day of the announcement of the successful appeal shares in Imperial closed up 12p at £23.63.

Cartels are held to be against the public interest in that they distort the efficient allocation of resources. The companies involved in cartels seek to reduce uncertainty for themselves – on the most benign view of what cartels do – but they can also use the arrangements provide by cartels to secure higher returns than would otherwise be possible in conditions of greater competitiveness. This is particularly the case where they are dealing with the public sector – where there are numerous instances of both national and international market distortion, brought about by a desire to maximise returns for shareholders at the expense of other stakeholders.

Building industry cartels – and one legal view

In September 2009, 103 building firms were found to have colluded to fix prices for public sector projects over many years. The number of firms involved allegedly accounted for 6% of the UK's construction industry. The cartel included Balfour Beatty, Kier and Galliford Try – all of which were listed companies – as well as many other smaller firms. The largest fine was levied on Kier which was ordered to pay £18m.

The investigation began after the OFT received complaints about the building of the Queens Medical Centre in Nottingham and spread throughout the East Midlands, Yorkshire and Humberside taking in thousands of projects.

A lawyer from a large firm of City solicitors, who had been involved in the defence against the charges wrote:

'If many businesses are "tipped over the edge" as a result of the fines, this will lead to reduced competition as opposed to increased competition – an outcome the OFT will surely not be looking for.

The rules are clearly there to be obeyed – but one can't help wondering whether this case could have been resolved more quickly and with fewer potential downsides.

Whilst genuine "bid rigging" – where rivals work out in advance who is going to bid aggressively for which contract – is clearly a questionable practice, to categorise the practice of "cover pricing" as "bid rigging" is rather misrepresentative in very many cases.

There is clearly a very big difference between a situation where several bidders know, early on in the tender process, which of them is not seriously bidding for the job and the situation where a bidder approaches a rival, a matter of hours before the bidding deadline, to ask for a cover price because it doesn't want to risk being excluded from the customer's tender list for failing to put in a bid.'

Source: A. Jurkiw, via *Press Association* (September 2009), available at http://news.sky. com/story/726108/builder-bid-rigging-fines-could-backfire

Other forms of governance abuse: concealment of information

Some counter-governance takes the form of concealment of information rather than active attempts to fix prices or conditions. The falsification of reserves by Royal Dutch Shell is a case in point – an action designed to produce an inflated view of the company in the eyes of investors and potential investors and therefore benefit the executives, either directly through financial reward (bonuses and options linked to share prices) or through merely maintaining their jobs.

For many years, until the practice was outlawed by changes in accounting regulations, the British construction equipment company Acrow used to sell large amounts of equipment to associated companies overseas just before the end of its financial year. Since the companies were associates rather than subsidiaries this enabled it to book profit from the sales. This then allowed an unbroken run of nineteen years of profit increase – an unheard of feat in the highly cyclical building industry. The trick lay in the fact that after the end of the financial year and just into the new one it would buy back some of the 'sold' equipment thereby relieving its associates of unwanted stock. Eventually, Acrow as a group was broken up into employee buy-outs since the perpetual ebb and flow of sales was unsustainable.

The Satyam affair

In 2009 Satyam Computer Services, a fast-growing computer services company in India and a major component of the Indian Stock Exchange's strong contemporary performance revealed that the accounting records for the company for the past six years had been falsified. In 2010 its accounts showed 'irregularities' totalling Rs78.5 billion ($1.7 billion) – nearly double the amount previously known. This included a 'diversion' of $41 million from a share issue made in New York in 2001. The accounts to that date had suggested a cash pile of $1 billion. Twenty-five thousand members of staff lost their jobs.

The forensic audit report included twenty-five pages of notes to the accounts and warned that the evidence was not complete since much information had been unobtainable, missing or falsified.

Other forms of abuse: environmental crime

Economists recognise externalities as the costs of completing contracts which fall on persons or things outside the contract, and therefore allow parties to the contract to escape some of the true costs of doing business. In many cases the costs fall on the environment, which, since it isn't a legal person and usually consequently can't afford lawyers or appeal to regulators, means that the perpetuation of the behaviour that caused the costs goes on unrestrained. Several instances of environmental crime have already been cited. The uncertain formulation of obligations under corporate responsibility – outside the limited view of shareholder supremacy – owes its developing prominence over the last few decades and has been boosted largely by increased sensitivity (mostly in the West) to the damage done by industrial processes, often in the developing world and often as a consequence of Western industrial practices.

The Trafigura case

Trafigura is an oil trading company based in Amsterdam which once was associated with the disgraced financier Marc Rich, who was pardoned in 1999 by President Bill Clinton, after being convicted of trading with Iran and on counts of tax evasion.

The company, which is privately owned, was convicted and fined €1 million in 2007 after a seven week trial in the Netherlands for illegally exporting and dumping toxic waste off the coast of West Africa. The company had originally claimed that waste held on board one of its ships was of lower toxicity than it was later shown to be, and then balked at the cost of processing the waste in Rotterdam. The company claimed that it had handed over the waste to a legitimate processing company in Abidjan, which then disposed of it illegally in the sea. Thirty thousand individuals have been held to be affected by the effects of the waste.

The company had already paid compensation of £30 million to those affected and had also paid £100 million to the Cote d'Ivoire Government to help clean up the mess.

The company had applied in the London courts for a super-injunction to prevent any discussion of the existence of the problem and had paid lobbyists and libel lawyers to pursue journalists who investigated the story.

Other forms of abuse: pension funds

Pensions are deferred income for employees – a form of insurance against ill-health, unemployment and reduction of income through retirement – that may constitute part of the contract of employment, if it is part of an employer-sponsored scheme. While final salary schemes – also and more properly known as defined benefit schemes – have fallen out of favour for a number of reasons (both social and economic), the defined contribution scheme has accelerated in popularity (at least among employers) and there are very few companies which do not run any sort of pension scheme – unless they are very small. The policy of governments in the UK for many years has been to encourage private provision for old age and enforced unemployment to relieve the pressure on public provision. Companies which do run pensions funds must treat them as trust property and are obligated to maintain certain conditions of stewardship. In maintaining their stewardship of pension schemes companies thus occupy a very particular position in terms of the set of responsibilities they owe to both past and present employees (and also future employees to some extent); to the company as a company (in respect of the size and sustainable continuity of pension payments competing with other resources); and to shareholders, in respect of the sustainable payments that do not drain too much out of the company's distributable resources and also provide for future growth.

It becomes possible, in consequence, for companies to incur substantial financial obligations in respect of the payment of pensions to a singularly important set of stakeholders – existing and past employees – which may run counter to the short-term interests of shareholders (since deficits on the scheme may have to be made up out of distributable funds). The law recognises this potential conflict and in the UK much of the nature of this set of obligations is reinforced by statute to protect the interests of pensioners.

As a consequence of this, companies may be the subject of a number of pressures caused by the state of their pension funds: these will differ according to whether they have large pension fund surpluses or have incurred large obligations to their funds.

As an indication of how pension fund obligations can affect company fortunes, British Airways is a good case. For many years after it became part of the private sector, British Airways was regarded by many City operators as a pension fund with an airline fortuitously attached to it. The age at which many flight crew retired (for safety reasons) and the legacy of public sector employment terms meant that the generous funding that the company had been given as a dowry when it was denationalised dwarfed its commercial asset values; only the police and fire brigades had equivalent retirement provision. The need to feed the pension pot had been partly responsible for the aggressive action that was taken in privatising the company and this required reducing the company's losses and turning it into profit before privatisation.[3]

Similarly, quoted companies with very large pension surpluses may find themselves pursued for the benefit their assets can confer on predators. This is what happened to Imperial Tobacco when its fat pension fund attracted the attention of the Hanson Trust in 1986. Hanson Trust eventually acquired Imperial in a $4.3 billion hostile takeover.[4]

By rolling up the Imperial fund into Hanson's existing provision, Hanson would have been able to give the combined group a holiday on pension contributions, thereby temporarily enhancing profitability and passing more money over to shareholders. The Imperial management sought to deflect the unwelcome (for them) attentions of the Hanson Trust by putting in place 'poison pill' provisions which denied an acquirer access to the surplus of the pension fund. The unforeseen effect of this was also to

---

[3] T. Bower, *Branson* (London: Harper, 2008), p. 109.
[4] M. Milner, 'German cement group captures Hanson', *The Guardian*, 16 May 2007.

deny access to beneficiaries of the fund, too, resulting in a landmark court decision[5] which identified pension fund beneficiaries as 'non-volunteers' in respect of their pension contributions (when the pension obligation formed part of a contract of employment) and that decisions affecting the future of pension fund members have to be made in good faith. The tenet of this ruling then became central to the character-isation of pension fund obligations for employers.

The fallout from the financial crisis – itself a failure of governance brought about by the unconstrained, supposed pursuit of increasing shareholder wealth – has had a substantial impact on company pension schemes. Many have recorded substantial deficits[6] and the accounting conventions which have to be applied to carry these provide a drag on the share price as far as managers intent on accelerating earnings growth are concerned. This has resulted in several companies attempting to get other sets of stakeholders to bear some of the burden, effectively preferring shareholders' interests over pensioners.

Trinity Mirror pension schemes take a hit

Bank de-leveraging is putting pressure on pension trustees to accept a poorer deal from their struggling sponsors. The unhappy trend is highlighted by Trinity Mirror, the underperforming newspaper publisher that on Thursday announced a 33 per cent slump in operating profits to £92.4m and a new £110m debt facility.

The company needs this credit to help pay off £168m in maturing loan notes. At one point it is understood to have offered lender Royal Bank of Scotland a preferential charge on its assets in the event of financial difficulties. But that would have damaged the covenant of the group's pension schemes, whose net deficit, as calculated by accountants, rose 43 per cent last year to £230m. The schemes have a claim of their own on the same assets.

The compromise was for the trustees to accept a wince-worthy 70 per cent cut in base contributions to £10m annually over the next three years. Trinity, whose market value has shrunk to £95m, may make extra contributions, either because it is performing well, or feeling generous. But the cut still weakens the schemes, albeit in a way more palatable to trustees than the alternative.

It was a striking coincidence that the Pensions Regulator on Thursday warned companies that it would take 'strong action' if it was unhappy with reductions in contributions.

The poor performance of Trinity Mirror is largely blameable on the long-run decline of printed newspapers. Digital substitutes show great promise. Trustees evidently

---

[5] *Imperial Group Pension Trust Ltd* v. *Imperial Tobacco Ltd* [1991] 1 WLR 589.
[6] N. Cohen, 'QE blamed for surge in pensions shortfall', *Financial Times*, 7 March 2012.

believe that chief executive Sly Bailey can lead a lucrative migration into cyberspace. If she does, she will have earned remuneration that – with her own pensions contributions included – stood at about £1.7m a year in 2006, 2007, 2009 and 2010.

Source: J. Guthrie, *Financial Times*, 15 March 2012

Trinity Mirror cuts pension payments

Trinity is the second company in a week to push its pension debt further back in the queue in order to obtain needed refinancing.

Premier Foods is deferring deficit contribution payments into its pension fund until 2014. The cash-strapped maker of Mr Kipling cakes announced the freeze as part of its refinancing package, under which 28 lenders granted it extended loan terms and new covenant terms on its £1.2bn of debt. Premier Foods says it is in dialogue with the pension regulator and that trustees had independent legal advice.

The pensions regulator must review each company's plans to fund scheme deficits and has powers, which it has never used, to force companies to follow a specific repayment schedule when it believes pension debts are subordinated to interests of other creditors.

'We will scrutinise any reduction in contributions or other actions that increase risks to the scheme, and are prepared to take strong action where necessary,' the regulator said.

Trinity made clear that securing an agreement from the trustees to lower its annual pension payments had 'assisted in securing' a new £110m bank facility in order to meet the £168m in payments of US loan notes.

John Ralfe, an independent pensions consultant, said: 'Reducing pension deficit payments from around £100m to just £30m for the next three years, so a US private placement can be re-paid in full, means the pension scheme is being pushed behind these other creditors, who are being repaid first.'

'It is very surprising that Trinity Mirror made the announcement without first agreeing it with the pensions regulator.'

Trustees secured agreement that if Trinity pays a dividend to shareholders a contribution of equal value will be made to its pension scheme.

Source: N. Cohen, S., Davoudi and L. Lucas, *Financial Times*, 15 March 2012

Qinetiq moves to slash pensions deficit

Qinetiq, the privatised defence technology contractor, pledged to slash its pension deficit by nearly 60 per cent through a package of measures agreed by trustees.

The former defence research agency said on Tuesday that changes to the way it measures pension contributions would result in a £109m reduction in its pension deficit to £74.7m.

The company has been struggling to tackle its deficit, which ballooned from £24m in 2008 to £183.7m, amid the market turmoil of the financial crisis.

Qinetiq will also make a one-off payment of £40m in cash to the pension scheme for the year ending March 31, and annual payments of £13m until March 31, 2018.

The news comes on the heels of a ruling from the High Court allowing the scheme to use the Consumer Price Index to measure increases in pension payments instead of the Retail Price Index.

Qinetiq said the changes would not affect its full-year forecast for operating profits of £160m for the year ending March 31, 2012.

The High Court ruled that a switch to CPI indexation could be applied retroactively from January 1, 2010. The company said RPI indexation would be applied for accrued pensions before that date.

David Luxton, national secretary of Prospect, a trade union Qinetiq will derecognise at the end of this month for collective bargaining purposes, said we 'believe the company has taken too short a view doing this in order to halve the deficit'.

Mr Luxton blamed Qinetiq's deficit on the 'unintended consequence of the Bank of England's monetary policy,' which he said would be less problematic over the longer term.

Qinetiq has created a new asset-backed structure, secured with its UK property, which it said would contribute to the £13m in annual payments into the scheme. This structure is expected to yield £2.5m in cash a year for 20 years.

It has also agreed on a 20-year deed, which will see Qinetiq take on the liability for the scheme in the event of insolvency of any part of the business.

Qinetiq's pension scheme consists of 2,300 active members, 3,500 deferred members and 2,400 pensioner members.

Source: A. Stevenson, *Financial Times*, 27 March 2012

In all three of the cases cited above, the deficits resulted from some past actions of the managers of the companies involved – either directly, or indirectly as a consequence of responses to (or failures to respond to) the actions of other companies' managers. Each of the remedial actions proposed will involve stakeholders who *were not* responsible for the actions being forced to take the consequences rather than the managers who *were* responsible or the shareholders on whose behalf the managers were working.

Traditional governance theory would suggest that failing managers might be subject to the 'market for control' and lose their jobs as shareholders rejected their continued employment in the event of such failure. Once again, it appears that the traditional theories do not explain well what actually happens, since none of the managers concerned have been subject to such a market test – and one in particular has received substantial benefits which appear out of kilter with the performance of the company.

Other forms of abuse: the utilisation of trans-national loopholes, tax avoidance and evasion

The distinction between tax avoidance and tax evasion is very straightforward: avoidance is legal while evasion is not. The problem lies – as ever – at the margin where action to avoid becomes so artificial as to constitute unreasonable activity undertaken to evade paying tax.

It might be reasonably contested that everyone – be they a human or a legal entity – has a moral obligation to pay no more tax than they are required to do on the two bases that to pay more merely allows greater scope to the State for intrusion into private affairs; and second, that no one actively enjoys paying part of his income in tax so paying tax reduces the sum of happiness for the individual (legal or human). So avoiding tax is legal but refusing to pay what you owe the State legitimately is not.

Traditional theories of governance have nothing to say about the issue. In common with other matters that they do not specifically address, they presumably imply (silently) that activities undertaken by managers in pursuit of shareholder wealth should conform to the prevailing morality and abide by regulatory and legal constraints on the activities undertaken by the company. The silence, however, allows great latitude to managers intent on pursuing the goal of shareholder wealth at the expense of other moral concerns that might reasonably be considered central to the long-term goal of maintaining and achieving shareholder wealth. Sometimes this latitude involves such corporate contortions that it appears that the schemes are so artificial they are really evasions, thereby destroying any claim that the companies may have to any form of responsible management. More importantly, such contortions can jeopardise shareholders' interests as the company applies complex structures which may be designed solely to prop up the share price (as allegedly is the case in numerous instances regarding the collapse of the Irish banks)[7] or attract opprobrium politically.

---

[7] Carswell, *Anglo Republic*.

Tesco and tax: a complex web of companies, trusts and partnerships

In February *The Guardian* published two articles about Tesco's tax practices. At the heart of the story was Tesco's stated desire to realise up to £5bn by cashing in on the rise in value of its massive UK property portfolio through sale and leaseback schemes – while maintaining control of the stores.

It was one of a series of *Guardian* investigations into the broader question of tax havens, tax avoidance and the problems governments have in collecting revenue in a globalised world, where sophisticated international companies can move their money and assets around.

Five weeks later the supermarket issued a libel writ. Tesco accused the paper of not only getting its facts wrong but having deliberately done so for dishonest and malicious reasons. The company said the allegations went to the heart of its business reputation and amounted to a 'devastating attack' on its integrity and ethics. 'An important and valuable aspect of its reputation, in which its directors, employees and shareholders take pride, is Tesco's commitment to its corporate and social responsibility,' it said ...

It now appears to be common ground between *The Guardian* and the retailer that Tesco has avoided taxes through a complex structure of artificial companies. The difference between the paper's original piece and Tesco concerns the nature of the tax avoided and the amounts which would have been denied the Treasury in the course of the property transactions ...

It is now clear to us that the Tesco schemes, designed over a period of years and in several different ways, were to avoid another tax than the one alleged – Stamp Duty Land Tax (SDLT). This was brought in by the government in 2003 worried about widespread avoidance of stamp duty on property and land deals. It is levied at 4% of the gross value of the property, in contrast to corporation tax, which is at a higher rate (30% until it was reduced to 28% from April 1 2008) on any gain and is payable by the purchaser. It is common practice in avoidance deals for the seller and the purchaser to split any saving between them.

We have now established that:

- On a property disposal programme totalling £5bn, the exchequer could be deprived of in the region of £100m of tax.
- Tesco has been involved in a game of cat and mouse with HM Revenue & Customs since 2003.
- On three occasions when the government has closed a loophole to prevent avoidance, Tesco has taken advantage of ingenious schemes to get around it.

- The firm's devices have centred on complex limited partnership arrangements and unit trust schemes based in Jersey, and have included offshore companies.
- Tesco still has 36 stores wrapped up in UK limited partnerships – with Cayman Islands registered partners – which were established in 2006 before the latest loophole was closed. These – called Tesco Blue, Tesco Fuchsia and Tesco Pink – are set up and ready to be used for large scale property deals, and would be free of the 4% SDLT.

On the day Tesco issued proceedings, a press release to the stock exchange from the company admitted tax 'savings' on two deals already done (for the first time after months of protracted exchanges with *The Guardian*): 'By structuring these transactions in this way Tesco expects to achieve savings of £23m in stamp duty-related taxes on the transactions completed to date. The maximum additional savings in stamp duty-related taxes that might be achieved from using these structures could be another £30m to £40m.'

This analysis makes it plain that the original *Guardian* articles did not correctly explain the effect of Tesco's tax schemes. It was wrong to state that they were designed to avoid corporation tax. It would have been correct to refer to avoiding SDLT.

As a result, the figure of 'up to £1bn' – calculated as the amount which could have been saved on the disposal of £5bn of property – is wrong. The loss to the exchequer is likely to be nearer the region of £90m–£100m ...

It is still not clear how much UK tax was paid since Tesco also said in the writ that these profits were subject to 'statutory relief exemptions'. It is possible that the gains arising from the sale of the 50% interests in the partnerships will qualify for statutory rollover relief (where assets are sold and the proceeds reinvested) and so any tax potentially due on the sales has been deferred (potentially indefinitely). The claiming of this relief is not tax avoidance.

Tax avoidance – as opposed to tax 'planning' or 'mitigation' – is commonly defined as the use of artificial or structured arrangements to frustrate the evident intention of parliament. The government brought in SDLT for UK land and buildings in December 2003 because of widespread avoidance of stamp duty.

In a consultative document, Ruth Kelly, then economic secretary to the Treasury, explained the thinking: 'The government is concerned about growing avoidance of stamp duty by a minority, at the expense of the majority of taxpayers. In particular, some companies are determined not to pay their full share of duty and structure property transactions in increasingly artificial ways to achieve that. This activity represents a significant threat to the tax base. We are determined to stop this abuse.'

But as one loophole closed, another opened. Transactions involving partnerships 'created opportunities for avoidance', said the government, closing that gap in 2004.

At the same time ingenious companies were using another way of getting around SDLT: transferring properties into a unit trust – usually in Jersey – which could take advantage of exemption, avoiding SDLT (as well as 0.5% UK stamp duty that would be payable if it was a UK unit trust). This is the arrangement Tesco came up with.

The exasperation felt inside the revenue was clear from an impact assessment of SDLT avoidance published in July 2005, which said: 'Tax avoidance costs the exchequer lost revenues each year. It also undermines government public spending objectives and brings unfairness into the tax system itself.'

In the budget of March 2006, that particular loophole was shut.

But the battle of wits between the Treasury and large companies continued. They found that by introducing an individual into a partnership along with offshore companies as limited partners they could circumvent the Treasury yet again. This is what Tesco did through one Philip Shirley, a tax consultant. He is named as a partner in at least four of the Tesco colour partnerships.

Again the government caught up, announcing in the pre-budget report of December 2006 measures to counter avoidance using partnerships, sub-sales and leases.

The Tesco schemes in waiting (with the relevant properties in them) were set up in October 2006 before the guillotine came down in December.

The stores could be worth £2.5bn. Because UK tax legislation is rarely retrospective, it seems unlikely SDLT will be triggered.

Source: *The Guardian*, 3 May 2008

In his 2012 Budget the Chancellor described tax avoidance and evasion as 'morally repugnant' and announced that stamp duty would be charged at 15 per cent in future (from midnight on 21 March) on properties over £2 million that are paid into a 'corporate envelope'. This closes the loophole that previously allowed some individuals to avoid stamp duty altogether.

Summary and conclusion

Overt acts of criminality are often undertaken by companies seeking to maximise their profits at the expense of some other set of stakeholders. These acts belong to a set of behaviours which can best be described as 'counter-governance' – actions which go beyond the usage of the set of ethical principles that are implicitly contained in concepts of good governance and are in conflict with the standards by which behaviour is 'normally' assessed. The actions are of course initiated by individual managers or groups of managers in conditions where the companies for which they work may subscribe nominally to 'ideal' sets of corporate governance statements.

The conclusion that is drawn from the existence of such counter-governance is that the goal of achieving maximum returns for shareholders exceeds in value the perceived penalties for behaving in accordance with the precepts of good governance. This is partly because the concepts of good governance in the conventional formulation do not adequately explain the workings of the real world, so the sanctions that are seen as operative are not regarded as meaningful in contrast with the rewards for pursuing increased shareholder wealth. Conventional expressions of governance – studiedly ethically neutral – are silent on the means by which such improvements can be achieved and therefore offer no support for ethically correct behaviour.

CHAPTER 17

Concluding remarks

Policy failure

The contention of this book has been that the failure of conventional, or traditional, expressions of corporate governance to adequately account for the operation of the relationships between companies, shareholders and other stakeholders, has resulted in policy failures.

These policy failures were brought about by a conceptual failure: the original definition of corporate governance – for convenience the 'Cadbury definition' – did not recognise changes in the way that companies were being used and developed as engines of wealth creation. Using the analogy employed in Chapter 1, the geography of the corporate landscape was recognised but the processes – the geology – which lay underneath the formation of that landscape were not accounted for adequately. Since the original definition had little explanatory value, successive committees set up to examine corporate governance have merely added layers of unsuitable recommendations to an unsound foundation – bringing about a practice of corporate governance that bears no relation to the actual practical circumstances of companies, shareholders or stakeholders.

Inadequate and outdated definitions

The conceptual failure arose because the 1992 Cadbury Committee definition of corporate governance was rooted in a view of the British economy which was largely out-dated even as it was formulated. Since this description was the first 'official' definition, was compiled by an authoritative committee, and appeared to be plausible in terms of the recommendations in which it was nested, it became accepted world-wide as the benchmark. In the past twenty years, the basic expression of corporate governance, as developed by the Cadbury Committee, has changed very little in its adoption by subsequent committees of investigation, who have all taken the original formulation as the basis for developing further recommendations. Yet the changes which were in train in the UK economy at the beginning of the 1990s have accelerated further and extended further in the Western economies, while the successive prescriptions of supposed best practice have only congealed around the original, unsatisfactory mechanisms, worsening the problem of the dislocation between the description and the reality of corporate governance.

The accretion of additional, unsatisfactory explanations and consequent recommendations is despite, in particular, the radical changes that have occurred in methods of investing in the fortunes of companies; the diminution of the significance of the individual shareholder; and in the rewards that various parties to the company contract expect to receive as their share of the wealth generated by companies. It is also despite changes in the structure of economic activity worldwide – particularly the growing concentration of financial activity in the Western world and the shift of manufacturing to the East – and the developing complexity of those economic structures.

The Cadbury-based definition of governance for listed companies – with its implicit acceptance of the primacy of the shareholders' interests and its failure to recognise the shift in ownership characteristics or the change in the weight of stakeholder influence – has been distorted to support a spurious concept of 'shareholder value' by linking misidentified 'agent' and misidentified 'principal' into an unthinking dance. This has had the unforeseen consequence of both enriching the supposed agents at the expense of the supposed principals and de-stabilising the economic structures founded on the supposed primacy of the shareholder. With a monocular view of governance as being an arrangement solely between three parties – directors, shareholders and auditors– the Cadbury definition and its subsequent enhancements both in the UK and abroad have failed to identify the correct linkages between both those three components of governance and others (in the form of the developing power of a multiplicity of stakeholders).

In concentrating on the formal definition as a fixed, unchanging distillation of corporate governance, too little attention has been paid generally to the additional comments that Sir Adrian Cadbury included in his remarks a few years after his main report:

> Corporate governance is involved in holding the balance between economic and social goals and between individual and communal goals … the aim is to align as nearly as possible the interests of individuals, corporations and society.[1]

Dimensions of governance

The traditionalist/conventional view has no capacity to describe how governance works inside an organisation. This then leads to a 'blunt instrument' approach which fails to account for the interactive nature of governance and distinctions in its form

---

[1] Cadbury, *Overview*.

between inward and outward facing variants (at the very least). This lack of an ability to distinguish does not permit the conventionalist view to recognise which parts of corporate governance have worked properly and which have failed. This weakness contributed to the cataclysm of the financial crisis, as an apparent adherence to the forms of governance prescribed by a view of the world based on 'Cadbury principles' fell short of ensuring effective governance.

Corporate governance is multi-dimensional in character – it has procedural, behavioural and structural components that operate inside the firm; a systemic component that links firms and the legal/regulatory structure; and operational and temporal/longitudinal components that reinforce all these. Managing these multi-dimensional aspects is the work of the board of directors of the company, assisted by appropriate advisers such as the company secretary – a task that is long-distance in nature and much more complex than simply 'setting the company's strategic aims, providing the leadership to put them into effect, supervising the management of the business and reporting to shareholders on their stewardship'.[2]

Stakeholders' importance – and problems

The problem with stakeholders is that there are so many of them. They consequently have a multiplicity of competing aims. The benefit of focusing corporate governance around the interest of shareholders is that they are a distinct, discrete group with very concentrated aims. Individuals may leave or join the ranks of the shareholding group but the objectives of the shareholders *in total* remain mostly unchanged. The same cannot be said for stakeholders who may have shifting priorities at different times, according to the constitution of their numbers and groupings.

This makes the pursuit of any form of what has come to be called 'corporate social responsibility' by a company a tenuous objective. The concept of corporate citizenship is merely risible, as was demonstrated in Chapter 3 (although if actively pursued it would become deeply disturbing in a political sense; another example of the need to infuse the study of corporate governance with a sense of history).

In many respects, Milton Friedman was absolutely correct when he criticised the diversion of corporate activity by management outside the pursuit of making profits: how are such activities to be determined and by whom? The conventional idea of the principal and agent relationship breaks down in the face of a detailed description of what many companies mistakenly regard as their social obligations. The social obligations of companies are to obey the law and not attempt to avoid – still less to evade – legal responsibilities in matters of tax; environmental behaviour; employee

---

[2] Cadbury, *Report*.

pay, rights and conditions; and the treatment of customers. That is surely a sufficient framework for most companies to behave properly. If a company tries to avoid or evade these obligations then, as Chapters 15 and 16 showed, such behaviour leads to a more significant breakdown of corporate governance in at least one dimension, with adverse consequences for shareholders.

If companies observe their legal obligations and provide for the development of their business in a sustainable fashion – in other words having appropriate and effective regard to minimising the external costs of their business that are borne by other stakeholders – they have gone as far as they need or should go in discharging any form of social obligation. It is the failure of the conventional definition of corporate governance to underline this ethical obligation that has led partly to the confusion over the fuzzy concept of corporate social responsibility.

The force of law

In the UK at least, the development of the attitude of the law to the problem of legal personality has outstripped the development of corporate governance – both in practice and in theory. In the Bribery Act 2010 and the Corporate Manslaughter and Corporate Homicide Act 2007, UK law now accords weight to the structural dimension of governance – the company culture and the cultural glue that pinions a company's procedural and behavioural governance dimensions. In this respect, it might be suggested that the law is moving towards a view of the company that further undermines the traditionalist/conventional concept of the directors as being the agents of the shareholders and correctly identifies the company as being the agent. In the conventional view, the shareholders supposedly appoint the directors to run the company on their behalf as their agent – but they have no direct contract with the directors so no agency relationship can exist between them (in legal terms at least). The contracts of both directors and shareholders are with the legal entity of the company which interposes between the other parties for reasons of efficiency, practicality and simplicity. The company's interest should be the directors' primary obligation – which is what the law says it is: directors owe a fiduciary obligation to the company in every instance and not to any partial consideration of shareholders.

Failure of the codes

The failure to correctly describe the mechanisms of governance and leave the description at the blunt level of 'Corporate governance is the system by which business corporations are directed and controlled. Boards of directors are responsible for the governance of their companies', has resulted in each successive committee investigation into the workings of corporate governance in the UK – the Greenbury Committee; the Hampel Committee; and the Higgs Committee – producing little of any value or worth. The accretions of recommendations merely brought about the death of lots of trees without any commensurate benefit to the practical operation of corporate governance. The result of this was 'light touch regulation' – which in its mildest manifestation was an impotent policy in conception and at worst a positive contributor to poor governance and the consequent crisis of the financial sector, when both regulators and regulated sat back and merely ticked boxes. While the scope for global damage caused by the failure of good governance in non-financial businesses is not so catastrophic, in the long term it is just as pernicious in terms of social and economic disruption. Vast increases in rewards for one class of stakeholders (directors and managers) have been achieved at the expense of other classes (employees in particular) all under the guise of pursuing increases in shareholder value.

The most damaging effect of this has been felt in the financial sector, of course. The prescriptions for improving governance in the UK which were developed as a consequence of the Walker Review of the Financial Sector, have been carried over into the UK Corporate Governance Code to apply to all listed companies. But the introduction of the stewardship provisions are simply misguided attempts to rebuild governance in the old image by bolting-on to the old structure out-dated concepts of shareholder ownership and primacy. Those charged with the exercise of such stewardship do not want it or should not have it (since it limits the freedom of action of institutional investors on behalf of their customers) or cannot exercise it (small shareholders are denied any power by virtue of such mechanisms as the non-binding vote on the remuneration report). A new form of stewardship has to be found with new characteristics if it is to work.

Intermediaries and their failings

In many ways the failure of the intermediaries – the regulators, ratings agencies, the brokers and the financial journalists – to sound the alarm about failures of corporate governance was the most egregious failure of all. The Press comes off least badly in that there were individual instances of journalists and commentators drawing the attention of the regulatory agencies to the problems: in the Madoff case for instance – the world's biggest fund swindle to date – the regulators received numerous warnings which they failed to heed.

The regulators and the ratings agencies proved themselves particularly unequal to the task. The regulators accepted both the precepts of the shareholder primacy argument unquestioningly and the undeveloped conventional view of corporate governance (apparently even encouraging some riskier practices according to some observers[3] to make the City 'more competitive'). Some regulators also made headway against instances of market abuse among firms but were then countered by political action (as in the case of the New York Stock Exchange and the American Savings and Loans scandals[4]). In the UK the FSA did little about market abuse for the first five years of existence and then seemed to wake up only after the event. Reports prepared on the responses of the Treasury and the FSA to the 2007–8 financial crisis indicate unpreparedness, incompetence or laxity.

The ratings agencies chose to play both sides against the middle: they determined to change the way that they charged for their services and then wriggled themselves into a position where end-users were compelled (under American regulations) to take formal notice of their ratings. They discarded the objectivity that was useful and valuable, in favour of increasing shareholder wealth themselves, thereby compromising their standing and reducing themselves to the status of 'valve doorkeepers' – closing stable doors long after the inmates had bolted – a function of little importance and even less worth.

The potency of regulatory involvement in the UK is likely to be improved by the introduction of the Bank of England's Financial Policy Committee which is supposed to scan the horizon for systemic threats – but this will be inadequate unless the power to intervene is also present and then properly utilised by the new twin arms of the old FSA. The FSA was, by the admission of Lord Turner in his review, not up to the task with which it was charged (see Chapter 10). The chairman of the Future Banking Commission David Davis described it as being 'limper than a wet lettuce in the cases that really mattered'[5] while seeking 'a tough reputation off the back of a number of cases where banks reported their own misdemeanours'.

The Treasury published its own report – in 2012, four years after the start of the financial crisis – which showed that it had only three members of its staff occupied with financial stability at the time of the crisis, an area it admits it had neglected. Because of a 25 per cent annual turnover of staff it lacked the basic financial skills to deal with the crisis and then spent generously on financial and legal advice from the private sector to try to make up ground – subsequently finding that much of the advice was poor value. The Bank of England, which alone of the triumvirate of UK regulators has yet to undertake a public review of its activities during the crisis, apparently squabbled extensively ('at the highest levels' according to the Treasury's Report) about how to handle the crisis.

The poor behaviour of the investment banks in pursuing profit at any cost to their reputations, as intermediaries between those requiring funds and those investing funds, is too well-rehearsed to require repetition. The investment activities of banks – either the

---

[3] D. Davis MP, 'Hannam is clearly a victim of injustice', *Financial Times*, 4 April 2012.
[4] Black, *The Best way to Rob a Bank*.   [5] Davis, 'Hannam is clearly a victim of injustice'.

specialised investment banks or the proprietary arms of universal banks – were cause, culprit and victim of much of what happened in 2007–8. Their behaviour is the most naked example of the poverty of substance in the forms of governance which could satisfy regulatory 'scrutiny' under the conventional view.

The Big Bang of 1986 radically altered the structure of the financial sector in the UK. Not all the pieces of the old structure that were thrown out were necessarily bad; some of the new structure was not necessarily good. The eliding of distinctions between market makers and brokers has probably been a bad development to substitute for a piece of the old structure that worked well in terms of the customers' interests. 'Chinese Walls' are no substitute for stretches of blue water.

Market imperfections

Stock markets do not behave in conformity with theory because, although they are the closest thing to the economists' perfect market ideal, they still possess a number of flaws which render them imperfect. More importantly, the traditional/conventional theory of shareholder primacy and its consequential thrust for the continual improvement of shareholder wealth is not well supported by the workings of the real world share marketplace.

Despite their general homogeneity of aim – to make a profit from the holding of shares – shareholders transact business in very different ways depending on their characteristics: the nature and activities of day traders differ from private investors which differ from those of institutional investors which differ again from hedge fund managers. High Frequency Traders are a type of investor almost entirely different from all the others in their behaviour and techniques. Yet the conventional theory assumes a long(ish)-term holder with a proprietorial interest in the company in which they have invested, prepared to spend time and effort in engaging with the management of that company to execute a stewardship function.

There are now fewer such investors based in the UK than when the Stewardship code was formulated: figures released by the Office for National Statistics in February 2012[6] indicated that UK institutional funds now hold less than 9 per cent of the shares of British listed companies; this is the lowest level since the beginnings of the 'cult of equity' in the early 1960s. The decline has been precipitate: in 1997 UK retirement funds held just over 22 per cent of the UK stock market; by the end of 2011 they held just over 5 per cent. Insurers now own 8.6 per cent of UK shares against 23.6 per cent in 1997. The balance has been taken up by overseas investors – as an example, Statens Pensjonsfond, Utland, the Norwegian sovereign wealth fund, owns just over 2 per cent

---

[6] www.ons.gov.uk/ons/rel/pnfc1/share-ownership—share-register-survey-report/2010/index.html.

of the entire European (collective) stock market. Overseas investors may well have similar concerns about corporate governance to their domestic counterparts but the extent to which they choose – or will be willing – to spend time and effort exercising that privilege is unclear.

Nor do markets allocate resources rationally as the conventional governance theory implies in its totem about shareholder primacy. There does appear to be a relationship between the share price of a company and its corporate governance reputation.[7] This is supposed to reduce the cost of capital for the company since shareholders will supposedly be happier to invest in companies with good reputations – but the relationship is not certain. Prior to the collapse of the financial market in 2007–8 most investors would have regarded the banks as bastions of appropriate corporate governance. While a rising tide certainly appears to lift all boats it is also the case that it submerges lots of flaws. Many companies are held up to be paragons of good governance only to be revealed as having feet of clay a few months later when events turn against them. A crisis exposes weaknesses in governance that may leave some companies beached in terms of both their share prices and their ability to pay returns to shareholders: the UK banks are a particular case in point.

Both the Efficient Market Theory and the Capital Asset Pricing Model have been exposed as seriously flawed after the events of 1998 and 2008. Both those theories have been used as philosophical underpinnings of the conventional shareholder primacy/ shareholder wealth idea. Developments in market technology have significantly affected trading behaviour. Elegantly discriminating choices in share selection are redundant against a tide of trades occasioned by arbitrage. Similarly, the intentional discrimination by market operators and companies against the small shareholder means that shareholders are not treated equally: the resources available to the professional render the private shareholder to a very subordinate position in terms of practical rights and significance despite legal equality.

Following the financial crisis of 2007–8 the FSA's enforcement division began to stir themselves and the pace of prosecutions for market abuse rapidly picked up – but it is difficult to accept that such infringements in market behaviour suddenly accelerated from a standing start and were not present in the years previously when the FSA took no action. The FSA's record of even investigating open book cases has not been impressive: in the investigation which it conducted into the failure of RBS it neglected to interview seven of the board members of the bank at the time of the crisis.[8]

---

[7] A. Shleifer and R. W. Vishny, 'A Survey of Corporate Governance', *Journal of Finance*, 52(2) (1997), 737–83; J. Treanor, 'Poor governance reduces profits, says ABI', *The Guardian*, 27 February 2008 (ABI Research Paper No 7).

[8] Davis, 'Hannam is clearly a victim of injustice'.

In 2010 the FSA fined Photo Me International plc £500,000 for failing to disclose contractual information to the market fast enough, a lapse which they claimed resulted in a false market in the company's shares for four days.[9] In the two years previously the FSA had also taken action against Woolworths plc, Wolfson Electronics plc and Entertainment Rights plc for similar offences, suggesting that such lapses are far from unusual and allow scope for those in possession of information to effect trades which will be of substantial benefit.

The market is demonstrably decidedly imperfect – listed companies should be well aware of their obligations in such matters and failure to notify is evidence of a procedural governance breakdown at least. By the FSA's own calculation and statistics,[10] up until recently one in three (now one in five) major transactions involving listed companies are preceded by 'unusual share price movements'. Proponents of conventional/traditional explanations of governance do not allow for this misbehaviour – since they have nothing to say about this dimension of governance – other than to mark down such lapses as unfortunate failures accompanied by the theoretical equivalent of a shrug of the shoulders as far as making adjustments to their chosen description of governance.

Accounting and audit

The 'conventional wisdom' is that the large banks which precipitated the financial crisis of 2007–8 were TBTF – 'too big to fail'. They were so systemically important that they could not be allowed to collapse collectively or individually. This bleak acceptance of a 'fact' is again a product of concentrating on the landscape of corporate governance and not the geology.

The reason that they had become TBTF was that they were also TBTA – 'too big to audit'. They had become so large that they could not be understood as entities and, in corporate governance terms, while their procedural governance may have been adequate (although the collapse of Lehman Brothers and the numbers of recent fines levied on banks for failing to separate clients' funds[11] showed this was also open to question) their behavioural governance was poor and their structural governance often non-existent. They appear to have behaved, with few exceptions, like a collection of satrapies rather than unified organisms – a product of their size and structure,

[9]   FSA Press release, 'Photo-Me fined £500,000 for delay in disclosing inside information', 21 June 2010 (FSA/PN/102/2010), available at http://www.fsa.gov.uk/library/communication/pr/2010/102.shtml.

[10] B. Masters, D. Schäfer and A. Sakoui, 'FSA tightens view of market abuse', *Financial Times*, 3 April 2012.

[11] T. Braithwaite, 'Telis Demos and Tracy Alloway "JPMorgan's practices bring scrutiny"', *Financial Times*, 5 April 2012.

which amounts almost to a federated union. The nature, causes and consequences of the financial crisis can be over-stressed in terms of the state of corporate governance in other sectors but experience and anecdote suggest that the circumstances in many other large listed businesses will be similar. Instances have already been cited of the managerial turmoil (and problems over share sales by directors) at Tesco in early 2012, the problems experienced by Premier Foods since at least 2007, the lack of a unified board response when BP's Macondo rig exploded, and the problems at Mitchell and Butlers over several years.

Reward issues

Chapter 14 dwelt at length on the market distortions caused by improper linking of shareholders' interest with those of directors and managers, in a misguided attempt to put into practical effect the concept of ever-increasing shareholder value. Such distortions not only affect the companies and their shareholders and stakeholders who are directly involved but often result in serious damage to market 'by-standers'.

The insider dealing activities of Raj Rajaratnam at the Galleon Fund distorted share prices for millions of other shareholders, with results that are incalculable. The attempts by Lewis Chester of the PCM hedge fund to persuade brokers in the USA to deal in mutual funds after the dealing deadline had passed distorted returns for other rule-abiding shareholders.[12] Both men were rewarded with record fines by US courts ($98.2 million and $99 million respectively). Similarly, the Paulson hedge fund – in active collusion with Goldman Sachs – cheated customers in the Abacus fund as a deliberate act to make more profit by exploiting asymmetries of knowledge in the most underhand fashion. These are ethical failings of market behaviour about which the conventional view of governance is silent – and consequently non-prescriptive.

Counter-governance

Eventually, if conducted for long enough, ethical failings become a policy in themselves. It is at this point that counter-governance supplants normal governance and markets become completely distorted in terms of all the objectives of corporate governance: shareholders are cheated; stakeholders are done down; the balance of reward between parties becomes dramatically skewed in favour of managers; resources are misallocated. Governance at all levels is functionally absent – procedure operates in a vacuum; behavioural obligations are mere conventions without substance; structural

---

[12] S. Jones, 'Pentagon hit with biggest US fine on foreign group', *Financial Times*, 3 April 2012.

governance has disappeared; systemic governance has no purchase. The outcome is a shift of the economy along the regulatory spectrum towards overt lawlessness and open banditry.

These major changes all begin with a modest infraction. Innocent breaches of procedure eventually become significant when customers' funds get mixed up with the company's money – and are then lost, as may have happened in the cases of Farepak or MF Global.[13] Behavioural prudence, as in the case of organising the company's affairs so as to avoid the payment of tax – legitimate, permitted, perhaps even socially-desirable – eventually at some point becomes so contrived and artificial that the boundary becomes indistinct and it looks to the ordinary stakeholder to be closer to evasion. Routine minor collusion with competitors to share information about bids in an attempt to smooth the uncertainty of the market, morphs into rigging the market against customers. A governance equivalent of Gresham's Law takes hold and bad practices drive out good.

Recognitions of inadequacies

Redefinitions

The problems with the existing regime of corporate governance and its underlying tenets, as captured in conventional definitions, have been identified in the preceding chapters and summarised in the remarks above. It is futile to believe that redefinitions of concepts will, by themselves, make participants in the great dance of governance behave differently. But to attempt to improve standards of governance by tinkering with a structure that does not work properly, when the context in which it is supposed to operate has changed so radically, is equally pointless. The environment in which corporate governance works is dynamic: the principles of governance must be sufficiently wide-ranging and flexible to deal with such contextual changes and are long overdue for a review after twenty years of creaking failure.

Dimensional recognition

In order to be effective, corporate governance must be recognised as operating across and through a number of different dimensions and levels; these are the concepts developed in this book – the dimensions of procedural, behavioural, structural and systemic governance, all of which operate across periods of time – with a longitudinal dimension – rather than being limited to specific periods as in the fashion of annual company reports.

---

[13] T. Alloway and S. Nasiripou, 'MF Global top executive pleads fifth', *Financial Times*, 28 March 2012.

Within these dimensions there are sub-sets of activity which relate to both inward-facing governance (concerned mostly with the interaction between shareholders, managers/directors and the company) and outward-facing governance (concerned mostly with the relations of the company with its external stakeholders). Again these extend through time rather than being limited to specific periods.

Failures of the structural dimension are far from being isolated incidents and those that become visible are usually always concerned with near catastrophic collapse – of an operating unit if not the whole organisation. In the case of Barings, the damage can result in the organisation suffering the business equivalent of a hole below the waterline. In the case of a UBS with an Adoboli or a Societe Generale with a Kerviel, then the damage may be limited to losses of billions of currency rather than cost the life of the organisation, but the reputational damage will be substantial and wide-ranging. Other individuals – close by-standers or silent witnesses not directly involved – may lose their jobs or their good names as the organisation goes through a spasm of ethical cleansing, whose depth may or may not extend to reversing the weakness of structural/cultural governance that prompted the discovered failing.

Federated governance

With some very large organisations it might be desirable to think of them as essentially federated bodies for the purpose of control, with the main method of external monitoring for outsiders – the audit – being similarly organised on a federal basis. Individual components of the federal structure might have to be subjected to much more searching and detailed analysis than was the case with the banks before 2007, given that they universally received clean bills of health from auditors, only days in some circumstances, before they became paralysed. The proposals to 'ring fence' certain activities in the financial sector come close to this arrangement but will require changes to accounting conventions to make any sense. This will further stretch the chronic tension that accounting information has to reconcile between usefulness and precision.

Ownerless companies

Listed companies are not really owned by their shareholders at all in any meaningful sense: the possession of one share certificate – or even several hundred thousand – among many millions confers no real proprietary rights. Company managers do not really behave as if they were working for shareholders except in the most abstract of senses. The balance of reward between the parties to the contract of incorporation has skewed very much in favour of managers. Obligations of stewardship cannot be successfully encouraged in such an environment – especially when the institutional investors have other and more direct obligations to their customers and beneficiaries.

Listed companies – but not private companies or unlisted plcs – might have to be recognised as having an ownerless nature in terms of their ultimate control.

Stewardship

The existence of 'ownerless plcs' does not mean that stewardship should be abandoned as a concept but that those investors who accept the obligations of undertaking a supervisory role should be given certain privileges and certain benefits to reward their involvement and the manoeuvring room they give up. The Alternative Investment Market suggests a potentially adaptable model in its use of Nomads – the brokers who are responsible for supervising the conduct of the company in respect of its obligations to the market. Such a structure could be adapted to the requirements of main market conditions, replacing brokers with institutional investors' committees with distinct and valuable rewards going to those institutional funds which accepted the steward-ship role. A dual share class structure would be required with cumulative, preferential and participative benefits to steward-shareholders. The property rights of other shares would then accord more with the current reality – the rights to participate in distributions and the growth in the value of the company; more like simply going to a horse race and betting than having to buy a chunk of the horse first.

The problem of counter-governance

One of the more outlandish responses to the impact of the financial crisis was the suggestion that MBAs might take the business equivalent of a Hippocratic Oath – a sort of business-based 'do no harm' pledge.

Facile and ill-conceived though this may be it touches upon a failing of the concepts of governance promoted by the conventional descriptions – they lack any form of moral framework. They limit their scope to shareholders, directors and Tail End Charlie auditors – with a more recent grudging acceptance of some undefined role for stakeholders among some definitions. Throughout this book the shorthand of 'the Cadbury definition' has often been used to identify this concept. But Adrian Cadbury was much more aware of the true purpose of corporate governance than the simplistic formulation which has provided the platform for subsequent reviews.

His remarks concerning the purpose of corporate governance have already been quoted in this chapter but bear repetition:

> Corporate governance is involved in holding the balance between economic and social goals and between individual and communal goals … the aim is to align as nearly as possible the interests of individuals, corporations and society.

It is necessary to recast the definition and mechanisms of good corporate governance to cope with the conditions of a changed world, in order to effectively restore that balance between economic, social, individual and communal goals. To that end, a new definition is needed that breaks the link between the exercise of corporate governance and the spurious claims of shareholder primacy:

Corporate governance is the governing structure and processes [procedural governance] in an organisation that exist to oversee the means by which limited resources are efficiently directed to competing purposes for the use of the organisation and its stakeholders; including the maintenance of the organisation and its long-run sustainability [behavioural governance], set and measured against a framework of ethics [structural governance] and backed by regulation and laws [systemic governance].

Bibliography

'A price on the priceless', *The Economist*, 10 June 1999

Adams, G., 'Chevron's dirty fight in Ecuador', *Independent*, 16 February 2011

Aglionby, J., 'Bumi governance problems "put to bed"', *Financial Times*, 27 March 2012

Allen, F. and Gale, D. M., *'Competition and Financial Stability'*, NYU Working Paper No. S-FI-03-06 (September 2003), available at http://ssrn.com/abstract=1297769

Alloway, T., 'Goldman's Tourre says show me the inexperience!', *Financial Times*, 1 February 2011

Alloway, T., Braithwaite, T. and Schäfer, D., 'Goldman battles "toxic" culture criticism', *Financial Times*, 14 March 2012

Alloway T. and Kaminska, I., 'UBS loss throws light on "synthetic" problem', *Financial Times*, 4 October 2011

Alloway, T. and Nasiripou, S., 'MF Global top executive pleads fifth', *Financial Times*, 28 March 2012

Armitstead, L., 'Serious Fraud Office criticised for closing Weavering Capital investigation', *Daily Telegraph*, 9 September 2011

Armstrong, A., 'Never Again – an evaluation of the ICB's proposals for structural reform', ESRC/NIESR Financial Stability conference, London, February 2012

Arrow, K., 'Uncertainty and the welfare economics of medical care', *Am. Econ. Review* (December 1963)

Arvedlund, E., *Madoff: The Man Who Stole $65 Billion* (London: Penguin, 2009)

Ashall, P., 'The new settlement under the Financial Services Act 1986', *Journal of Financial Regulation and Compliance*, 1(1) (1992), 47–55

Audit Firm Governance Code, available at www.icaew.com/en/technical/corporate-governance/audit-firm-governance-code

Augar, P., *Chasing Alpha* (London: Bodley Head, 2009)

   The Greed Merchants: How the Investment Banks Played the Free Market Game (London: Penguin, 2006)

Australian Stock Exchange, *Principles of Good Corporate Governance and Best Practice Recommendations* (Sydney: Australian Stock Exchange, 2007)

Avallaneda, M. and Stoikov, S., 'High-frequency trading in a limit order book', *Quantitative Finance*, 8(3) (2008)

Avrahampour, Y., 'George Ross Goobey and the cult of equity', *Professional Pensions* (2005)

Bagehot, W., *Lombard Street: A Description of the Money Market* (New Jersey: Wiley, 1999)

Bakan, J., *The Corporation: The Pathological Pursuit of Profit and Power* (London: Constable and Robinson, 2005)

Balen, M., *A Very English Deceit* (London: Fourth Estate, 2002)

Bank of England, *Financial Stability Report* (December 2011)

Barber, B., Lehavy, R., McNichols, M. and Trueman, B., 'Can investors profit from the prophets? Security analyst recommendations and stock returns', *The Journal of Finance*, 56 (2002), 531–63

Barker, A., 'European rules alarm fund managers', *Financial Times*, 1 April 2012

Berle, A. A. and Means, G. C., *The Modern Corporation and Private Property* (New Jersey: Transaction, 1999)

Bethel, E. W., Leinweber, D., Rübel, O. and Wu, K., 'Federal market information technology in the post flash crash era: roles for supercomputing', Lawrence Berkeley National Laboratory, Proceedings of the fourth workshop on High performance computational finance (2011), pp. 23–30, available at www.lbl.gov/cs/html/CIFT-LBL-report.pdf

Black, W. K., *The Best Way to Rob a Bank is to Own One* (University of Texas Press, 2005)

Blas, J., 'Time nears for a Glencore and Xstrata deal', *Financial Times*, 11 October 2011

Blas, J. and Kerr, S., 'IPO values Glencore at $48bn–$58bn', *Financial Times*, 4 May 2011

Blowers, S. and Treanor, J., 'RBS "gamble" on ABN Amro deal: FSA', *The Guardian*, 12 December 2011

'Boardroom practices under the microscope', *BBC website* (archived), 4 March 1998

Bøhren, Ø., Priestley, R. and Ødegaard, B. A., 'The Duration of Equity Ownership', BI Norwegian School of Management Working Paper 2006, available at http://finance.bi.no/~bernt/wps/ownership_duration/durationpaper_dec_2005.pdf

Boland, V., 'Anglo Republic', *Financial Times*, 9 October 2011

Bower, T., *Branson* (London: Harper, 2008)

Bowers, S., 'DSL faces court case over Simon Cawkwell's gains from short-selling Northern Rock and Eurotunnel', *The Observer*, 30 January 2011

   'Thomas Cook investors express anger at high levels of executive pay', *The Guardian*, 8 February 2012

Boyde, E., 'Fund file: a Chinese opacity problem', *Financial Times*, 28 November 2011

'BP faces storms of protest at annual meeting', *The Guardian*, 14 April 2011

Braithwaite, T., 'Banking costs more for small businesses', *Financial Times*, 14 October 2005

   'Telis Demos and Tracy Alloway "JPMorgan's practices bring scrutiny"', *Financial Times*, 5 April 2012

Braithwaite, T. and Masters, B., 'AIG set to sue BofA for $10.5bn', *Financial Times*, 8 August 2011

Braithwaite, T., Scannell, K. and Bryant, C., 'BofA and JP Morgan sued over securities', *Financial Times*, 30 September 2011

Brief, A. P., Dukerich, J. M., Brown, P. R. and Brett, J. F., 'What's wrong with the Treadway Commission report?', *Journal of Business Ethics*, 15(2) (1996), 183–98

Broadberry, S. and Crafts, N., 'British economic policy and industrial performance in the early post-War period', *Business History*, 38(4) (1996)

Brown, K., 'FSA issues further reprimand to analysts', *Financial Times*, 13 August 2004

Bruce, A., Skovoroda, R., Fattorusso, J. and Buck, T., 'Executive bonus and firm performance in the UK', *Long Range Planning*, 40(3) (2007)

Bryce, R., *Pipedreams* (New York, NY: Public Affairs, 2002)

Buhr, N., 'History of and rationales for sustainability reporting' in Unerman, J., Bebbington, J. and O'Dwyer, B. (eds), *Sustainability Accounting and Accountability* (Abingdon: Routledge, 2007), pp. 57–69

Bulletin of the Business Historical Society, 27 (1) (March 1953), 1–25

Burgess, K., 'Cable outlines plans on executive pay', *Financial Times*, 23 January 2012
   'FTSE considers tougher listing rules', *Financial Times*, 1 November 2011
   'Pond Life', *Financial Times*, 24 July 2012
   'Sants gets wish and heads for FSA's door', *Financial Times*, 16 March 2012

Burgess, K., Blas, J. and Burgis, T., 'Glencore and Xstrata face blocking threat', *Financial Times*, 7 February 2012

Business Strategy Review, *London Business School Journal*, 10(2) (June 1999)

Cable, V., House of Commons Debates, *Hansard*, 10 April 2002, col. 63–68

Cadbury, Sir A., *Corporate Governance Overview*, World Bank Report (Washington, DC: World Bank, 1999)
   Report of the Committee on the Financial Aspects of Corporate Governance (London: Gee, 1992)

Campbell, A., Fishman, N. and McIlroy, J. (eds), *The Post-war Compromise: British Trade Unions and Industrial Politics 1945–64* (London: Merlin, 2007)

Cannon, L. M. and Adams, P., 'Twin peaks regulation', *New Law Journal*, 162(7507) (2012)

Carr, A., 'Is business bluffing ethical?', *Harvard Business Review*, Jan–Feb 1968

Carr, Sir R., 'Let's end the executive greed debate and focus on growth', *Sunday Telegraph*, 12 February 2012

Carswell, S., *Anglo Republic: Inside the bank that broke Ireland* (Dublin: Penguin Ireland, 2011)

Cassidy, J., *dot.con* (London: Penguin, 2002)

Chancellor, E., *Capital Account* (New York, NY: Texere, 2004)

Chandler, A., *The Visible Hand* (Cambridge, MA: Harvard University Press, 1977)

Chapman, J., 'The truth behind short selling's public face', *Financial Times*, 24 April 2011

Cheffin, B., *Corporate Ownership and Control* (Oxford University Press, 2008)

Cheques with Balances, Report of the High Pay Commission, available at http://highpaycommission. co.uk/facts-and-figures/final-report-cheques-with-balances-why-tackling-high-pay-is-in-the-national-interest/

Clark, A., 'Browne speaks of Elton, elves and etiquette – but little of Texas City', *The Guardian*, 24 July 2008

Coase, R. H., 'The lighthouse in economics', *Journal of Law and Economics*, 17(2) (1974)
   'The nature of the firm', *Economica*, 4(16) (November 1937), 386–405

Cohen, N., 'QE blamed for surge in pensions shortfall', *Financial Times*, 7 March 2012
   'Takeover panel urged to consider M&A pension toll', *Financial Times*, 30 May 2011

Cohen, N., Davoudi, S. and Lucas, L., 'Trinity Mirror cuts pension payments', *Financial Times*, 15 May 2012

Cohen, N. and Routledge, P., '£5 million pension for Cedric Brown', *The Independent on Sunday*, 17 December 1995
   Company Law Reform Steering Group Report, June 2001, vol. 1, s. 2.13

Conyon, M. J. and Murphy, K. J., 'The Prince and the Pauper? CEO pay in the United States and United Kingdom', *The Economic Journal*, 110(467) (2000), 640–71

Cookson, R., 'Sino-Forest suffers another blow', *Financial Times*, 6 April 2012

Coopey, R. and Clarke, D., *3i: Fifty Years Investing in Industry* (Oxford University Press, 1995)

CPS Press Release, 15 February 2011

Croft, J., 'Clerk first to be prosecuted under Bribery Act', *Financial Times*, 31 August 2011

Crooks, E. and McCrum, D., 'GE Changes share option plan for Immelt', *Financial Times*, 20 April 2011

Crosland, A., *The Future of Socialism* (London: Robinson, 2008)

Cruver, B., *Enron: The Anatomy of Greed* (London: Arrow, 2003)

Curtis, A., *The Mayfair Set*, BBC video, first broadcast 1999

Daneshkhu, S., 'Kerviel found guilty in SocGen scandal', *Financial Times*, 5 October 2010

Darling, A., *Back from the Brink* (London: Atlantic, 2011)

Das, R., Hanson, J. E., Kephart, J. O. and Tesauro, G., 'Agent-human interactions in the continuous double auction', *Proceedings of the IJCAI* (2001)

Davies, H., *The Financial Crisis: Who is to Blame?* (London: Polity, 2010)

Davies, H. and Green, D., *Global Financial Regulation* (London: Polity, 2008)

Davies, N., *Flat Earth News* (London: Chatto & Windus, 2008)

Davis, D., 'Hannam is clearly a victim of injustice', *Financial Times*, 4 April 2012

Dembe, A. E. and Boden, L. I., 'Moral hazard: A question of morality?', *New Solutions*, 10(3) (2000), 257–9

Dewing, I. P. and Russell, P. O., 'Accounting, auditing and corporate governance of European listed countries: EU policy developments before and after Enron', *Journal of Common Market Studies*, 42 (2004), 289–319

Dickson, M., 'Fair destination, shame about the driving', *Financial Times*, 9 September 2004

DoT, 'Report of Court of Enquiry 8074 under the Merchant Shipping Act 1894; mv *Herald of Free Enterprise*' (Norwich: HMSO, 1987)

Dubow, B. and Monteiro, N., 'Measuring market cleanliness', *FSA Occasional Paper* 23 (September 2006)

Eaglesham, J., Jopson, B. and Tucker, S., 'Investors disappointed by audit reform', *Financial Times*, 20 July 2005

EIU/KPMG, *Corporate Governance The New Strategic Imperative* (EIU, 2002)

Elder, B. and Hume, N., 'Oil spill continues to put skids under BP's share price', *Financial Times*, 25 May 2010

Elkington, J., *Cannibals with Forks* (Bloomington, MN: Capstone, 1997)

'Enron's board of directors', *The Guardian*, 1 February 2002

Evaluation of the Companies Act 2006, BIS December 2011

'Familiar sins', *The Economist* 13 March 1997

Felsted, A., Kuchler, H. and Burgess, K., 'Investors censure Tesco on pay plans', *Financial Times*, 2 July 2010

Finch, J., Treanor, J. and Wachman, R., 'Critics unite over executive pay to force the "aliens" of business down to earth', *The Guardian*, 31 March 2010

Fletcher, N., 'Shareholder group attacks bonus payments at property group Conygar', *The Guardian*, 5 January 2012

Flood, C., 'ETF providers attack systemic risk warnings', *Financial Times*, 17 April 2011

Flower, J. and Ebbers, G., *Global Financial Reporting* (Basingstoke: Palgrave, 2002), Chapter 19

Fontanella-Khan, J., 'Timeline: the Satyam scandal', *Financial Times*, 7 January 2009

FRC, *Audit Committees Combined Code Guidance* (London: FRC, 2003)

Freeman, R. E. and Evans, W. M., 'Corporate Governance: a stakeholder interpretation;' *Journal of Behavioural Economics*, 19(4) (1990)

Freeman, R. E., Harrison, J., Wicks, A. and Parmar, B. L., *Stakeholder Theory* (Cambridge University Press, 2010)

Frey, B. S. and Jegen, R., 'Motivation Crowding Theory', *Journal of Economic Surveys*, 15 (2001), 589–611

Frey, B. S. and Osterloh, M., 'Stop tying pay to performance', *Harvard Business Review*, Jan–Feb 2012

Friedman, M., 'The social responsibility of business is to increase its profits', *The New York Times Magazine*, 13 September 1970

FSA, *The Failure of the Royal Bank of Scotland* (London: HM Treasury, 2011)

    The FSA Handbook: Listing Rules, available at www.fsa.gov.uk/pubs/other/listing_rules.pdf, continually updated

    The Turner Review: A Regulatory Response to the Global Banking Crisis (March 2009)

    Market Watch, Issue 37 (September 2010)

    Press release, 'FSA consults on changes to the Listing Rules', 26 January 2012 (FSA/PN/006/2012), available at www.fsa.gov.uk/library/communication/pr/2012/006.shtml

    'FSA fines stockbroker £250,000 for using high pressure sales tactics', 14 January 2008 (FSA/PN/002/2008), available at www.fsa.gov.uk/library/communication/pr/2008/002.shtml

    'FSA secures €77,000 for victims of boiler room fraud', 17 February 2012 (FSA/PN/016/2012), available at http://www.fsa.gov.uk/library/communication/pr/2012/016.shtml

    'New deposit guarantee limit to be £85,000', 17 December 2010 (FSA/PN/181/2010), available at http://www.fsa.gov.uk/library/communication/pr/2010/181.shtml

    'Photo-Me fined £500,000 for delay in disclosing inside information', 21 June 2010 (FSA/PN/102/2010), available at http://www.fsa.gov.uk/library/communication/pr/2010/102.shtml

Giddens, A., *A Contemporary Critique of Historical Materialism* (Basingstoke: Palgrave, 1981)

Goff, S., 'Barclays' PPI complaints soar', *Financial Times*, 22 February 2012

    'Diamond vows to try harder as Barclays disappoints', *Financial Times*, 10 February 2012

Goff, S. and Murphy, M., 'Lloyds 13 to lose total of £1.5m', *Financial Times*, 20 February 2012

Goff, S., Murphy, M. and Parker, G., 'RBS bonus cuts offset by big salary increases', *Financial Times*, 22 February 2012

Goibert, J., 'The Corporate Manslaughter and Corporate Homicide Act 2007 – thirteen years in the making but was it worth the wait?', *Modern Law Review*, May 2008

Gomber, P., Arndt, B., Lutat, M. and Uhle, T., 'High-Frequency Trading' (2011), available at http://ssrn.com/abstract=1858626.

Goodhart, C., *Monetary Theory and Practice* (Basingstoke: Palgrave, 1983), p. 96

Grant, J., 'D Börse to sue Brussels over NYSE block', *Financial Times*, 20 March 2012

    'UK study questions liquidity claims of HFT', *Financial Times*, 29 February 2012

Grant, J. and Demos, T., 'Superfast traders feel heat as bourses act', *Financial Times*, 5 March 2012

Grant, J. and Sanderson, R., 'Italy to limit high-frequency orders', *Financial Times*, 20 February 2012

Grant, J. and Stafford, P., 'France wants tougher HFT regulation', *Financial Times*, 19 December 2011

    'Studies say no link between HFT and volatility', *Financial Times*, 8 September 2011

Grant, J. and Tait, N., 'Europe set for overhaul of rules on share dealing', *Financial Times*, 29 July 2010

Gray, A., 'Insurance body cautious on solvency deal', *Financial Times*, 21 March 2012

'Greater transparency in company pay and reporting', available at www.bis.gov.uk

Greenbury, R., *Directors' Remuneration: Report of a Study Group Chaired by Sir Richard Greenbury* (London: CBI, 1995)

Grene, S., 'ETF Q&A: The good the bad and the synthetic', *Financial Times*, 31 January 2010

Gribben, R., 'FSA wants reform of listings rules', *Daily Telegraph*, 15 January 2008

Groom, B., 'Executive pay: The trickle-up effect', *Financial Times*, 28 July 2011
    'UK directors' earnings doubled in 10 years', *Financial Times*, 5 September 2011

Guerrera, F., 'Welch condemns share price focus', *Financial Times*, 12 March 2009

Guthrie, J., 'MG Rover auditor given clean bill of health', *Financial Times*, 13 September 2009

Hall, B. and Murphy, K. J., 'The trouble with stock options', *NBER Working Paper* 9784 (2003)

Hall, P. and Soskice, D., *Varieties of Capitalism* (Oxford University Press, 2001)

Hamilton, S. and Mickelthwait, A., *Greed and Corporate Failure* (Basingstoke: Palgrave, 2006)

Hampel, R., *Report of The Committee on Corporate Governance* (London: Gee, 1998)

Harris, L., *Trading & Exchanges* (Oxford University Press, 2003), Chapter 29, pp. 591–7

Hennessey, J., *Economic Miracles* (London: IEA/Andre Deutsch, 1964)

Heron, R. A. and Lie, E., 'On the use of poison pills and defensive payouts by takeover targets', *Journal of Business*, 79(4) (July 2008)

Higgs, D., *Review of the Role and Effectiveness of Non-Executive Directors* (London: DTI, 2003)

Hill, A., 'All I am saying is give CEOs a chance', *Financial Times*, 23 May 2011

Hirschman, A., *Exit, Voice and Loyalty: Responses to Decline in Firms, Organizations and States* (Cambridge, MA: Harvard University Press, 1990)

Holmstrom, B. and Kaplan, S. N., 'Corporate Governance and Merger Activity in the U.S.: Making Sense of the 1980s and 1990s', NBER Working Paper No. 8220, issued in April 2001

Horack, S., Leston, J. and Watmough, M., 'The Myners principles and occupational pension schemes, Volume 1 of 2, Findings from case study research', DWP Research Report No. 195 (London: HMSO, 2004)

Hunter, M., 'FTSE 100 enters correction territory', *Financial Times*, 4 August 2011

Hurley, J., 'Venture capital "gap" between US and UK closes', *Daily Telegraph*, 1 June 2011

ICAEW, *Internal Control: Guidance for Directors on the Combined Code* (London: ICAEW, 1999)

ICGN, *Second Statement on the Global Financial Crisis* (London: ICGN, 2009)

'In brief', *The Guardian*, 10 January 2005

'India PM to ask US to extradite ex-CEO in Bhopal case', *The Economic Times*, 29 June 2010

IoD, *Evidence to FRC Consultation*, available at www.iod.com/MainWebSite/Resources/Document/Takeover_Panel_Review_0710.pdf

Jacomb, M., 'Taming the banks: long overdue or utter folly?', *Financial Times*, 13 September 2011

Jenkins, P., Goff, S. and Sakoui, A., 'Hester has task of selling off "risky" divisions', *Financial Times*, 4 January 2012

Jones, A., 'Auditors urged to be more medieval', *Financial Times*, 30 March 2012

Jones, E., *The Business of Medicine: A History of Glaxo* (London: Profile Books, 2001)

Jones, M., *Creative Accounting* (Chichester: Wiley, 2010)

Jones, S., 'Cypriot court rules for Martin Coward', *Financial Times*, 22 March 2012
    'Pentagon hit with biggest US fine on foreign group', *Financial Times*, 3 April 2012
    'Synthetic eurotrash', *Financial Times*, 22 January 2009

Judge, S., *Business Law*, 4th edn (Hampshire: Palgrave Macmillan, 2011)

Jung-a, S., 'Hanwha chairman sentence suspended', *Financial Times*, 11 September 2007
    'S Korea: the tiny roar of the NPS', *Financial Times*, 14 February 2012

Jurkiw, A., *via Press Association* (September 2009), available at http://news.sky.com/story/
    726108/builder-bid-rigging-fines-could-backfire

Kahneman, D., *Thinking Fast and Slow* (London: Allen Lane, 2011)

Kay, J. and King, M., *The British Tax System* (Oxford University Press, 1978)

King, M., *The King Report on Corporate Governance* I (South Africa: IoD, 1994)
    The King Report on Corporate Governance II (South Africa: IoD, 2002)

Kirkup, J., 'Bribery Act to be reviewed after business fears', *Daily Telegraph*, 14 January 2011

Kollewe, J., 'Hector Sants quits FSA', *The Guardian*, 16 March 2012

Kynaston, D., *Austerity Britain, 1945–1951* (London: Bloomsbury, 2008)
    The City of London (London: Chatto, 2003), vol. IV

Le Grand, J., *Motivation, Agency and Public Policy* (Oxford University Press, 2003)

Leader Column, *Financial Times*, 12 June 2011
    Financial Times, 10 April 2012

Lewis, M., *Boomerang; the Meltdown Tour* (London: Allen Lane, 2011)
    Liar's Poker (London: Hodder, 2006)

Lex Column, *Financial Times*, 23 June 2011
    Financial Times, 16 February 2012

Lowe, E. and Tinker, A., 'Siting the accounting problematic: towards an intellectual emancipa-
    tion of accounting', *Journal of Business Finance & Accounting*, 4 (1977), 263–76

Lowenstein, R., *When Genius Failed* (London: Fourth Estate, 2002)

LSE Statistics for new issues, Main Market and AIM, www.londonstockexchange.com/statistics/
    markets/markets.htm

Lysandrou, P., 'The real role of hedge funds in the crisis', *Financial Times*, 1 April 2012

Macey, J., *Corporate Governance* (Princeton University Press, 2008)

MacKenzie, M. and Grant, J., 'The dash to flash', *Financial Times*, 5 August 2009

Main, B. G. M., 'The Question of Executive Pay' in Owen, G., Kirchmaier, T. and Grant, J.,
    Corporate Governance in the US and Europe (Basingstoke: Palgrave, 2006)

Masters, B., 'Suspicious trades mar 30% of UK takeovers', *Financial Times*, 10 June 2010

McDermott, J., 'Dick Fuld and E&Y fail to dismiss Repo 105 case', *Financial Times*, 27 July 2011

McNeal, K., *Truth in Accounting* (Houston, TX: Scholars Book Co., 1939)

MacNamara, W. and Jenkins, P., 'Third independent director to quit ENRC board', *Financial
    Times*, 9 June 2011

Masters, B., 'Financial regulator seeks 15% rise in budget', *Financial Times*, 2 February 2012
    'FSA raises hackles over Hannam', *Financial Times*, 5 April 2012

Masters, B. and Jones, S., 'Einhorn and Greenlight fined £7.2m', *Financial Times*, 25 January 2012

Masters, B., Schäfer, D. and Sakoui, A., 'FSA tightens view of market abuse', *Financial Times*,
    3 April 2012

Mickelthwait, J. and Wooldridge, A., *The Company: A Short History of a Revolutionary Idea*
    (London: Wiedenfield and Nicholson, 2003)

Milner, M., 'German cement group captures Hanson', *The Guardian*, 16 May 2007

Mokoaleli-Mokoteli, T., Taffler, R. J. and Agarwal, V., 'Behavioural bias and conflicts of interest
    in analyst stock recommendations', *Journal of Business Finance & Accounting*, 36 (2009)

Monteiro, N., Zaman, Q. and Leitterstorff, S., 'Updated measures of market cleanliness', FSA Occasional Paper 25 (March 2007)

Moore, E., 'Banks face £3bn bill in PPI Scandal', *Financial Times*, 6 March 2012
'Davies raps bank boards' "fatal mistake"', *Financial Times*, 22 February 2012
'Sales of structured products soar', *Financial Times*, 13 March 2012

Moore, S., Grunberg, L., Anderson-Connolly, R. and Greenberg, E. S., 'Physical and mental health effects of surviving layoffs: a longitudinal examination', Institute of Behavioral Science Working Paper PEC 2003–0003, University of Colorado

'Morgan Stanley in hot water over HBOS short', *The Independent*, 23 July 2008

Moscati, S., *The World of the Phoenicians* (New York, NY: Praeger, 1965)

Monks, R., *Corpocracy* (New Jersey: Wiley, 2008)

Moran, M., 'The rise of the regulatory state in Britain', *Parliamentary Affairs*, 54(1) (2001)
The British Regulatory State: High Modernism and Hyper-Innovation (Oxford University Press, 2007)

Murphy, K. J., 'Executive compensation: Is Europe catching up with the US and should it do so?' in Owen, G., Kirchmaier, T. and Grant, J., *Corporate Governance in the US and Europe* (Basingstoke: Palgrave, 2006)

Murphy, M., 'Compensation ratios become latest jargon', *Financial Times*, 12 February 2010

Murphy, M., Burgess, K. and Jones, S., 'UBS trader held over $2bn loss', *Financial Times*, 15 September 2011

Murray, S., 'Making the business case: a growing body of evidence', *Financial Times*, 7 June 2011

Myners, P., *Institutional Investment in the UK: A Review* (London: HM Treasury, 2000)

Nadar, R., *Unsafe at Any Speed: The Designed-In Dangers of the American Automobile* (New York, NY: Grossman Publishers, 1965)

Nakamoto, M., 'Olympus is litmus test on governance', *Financial Times*, 22 February 2012

Nakamoto, M. and Wighton, D., 'Citigroup chief stays bullish on buy-outs', *Financial Times*, 9 July 2007

Napier, C., 'Intersections of law and accountancy: unlimited auditor liability in the United Kingdom', *Accounting, Organizations and Society*, 23(1) (1998), 105–28

Newlands, C., 'Crime and the City', *Financial Times*, 30 March 2012

Nolan, Lord R., *First Report of the Committee on Standards in Public Life* (London: Committee on Standards in Public Life, 1995)

Norman, W. and MacDonald, C., 'Getting to the bottom of the Triple Bottom Line', *Business Ethics Quarterly*, 14(2) (2004), 243–62

Nozick, R., *Anarchy, State and Utopia* (New Jersey: Wiley-Blackwell, 2001)

OECD, *Principles of Corporate Governance* (Paris: OECD, 1997)
Corporate Governance: Lessons from the Financial Crisis (Paris: OECD, 2009)

Office of National Statistics, February 2012, available at www.ons.gov.uk/ons/rel/pnfc1/share-ownership—share-register-survey-report/2010/index.html
Table MQ5. www.ons.gov.uk/ons/rel/fi/mq5–investment-by-insurance-companies–pension-funds-and-trusts/2nd-quarter-2011/stb-mq5-statistical-bulletin.html

Owen, G., *The Rise and Fall of Great Companies: Courtaulds and the Reshaping of the Man-Made Fibres Industry* (Oxford University Press/Pasold, 2010)

Owen, G., Kirchmaier, T. and Grant, J., *Corporate Governance in the US and Europe* (Basingstoke: Palgrave, 2006)

Oxlade, A.. 'How the News Corp crisis might affect Rupert Murdoch's Wealth', *Thisismoney.co.uk*

Parker, A., 'Deloitte blames Grant Thornton', *Financial Times*, 3 January 2005

Peel, M. and Croft, J., 'British Airways price-fixing trial collapses', *Financial Times*, 10 May 2010

Peston, R., *Who Runs Britain?: and Who's to Blame for the Economic Mess We're in?* (London: Hodder, 2008)

Pfeifer, S., 'Shell settles last reserves misreporting claim', *Financial Times*, 6 March 2008

Power, M., *The Audit Society* (Oxford University Press, 1997)

PriceWaterhouseCoopers, *A Practical Guide to the Companies Act 2006* 2nd edn (Kingston upon Thames: CCH, 2010)

Puckett, A. and Yan, X. S., 'Short term institutional herding and its impact on stock prices', University of Missouri Working Paper 2005

Quinn, J., 'Goldman Sachs, Fabrice Tourre and the complex abacus of toxic mortgages', *The Daily Telegraph*, 16 April 2010

Randall Woolridge S. J. and Dickinson, A., 'Short selling and common stock prices', *Financial Analysts Journal*, 50(1) (1994), 20–28

Raw, C., *Slater Walker* (London: Andre Deutsch, 1977)

Rawls, J., *A Theory of Justice* (Cambridge, MA: Harvard University Press, 1999)

Reid, M., *The Secondary Banking Crisis, 1973–75: Its Causes and Course* (London: Palgrave Macmillan, 1982)

Reisberg, A., 'Corporate Law in the UK after Recent Reforms', *Current Legal Problems*, 63 (2010), 315–374

Report of the Independent Committee set up to review Sino-Forest, 1 February 2012, available at www.newswire.ca/en/story/913801/sino-forest-releases-final-report-of-the-independent-committee

Rheinhart, C. and Rogoff, K., *This Time is Different* (Princeton University Press, 2011)

Sampson, A., *Who Runs This Place?: The Anatomy of Britain in the 21st Century* (London: John Murray, 2005)

Sanderson, R., 'Machiavellian corporate princes resist Monti reforms', *Financial Times*, 17 February 2012

Sandland, M., *correspondence in CAD-0121, Cadbury Archives, Judge* Business School, University of Cambridge

Scannell, K. and Reddy, S., 'Greenspan admits errors to hostile House panel', *Wall Street Journal*, 24 October 2008

Schumpeter, J., *Capitalism, Socialism and Democracy* (Basingstoke: Routledge, 2010)

Schwed, F., *Where are the Customers' Yachts?* (New York, NY: Wiley, 1995)

Securities and Exchange Commission, *The October 1987 Market Break* (Washington DC: SEC, 1988)

Shleifer, A. and Vishny, R. W., *A Survey of Corporate Governance*, NBER Working Paper 5554 (Cambridge, MA: NBER, 1996)

  'A Survey of Corporate Governance', *Journal of Finance*, 52(2) (1997), 737–83

Shleifer, A., Vishny, R. W., Laporta, R. and Lopez de Silanes, F., 'Investor protection and corporate governance', *Journal of Financial Economics*, 58(1–2) (2000), 3–27

Shonfield, A., *Modern Capitalism: The Changing Balance of Public and Private Power* (RIIA/ Oxford University Press, 1965)

Simon, H., 'A behavioral model of rational choice' in Simon, H., *Models of Man* (New York, NY: Wiley, 1957)

'Sir Richard Greenbury, the chairman and chief executive of Marks and Spencer, has discovered how much corporate governance matters when things go wrong', *The Economist*, 19 November 1998

Skovoroda, R., Main, B. G. M., Buck, T. and Bruce, A., 'The minimum assumed incentive effect of executive share options', ESRC Paper 2003

Smith, A., 'Crisis highlights need to step up governance', *Financial Times*, 27 March 2011

The Wealth of Nations; Book IV-V (London: Penguin, 1995)

Smith, A. and Burgess, K., 'Peer pressure matters with executive pay', *Financial Times*, 18 January 2012

Smith, A. and Saigol, L., 'Panel gets mixed response to change', *Financial Times*, 21 October 2010

Spivack, P. and Raman, S., 'Regulating the "New Regulators": Current trends in deferred prosecution agreements', *American Criminal Law Review*, 45 (2008)

Staff Reporters, 'Coopers and Deloitte face Barings suit', *The Independent*, 8 June 1996

'Former BP chief explores the final oil frontier', *Financial Times*, 7 December 2011

'Fund managers should stay out of Boardrooms', *The Independent*, 2 March 2004

'The 10 biggest IPOs in history', *Daily Telegraph*, 14 May 2011

Stafford, P., 'LSE calls for smaller IPO syndicates', *Financial Times*, 8 December 2011

'Sweden finds HFT effects "limited"', *Financial Times*, 21 February 2012

Sterngold, J., 'AIG writedowns may rise $30 Billion on European swaps', *Bloomberg.com*, 17 December 2008

Stevens, P., 'It is time to abandon imprudent caution', *Financial Times*, 6 October 2008

Stevenson, A., 'Qinetiq moves to slash pensions deficit', *Financial Times*, 27 March 2012

Sullivan, R., 'Brussels drubs managers over short-termism', *Financial Times*, 24 April 2011

Tait, N. and Clark, P., 'Global airlines hit with $1bn cartel fines', *Financial Times*, 9 November 2010

Tambini, D., 'What is financial journalism for?', POLIS (LSE, 2008)

'Tesco and tax: a complex web of companies, trusts and partnerships', *The Guardian*, 3 May 2008

'The National Homeownership Strategy: Partners in the American Dream', US Dept of Housing and Urban Development (1995)

The Royal Mail Case; Notable British Trials (Edinburgh and London: Wm Hodge & Co, 1935)

Tosi, H., Gomez-Mejia, L. R. and Hinkin, T., 'Managerial control, performance, and executive compensation', *The Academy of Management Journal*, 30(1) (1987) and *Journal of Management*, 26(2) (2000), 301–39

Treanor, J., 'Are banks heeding King's bonus call?', *The Guardian*, 5 December 2011

'HSBC chief Mike Geoghegan ousted after brutal boardroom battle', *The Guardian*, 23 September 2010

'Pirc takes on banks over "true and fair" reporting', *The Guardian*, 11 April 2012

'Poor governance reduces profits, says ABI', *The Guardian*, 27 February 2008

Treanor, J. and Stewart, H., 'Anger at further RBS bonus payouts', *The Guardian*, 28 January 2012

Treasury Select Committee, *The Banking Crisis: reforming corporate governance and pay in the City* (May 2009)

Trefgarne, G., 'Railtrack told to freeze final dividend', *Daily Telegraph*, 21 May 2001

Tricker, R. I., *Corporate Governance* (London: Gower, 1984)

Van der Weyer, M., *Falling Eagle* (London: Wiedenfield, 2000)

van Duyn, A., 'CDO fees flow to ratings agencies', *Financial Times*, 29 April 2010

Véron, N., *Financial Times*, 5 February 2009

Vickers, Sir J., *Report of the Independent Commission on Banking* (London: HM Treasury, 2011)

Villiers, C., *Corporate Reporting and Company Law* (Cambridge University Press, 2006)

Wade, M., 'Lloyd's of London's collapse has lessons for today's crisis', *Daily Telegraph*, 13 February 2009

Walker, Sir D., *A Review of Corporate Governance in UK Banks and Other Financial Industry Entities: Final Recommendations* (London: HM Treasury, 2009)

'Who pays for unions?', *The Economist*, 9 July 1998

Wiggins, J., 'The Inside Story of the Cadbury Takeover', *Financial Times*, 12 March 2012

Wigglesworth, R., 'Listings: Gold standards', *Financial Times*, 6 December 2011

Williamson, O., *The Mechanisms of Governance* (Oxford University Press, 1996)

Wilson, J., 'Ex-IKB chief guilty of market manipulation', *Financial Times*, 14 July 2010

Wilson, J. and Benoit, B., 'Berlin agrees second package to save Hypo', *Financial Times*, 6 October 2008

Wolf, M., 'Of course it's right to ringfence rogue universals', *Financial Times*, 15 September 2011

Zweiniger-Bargielowska, I., *Austerity in Britain: Rationing, Controls, and Consumption, 1939–1955* (Oxford University Press, 2002)

Further Reading

Accounting and Technical

Armour, D., *The Company Secretary's Handbook* (London: ICSA, 2010)

Barber, B., *The Good Governance Handbook* (London: ICSA, 2010)

Berenson, A., *The Number* (London: Pocket Books, 2004)

Bookstaber, R., *A Demon of Our Own Design* (New Jersey: Wiley, 2007)

Brewster, M., *Unaccountable* (New Jersey: Wiley, 2003)

Du Plessis, J. J., Hargovan, A. and Bagaric, M., *Principles of Contemporary Governance* (Cambridge University Press, 2011)

Ferran, E., *Principles of Corporate Finance Law* (Cambridge University Press, 2008)

Ferrarini, G. and Wymeersch, E., *Investor Protection in Europe* (Oxford University Press, 2006)

Gray, J. and Hamilton, J., *Implementing Financial Regulation* (Chichester: Wiley, 2006)

Griffiths, I., *Creative Accounting* (London: Sidgwick and Jackson, 1986)

King, T., *More than a Numbers Game: A Brief History of Accounting* (New Jersey: Wiley, 2006)

Morgan, B. and Yeung, K., *An Introduction to Law and Regulation* (Cambridge University Press, 2007)

Stevens, M., *The Big Eight* (New York, NY: Macmillan, 1981)
    The Big Six (New York: Simon and Schuster, 1991)

Toffler, B. L., *Final Accounting* (New York, NY: Broadway, 2003)

Economics and Theory

Albert, M., *Capitalism against Capitalism* (London: Whurr, 1992)

Blair, M., *Ownership and Control* (Washington DC: Brookings, 1995)

Clarke, T., *International Corporate Governance* (Abingdon: Routledge, 2007)

Cooper, G., *The Origins of Financial Crises* (Petersfield: Harriman, 2010)

Crane, A., McWilliams, A., Matten, D. and Moon, J., *The Oxford Handbook of Corporate Social Responsibility* (Oxford University Press, 2009)

Crosland, A., *The Future of Socialism* (London: Constable, 2010)

Davies, N., *Flat Earth News* (London: Chatto & Windus, 2008)

Delves Broughton, P., *What they Teach You at Harvard Business School* (London: Penguin, 2008)

Elliott, L. and Atkinson, G., *Fantasy Island* (London: Constable, 2007)

Ferguson, N., *The Ascent of Money* (London: Allen Lane, 2008)

Galbraith, J. K., *The Economics of Innocent Fraud* (New York, NY: Houghton Mifflin, 2004)
  The Great Crash (London: Penguin, 2009)
  The Affluent Society (London: Penguin, 1999)

Glyn, A., *Capitalism Unleashed* (Oxford University Press, 2006)

Gourevitch, P. and Shinn, J., *Political Power and Corporate Control* (Princeton University Press, 2005)

Hawken, P., *The Ecology of Commerce* (London: Harper Collins, 1993)

Kindleberger, C. P., *Manias, Panics and Crashes; a history of financial crises* (New Jersey: Wiley, 1978)

Plender, J., *Going Off the Rails* (Chichester: Wiley, 2003)

Turner, A. and Dahrendorf, R., *Just Capital* (London: Macmillan, 2001)

Tricker, R., *Corporate Governance Principles and Practice* (Oxford University Press, 2008)

Wolf, M., *Fixing Global Finance* (New Haven, CT: Yale University Press, 2009)

Corporate Battles, Scandals and Takeovers

Ahamad, L., *Lords of Finance* (London: Windmill, 2010)

Barnett, C., *The Verdict of Peace* (London: Macmillan, 2001)

Bevan, J., *The Rise and Fall of Marks and Spencer* (London: Profile, 2001)

Bouquet, T. and Ousey, B., *Cold Steel* (London: Little Brown, 2008)

Bower, T., *Maxwell* (London: Harper Collins, 1996)

Burrough, B., *Vendetta* (New York, NY: Harper Collins, 1992)

Burrough, B. and Helyer, J., *Barbarians at the Gate* (London: Cape, 1990)

Cohan, W., *The Last Tycoons* (London: Allen Lane, 2008)

Coll, S., *Taking Getty Oil* (London: Unwin Wyman, 1998)

Connell, J. and Sutherland, D., *Fraud: the Amazing Career of Dr Savundra* (London: Hodder, 1978)

Cornwell, R., *God's Banker: an Account of the Life and Death of Roberto Calvi* (London: Gollancz, 1983)

Elliott, G., *The Mystery of Overend Gurney* (London: Methuen, 2006)

Fay, S., *The Collapse of Barings* (London: RCB, 1996)

Ferris, P., *The City* (London: Gollancz, 1966)
  Gentlemen of Fortune (London: Wiedenfield, 1984)

Jetter, L., *Disconnected* (New Jersey: Wiley, 2003)

Johnson, J. and Orange, M., *The Man who Tried to Buy the World* (London: Penguin, 2003)

Kennedy, C., *The Merchant Princes* (London: Hutchinson, 2000)

Lever, L., *The Barlow Clowes Affair* (London: Channel4/Macmillan, 1992)

Raw, C., Page, B. and Hodgson, G., *Do You Sincerely Want to be Rich?* (London: Andre Deutsch, 1971)

Truell, P. and Gurwin, L., *False Profits* (New York, NY: Houghton Mifflin, 1992)

Index